MEXICO'S "GOLDEN AGE"

THE FIRST HALF CENTURY

HERNÁN CORTÉS, THE BELVÍS FRANCISCAN FRIARS, AND THE CUERNAVACA CHIEFTAINS

WILLIAM H. KATRA

Copyright © 2025 William H. Katra.

Cover: Adapted from the Código de Xicotepec.

All rights reserved. No part of this book may be reproduced, stored, or transmitted by any means—whether auditory, graphic, mechanical, or electronic—without written permission of both publisher and author, except in the case of brief excerpts used in critical articles and reviews. Unauthorized reproduction of any part of this work is illegal and is punishable by law.

ISBN: 979-8-89419-518-6 (sc)
ISBN: 979-8-89419-519-3 (hc)
ISBN: 979-8-89419-520-9 (e)

Because of the dynamic nature of the Internet, any web addresses or links contained in this book may have changed since publication and may no longer be valid. The views expressed in this work are solely those of the author and do not necessarily reflect the views of the publisher, and the publisher hereby disclaims any responsibility for them.

THE EWINGS PUBLISHING

One Galleria Blvd., Suite 1900, Metairie, LA 70001
(504) 702-6708

For Raimundo, Ofelia, Ramiro, Kari, Sandra, Marta, Estela, Angi, Ari, Momo, Javi, Rosa, José Luis, La china, Miquis, La mera, Josué, Michita, Kiko, y Mari—Through all of you I have "lived" Morelos.

The conquest of the earth, which mostly means the taking it away from those who have a diffeerent complexión or slightly flatter noses than ourselves, is not a pretty thing when you look into it too much. What redeems it is the idea only. And idea at ther back ofi t; not a sentimental pretense but an idea; and an unselfish belief in the idea—something you can sett jup, and boew down before, and offer a sacrifice to . . . .

—Joseph Conrad, *Heart of Darkness*

Finally, he commanded total control of the terrain—which had been won through bloody combat. Facing no restriction or limitations, Cortés now faced an entirely open field; he was free to act; to bring into being that new society about which he had dreamt for years. Yet he dreamt of another type of world, one the result of a complex mixture of rejections and attractions. First, he rejected on principle the old Spain and a decrepit Europe, both recently emerging from their feudal pasts. Second: he harbored visceral attraction to this tropical America that was populated by mysterious and taciturn Indians.

—Christian Duverger

CONTENTS

Introduction vii

Chapter 1 **A Different Type of Conquistador, a Different Type of Conquest**..................................... 1
  Cortés's Leadership Put to the Test 10
  Conquering the Aztecs in Morelos (1520) 12
  A "Conquest" or "An Indigenous Civil War"? 19

Chapter 2 **Cuernavaca's Chieftains Submit to Cortés**............. 21

Chapter 3 **1521: The First Two Months** 30

Chapter 4 **Cortés and the Spanish** 45
  Encomiendas 49

Chapter 5 **Indian Society**... 58
  Natives' Views 64
  Spanish Views of More "Backward"
    Indigenous Communities... 66
  Perspectives of Franciscan Friars 68
  Mexico's "Golden Age"?.. 71
  Cortés' Benevolent Treatment of
    Moctezuma's Daughters 73

Chapter 6 **Beginnings in Cuernavaca (1521-1524)**................ 77
  Cortés Returns to Cuernavaca 82
  Cuernavaca's Nobles 94

Chapter 7 **Mexico's Evangelization Campaign** 102

Chapter 8 **1524-1526: Years of Crisis, Absence from Mexico**... 131
  The Honduras Expedition 132
  The First Audiencia 135

Chapter 9 Cortés in Cuernavaca, 1526-1528 140
    The Friars at Work in Cuernavaca 146
    El Colegio de Tlatelolco... 150
    The Cuernavaca Church.. 155
    Further Evangelization Activities 161

Chapter 10 Visits with the King, 1528-1529 166
    La Segunda Audiencia 171

Chapter 11 Cortés in Cuernavaca, 1530-1536 175
    Constructing a Community 180
    Law Suits: Cortés's Treatment of Cuernavaca Indians .. 184
    Chapter Conclusion.. 190

Chapter 12 Cuernavaca: Agriculture, Mining,
    Cattle, Industry 195

Chapter 13 Aftermath of Mexico's "Edad Dorada" 202
    End of the Golden Age 207
    The Deadly Epidemics 213
    Other Causes... 214
    The Eroding Situation of the Encomenderos 215
    Tensions Affecting the Franciscan Order 220
    Las Casas Demoralizes the Franciscans.......................223

Appendix A: Bartolomé de las Casas and the Disputes
    between Franciscans and Dominicans 228
Appendix B: Tlaxcala: The Ideal Indian Community
    and Charles Gibson 241
Appendix C: Códices de Cuernavaca..245

Bibliography... 251
Notes About Sources 259
About the Author 269
Endnotes...271
Index...307

INTRODUCTION

Only recently there came and went the five hundredth anniversary of the Mexican Conquest, when, back in 1521, a relatively small band of Spanish *conquistadores* combined with nearly a half-million Indian warriors to force the submission of the brutal Aztec regime. A handful of informed observers today realize that this marked the beginning of a historical period, the half century or so immediately following the conquest, that has remained almost unstudied because of its relatively short duration and scarcity of surviving documentation. This was when an enlightened team of leaders embarked on the construction of a benevolent, bicultural society that several informed observers have called Mexico's "Golden Age."[1] This book is my attempt to cast new light on that nearly forgotten early chapter of Mexican history.

Worth noting is the positive appraisals that many of the Spanish held for their own works during those first few decades. They took pride in belonging to that special group of "true conquistadors" whose lives were marked by fortune and honor unequaled in their century. They celebrated the fact that their battlefield success marked the liberation of thousands of their Indian allies from cruel Aztec bondage and the latter's entrance into a better life that would result from their conversion to Catholicism, improved diet and material circumstances, and new status as subjects of the Spanish king. The chronist Bernal Díaz del Castillo, a young participant in the conquistador army, communicates what both Spanish and Indians must have felt at the time. This was because together they transformed into lived reality the most ambitious dreams of their monarch, their pope, and their medieval society:

> We survived... battles and dangers that could have ended in our death.... We discovered these people and conquered them, with the result of turning them away from their former idol worship and leading them to embrace the holy doctrine.... We brought them a good political order, helped them to overcome former bad traits, and taught them the holy doctrine. The truth is that, in contrast to their former life [under the cruel domination of the Aztecs], they now live in peace; they are members of a new society and enjoy a good life—as I've explained. [Much credit is due to] the good Franciscan monks... and later those of the Dominican order... who have provided [for the Indians here] their good personal examples and have taught them the holy doctrine. ... Any reader of these words [would agree with me] that we have brought to New Spain a benevolent social order, justice, and Christianity.[2]

In this last statement, Bernal's optimistic appraisal was correct for his own century, but not for most readers today. I briefly explore this fall from favor in both the paragraphs below and in "Notes about Sources."

In the chapters of this book, I focus on three different groups constituting New Spain's early leadership team. The first pillar were New Spain administrators, some of the most competent and respected individuals of their century: the first two viceroys, Spanish nobles Antonio de Mendoza and Luis de Velasco; respected lawyer and founder of missions Vasco de Quiroga; the country's first archbishop, Juan de Zumárraga; and the ex-conquistador-turned-civic-leader Hernán Cortés.[3]

The figure of Cortés will be featured in many of the pages that follow. During the period in question, he assumed several different roles: Mexican governor, director of Indian labor and commercial enterprises, and civic leader. He enjoyed the unrivaled influence over both ex-soldiers and Indians all across Mexico. He sparked controversy then, and his figure continues to do so today. On the one hand, it is impossible to ignore the negative aspects of his career. Both peers and posterity have held Cortés in contempt on account of his personal greed, the favoritism he demonstrated in distributing the fruits of the conquest, and the execution that he ordered to be carried out of Cuauhtémoc and several other rebellious Indian chieftains.[4] He was a product of the violent century in which he lived. We citizens of the present may find many of his acts reprehensible.

Yet noteworthy individuals of his own time, both in Spanish and Indian circles, held him in the highest esteem. In different chapters of the book, I treat aspects of Cortés's postconquest career that the contemporary reader will find worthy of praise: his sincere religious convictions, his "humanist" ideas, and an unequaled ability to plan and get things done. I also treat lesser-known acts of his that the contemporary reader will find worthy of praise: his efforts to assure a permanent place in Mexico's future for the Indian daughters of Moctezuma, and his supervision of Cuernavaca's Indian elders to draw up and preserve documents designed to protect their communal lands. The evidence is clear that Hernán Cortés was a dreamer as well as a "doer." Truth be told, he was the author of a nation.

The second leadership pillar of Mexico's Golden Age was the Belvís Franciscan friars. In 1524, three years after the submission of the Aztecs, twelve of them arrived at Mexican shores to head up the evangelization campaign. In short order, they would be joined by nearly a thousand other mendicant monks hailing from different religious orders and several countries. Admirers all across Europe realized that this would be the most noble "crusade" of their century. The participating monks, over several decades, baptized millions of willing Indians and, in doing so, facilitated their moral and material improvement. Several of these head the list in Mexico's pantheon of national heroes: Friars Martín de Valencia, Toribio Benavente Motolinía, and Pedro de Gante, who all initiated the evangelization campaign. Added to this list are Gerónimo de Mendieta, the country's most important early historian, and Bernardino de Sahagún, Mexico's first "anthropologist."

MEXICO'S "GOLDEN AGE": THE FIRST HALF CENTURY

The last pillar of this new society was the native chieftains (this work focuses on those from Cuernavaca) that led their communities to join the Spanish conquistadors in bringing about the defeat of their historical enemies, the Aztecs. Then they partnered with the Spanish in administering their communities and seeking ways to uplift their people. As a result, their cities and regions became showcases for intercultural cooperation and a multitude of enterprises involving the foundation of places for Christian worship; the cultivation of new agricultural products; the introduction of horses and cattle; and the creation of new commercial networks for wheat, sugar, cotton clothing, etc.

This book concentrates on the geographical area in and around Cuernavaca[5] (and the current State of Morelos for which it is the capital city). There are two basic reasons for this: First, that is where Cortés, the conquistador-turned-civic-activist, chose to build his palace, raise his family, and direct his multifaceted activities.

And second, that is where perhaps the most important of relevant documents have their locus of attention. The recently "rediscovered" Cuernavaca *códices* provide convincing information about how the chieftains of that region chose to ally their communities with Cortés's army to wage war against the Aztecs; about their baptism and then participation in the Catholic Church; and how they protected their communities' public lands by measuring, recording, and then filing the resulting documents in local archives. Another set of historical records demonstrate how, during the period in question, many of those same Cuernavaca chieftains sought and then found, via the Spanish courts, the needed protection for their communities against exploitation on the part of the most unprincipled of their new feudal lords. In the past few decades, we also have in hand, for the first time, a letter to the king written by Indian leaders of an Indian community who praise the leadership of Cortés. Also new to researches only in recent decades are the letters written by three renowned Franciscan monks who, having served in and around Cuernavaca, display their pride in having led the remarkable evangelical campaign to bring Christianity to millions of Mexican Indians, and defend the role of the conquistador-turned civic leader, Hernán Cortés, in bringing about that exceptional biracial society that existed in the first half-century of post-conquest Mexico.

The above paragraphs might surprise those readers familiar with any one of an abundant number of books that condemn the actions of conquistador leader, Hernán Cortés, as well as Mexico's early Spanish religious and colonial leadership. As a result, those readers might legitimately question motives and results of this author in undertaking this new historical inquiry aimed at countering two centuries of here-to-fore highly regarded scholarship both in Mexico and the United States. In "Notes About Sources," at the end of this book I address this issue in greater detail.

Understandably, even the informed reader is apt to condemn many of the customs and belief systems commonly held or practiced during those conflictive times, such as "conquest," colonialism, white supremacy, feudalism, and slavery (even George Washington, two centuries after Cortés, would embrace, whether explicitly or implicitly, most of these institutions!). Tuchman's conclusions about her studies of Western Europe also can be seen as relevant to my own focus on Mexico's early sixteenth century: the period's "political and moral degradation and vicious behavior . . . walked . . . to an unusual degree . . . with [a few] wonderous developments."[6]

A most unusual circumstance underlies my choice to offer a new perspective of Mexico's early Sixteenth-century history: the recent appearance of several important documents that were totally unknown to the outstanding scholars treating these and related issues over the past century. Some of these documents had laid totally undisturbed for centuries in a handful of important archives, perhaps because they were written in Náhuatl, the nearly-forgotten language of the Aztecs. Add to these other documents that were known to early researchers and writers, but later—at the beginning of the 19th century—were "devalued" and then relatively "forgotten" given the sometimes-rabid anti-Spanish views that came to predominate throughout Mexico and elsewhere. Only since the 1970s were these documents either translated into Spanish for the first time, or reevaluated and made newly available to a new generation of readers.

The recent availability of these important historical documents (which I detail in *Notes about Sources* at the end of this book) justifies the need for a reexamination of events and society during this period: the first half century following the submission of the Aztecs. Indeed, the informed reader will realize that the contents of this book represent an abrupt departure from many studies published by accomplished researchers over the past two centuries.

In Chapter 1, I provide important reasons for why readers should regard Hernán Cortés as not just "one more conquistador" and why the vanquishing of the Aztecs should not be regarded as merely one more instance of European "conquest." As a young man venturing to the newly discovered Caribbean islands, Cortés was moved by the cruelties inflicted on the island Indians serving under his fellow Spaniards. With uncommon personal skills, he maneuvered to take charge of the expeditionary force sent to (what we now call) the Mexican mainland. At the head of five hundred soldiers, he and the Merced priest Bartolomé Olmedo enacted practices of "conquest" that won the trust of local chieftains. Acting together, the combined Spanish-Indian army brought about the definitive defeat, first of the Aztec-dominated communities located in today's state of Morelos and then of the powerful confederation headed by the ruthless Aztec oligarchy.

In Chapter 2, I treat a topic only alluded to in a few known sources: how, even before the final submission of the Aztecs, a delegation of Cuernavaca's Indian chieftains traveled two days to the Spaniards' army's base near Mexico City to offer support for the latters' campaign against their hated masters, the Aztecs. They were not alone: the leaders of tribe after tribe would join with the band of determined white-skinned adventurers, mounted on (what for them must have appeared as) "magical" four-legged beasts and wielding smoky arms that silently killed their enemies from a substantial distance. Uniting together, they would put asunder the Aztecs' oppressive domination. In this chapter, I focus on the testimony of one of those chieftains, as contained in *Códices de Cuernavaca*, that only thirty years ago was translated from Náhuatl to Spanish, published, and made available to a world public.

In Chapter 3, I give careful attention to an intriguing section of the here-to-fore vastly undervalued chronical of the Cortés-led activities in Mexico: Bernal Díaz del Castillo's *Historia verdadera* de *la conquista de México*. In this history, the octogenarian author captured with his uncanny powers of memory a thousand details about his participation, when as a youth a half-century before, he had accompanied Cortés in Mexico. In light of the information provided by the recently discovered Náhuatl documents, the work by Bernal Díaz, previously undervalued, acquires a new and deserved importance as a reliable historical document. In this chapter I focus on only one episode treated by Díaz.[7] Díaz's commentary reveals startling information about a few of the protagonists in those and subsequent events: the haughty Aztec prince Cuauhtémoc; the conniving Crown representatives who would join with personal enemies to thwart Cortés's initiatives; the young Indian concubines choosing to remain with their new Spanish mates; and the common soldiers who, throughout the post conquest period, would remain loyal to the prerogatives and council of their leader, Hernán Cortés.

Chapters 4, 5, and 8 present brief background information about the soldiers participating in the conquest, the advanced Indian civilization in some of Mexico's cities, and Cortés's dealings with the Crown. All of this information will assist the reader in "contextualizing" the new material treated in the remaining chapters.

In Chapter 6, I treat the constructive relationship that came to exist between Cortés and the native leaders of Cuernavaca during the first post-conquest years, after those chieftains accepted Cortés as Cuernavaca's new "feudal baron." I base my study on the ground-breaking work, first published in 1991 by Juan Dubernard Chauveau, who collects and translates to Spanish the recently recovered *Códices de Cuernavaca*. Among the many documents included in this work, I focus on those which were dictated in Nahuatl by the Cuernavaca chieftains under Cortés's direction. I highlight the motivations behind Cortés's choice of Cuernavaca as the center for his future activities. He would spend time with the Indian nobles and assess their special qualities. On the basis of this, he would make the momentous decision of assigning them to continue in their previous role of governing over the nearby communities. He would survey regional resources and commercial possibilities. He would make initial plans to invest resources and harness the labor of native workers to found dozens of successful modernization projects and agricultural enterprises. Cuernavaca was where Cortés chose to build his "palace," which would also serve as administrative center for his multiple enterprises as well as residence for himself and his growing family.

In Chapter 7, I treat the organization of the evangelization campaign—one of the most celebrated religious "happenings" of the sixteenth century, when almost a thousand monks, born and formed in Europe, dedicated their energies for over a half century to bring millions of Mexicans into the Catholic fold. My primary sources are several texts written by the Belvís Franciscan friars—the honored leaders of that campaign—which have never before been translated into English. In this chapter (also in Appendix A), I treat a topic that no previous historian has treated: the positive relationship of over twenty-five years between the ex-conquistador Cortés and several of the Franciscan friars.

In Chapters 9 and 11, I continue to recount important events in Cuernavaca's early history, again using as my main source the newly-recovered *códices* dictated by the Cuernavaca chieftains. Following Cortés's instructions, these chieftains performed the measurements and then dictated in Náhuatl their descriptions of the physical boundaries for their respective communities and provide information about their church activities and governance during the initial decades of the post conquest period. Also important are official summaries of little-known court cases through which the natives succeeded in moderating the conditions of their servitude to Cortés; in these, for the first times ever, the Náhutal testimonies were translated to Spanish and then preserved official court documents. I also return to the writings by the Franciscan monks, but now to focus attention on how the decades-long evangelization campaign played itself out specifically in and around Cuernavaca. I end the chapter by quoting from letters written by three of these friars who, toward the end of their respective lives, saw fit to defend before both the sitting king and posterity the character and legacy of their deceased friend and associate, the conquistador leader Hernán Cortés.

In Chapter 12, I summarize existing studies to present an abbreviated history of the modernization projects initiated during this time period in Morelos, the present-day Mexican state whose capital city is Cuernavaca.[8] Cortés, taking advantage of Indian labor and tributes, proved to be a resourceful entrepreneur. He spearheaded the construction of new roads, water sources, churches, and monasteries. He founded sugar-making enterprises. He was the first person in New Spain to plant and grow wheat, fruits, grapes (vineyards), and vegetables. He initiated operations to produce silk and to raise horses, pigs, cattle, and mules. (In other regions of New Spain, he was a leader in mining, shipbuilding, and the commercialization of clothing.)

In Chapter 13, I explain how and why Mexico's Golden Age, this interesting and largely unstudied chapter of national history, was short-lived. The reasons are varied and complicated. A brief anticipation: New Spain (Mexico) suffered from the growing opposition in official Spanish circles to "humanist" ideas and practices, the fall from favor of the Franciscan monks, and the growing corruption in colonial government. Paralleling these factors was the steep demographic fall caused by recurring epidemics (beginning in 1545, a quarter century after the final submission of the Aztecs); the retirement of emperor Charles V and replacement by his son, Felipe II; and the Crown's implementation of policies in New Spain that invited increased Indian oppression. In short, the so-named Golden Age passed into history, only to be replaced by the oppressive colonial system that was to remain for four more centuries.

The three appendices treat related material. In Appendix A, I discuss the serious rivalries that erupted between the Franciscans and the Dominicans during the period under study. I also treat (for the first time, to my knowledge) the complicated role played in Mexico during those very years by Friar Bartolomé de las Casas, the famed Indian defender. In Appendix B, I present information about Tlaxcala, one of the several sixteenth-century Mexican cities ruled by Indian chieftains but the only one treated adequately by the criticism.[9] In Appendix C, I present detailed information about the most important source of new documents that I have drawn upon for writing this book: Juan Dubernard Chauveau's *Códices de Cuernavaca*.

In "Notes on Sources" I present a rough chronology of the important studies that, over the past five centuries, have been done about the acts, events, and personages treated in this book. Most surprising is the "rediscovery"—beginning only in the 1970s—of important documents (most written in Náhuatl, the language of the Aztecs), most of which were unknown and unavailable to important 20th century investigators, whose contents justify the new appraisals that I offer in this book.

The material included in the text of the book has a target public of interested readers. In contrast, much of the information included in the notes and appendices is intended for those specialists who, like myself, have spent months, if not years, dealing with the subjects at hand.

I have chosen to preserve most of the original place-name spellings as they appear in the quoted material. All translations to Spanish are my own unless otherwise indicated.

CHAPTER 1

A DIFFERENT TYPE OF CONQUISTADOR, A DIFFERENT TYPE OF CONQUEST

In this chapter I treat three different moments before Cortés and his soldiers achieved the military defeat and then the submission of the Aztecs.[10] Of particular interest is the campaign to defeat the Aztec-led garrisons located in (today's) state of Morelos, which a year later would become part of the Marquesado granted to him by the king.

Hernán Cortés was perhaps the most enterprising individual of his conflictive century. Historians have pointed out his superb faculties of manipulation, intelligence, and intuition, and no one doubts the "genius" of his conquest, which—in purely military terms—was matched only by the deeds of Caesar and Alexander. Then, after the submission of the Aztecs, the man to all appearances continued to be motivated by the same mixture of self-interest and striving for glory. While he had an uncanny ability to create enemies, he also inspired life-long loyalty in a core group of soldiers and, after a few years, hundreds of thousands of natives and dozens of principled Franciscan monks.

Much could also be written about the Spanish men who formed the core of his fighting force. Often repeated by historians is what they shared with Cortés: their primary motivation of obtaining gold and winning for themselves a comfortable future life commanding Indian servants and farm workers. When finally victorious, they would expect to receive not only riches, but also honor and fame; they would expect to be recognized as "hijos de algo."[11] Before setting off for the Americas, most had lived as serfs in poor villages of drought-inflicted southern Spain. Few possessed literacy skills. Their manners were rough and hearty. Among their numbers there were those who would come to demonstrate unmitigated greed as well as cruelty to the Indians placed into their charge. But most also had positive qualities: in their marches or when engaged in battle, they had carried themselves with pride. As Cortés proudly wrote in his first letter to the king, "And we always had the custom, in whatever place we'd be, to present ourselves as Christians, as servants of the Church, as Spaniards, and as vassals of the emperor don Carlos who was the best leader then existing in the world."[12] Those choosing to follow Cortés were the type of men who, when led by a principled leader, would demonstrate constructive conduct, whether in war or peace. With regard to their mission, they were not plagued either by doubts or dissension, because they knew that the principles guiding them in war and peace were sanctioned by both their king and their Church.

Ignored by many previous commentators is the deep loyalty of a significant number of those soldiers to their captain during the bellicose encounters, which would continue for decades after the submission of the Aztecs. They, following the example established by Cortés, would demonstrate time and again their support for the new regime headed up by the first two viceroys and the Franciscan leaders. All together, they would defend Indian rights and would support the decades-long campaign to lead Mexico's entire population into the Christian fold.

In contrast, most of the army's officer class had been low-level feudal lords back in Spain. They did not see themselves as exploiters; their formation was in the management of manors, with few having enjoyed significant wealth or comfort. Some—like Cortés himself—were *secondones* who would not inherit either land or wealth, meaning that they had little to lose in their American adventures.

A DIFFERENT TYPE OF CONQUISTADOR, A DIFFERENT TYPE OF CONQUEST

In 1519, the initial group of 400+ Spanish soldiers and officials spent several months near the current-day city of Veracruz organizing their forthcoming march inland toward the Aztec capital. Most were favorably inclined to the likable Cortés, whom the irascible Cuban governor Diego de Velázquez had named, perhaps reluctantly, as their Captain-General. But few observers would have imagined how quickly this vague acceptance grew into respect and—in even a few cases—devotion. Historians expounding on those events have speculated that this was due to favorable circumstances, when added to Cortés' force of character and charisma. It's also important to note that the growing confidence in his leadership was accomplished across class lines: this relatively untested leader was to gain the deep trust of not only common soldiers, but also that of at least four war veterans hailing from the same low-nobility strata as Cortés himself: Andrés de Tapia, Cristóbal de Olid, Pedro de Alvarado, and Gonzalo de Sandoval. It must have impressed everyone that Cortés had been willing to invest his worldly possessions to outfit the expedition, to buy arms, armor, horses, and food supplies, and to offer assistance for willing recruits too poor to provide for themselves. Then, in the face of Governor Velázquez's attempts to withdraw the previous commission naming him as leader, Cortés received the support of all to free his command from immediate interference. One biographer:

> With his gayest humor there mingled a settled air of resolution, which made those who approached him feel they must obey; and which infused something like awe into the attachment of his most devoted followers. Such a combination, in which love was tempered by authority, was the one probably best calculated to inspire devotion in the rough and turbulent spirits among whom his lot was to be cast. . . . Such is the portrait left to us by his contemporaries of this remarkable man . . . .[13]

Let there be no doubt: when that armed group with three score horses set off from the coast, Cortés was firmly in command.

As the days passed into weeks, all must have come to appreciate Cortés' hands-on style of leadership; he always insisted on being at the center of the action. He would willingly join common soldiers in accomplishing the most undesirable of tasks. When it came to military confrontations, he would not hesitate to lead by example, positioning himself at the front of the lines. And luck always seemed to accompany him: only a few times during the three years of belligerent activity did he suffer the slightest of wounds.

Add to that his ability to maintain his soldiers' incentive and discipline. There is no surviving record of veterans having served formerly in other military campaigns now voicing exasperation or frustration before the decisions of their "green-horned" leader. Experienced eyes must have admired the natural way that he surmounted common problems or speedily resolved minor disputes. Early on, he must have demonstrated a unique ability to humorously defuse even the most minor of challenges to his authority.

As far as we know or can surmise, Cortés had few problems with the common soldiers—the *peones* as he called them. Some constituted a swarthy bunch and a few had a criminal past. Wisely, he imposed strict rules of conduct. Seldom did he have to resort to severe punishment for a foul deed committed by an individual who, in another moment, would take the sword in hand to perform fearless feats of war.

Yet sternness alone—Cortés intuited—was not sufficient. He had to be a master at balancing punishment with reward in order to assure their unquestioned loyalty. The chronicler, Bernal Díaz del Castillo—himself a young participant at that time—would capture well this aspect of Cortés' uncanny leadership abilities in writing his *Historia verdadera* some fifty years later:

> when he got angry with of the soldiers in our circle of friends, he would say: 'You're much better than that;' and when he got really mad, the veins on his throat and forehead will swell up; and when he got furious, he would slam a piece of firewood to the ground, but he wouldn't say any angry or offensive word, whether it be to a captain or a common soldier. But we could

tell he felt hurt—especially when soldiers were inconsiderate or when they showed their anger or frustration. Even then, he wouldn't respond with either anger or offensive language—even when he might have been justified to do so. In that type of situation, I heard him say on at least a few occasions: 'Just shut up now' . . . or 'Get over it. God will be with you if you're more considerate next time in what you say. Otherwise, I'll be the first to punish you. And understand this: I won't go easy on you.'[14]

Cortés must have demonstrated, from the very start, signs of an extraordinary leader.

Another factor which—from the distance of posterity—sets his legacy apart from that of other conquistadores: Cortés' religiosity. In an early instance, this took the form of his anger upon first viewing the gross idolatry of the natives' worship—a reaction which was tempered by the moderate council of one of the figures accompanying his group, the Merced monk Bartolomé de Olmedo. In his own letters written to the King (known to us as *Cartas de relación*), Cortés hardly mentions this man. In the always informative pages of *Historia verdadera*, the chronicler Díaz del Castillo, although mentioning Olmedo's name on several occasions, only suggests his growing importance as Cortés' strategic and well as "theological" advisor. Years later, Cervantes de Salazar, writing his own history on the basis of interviews with many of the actual participants, characterized Olmedo as "muy sagaz y de buenos medios," de "muy buenas razones", de "astucia y maña", "muy regocijado", "hombre entendido."[15] All in his band came to realize that Cortés and Olmedo shared a common, dual, orientation: fervent Christian zeal and charity.[16]

According to Díaz del Castillo:

[Cortés] explained to the men why our great king had sent us to this new lands and what he expected us to accomplish: to put an end to the sacrifices that one group did to another, to end all those evil sacrifices, to make so that they don't continue robbing one from another, that they cease adoring those horrendous idols, and that we plead with them to place throughout their cities and on their alters the figure of the cross . . . and an image of Our Virgin Señora. And they will see what good will come of it, and what our God will do for them. [17]

Cortés, almost from the first, had realized the tyrannical bondage by which the Aztecs, from their as-of-yet unknown capital located a two-week's march inland, exercised over almost all the Indian groups they were encountering. He had witnessed signs of the fear that the latter demonstrated before the Aztecs' representatives periodically visiting their communities. He had also observed how the local leaders trembled in fulfilling their terrible responsibility of rounding up and then delivering, twice a year, several hundred captives—which included their community's slaves, workers, and most prized virgins and athletic youth—who were destined to be sacrificed upon the Aztecs' sacrificial altars.

These Indians were simple people. They were obedient; they were respectful. Many—but not the fiercely autonomous *tlaxcaltecas*— were meek before the bloodthirsty demands of their Aztec overlords. In contrast to the encomienda Indians Cortés had controlled in both Hispaniola and Cuba, most of Mexico's indigenous communities were organized and accepted their place in the stratified, hierarchical order. In the most advanced communities, upper-class Indians governed with unquestioned authority, favoring the values of fairness and justice. In turn, the lower classes responded faithfully to the instructions of their superiors. Cortés and Olmedo intuited one factor about them, and then based their war campaign on it: that once these Indian communities submitted to the authority of Cortés and the Spaniards, they would prove to be reliable combat allies. What's more, they were pious—in contrast to the Moorish "infidels" back in Spain. Most had a strong "religious orientation." In all probability the Spanish would be successful in converting them to the "True Faith." [18]

Cortés and Olmedo must have brainstormed: how could a military alliance with the *tlaxtaltecas* and other Indian communities be transformed into something far more lasting? How—when the tyrannical Aztecs were defeated—would they motivate the Indians to willingly convert to Catholicism and then accept instruction in Catholic belief and rituals? How would they, as protagonists in this divine mission, save millions of Mexican Indians from eternal perdition? How would they bring into the world community of Christian states a new Mexican nation?

First priorities first. If they were to forge a peaceful alliance with the local Indian tribes, then that would dovetail conveniently with their rapidly evolving military strategy to combat, and then vanquish, the Aztec overclass. In no way could the 400+ well-armed Spanish soldiers, if forced to operate alone, pull off the military victories that would be needed to bring to their knees the several hundred-thousand Aztecs. Their task required the assistance of Indian allies. They would need many.

Tlaxcala. It was an impressive city! Cortés was most favorably impressed with its competent leaders and the deep respect that the ordinary citizens had for them. This Indian community was prosperous and organized—nowhere did the Spanish see signs of the abject poverty that proliferated among the lowest classes of Indian communities near the coast. Furthermore, thousands of their warriors were not only well armed; their hatred of the Aztecs motivated them to support his army in every way for the inevitable struggles that lay ahead. Cortés instantly realized that if he could forge a positive relationship, it could serve as an example for the tribes or communities they would meet on the road ahead. Playing his cards well, he could multiply ten-fold, a hundred-fold, the number of soldiers constituting his fighting ranks.

In concert with Father Olmedo, Cortés and his war lieutenants forged a plan that they would follow in marching toward the Aztec capital (and relatively the same plan would be followed a decade later in yet-to-be visited regions of the subcontinent.)[19] First, at the moment of initial contact, Cortés would send out overtures for the new Indian community to submit peacefully to the authority of the

Spanish. Second, if the Indian leadership refused, then swords would be drawn and a battle would ensue; the Spanish forces under Cortés, with superior arms and unbreakable determination, almost always ended up victorious. Depending on the resistance that had been offered, the Spanish would punish (and sometimes execute) the resisting leadership and, on occasion, burn weapons or whole neighborhoods as punishment. Then, the Spaniards would demonstrate their willingness to accept the submission of a more willing Indian leadership. This is where Father Olmedo would step forward to do his part.

Using the translation services of Doña Marina and Jerónimo de Aguilar, the Merced monk would stand before the now compliant Indian leadership and explain to them that the Spanish soldiers had done battle with their Indian warriors "in compliance with our holy faith and with the instructions of our own rulers, who were the best princes in the world, and that both the Spanish soldiers present, as well as their king in Spain, acted on behalf of an even greater and more holy authority," that of the Christian God.[20] He would explain that the objective of the Spanish leader Cortés was for the Indians to give up their former gods and rituals and receive baptism as Christians. Their submission would bestow upon them a new status as vassals of the emperor, with all the rights and obligations entailed: first, they—including women and children—would enjoy the same legal status as all Spaniards; and second, they would be subject to the same obligations of rendering services, paying tribute, and bearing arms in defense of the regime. Then, following the delivery of that basic message, Olmedo would begin to instruct the very basics of the Christian religion.

As Cortés quickly found out, the above plan would not be easy to achieve. The example of Tlaxcala is again instructive. Initial native resistance to any Spanish prerogative proved to be intense. The Spanish were forced to fight long, protracted battles and then performed the exemplary punishment of cutting off the hands of native spies or those who had feigned allegiance. Even after an alliance had been forged, *tlaxcalteca* dissidents would continue to cause problems. But, when it came to the final military campaign launched against the Aztecs, that community was to assume a huge role: the provision of 50,000 warriors and other important services.

It is to be noted that Olmedo's message to the Indian communities was also aimed at impacting the "spiritual formation of Cortés and his army. . . . Their service on behalf of the Heavenly Father, in the form of the conversion of the Indians, went hand-in-hand with the mental set progressively embraced by this now autonomous army. . . . This missionary consciousness progressively motivated, informed, and regulated the soldiers involved in the campaign; it came to influence and determine their conduct as they advanced."[21] Following successful battles and winning the compliance of the *tlaxtalteca* community, the Spanish soldiers "became very enthused" upon listening to the speech made to them by their Captain Cortés, who instructed that in order for all of them to "act like Christians, we are obligated to battle against the enemies of our religion; that we must pray for God to bless us with his grace and intercede on our behalf and save us from any danger." Bernal Díaz, at that time a common soldier participating in that campaign, concluded: "all of us promised . . .. that in high spirits we would be very willing to die on behalf of our Catholic religion." Olmedo's wise and benevolent counsel served "to mitigate the attitude of the cruelest of the soldiers, convincing them to hold back the sword in dealing with the unfortunate natives." As a result of that spiritual leadership, no soldier in that army was to doubt the high mission which they were to accomplish as soldiers of the Cross.

Almost all of those Spanish soldiers, we can safely assume, embraced in name and most probably in daily practices an outward commitment to Catholic ideals. Their initial adherence to Cortés' leadership would grow into a life-long loyalty to both his figure and ideas. It is important to emphasize that Cortés' humanistic brand of Catholicism was deep and authentic, and that it touched the deepest strands of religious sentiment in a great many of the soldiers under his leadership.

Cortés's Leadership Put to the Test

Here I skip over important events: the Spanish army's bold march to the Aztec capital and then their success in taking the Aztec leader, Moctezuma, as their puppet/captive. After several weeks the soldiers' trust in their inspired leader would be put to an extreme test. This is the part of the conquest history when Cortés and his men learned the perhaps not unexpected news that two dozen ships carrying a thousand Spanish soldiers had arrived at Mexican shores a hundred leagues away, and that the latter were commanded by Pánfilo Narváez, under orders from Cortés' jealous ex-employer, Cuban governor Velázquez, to oust Cortés from the leadership position of the Mexican campaign.

Cortés was not naïve; he knew that in Spanish society "might makes right," that if the command of the Mexican campaign ever became a court issue, then a powerful noble such as Velázquez would win the backing of Crown authorities, if he did not enjoy it already. Furthermore, he intuited that the "legal fiction" by which he, backed by his inner circle, had assumed control over that small army would not withstand a power-backed scrutiny in official circles. So he had to take immediate and effective action in order that the issue of command over the Spanish army would never appear in a judge's docket. He intuited correctly that if he were successful in the months ahead, then that would relegate to irrelevance any other consideration. So it meant that he had no other option than to take immediate action in order to parry the threat then offered by the sudden appearance of the Narváez-led army. Given the disparity between the huge number of soldiers at the latter's command and the limited number of his own—which were already stretched thin in his growing commitments between Veracruz and Mexico City—he had to avoid direct confrontation of any type. So whatever he might decide to do, it would have to involve stealth and surprise.

Another consideration: there, in that moment, he had high confidence in three important issues: own leadership abilities, the God-ordained mission he had assumed, and his men's shared feelings on both accounts. Also, he had learned about the dissension that divided the men commanded by Narváez. That meant that if he were to play his cards right, then many of those soldiers might be willing or persuaded to abandon that force and join his own.

Cortés' best biographer, William Prescott, opines that "It was one of those occasions that proved the entire influence which Cortés held over these wild adventurers."[22] His audacious plan required absolute obedience and unified action; there was no room for error. Cortés once more called upon the friar Olmedo, who had proven to be as sly as he was holy, to carry out a most delicate mission: to travel to Veracruz, meet personally with Narváez, and confuse him by offering false assurances. Cortés then left the Aztec capital with seventy carefully chosen soldiers to accompany him—those who had demonstrated both "mettle" and strong loyalty. He left the remaining 150 soldiers under his lieutenant Pedro de Alvarado, who would have to withstand the growing Aztec opposition in Mexico City. His select team travelled rapidly, recruiting on the way another hundred trustworthy soldiers. Taking advantage of stormy weather and flood conditions, they were able to approach Narváez's camp undetected. Their surprise tactics worked as they had hoped: Narváez was taken prisoner and the latter's 1500 men were either forced or induced to join the Cortés-led command.

In subsequent chapters I treat how, during the 25 or so years following the submission of the Aztecs, this same important factor came to the fore time and again: the total respect which a significant body of Spanish soldiers continued to hold for their one-time captain. Although court officials would see fit to remove Cortés from actual control over the day-to-day governance of New Spain a short four years after the Aztec submission, he would continue to be revered and respected by the men he had once led. This also included Mexico's Indian population. The ex-warriors and their communities would treasure till the end of their lives the figure and authority of that leader of men, Hernán Cortés.

In fact, historians looking back at those first decades of Mexico might conclude that whenever the influence of Cortés was either muffled or absent, then dissension burst forth and chaos ruled. And then, when the authority of Cortés was once more in force, order became restored. This situation stands in stark contrast to the strife between Spanish leaders that typified society, politics, and government in the great majority of American lands under the dominion of the Spanish King.

Conquering the Aztecs in Morelos (1520)[23]

After Narváez's humiliating defeat, Cortés hurried back to the Aztec capital. The Aztecs, furious over the indignities they had suffered over the previous two months, had killed their humiliated ruler Moctezuma and had risen in revolt. The Spaniards miraculously escaped, suffering considerable casualties.

Back at Mexico's Caribbean coast Cortés, like the classical Phoenix, was able to lift himself up from defeat. With his customary resourcefulness and determination, he recruited yet another army of Spaniards, several dozen more horses, and a sufficient supply of munitions. He and his army spent months between Veracruz and Tlaxcala recuperating and formulating a new plan for conquest.

An integral part of that new plan involved constructing in Tlaxcala a fleet of small, maneuverable boats, the *bergantines*, so that his forces' attacks by water would supplement the battles his soldiers would wage on the causeways stretching from dry land to the Aztecs' island-city capital. Over those months Cortés assembled a team of skilled craftsmen to carry out the hundred different specialty tasks involved in ship building. In addition, allied Indians had to be specially trained in the less-skilled labors of rope making, lumber cutting, boat carpentry, metal forging, and sails stitching. He recruited porters and then directed them in ferrying the thousands of pieces of essential equipment and munitions from Veracruz to the central highlands. Could gun power be made locally? Housing for his soldiers had to be obtained. And—how to guarantee the continuous supply of food for the hundreds of workmen and soldiers? A whole network of production, supply, and transport had to be devised, supervised, and maintained. Only one person possessed those organization skills: Cortés himself.

Add to that the problem of maintaining his soldiers' incentive, discipline, and continued loyalty. Some of his officers, formerly serving under rivals Diego de Velázquez and Pánfilo de Narváez, had been forced to participate, and rebellion on their part was always a possibility.

Finally, Cortés and his combined Spanish-Indian army began—once again—their march toward the Aztec capital. Indian porters carried on their backs the weapons, munitions and supplies they would need, in addition to the dissembled bergantines. This time, along the way, willing Indian warriors from dozens of communities added considerably to their ranks. Their route led them past the native city of Chalco, and then to Texcoco, located on the eastern shore of the great lake in the middle of which was located the Aztec island-capital of Tenochtitlán.

On that shore, Cortés directed his craftsmen to assemble, once again, the fourteen *bergantines*. There would be no time to alter any important feature of the sailing ships being reconstructed. Even with the supervision of skilled master-builder Martín López, Cortés insisted on his own involvement to mount tillers to each of the reassembled hulls.

Meanwhile he coordinated with his new Indian allies to supply the food and supplies that would be necessary for the combined Spanish-Indian forces to launch the final water-land onslaught.

At the beginning of July, when preparations were well underway, his Indian allies made known to him that, two days to the south, hostile warriors were amassing to launch a surprise attack against his army. An instant response was called for. Although lusting—as always—to assume the leadership position in this new campaign, he decided to assign the leadership position for this new campaign to his most reliable lieutenant, Gonzalo de Sandoval.

The chronicles treating these events provide the following details. The army, under the direction of Sandoval, left from the Spanish stronghold located at Texcoco. Among their number were 15 mounted Spaniards, 300 foot soldiers (several of whom were archers—*ballesteros*—and blunderbuss shooters—*escopeteros*), and thousands of armed Indian allies hailing from the regions of Tlaxcala and Tascuco. Heading east, they passed Chalco and then turned south to continue along the Aztec route to military strongholds at Oaxtepec and Yecapixtla. They passed through (today's) Milpa Alta, then chose a lesser-traveled road that led to either Totolapan or Atlatlahuan—or both. Still a half-day's travel from Oaxtepec, they had their first military encounter, with Spaniards equally matched with the Aztec-led enemy forces. Díaz del Castillo describes the "real difficult terrain and deep gullies . . . it was difficult to proceed, especially on account of the ravines."[24] These stretches of irregular terrain lessened the effectiveness of their own horse-mounted warriors. On one stretch of the "rough road," the horse under captain Gonzalo Domínguez "lost its footing and fell, falling on top of him. Seriously injured, he died a few days later."[25]

Arriving at the outskirts of Oaxtepec, they fended off the attack of 15,000 enemy forces. Several of their infantrymen were wounded as well as five of their horses. Their only consolation was being able to pass the night among the trees of a huge, fenced-in garden—occupied today by the famous water park. Both Díaz and Cortés, in their respective chronicles, described those gardens as more elegant than any other in the known world.

In the next few days, the struggle only intensified when Sandoval's Spanish-Indian army arrived at the outskirts of Yecapixtla. There the enemy troops, throwing rocks from the "top of a high mound," made impossible an attack by the Spaniards' mounted soldiers. The struggle was fierce, with both sides suffering casualties. Díaz, in his written account, describes the nearby stream turning red with the spilt blood of the fallen. By day's end, the locals under the direction of Aztec war lords again succeeded in repelling the Spanish attack. Sandoval, returning with his troops to the Spanish base near Texcoco, was scolded by Cortés for his failure to gain total victory.

The chieftains in and around Chalco, still fearing an Aztec-led attack, pleaded once again for the Spanish to wield their military might and eliminate that threat from the south. The number of Spaniards would be doubled, and accompanying them would be 20,000 native warriors from Tesuico. This time Cortés himself would command, and he would take no chances: accompanying him would be three of his most important lieutenants: Alvarado, Tapia, and Olid.

Cortés knew that he had to choose a different land route than that followed by Sandoval, one that offered fewer obstructions for their horse-mounted cavalry. They passed near the Indian villages of San Felipe Neri and Tlalnepantla (today's national highway 142). Upon descending the steep hillside and arriving at the gently sloping plain (now planted, almost everywhere, with nopal) they met with thousands of Indian soldiers that had been dispatched from the Aztec stronghold at Oaxtepec. The latter also occupied the summits of several "peñoles"—steep mini-mountains or outcroppings—immediately to the west (which locals today know as Cerros Ayotzín, Tepozoco, and Tonantzín.[26]) As the Spanish advanced, they met fierce resistance. But they had a technical advantage with their blunderbusses, crossbows, and horse-mounted warriors. They slaughtered the enemy in their path, and in doing so suffered a few casualties (as duly noted by the three chroniclers treating these events: Cortés, Gómara, and Díaz del Castillo). A great number of their Indian allies also fell before the enemy's resistance. But with their overwhelming might they successfully took possession of several of the enemy's "fortalezas y mamparos"—fortified outposts. During hours of heated battle near (today's) San José de Los Laureles, the enemy progressively retreated.

The chronicles provide detailed and colorful descriptions of these tense battles to the north of the town of Tlayacapan, with indigenous warriors occupying the tops of the surrounding *peñoles*, continuing to obstruct the Spanish advance. In his account, Díaz del Castillo impressionistically describes that terrain: it was "quite flat, but every so often there arose small, pointed summits, and we continued driving them in front of us until we came to yet another, this time immense and well-defended *peñol*."[27] The Spanish, although dominating the plain below, still had to struggle against the vegetation: "a particular tree growing everywhere in that area has a thick trunk covered with thorns." But the Indian forces, intimidated by the Spaniards' unrelenting attacks and without water sources, soon surrendered and sued for peace.[28]

The local women urged their warriors to put down their arms, communicating through signals their willingness to provide bread and tortillas to the Spanish soldiers. Under these circumstances, Cortés began his now-routine practice of winning their allegiance. Through his translators, he communicated his generous proposals for peace: He would pardon their recent belligerency and protect them from future Aztec reprisals if they would work to convince neighboring tribes to submit. Then, it was Fray Melgarejo's turn: he instructed the locals to cast aside their idols, cease performing the bloody rites of Aztec worship, and accept the True Religion that offered them consolation in their daily sufferings and salvation in the afterlife.

The events just related at Tlayacapan were the climax for this military expedition: the Spanish had demonstrated to the indigenous locals several important things: first, their superiority in military might; second, their determination to apply that might, without mercy, until victorious in the field; third, their willingness, as demonstrated in both word and deed, to accept the submission of any and all indigenous communities; fourth, the Spaniards' willingness to protect their new indigenous subjects from future reprisals on the part of their former masters; and fifth, the Spaniards' offer to accept the natives, of any social class, into not only their new political system, but also into the folds of their benevolent religion.

Word about all this must have spread quickly from community to community, because within days, when the Spanish forces proceeded to Oaxtepec and Yecapixtla, the local forces welcomed them as their new masters, laying down their arms and pledging obedience.

Our sources provide no information about the Spanish army's passage to the west. We can assume that they spent a least a day travelling along the well-worn path (following the route of today's *libramento*) to arrive at Yautepec; and then at least another day passing through *El Valle de los lobos* that led to Tepoztlán and then to Cuernavaca and Juitepec. Apparently, news of the Tlayacapan pact of rendition had failed to impress the locals who were determined to resist.

Arriving at the outskirts of Cuernavaca, the Spaniards perceived that enemy warriors were stationed throughout the city's hills and ravines—a few being sixty feet in depth. The Díaz narrative captures the excitement how a few Spaniards and their Indian allies succeeding in climbing over tree branches to bridge the chasm and launch a surprise attack—which turned out to be the prelude to their total victory. On account of that military resistance, Cortés ordered the execution of dozens of the indigenous leaders and the burning of whole neighborhoods before offering peace:

> And Cortés then showed them his generous face and said all of us were vassals of a great master, the emperor Don Carlos, under whom all of us were happy to serve, that every single one of us felt blessed by his leadership, and that if they were to admit him, like us, as their leader and show him obedience, then he would receive them in peace. And I remember that those chieftains then said to us that because they had originally not come in peace, then our gods were justified in punishing not only their gods, but also in punishing them and their communities, and confiscating their possessions.

That night the Spaniards and their Indian allies celebrated a victory feast: for the former, the dog meat, corn, and beans that they had confiscated from the locals' well-stocked markets; for the latter, human flesh cut from the bodies of the fallen enemy. But an even greater treat must have been their lodgings: a spacious and well-tended garden belonging to the master of that town—huge, but still small in comparison to the protected garden of Oaxtepec. According to Díaz,

> There was room for all of us to bed down for the night; it was a real special place—with none of the bothers or irritations that I've told about in other parts of this history. In that immense garden our candles burnt steadily without the bother of breezes. There was no bothersome barking from the ever-present dogs; no mice scurried over our bodies spread out on the manicured grass. . . .

Of equal interest for the contemporary reader is the route chosen by Cortés to return back to the Valley of Mexico: a straight line uphill from the central plaza of Cuernavaca heading toward the Sierra de Ajusco, traversed the summit meadows, and then descended down to the central plain near the village of Tasqueña (this route offers no surprise to the contemporary reader: it is the path of the "regular highway" followed by every car before the construction of the modern "toll" freeway linking Cuernavaca to Mexico City). But Cortés's return along this route was not so easy. At the time, it must have consisted of nothing more than a faint pathway. A small horse-mounted party was sent ahead to scout the way, searching for any stream or sign of human habitation. Hiking up the endless slope, foot soldiers and Indian allies suffered extreme fatigue while passing "through totally uninhabited pine forests totally devoid of any water source." All the foot soldiers—Spaniards and Indians alike—suffered faintness; some fell unconscious in their tracks. A few were even left there to die. This certainly constituted one of the low points of the whole Spanish experience in Mexico.

But for Cortés himself, this must not have been the case. After a long day's ride, he and the few dozen horse-mounted Spaniards returned to the southern stretches of the great lake, and then another long day's ride back to *bergantín* construction site at Texcoco.

He must have returned enthused by what they'd seen: well-ordered Indian communities throughout, whose leaders were now eager to obey his slightest wish and command.

And equally impressive: the well-maintained, exotic gardens where his soldiers had found rest and solace—at both Oaxtepec and Cuernavaca. Cortés, in his written account, offers an enthusiastic description of the latter:

> That garden is the best, most extensive, and most beautiful and fresh that has ever been seen. Its perimeter must measure two leagues around, and you couldn't reach one end to the other with two bow shots. Water abounds: you find gentle streams of crystalline water every short distance. There are several perfect places to sit or even lie down—all surrounded by green: an infinite number of trees bearing different fruits, and underneath a variety of herbs and fragrant flowers. Believe

me, everything here is so well done; this garden is nothing less than spectacular.²⁹

The Indigenous cities in the Cuernavaca area were all blessed with sparking streams, unlike the dry countryside of almost all other regions of this New Land. And—what's more—Cuernavaca's bountiful natural landscapes invited the aesthetic inclinations of a benevolent population.

Gardens beckoned them; an honest, diligent community attended them. Cortés would return. He would want to return.

A "Conquest" or "An Indigenous Civil War"?

The military struggle leading to the defeat of the Aztecs has been called—perhaps incorrectly— "a conquest" by a great number of commentators and historians. But the fact of the matter is that the composition of the fighting forces serving under Cortés contained an overwhelming number of Indian warriors: the 1000 Spanish soldiers joined arms with 200,000+ indigenous warriors.³⁰ A apropos, a few historians have recently stated a truth largely hidden in so many previous accounts: "The Spanish victory was due totally to the alliances between Europeans and Mesoamericans." And: "Hernán Cortés was involved in . . . an indigenous civil war. . . . Those who won out in 1521 participated in an inter-ethnic coalition, 99% Mesoamerican, with numerous allied groups like the *tlaxcaltecas* y *texcocos*, who destroyed the Mexicans for their own reasons and objectives." And: those Indian communities previously living under the cruel tyranny of the Aztecs were motivated by their desire for "revenge, humiliation."³¹ In summary: "[I]t is pretty clear that Cortés was able to carry out his really awe-inspiring feat only because the bulk of the Mexican people welcomed him as a deliverer from the unbearable oppression of the Aztecs."³²

The important point has been made that the belligerency leading to the downfall and defeat of the Aztec empire was accomplished through the collaboration of two groups: the intrepid Spanish army led by Cortés, and an overwhelming number of Indians seeking revenge and liberation from their former Aztec overlords. So, "conquest" it was not. Might it more appropriately be called a "rebellion" or "civil war" in which the Spanish intervened? Yet other historians use the term the "Spanish interruption."

The rest of this book attempts to capture the largely fortuitous circumstances which resulted. At least for the first fifty years.

CHAPTER 2

CUERNAVACA'S CHIEFTAINS SUBMIT TO CORTÉS

Chroniclers would describe wholly different types of Indian communities existing across the expansive area that today we call Mexico. On the one hand, there were the violent barbarians inhabiting the hot coastal lands of Jalisco and the desert-like expanses to the north. But, on the other hand, and in great contrast, in New Spain's central highlands Cortés's army of conquistadores found prosperous people inhabiting well-managed cities. That is to say: the Indian principales *governing over a city such as Cuernavaca were, in almost every way, the social equivalents of the nobles occupying the higher rungs of Cortés's army (Alvarado, Olid, Sandoval). In those cities the Spanish soldiers marveled upon observing the expansive, orderly marketplaces and clean residential neighborhoods. Even those soldiers who had served the King in Constantinople or Rome (according to chronist Díaz del Castillo) had never before witnessed such comforts or splendor as those enjoyed by the* principales *in their residences and dress.*

Cortés's first visit to Morelos occurred in the early months of 1521—as recounted in Chapter 1—when his army, assisted by Indian allies, subdued all the Indian communities in the northern part of today's State of Morelos. Then, his final victory over the Aztec hierarchy would occur in August of that same year. In between those two happenings, a most important event occurred: the visit to his military headquarters in Coyoacán by a group of Indian chiefs from the region of Cuernavaca.

Only since the latter decades of the twentieth century, with the "rediscovery" of the *Cuernavaca códices*, do we know the following information: The "great noble" of Cuernavaca at that time was Don José Axayacátzin (we know him only by this Christianized name). The victorious Spanish had just departed, and the contingent of Aztec war chiefs directing the local warriors in battle had made haste to return to Tenochtitlan. Don José, remaining in Cuernavaca, must have realized the unique opportunity that the situation presented. He must have been impressed by Cortés's peace offer, that on the condition of his and his community's willing submission, the Spaniards henceforth would treat them as loyal vassals and would protect them against reprisals from their previous overlords, the Aztecs. Calling a council with the *principales* of his community, he proposed and then convinced them to follow his lead in carrying out a daring plan.

Over the next several weeks he and his warriors set off to force the compliance of the nobles predominating in 21 of the neighboring communities ("those who had fled"—?). We read his own words (written in the original Nahuatl language and now translated into Spanish), as found in one of the Cuernavaca codices that has recently come to light: ""I, at the head of my warriors, set out to do battle with the all the rest of the local chieftains. It took us two months and twenty days of tenuous battles, but we finally succeeded in defeating all of them and forcing their compliance to my plan."[33] Then, he and his warriors coerced the now-compliant *principales* from those communities to march with them to the Spaniards' camp near Texcoco in order that they, all together, demonstrate their willing submisson to the chief of the Spanish conquistadors. They traveled by foot, a journey that, each way, must have taken the better part of two or three days.

Don José provides a list of those towns under jurisdiction whose leaders participated in that ceremonial act of submission: "Huilanca Tlahualtepec, Ceptonco, Tlacotepec, Xocotitlan, Meyocan, Tlacichilpa,

Cuitlapilco, Calehuetepec, Tilsoyucan, Pilcayan, Macuicicluco, Petlatla, Tlapechco Tequanichan, Chichimecapa, Tequeactepec, Ahuixoapa, Xolotenamic, Tlamacayaca, Tonatiuhco, Quehuacentepic, y va a encontrar con Ahuexotla Cochtepec."[34] None of the place names are recognizable today.[35]

This chieftain, in the same document, also provides a list of the Cuernavaca elders participating in those events: ""all the mayors and officials serving under me . . . All are all *principales* of Panchimalco. . Don Christoval, Don Mateo Nezahualcoyotzín, Don Santiago Tecuipilzintli, Don Joseph Acamapitzín."

Aside from these recently rediscovered códices, I have not been able to identify a single historical source that mentions any of these names.[36] Mysteries deepen upon noting that this list of notables does not include two important historical figures whose names do appear in histories and legal documents: Yoatzín, "señor of Cuernavaca at the time of the arrival of the Spanish," and Don Hernando, "the señor's heir and successor, who was still a minor" and for whom "Cortés named himself guardian."[37] Is it possible that Don José's initiatives resulted from a "revolt" of his faction of Morelos nobles against Yoatzín, who had previously served as the Aztecs' point-man controlling Cuernavaca? I present further evidence of this assumption in the next chapter.

Immediately following this ceremonial submission at the Spaniards' Texcoco camp, Cortés saw fit to organize a baptismal ceremony, most probably conducted by one of the two priests who customarily served his army as chaplains, Father Bartolomé de Olmedo (of the Merced Order), or Juan Díaz. In organizing this event, Cortés once again was defying conventional procedures and venturing into terrain that, he knew, might cause him political problems in the future. Over the past half-century the standard practice for peninsular Spaniards had been to confer baptismal rights only to those Moors or Jews who had been able to demonstrate a firm understanding of Christian doctrine and practices, and who had already learned by memory, and could recite in Spanish, many of the standard orations and mass verses. But this was clearly not going to be the case with the Mexican nobility—and later populace. It was Cortés's decision—which would later be embraced by the Franciscan friars—that the good intentions and willingness of the Indians was qualification enough. In the months and years after the subjugation of the Aztecs, the natives would have time enough to learn what every Spanish-speaking Christian was required to learn. A *sine qua non* of the post-conquest society—which Cortés was already planning—would be the leadership role of a whole class of Spanish religious, who would instruct the natives in Catholic rites and beliefs.

The friars, which his allies back in the home country were already in the process of recruiting, would serve another essential function: through instruction and personal example, they would guide the Indian communities in the assimilation of new and acceptable practices that were standard for Christians everywhere. He mandated that all aspects of indigenous culture having to do with the rites of human sacrifice would cease immediately. A similar prohibition would also be in force against future acts of sodomy and bigamy. But he and those religious personnel at hand decided that they would willingly tolerate, at least until pacification were achieved across the continent, the common practice of warriors consuming the slain bodies of their enemies (he needed to count on the willing participation of warriors from both Tlaxcala and other indigenous communities). With all this decided, plans for baptismal rites went forward.

According to the Cuernavaca chieftain: "It was I who reduced the lesser chieftains to obedience in order lead them, en masse, to the presence of the *Señor Marqués* where they received the *Santo Bautismo*." According to the customary practice of the time, Indians—upon being baptized—accepted Christian names as substitutes for their birth names, while at the same time retaining their indigenous last names. (Within decades this practice would be modified: by the mid-1600s many leading Indian leaders, or their mestizo descendants, would also drop the Nahuatl last name in favor of Christian ones in their place.) Those high-ranking Spaniards present served as padrinos, or god-fathers: Cortés (of course), and also Alvarado, Tapia, Olid. A fiesta featuring food and drink then followed. Bernal Díaz wrote: "This is what I personally witnessed, and in other provinces of this land we Spaniards were diligent in doing the same."

CUERNAVACA'S CHIEFTAINS SUBMIT TO CORTÉS

We can assume that—as almost always—Aguilar and Doña Marina were present to serve as translators for the submission and baptism ceremonies. Most probably the native elders began by reminding Cortés about what they had communicated to him only weeks earlier—during Cortés's military excursion to Cuernavaca—that they had originally offered armed resistance to the Spanish because they were under orders from their Mixtec overlords to do so, that a large contingent of Aztecs had been present, intermixed with local soldiers, intimidating them, and directing the armed resistance to Cortés and his army entering into their communities.[38] They must have reminded Cortés of the promises he had then made to them, that if submitted to both the Spaniards' civil and religious authorities, and if they pledged obedience to the King Don Carlos, then Cortés would forgive them for their former resistance and would accept them as vassals.

The Cuernavaca chiefs must have been impressed with that initial offer. Most probably, they stood in "awe" before Cortés's powerful war machine; they were impressed that Cortés himself—according to his own words—was an obedient servant to yet a higher authority. Could they believe his generous offer, that of accepting them as equals before the Christian God and His Majesty, the Catholic King (and future emperor)? Their faith in his words, at this early moment, must have been nearly total.

All the above is evidence that even before the final submission of the Aztecs in Mexico City, the Indian leadership of Cuernavaca had already acquired the status of Cortés's faithful allies.

Viewed critically, this was a most startling series of events: a local chieftain, totally on his own initiative, had gone out of his way to force neighboring community leaders to participate in his—also most exceptional—plan: he would willingly lead the thousands of Cuernavaca residents in submitting to the will of the potent Spanish captain. This Cuernavaca chieftain had seen or intuited algo about the character of Cortés—in the days after the native peoples' military defeat in the latter months of 1520—that explains his willingness, only weeks later, to commit his own future and that of his people to the will of the Spanish commander.

One reliable history book calls them the Acolhuas, those people occupying the Cuernavaca Valley who came to be dominated by the Aztecs (called by some sources as Mixtecs).[39] This had occurred a whole century before the arrival of the Spanish. Theirs had resembled other Indigenous communities across the sub-continent, in that it was hardly an egalitarian society: a privileged group of nobles commanded vast numbers of commoners—the latter constituted about three-quarters of the total population. It is estimated that, at the beginning of the sixteenth century, the areas surrounding both Cuernavaca and Oaxtepec supported populations approaching 50,000 each, and other urban centers such as Yautepec, Tepoztlán, and Totolapan had between 20,000 and 30,000. The smaller communities of Tlayacapan, Tetela del Monte, Yecapixtla, and Ocuituco had about 12,000 each.[40]

Moctezuma I (some sources call him Motecuhzoma I) reigning from approximately 1440 to 1469, had imposed bloody measures, both in civic as well as religious practices, upon the Acolhua. He, as well as his successors waged continuous war against not only their unconquered enemies, but also against tribes such as the Acolhua that had already submitted to their authority. This was the Aztecs' means for obtaining hundreds, if not thousands, of prisoners to slay in blood rites on the sacrificial stones located at the top of the pyramids they had dedicated to the war god, Huizilopoxcli. According to one historian:

> Three times a year the Mixtec chiefs invited to their fiestas the leaders of Tetzoco, Tlacopan, Chalco, Xochimilco, the Indian communities later constituting the Marquesado (¿Cuauhnahuac?), and Couixco. They did the same with the matlatzinca and mazahuala [people inhabiting other regions]. On those occasions Moctezuma and his successors, if they were to succeed in terrifying those invitees, they would please, and therefore maintain the support of the principal leaders, as well as the plebian masses, of their own community. Through

this practice they also succeeded in snuffing totally out any desire for rebellion on the part of the subjugated communities surrounding them. Intimidation worked. Few times during the previous century had the dominated tribes even braved to voice minimal criticisms of their treatment at the hands of the dreaded Aztecs.[41]

Historians are familiar with surviving historical chronicles, which Mixtec scribes had composed a few years before the Spaniards' arrival—that is, during the period of their maximum power. (Also known to posterity are the histories and "literary" creations that Aztec elders later would dictate to the Franciscan intellectual and fraire, Bernardino de Sahagún—texts with a decidedly different "tone.") These project a fierce and bloody image of themselves and their own culture. They transmit a basic Aztec idea that, by inflicting the cruelest measures possible upon other communities, then their dominance would remain unchallenged. Each increase in the number of their sacrificial victims would further cement their strangle-hold over the neighboring tribes. "Their gods' insatiable appetite for massive human sacrifices engendered . . .in the Mixtec armies an indefatigable dynamism and tenacity in waging war against their enemies."[42]

The Acolhua in Cuernavaca must have suffered nightmares every night due to the cruel domination which they and their forebearers, over almost a century, had suffered under the cruel domination of the mixtecas. Their chieftains were required to be present in the Aztec capital to bear personal witness to those bloody ceremonies; at least once a year they had to round up hundreds, if not thousands, of local worker—if they lacked prisoners of war—to be slaughtered by the Aztecs' high priests in sacrificial rites. All this served to reinforce in their minds their subjugated status. The chronists make clear that if the Acolhua chieftains were to even contemplate not attending, the Aztec prince would interpret this as a challenge to his authority and would launch a bloody military campaign to "punish" the perceived rebellion.

One's familiarity with this history of anguished submission of the Cuernavaca Acolhua to the cruel Aztec regime helps to understand their willingness to ally themselves with the Spanish conquistador. They must have celebrated upon seeing Cortés's determination, as well as his military potential. By joining forces, they would become participants in putting asunder the cruel Aztec dynasty whose power base was Tenochtitlan. Not only that: the Cuernavaca chiefs—through their visit—were tacitly making known to Cortés their willingness to leave behind cultural and religious practices imposed upon them by the Aztec overlords. Also, they would willingly put aside aspects of their Chinameca cultural inheritances that their new masters, the Spanish, found offensive.

Cortés, from his own perspective, must have understood the profound implications of this offer of friendship and submission. That it meant—first of all—these chieftains' willingness to lead their communities in rejecting previously-embraced cosmologies, with related rituals and beliefs, and accept in their stead what Cortés and has cohorts believed to be the only true religion: Catholicism. Vitally important for Cortés was yet a second reason for celebration: a competent, yet pliant, indigenous leadership in Cuernavaca would guarantee full collaboration in ambitious projects that he already was envisioning. The nobles would organize, control, and discipline the thousands of lower-class, as well as technical, workers from the Morelos communities—these would constitute an essential component for his vast reconstruction, and development projects, as well as for his economic enterprises. Furthermore, these leaders, submissive to him, would become effective leaders in the insemination of new cultural and religious values among the Indian masses of the entire Morelos region. Also, they would make governance and tribute collection easy, if not automatic.[43]

Did Cortés "hide" details about the visit by Cuernavaca's chieftains from his lieutenants? (Bernal Díaz del Castillo, usually exact with his remembered facts, wrongly identifies these chieftains as coming from Oaxtepec, Yecapixtla, and Chalco[44]—as would the usually thorough Prescott some three centuries later). That is to say, Cortés might have intentionally decided to not divulge to others detailed information about the special linkages that he, even before concluding the conquest of the Aztecs, had formed with the chieftains governing Cuernavaca. If this were indeed the case, then why? In his letter-report to the king, he dedicated only seven words to the event. Then, in the 1540s, when he would dictate to yet another historian, López de Gómara, information about events relevant to the conquest, the latter would mention in his own text "a visit by Indian chieftains," but not provide further details. It is through the Indian testimonies, as recorded by Franciscan scholar Fray Bernardino de Sahagún, that posterity has learned more about this matter. Sahagún recounts that while Cortés was nursing a painful injury received during a skirmish with the Aztec army, "there arrived at his lodgings a delegation of ambassadors from Quauhnáhuac . . . pleading—almost begging—him to send Spanish troops to their region to protect them. Responding to that request, he ordered Andrés de Tapia to lead a force of 80 foot-soldiers, accompanied by ten horse-mounted soldiers, who spent ten days in that region securing the native communities [from any further Aztec threat]" . . . ."[45]

The Cuernavaca manuscripts make vague references to yet a further level of commitment on the part of the Cuernavaca chieftains to Cortés: their enthusiastic offer to lead their warriors in military campaign against any community within a hundred leagues that resisted submitting to the Spanish.[46] Sahagún offers details: Spanish captain Tapia, "together with the warriors from Quauhnáhuac—their total force might have come to forty thousand—set off in the direction of Malinco; on the road there they came upon an enemy army, fought against it, inflicted serious casualties, and sent the rest fleeing for their lives. Then, they made their way to that city, which they found to be quite large and heavily populated."

Did these military excursions occur before the August 1521 rendition of Cuauhtémoc—or after? About this detail, the historical record is silent. But beyond doubt is the fact that the Cuernavaca chieftains did lead their warriors in at least one, and most probably a few, of the expeditions ordered by Cortés to subdue Indian tribes or communities in other regions of New Spain. No independent sources confirm what the Cuernavaca chief vaguely suggests in the quoted Cuernavaca codex, that he himself had gone out "everywhere accompanying Cortés" in the months either before or following Cuauhtemoc's submission.

CHAPTER 3

1521: THE FIRST TWO MONTHS

Most of the information in this chapter draws from one of the most impressive, intriguing, and mysterious works ever written by a Latin American: Bernal Díaz del Castillo's Historia verdadera de la Conquista de la Nueva España: *"Impressive" for the overabundance of reliable facts and details that the work gives about the conquest, "Intriguing" for the octogenarian author's incredible recall of events and individuals that he himself had either known or witnessed a half century before, and "mysterious" because so much about the work leaves the informed reader perplexed about how the historical Díaz was capable of authoring such a text. Also mysterious was where and how the (three versions of the) manuscript survived for centuries before its first publication in 1877 and how it came to contain chapters treating events occurring even after Díaz's natural death.*

The submission of Tenochtitlán's Aztecs marked a notable transition in the lives of both soldiers and citizens, but it would not be simply the imposition of white-skinned victors over bronze-faced vanquished. Instead, two medieval ideas governed what was to happen. First, in accordance with the feudal traditions of their age, the Spaniards would replace Indian *principales* as the "lords" ruling over hundreds of Indigenous communities. And second, "to the victors belong the spoils," which is to say that the Spanish, elevated to the status of *encomenderos,* would receive from the Indians both tributes and free labor.

In the new society, native intermediaries would play an integral part. Months before, the conquistador army had accepted as essential allies the *tlaxcaltecas.* More recently, Cortés had given his assurances of co-governance to the Cuernavaca chieftains. Similar, it was already apparent that hundreds, if not thousands, of common Indians would be willing to follow Spanish guidance in rejecting the more onerous practices associated with the Aztecs' idol worship and in accepting the benign promises of the Spaniards' Christianity. Another plus: in the initial months the now-captive Aztec captain Cuauhtémoc verbally accepted a subservient role in governing the Indian community.

Commentators today might use the term "regime change." Within Cortés's hands was a magnificent opportunity: he had at his disposal the whole spectrum of resources that could be found in the newly conquered land. Where to begin? According to what plans?

The surviving source that best treats this issue is Bernal Díaz del Castillo, in his *Historia verdadera,* This narrator recounts that within hours of the Aztecs' final submission, Cortés ordered Spanish and Indians alike to rid the city's streets of the human gore and rubble left over from the destructive military struggle. He directed thousands of workers to repair or fortify the city's bridges and streets. He sent special teams of men with the urgent task of restoring the canals and aqueducts that carried drinking water to Mexico City's neighborhoods Note Díaz del Castillo's "spicy" style:

> Let's leave that subject—I want to address now what Cortés did after having won Mexico. The first thing was Cortés ordering Cuauhtémoc [the captive chieftain who had replaced the deceased Moctezuma as head of the now defeated Aztecs] to rebuild and clean out all the ducts carrying fresh water to the city from Chapultepeque and restore them to the condition they had been in before, so that water would flow again into Mexico City, so that all the streets could be totally cleaned of all the dead bodies and decapitated heads, that all the latter be

properly buried, so that public places be clean, and that none of the offensive smells remained, and that all the bridges and access roads be straighten out and restored to the condition that they had been before, and that new palaces and houses be rebuilt, and that all this be accomplished within two months so that the city's people would be able to move back and reoccupy them . . . .[47]

Cortés was in a hurry—as the same chronicler makes clear.[48] Immediately he had to assure the safety of his army which involved, among other tasks, the fortification and storage of their arms, munitions, and boats.[49] It was imperative to send out patrols to nearby communities in order to protect against any immediate resurgence of Aztec resistance and to demand obedience of all Indian communities to the new Spanish authority. Then, within a week, he sent out larger armed groups of both Spanish and Indians to more distant regions.

Only after taking measures to guarantee his army's security could Cortés embark on other initiatives. But all had to be done with an eye to his back-side: he was surrounded by potential threats—not only from the conquered, and now disarmed, Aztec soldiers, but also from within his own ranks. Although he could count on the loyalty of a majority of the soldiers—what Bernal Díaz calls "su banda"—his army contained several individuals who would attempt to usurp his authority at the slightest cause. He would have to act with extreme care.

But, as the stars or the gods decreed, luck always seemed to accompany him and favor his cause. One such opportunity presented itself to him in those first hours. This was a situation that he quickly realized would serve not only to discredit his enemies, but also to fortify his leadership position before both soldiers and Indian masses.

The involved the dozens young Indian concubines who had been taken during the recent period of belligerency and were now quartered with their new mates in the nearby Spanish encampments. It was a bombastic demand made by Cuauhtémoc, the headstrong leader of the defeated Aztecs, that precipitated the situation. With arrogance, he publicly accused Cortes of hypocrisy. "You promise the Indian communities merciful treatment. Verbal promises, nothing but empty words! Demonstrate your supposed generosity through real actions. Begin with this: liberate all the Indian concubines that your soldiers have captured and now treat as sex slaves."

What Cuauhtémoc ignored was Cortes's total familiarity with the issue of Indian concubines, that for the past twenty-two months this was precisely the issue that had played a significant role in the discord within his own ranks. Cuauhtémoc ignored the fact that even though a few of Cortes's powerful Spanish rivals had done their part in the battles against the Aztecs over the past several months, those rivals had recently drawn their knives in an attempt to assassinate him. Even while facing this possible rebellion to his authority, Cortés still enjoyed full support and unflinching loyalty from perhaps a majority of the common Spanish soldiers. In secret meetings over recent weeks, he and his core of loyalists had planned measures to deal with those rivals which involved, coincidentally, the same issue of the Indian concubines. His loyalists had been taken aback by the violent tactics with which those "representatives of the king" had treated the native *naborias*. They knew of many instances when those officers advocating harsh treatment, especially the forehead branding of the native women, were—precisely—from the ranks of Cortes's most dangerous enemies. The concubines had confided in them, and these loyalists had taken actions taken on their behalf. Cortés knew that the concubines appreciated those efforts and treasured their new situation as the favored women or common-law wives of many Spanish soldiers.[50]

Cuauhtémoc also ignored Cortés's uncanny intuition about human psychology. Over the past two years his crafty calculations, fueled in part by those intuitions, account—at least in part—for his effectiveness in dealing with both supporters and detractors and pulling off perhaps the most audacious military enterprise in history. And now, he would exercise those same skills to out-maneuver two different sets of potential enemies.

So, Cortés let Cuauhtémoc shoot off his mouth. He even pretended to ally with the defeated prince so that subsequent events would attain the status of a public spectacle which would be witnessed by every single inhabitant—whether Spanish or Indian—in Mexico City and the Valley of Tenochtitlan. Cortés had little to fear; he had information that Cuauhtémoc ignored. It would be great drama! Events would unfold in a very predictable course. Cuauhtémoc would be humiliated; he would be exposed for what he was: a verbal buffoon. Furthermore, Cortés would "flush out" those potential opponents from the ranks of his army and publicly discredit them, those who—otherwise—might offer problems at a future date.[51] The whole affair would benefit the young and vulnerable Indian *naborias* by assuring them legal protection in their new liaisons with the Spanish soldiers. And—finally—it would constitute concrete evidence that, in the next period of New Spain history, Cortés would prioritize the welfare of the common Indians in everything that he would attempt to accomplish.

All that Cortés must have had in mind what would happen.

Again, we rely upon Díaz del Castillo's written account as the only source of information about the *denouement* of these events:

> Because many of the king's representatives [who accompanied our army] had as their personal possessions [a number of the young female captives], and they listened to nobody about the way they treated them, they did to them what they wanted, that if on Monday they treated one of them badly, then on Tuesday it was even worse, and for that reason, from that time on, many of us soldiers began taking, after a battle, some of the better-looking girls—unlike what had been happening before, because if we didn't take them and hide them away in our own quarters, then the others would take them aside to mark their foreheads with hot branding irons, and we would then say that the girls had escaped. . . . I also want to say that beginning about two or three months earlier, that some of the girl slaves we were protecting from those representatives of the royal house, the girls let us listen in on their conversations, they knew which of the soldiers had a reputation for treating the girls well, and which abused them, which treated well the Indian girls and the *naborias* that they owned, and which treated them badly,

which had the reputation of being "gentlemen" and which did not, or when one had the plan of selling one of his girls in the marketplace, or if this or that soldier had plans to buy a girl or was unhappy with the favors received from a different girl, which [Spaniard] treated his slaves badly, about a case or two when a girl simply "disappeared" and was not seen again, and if one of us made inquiries about that girl then the chances of finding her or about her whereabouts was like searching for a person named Moses in a Moorish community like you'd find in the city of Granada, or to have your letter arrive at the hands of your son in Salamanca if you only addressed it 'To Mr. Student' . . . ."[52]

Díaz—in another passage—suggests that the defeated Aztec prince Cuauhtémoc had taken the initiative to involve himself in this issue. According to Díaz,

Cuauhtémoc and all his captains said to our Captain Cortés, that many captains and soldiers who had been fighting in the bergantines, and also those of us who were in the streets doing battle, that we had taken many daughters, even the wives, of the Indian nobles; and Cuauhtémoc and his people pleaded that he return those women to their Indian homes: and Cortés obliged them by ordering that all the affected women be brought before him . . . .

Not only did Cortés's orders regarding the concubines cause anger among some of the soldiers; equally offensive for them was the manner in which they were to be carried out. Cortés's plan, which he probably formed with the most trustworthy of his associates, was to publicly grant Cuauhtémoc and his men his permission for the captive Aztec princes, themselves, go through the three encampments of Spanish soldiers looking for the *naborias*. Apparently, the young soldier "Bernal" was uninformed about Cortés's intentions in concocting that plan. Because the elderly narrator relates his irritation that Cortés publicly ordered that "any soldier possessing girls had to turn them over immediately.... A number of the [Aztec] *principales*, arrogantly carrying out the search through every single Spanish residence, ended up finding all the girls."[53]

But Cortés's allies—the soldiers in "his band"—knew they had nothing to fear.[54] Because Cortés, from the very beginning, had made it clear that he would not allow Cuauhtémoc or any of the other Aztec males to force a concubine—or any woman—to return against her will to the servitude of either family of origin or former husband. And—to the embarrassment of Cuauhtémoc—when the young women had the opportunity to plead their individual cases before Cortes himself,

> the great majority of the girls did not want to return to be with their fathers or mothers, not even with their former Indian husbands. Instead, they wanted to remain with the soldiers they were then living with; other concubines, fearing their forced return, had fled into hiding, and others said that they did not want to return to the worship of idols, and some of them were even pregnant with child; and as it turned out [Cuauhtémoc and his captains] ended up carrying away only three young women;[55] only in the case of these three had Cortés been force to recur to the distasteful situation of ordering the corresponding Spanish soldiers to release them.

Cortes had known all along that this would be the result. And Cuauhtémoc demonstrated in the public forum that his verbal challenge to Cortés had consisted of empty huff.

Through this adroit maneuvering, Cortés successfully reinforced his leadership position: he had publicly exposed the "domestic" side to Aztec tyranny—and therefore provided a justification to both Spanish and Indians alike for the harsh measures he would be forced to take within three years with the headstrong Cuauhtémoc and two dozen of the most powerful Aztec princes. He also succeeded in bolstering his prestige among the non-Aztec natives. In addition, he had inconvenienced the powerful Spanish enemies within his ranks. Furthermore, he had reinforced his prestige before the rank and file of the Spanish soldiers.

He had demonstrated once again his commitment to fairness in all matters and with all social levels. And he had provided a golden example of his effectiveness in containing dissent, fortifying his own authority, and guaranteeing a level of social order conducive to the wellbeing of the most principled individuals among the ranks of the Spanish.

The prestige he had won in the "concubine issue" would "save his hide" only weeks later, when Cortés would demonstrate—once again—that he was his own, worst enemy.

Orders emanating from those same court officials included in his ranks would cause new irritation, if not anger, among the Spanish soldiers. Cortés must have been pressured by the *procuradores del rey* when he issued instructions that all members of the army had to turn over to the appropriate officials any valuables, but especially the gold, that they had seized over the previous year.[56] Bernal Díaz recounts that this involved what many soldiers considered to be their "legitimate" personal possessions. Cortés justified the need for yet a new division of the seized goods with the explanation that the previous "king's fifth," which had been gained from previous booty division, had been seized by French pirates on the high seas.

It is possible that this new division, although seemingly distasteful at first glance for all personnel, might—in actual fact—have fallen the hardest on Cortés's enemies. That is to say, the common soldiers in all probability had had followed Cortés's strict orders in not confiscating goods in the aftermath of a victory over Indian warriors. But was not the case with many of the hidalgo captains, who had been unwillingly impressed into the Spanish army after Cortés's surprise maneuvers against Narváez less than a year before. We can assume the same about the "king's representatives"—those who had muscled their way into the position of controlling the fate of captured native girls (and whatever else). These two groups, whom Cortés's loyalist soldiers distrusted, were most probably those who complained the loudest about the mandate to hand over all the confiscated valuables.

Díaz (who is silent about the points I have made in the previous paragraph) provides details about the effect of this new goods division over the soldiers in general. They would follow pre-established procedures: The first fifth would be earmarked—again—for sending to the king back in Spain. The second fifth, according to established procedures, would go to Cortés himself (again!). Then, the third fifth would be yielded to Cortés (yet once again!) as compensation for his own out-of-pocket expenses—that is, the monies he had spent to purchase ships, munitions, horses, food, etc. After officials removed from the aggregate collection of goods these three-fifths, then little remained to be apportioned to the soldiers: 3X amount for a *caballero*, a 2X quantity for a gunner, and the smallest—an X portion for each foot soldier (those who constituted the vast majority of Spanish soldiers present). A typical "salary" for two years of risk and warriorlike toil: less than a small pittance.

When the soldiers—from the highest to the lowest in rank—were finally allowed to view each's paltry share, they erupted in fury. That small recompense for so much suffering and sacrifice? Some of the common soldiers expressed the belief that, even before the supervised division, the higher-ups—had absconded with unreported booty. The first reaction was disbelief. Then, widespread grumbling about the possibility that the higher-ups—whether allied Indian chieftains, Spanish lieutenants, or the king's representatives in their midst—had "hoodwinked" them all. Predictably, many were furious. A few of the soldiers openly expressed their despise for the "money-grubbing" king, knowing full well that Cortés might take stern measures to punish them for doing so.

Yet another result, days later: the Spanish soldiers took Cuauhtémoc captive, fully convinced that the latter had found a hiding place for his deceased uncle's (Moctezuma's) treasures in the few days before his own submission. They tied him to a stone bench and burnt his feet with burning torches, all with the idea that this physical torture would induce a confession. According to Bernal Díaz, "all this certainly caused Cortés pain." But because no words of his could appease his soldiers' anger "and because he could not prevent them from doing it, he—in effect—consented to the torture."

In addition, the great majority of the soldiers shared the belief that Cortés himself—their commander—had played a major role having the treasures disappear. According to Díaz, "all thought the worst about Cortés's role in all that, and they did not hesitate to demonstrate their resentment, which saddened him."

Bernal Díaz relates yet another consequence—which at first irritated Cortés, but in the end amused him: the soldiers' anger took the form of clever ditties repeatedly scrawled in the middle of the night onto one of the white-washed walls of Cortés's new sumptuous palace in Coyoacán. Here I'll repeat only one example of this anger-fueled graffiti, written by a highly disgruntled soldier in the cover of darkness: "that [the soldiers] felt themselves to be more 'conquistados' than 'conquistadores;' that although they might have vanquished Mexico, they now felt themselves to be more 'vanquished' by none other than their leader, Hernando Cortés . . . ." Was the anger directed by the soldiers at their commander justified? About one related issue there is no doubt: Cortés's role in all this had produced scores of new enemies.

His soldiers and other observers began to note a significant "change in the personality" of their leader—that "he no longer appeared before them as a sober and daring conquistador, but as a monarch"—as one historian has noted.[57] Other measures enacted by Cortés added to the suspicions about his questionable leadership ethics.

First, he redirected the flow of tributes and gifts which the different Indian communities had been required to pay to their former Aztec masters; now Cortés—working through a small group of confidants including members of his own family—made arrangements so that the tributes now streamed into accounts under his direct control.

Second: he appropriated for his own use several residential land plots in and around the vanquished Aztec city, Tenochtitlan—soon to be rebaptized as Mexico City. Months earlier he had designated for himself the luxurious Aztec palace, in addition to a comfortable residence in the nearby village of Coyoacán—near where a new Spanish military base had been established. Now, within hours after Cuauhtémoc's final rendition, Cortés appropriated important buildings and real estate around Mexico City's central plaza (today's Zócalo).

And third, he, acting as governor, imposed new taxes upon many money transactions. Díaz—again the primary source for this information—recounts that Cortés and his team had ordered the payment of "three *quilates*" to the new municipal authorities each time a Spaniard melted booty objects to produce a gold bar. Then there followed an ordinance requiring merchants, upon selling a certain quantity of market goods, to pay the same amount. "And they justified the new tax by saying that it would pay for benefits that would go for the community and needy conquistadores; and in the end that turned out to be just another lie." "Bernal"—the young soldier—might have originally believed in these promises made by his commander. But not for long. The chronicler remembers that the new tax ended up worsening the situation of the common soldiers: merchants, formerly charging 12 *quilates* for a measure of wheat then began charging 18: the original price plus three *quilates* for the tax, and two additional *quilates* to line their own pockets. The resulting situation had the appearances of yet another form of exploitation imposed upon them by their former commander.

Were these measures evidence of Cortés's personal greed? Learned opinions over the last four centuries are mixed.[58] Beyond dispute is the fact that Cortés needed money—lots of it. He needed to fund his grandiose plans for the reconstruction of the country. Second—according to several detractors—he had to pay dearly to certain individuals who became his personal supporters. And finally, he needed vast sums to fund his new "princely" life style. One telling example: a whole page of the Bernal Díaz text details the "opulence" displayed by Cortés in outfitting the "military" expedition he would lead in 1524 to Higueras (Honduras): in addition to the 250 foot soldiers and ten mounted warriors, there were court "jesters, acrobats, musicians, servants to attend to his wardrobe and table, cooks, and a very long etcetera list of superfluous persons."[59]

In short, the measures taken by Cortés in the first several weeks following the final submission of the Aztec armies had the effect of dividing the Spaniards into two contending camps. One group included his most reliable lieutenants and devoted followers; they were willing to overlook Cortés's excesses, knowing well that any alternative leadership in New Spain would unleash dangerous passions and unchecked rivalries.

The rival group of Spaniards—in contrast—included the leaders whom Cortés had out-maneuvered in seizing leadership of the Spanish army. Add to their number the corrupt officials representing the crown; many from either of these two groups would threaten any leader limiting their pursuit of gold and instant wealth; they shared in their intent to bring about Cortés's downfall. (As long as Cortés exercised the power of New Spain's governor, he was able to out-maneuver these dissidents and keep them under control. But when he imprudently absented himself from New Spain in 1524, and then when a feckless, uninformed, and possibly uninterested monarchy then removed him from power, violence between his supporters and these dissident groups would become inevitable).

Were these conflicts inevitable? Or should the observer blame Cortés himself on account of an appetite for power and riches, the favoritism he demonstrated to family and intimates, and the stern—if not harsh—measures he had taken to control Spanish behavior? The chronicler Díaz del Castillo offers a neutral appraisal of this and related issues:

> One could look at all this from two different perspectives. On the one hand, many people who have travelled to different parts of Christendom would see that Mexico City, at breakneck speed, was becoming transformed into one of the most populated and beautiful cities in the whole world—with its fine houses and goodly number of exclusive neighborhoods. But on the

other hand, imagine the contrasting situation of the poor conquistadores.[60]

Cortés, very concerned about this growing hostility among his now ex-soldiers, decided to act. First, he would rid the area of future troublemakers; he would "kill two birds with one stone"—these same individuals would fulfil the needed task establishing a Spanish presence in other areas of New Spain. These individuals would be charged with keeping a wary eye on potentially rebellious native chiefs or groups and would facilitate the wellbeing of new Spanish settlers soon to arrive, as Díaz explains:

> Cortés saw that many soldiers grew so bold as to demand from him a more just share of all that—tributes, booty, land—and even to accuse him of having taken for himself too large a share or having robbed the rest, and others were asking him for loans, and he singled out those individuals to send as settlers, these were people he wanted out of Mexico City, people he didn't want to settle anywhere nearby.

Bernal Díaz provides a telling example of Cortés's adroitness as a leader: not only did he successfully remove potential enemies from Mexico City and its proximities (and from his future center of operations in Morelos), but he also was able to neutralize their hostility; he had the good sense to motivate their departure by offering them some form of material compensation. Although nursing grudges, many willingly accepted Cortés's assignments—in the form of encomienda grants, bureaucratic appointments, or rights to mines, etc. Díaz writes:

> I don't want to write from memory how many horses, nor crossbow or shotgun shooters, nor foot soldiers there were. Nor how many days passed nor in what month it occurred when Cortés dispatched the army's captains to head the settlement

efforts of the different provinces . . . because all that would constitute a long history. It's enough to write here that only a few days passed after the having won Mexico, and after having taken Guatemuz prisoner; and two months had not passed before he sent yet another Captain to other provinces.

Also, interesting to note: the sly Cortés must have had a part in creating their *positive motivation* for departing. Telling are the words of Bernal Díaz, still gullible after the fifty or so intervening years. He writes that the young "Bernal" had not been *ordered* to depart; "he" *chose* to leave:

> Let's leave this topic to get to another, and it's necessary that I have the opportunity to make this declaration, because many readers have expressed their curiosity about this: they ask, what is the reason why us, the true conquerors, we who won New Spain in battle, why didn't we stay there to form new homes, and why did we choose to go to other provinces? This is a reasonable question. And I wish to express here our reasons for leaving; I'll write it right here. We were able to see in Moctezuma's own tribute books where precisely the gold came from, in what provinces were located his mines, where the chocolate beads came from, and the rich linens. And in those books, we learned precisely which community paid their tributes in gold, and we wanted to go there.

Only the gods know how those tribute records of the deceased Aztec king, Moctezuma, fell into the hands of the victorious Spanish soldiers. But it is not beyond the realm of the possible that the super-intuitive Cortés, accurately predicting its possible result, facilitated their circulation.

During these first two post-conquest months, the huge contradictions in Cortés's spirit became visible to those surrounding him. The previously rough, frugal warrior-chief now demonstrated signs of craving a regal life style and unlimited power. And—of special interest here—his intensity in thought and activity now shifted from things of war to plans of peace. He enjoyed unrivaled popularity among both the common soldiers and the Indian masses. He had demonstrated, time and again, his effectiveness in getting things accomplished. He was unsurpassed in making bold plans and then carrying them out. With so much faith in his own views, he resisted the council of others. In so many of his acts and activities, Cortés demonstrated that he would accept no middle ground; he demanded all and expected all.

CHAPTER 4

CORTÉS AND THE SPANISH

After victory, hundreds of Spanish soldiers were elevated to the status of encomenderos. Many, and their descendants, would come to constitute a segment of Mexico's new class of feudal lords. Yet in character, the majority remained serfs at heart. One historian writes that they were "greedy because poor, cruel because fearful, violent because repressed, churlish because treated as churls."1 But Cortés, having forged strong affective links with many, had confidence that they, in their new social roles, would dutifully respond to his leadership. Yet he also prepared for the worst by imposing over them a strict body of rules to guard against unjust or cruel treatment of the natives entrusted to their care. For two generations, this type of management yielded positive results. Indeed, this is one reason why Franciscan historian Friar Gerónimo de Mendieta, would praise New Spain's first postconquest decades, calling them the country's Golden Age.

It was a period of "paradigm" transition. While most New Spain leaders embraced feudal beliefs and institutions, the young Spanish king would seek new solutions to societies' age-old problems. Specifically, Cortés, his soldiers, the Franciscan friars, and New Spain's otherwise enlightened leaders would continue defending the merits of the feudal encomienda while the king and his advisors would search for a new type of colonial governance. Conflict, well into the next century, was inevitable.

Before the Mexico campaign, when Cortés had enjoyed the benefits of free Indian labor in both Hispaniola and Cuba, he had been a personal witness of the "hypocrisy" of state policy with regard to the Spaniards' treatment of the native populations. Although some historians call attention to the "benign" guidelines issued by previous monarchs for the treatment of American natives, in truth, most Spanish soldiers and settlers in Hispaniola and Cuba had seen fit to ignore them. Instead, their primary interest had been the accumulation of gold and material wealth—and as rapidly as possible. Having been named *encomenderos*, meaning "the legitimate recipients of free Indian labor," most had ordered their native charges to work long hours and under subhuman conditions, mainly in the mining of precious metals. They had rapidly learned that feeding their Indian charges with a sufficient quantity of food cost more than the purchase of new workers. The result: the extreme mistreatment and the early death of thousands.

Jump ahead fifteen years to the final months of 1521. Cortés's army, with the assistance of thousands of natives, had reduced the Aztecs to submission. Now he was faced with the task of rewarding his victorious soldiers. He knew that royal policies with regard to the treatment of the natives were ineffective fantasies; that—in the Antilles—they had served as an invitation for genocide. Far surpassing in wisdom and decisiveness of any of his contemporaries, he had the good sense of either ignoring, or contradicting, the detailed instructions emanating from the court.

Almost immediately, he decided to put aside the monarchy's instructions to co-mingle the Spanish and natives. Instead, he had judged that a strict separation of the two races was the best, and perhaps only, way to protect the native population from Spanish abuses. He was convinced that the latters' vice-ridden conduct would set a terrible moral example for the natives who were eager to embrace a new life. Here are his frank but discrete words, written in a letter to the king:

> We know that the natives would be the target of the Spaniards' mistreatment, that the latter would rob them, require harmful labor, and other abuses; because . . . everyone knows that the

great majority of Spaniards here are of low social extraction, some are extremely brutal individuals, others if they could would drink till they fall, and embrace any type of immoral or sinful behavior. And if we were to permit these free movement among the Indian communities, then the end result would be the Indians themselves learned from them those same vice-ridden and even sinful behaviors. One result would be even greater difficulties than already exist to attract the Indians to the new faith.[61]

What to do with the Spaniards? Their presence was needed, especially in strategic places, in order to protect against a resurgence of the defeated Aztecs or a local native rebellion. Military imperatives dictated that New Spain would survive and prosper only if the Spaniards had a significant demographic presence. With that in mind, he sought the means to entice permanent settlement, not only for his now unemployed soldiers but also for the "adventurers" who were beginning to arrive by the hundreds. To this end, he engaged specialists to design new, attractive neighborhoods in the areas in and around Mexico City that were outfitted with streets, plazas, and churches. He put into writing the new ordinances that would restrict potentially harmful practices such as the indiscriminate presence of horses, hogs, and sheep; and he imposed conditions to govern the location of butcher shops and their disposal of wastes. Then he assigned lots for Spanish residents and distributed written instructions about the proper construction of houses and sheds. He appointed officials to implement regular municipal functions and to enforce strict laws aimed at controlling the sometimes-rude behavior of the worst of the Spanish settlers.

After taking measures to guarantee the strict separation of Spanish and native populations in and around Mexico City, Cortés set about deciding how to organize the other—numerous—regions of New Spain. His pragmatism is on display—once again—in the secret communication he sent to the king. The major problem, as he saw it, was how to motivate ex-soldiers and newly arriving settlers to remain in New Spain to raise their families. They would wish to do so only if they had the means for material advancement.

His thought on this issue had two main influences: first, the bitter lessons learned from his family's economic trials in Extremadura; and second, the "humanist" tendencies then gaining prominence in Europe's intellectual circles.[62] These influences are visible in his description of an ideally structured New-Spain society:

> It seems to me that, in order for these ideas to prosper; that is, in order to construct [a new society] that will thrive as long as the world might last, it would be convenient for Your Majesty (maintaining respect of all the people and agencies involved) to retain final control over all that might happen here; because if not, then each one of the actors here would judge things only in light of their own private interests and would act primarily with the objective of favoring their own heirs or descendants [and not the good of the community itself]. That would work against what I alone, [as governor] am attempting to accomplish—as I understand my responsibilities as the person appointed by Your Majesty to govern these lands, that I should seek ways to provide a common direction for all the collective and private initiatives. That I should be diligent in assisting each party or group to take full advantage of their respective situations, so that each might find their path to achieve what they might and, in the time, available to them. That I should give special care to assist those individuals taking initiatives on their own account, so that they might feel secure in expending their energies and attentions to that effect.[63]

Private initiatives brought together by a common vision: that was how Cortés envisioned the mechanism for New Spain's future.

How might he convince the king about this idealistic (and possibly "radical") idea? He had to choose words that would appeal to a monarch who, above else, would not be eager to allocate the necessary funds (everyone knew that the first priority of the young emperor were his military interventions all across Europe and the Mediterranean). Cortés knew who he was addressing; he presented to the king the argument that the more prosperous the colony, then the more abundant would be the monies available for the king's own enterprises.

Encomiendas

The encomienda had a long history in Spain. Throughout the medieval period, the Crown made temporary grants to individuals for territory recaptured from the Moors. In most cases, this was not a landed estate, meaning that it had nothing to do with ownership of land; in contrast, the *encomendero* was given, on a strictly temporary, non-hereditary basis (at least in theory) a grant of lordship over a certain number of serfs—in the case of the Americas, Indians. In the New World, the *encomendero* accepted the obligation to protect a specific group of Indians and to instruct them in the ways of civilization and the Catholic faith, in exchange for the Indians' labor services and/or tributes. In theory, the institution appeared to harmonize the Castilian ideals of lordship and the demands of pastoral care.[64]

But in practice—especially in the first decades of Hispanic occupation of Canary Islands, and then Hispaniola, the encomienda system came to assume characteristics that barely distinguished itself from outright slavery. Queen Isabel, in reaction, had prohibited the enslavement of the Indians in 1500, while allowing exception for those Indians attacking Spaniards. Her grandson, Carlos, upon assuming the throne about the time of Cortés's arrival at New Spain, followed his predecessors in his theoretical opposition to slavery, which was added to the growing sentiment in court circles that the Crown should do everything possible to discontinue the practice of distributing new *encomiendas*. Their dual objectives were to protect the Indians and thwart the formation of a permanent, landed class of grandees.

Come 1521, with the Aztecs subdued, Cortés was under intense pressure to reward his soldiers for their huge sacrifices, the time and energy they had "invested," and—in some cases—the financial debt some had accrued. If they would not receive compensation in the form of gold or species, then many had full expectation of receiving encomiendas to harness the Indian labor to guarantee their material enrichment and a comfortable lifestyle. Díaz del Castillo's narration reminds the reader about the Veracruz agreement, at the beginning of their first march toward the Aztec capital, when all the soldiers had voted for Cortés to assume the position as their *capitán general* on the condition that he would "favor" them if and when their campaign yielded positive results. The young "Bernal," like the other common soldiers, had believed that Cortés would be following through with in his promises, as well as the written agreement all had signed in Veracruz at the beginning of the Mexico campaign, for him to distribute encomiendas to his "buenos y leales" soldiers who, for their part, had totally fulfilled their side of the agreement in winning the necessary battles.[65]

All his soldiers knew that the granting of encomiendas had a long history, that it was a common, and accepted, practice in the hierarchical feudal society of the time: the sovereign authority—Cortés in this case—was empowered to reward faithful servants for special services.[66]

He silently held another, equally persuasive, reason for the issue of encomiendas: he could remove from the central plateau any and all of his Spanish enemies; he would disburse them to made difficult their organization his authority, their soldiers' lust for material gain would be satiated by the grant of Indian laborers. In short, this pragmatic man recognized a truth that his king and future religious leaders resisted comprehending: that—according to the 'dean" of American hispanists, Charles Gibson, the "encomienda was ... an appropriate institution for [New Spain's] early years."[67] He realized that, apart from granting *encomienda*s, he had no other practical way of defending the newly imposed Spanish order and compensating his soldiers for their services.

However, what to do with specific instructions he had recently received from the Crown, that he was not to proceed with the issuing of encomiendas? Cortés must have realized that those orders emanated from individuals, advising the Crown who had little idea about either his own situation vis-a-vis the victorious soldiers, or the practical side of government. He realized that, apart from granting encomiendas, he had no other practical way of compensating his soldiers for their services.

Given the above reasons, he decided to act quickly, assigning encomiendas even before the final rendition of the intrepid Aztec leader, Cuauhtémoc. He knew that in a future moment he would have to deal with the Crown's disapproval. But he also knew that his own survival as *capitán*, and now as governor, depended upon the continued support of his loyal soldiers.

We see a confirmation of all this in the account rendered by the chronist, Bernal Díaz del Castillo. In at least ten different passages of his long history,[68] he returns to his "thesis" that he and the other soldiers who had successfully brought the Aztecs to submission merited a just compensation in the form of encomienda grants. Perhaps typical for his time, he repeatedly refers to the "Indians" or "Indian communities" as if they constituted mere "possessions" or "accidents" attached to or present on the land-masses mentioned. That is to say, if he mentions Indians, he might as well be writing about "trees" or "valuable forests." Absent is any indication that the chronist considered the natives as anything other than yet one more form of property.

Should this surprise the contemporary reader? Did nineteenth-century plantation owners in the American south consider their slaves any differently? We assume that the attitude of a perhaps a majority of the Spanish encomienda recipients—and perhaps Cortés himself—shared this view of New Spain's native population.

Contemporary readers might regard Cortés's role in awarding encomiendas as hypocritical. Indeed, he himself demonstrated in his letters to the king that he was well aware that, in the Antilles, a badly administered, and poorly supervised, encomienda system had invited Spanish settlers to commit horrendous abuses against the natives. Nor did he ignore the greedy inclinations of many of his—otherwise—trusted soldiers. He knew that their foremost interest, once peace were at hand, would be to obtain gold and pearls and to live a pampered lifestyle surrounded by obedient servants. He knew that among the hundreds of ex-soldiers clambering for a portion of the victory spoils, only a handful of them would treat the Indians decently and would seriously consider becoming effective managers of agricultural enterprises. He could have predicted that these individuals, once in control of the lives and livelihoods of Indian workers, would exploit them to the maximum.

So it's important to understand that Cortés was not a "blind" supporter of the encomienda institution (his views were shared by those who would become New Spain's governing team during the next half century). He saw no feasible alternative. But the encomienda would function to the benefit of all only if the new "managers" of land and Indian serfs operated under detailed conditions that would have to be strictly enforced.

In a subsequent letter to the king, he explained his intention of maintaining that "strict control." The ordinances that he drew up mandated the form and manner according to which each new encomendero would be required to treat the natives entrusted to his care.11 The thirteen provisions explained in detail what would or would not be permitted with regard to the Indian tributes, labor, food provisions, rest days, and residency. Following earlier stipulations emanating from both papal and Crown sources, encomenderos would be required to teach the Indians in the practices of Christian rituals and customs. In all this, Cortés was mandating much more stringent measures than had any previous governor in the different Antilles colonies. He appointed inspectors (*visitadores*) to enforce those ordinances and assess whether any particular encomendero was abusing Indians' rights or imposing excessive tribute or labor obligations.

Other clauses aimed at creating the conditions whereby encomenderos would see it in their interest to settle permanently in the newly conquered land. Each, within two years, was obligated to either marry or transport his wife from Spain to the new home. Each was required to begin residential construction and reside there for a minimum of eight years before receiving an encomienda title. Cortés envisioned a land where even the most impoverished of Spanish settlers would manage their own property, profit according to their diligence, and be empowered to bequeath to their children both the granted rights and the accumulated fruits of their labor.

Only in 1524, three years after commencing the assignments of encomiendas, would he publish and distribute throughout New Spain a revised copy of those ordinances and then file a copy in his archives. As long as he exercised the authority of New Spain's governor, he sought measures to promote the emergence of a lord-vassal relationship designed to promote social stability, much as what the encomienda institution had accomplished in Castile since time immemorial.

In the "Carta reservada" to the king, he stated what he had done and provided a vague justification for having done so. The king would delay some five years before sending a document that, in effect, approved Cortés's measures.

New Spain's scribes must have been occupied night and day in writing out for each newly-named encomendero a personal copy of these or similar requirements.

While Cortés was granting encomiendas to ex-soldiers and crown officials he, at the same time, was reserving some of the most lucrative for himself. Exercising the powers as New Spain's maximum authority, he made sure that he himself would benefit most from Indian tributes and labor. This, for him, was a dream come true: he'd be proud to communicate to his father back home his dramatic ascent in social rank. He would become the lord and master of more vassals than even the most powerful noble of Extremadura. He also dreamed of following the conventions of his century in adapting an ostentatious lifestyle well in keeping with his new princely position.

In the days immediately following the submission of the Aztec army, Cortés appropriated for his own use several of the Mexico City buildings formerly owned by the now deceased Aztec emperor. (At a future moment, one of his lawyers would argue, unsuccessfully, that similar circumstances entitled him to the terrain, near Cuernavaca's city center, where he would build his palace residence.)

Cortés would also derive personal benefit from his control over the tributes that subdued Indian communities had provided to the Aztec authorities. Possessing the written tabulations formerly used by Moctezuma, he jealously reserved for himself the most populated and potentially lucrative of those encomiendas. Only then did he set about to distribute the other grants to his soldiers. One historian explains:

The 42,800 pesos de oro of annual revenue in tribute payments which his attorneys reported as the minimum figure he was receiving in 1524 suggests the value of these holdings . . . located in practically every area . . . of the colony. . . . Those encomiendas [were all across New Spain, but perhaps the most populated and best were located in the current state of Morelos. There,] Cortés reserved for himself . . . Cuernavaca, Oaxtepec, Acapistla, Tepoztlán, and Yautepec . . . . Before the Spanish arrived, [the natives in those communities] had paid their tribute directly to Aztec agents. . . . These assignments reflect Cortés' use—with significant alteration—of the Aztec taxation system in making his repartimiento-encomienda grants.[12]

In distributing encomiendas, Cortés followed the accepted and mandated procedures, similar to the way he directed the division of booty or land. First, he "separated" all encomiendas into five equal shares, as explained by the chronist Díaz del Castillo: the first

> fifth of the best cities and cabeceras were reserved for His Majesty; the second fifth would become grants for those gentlemen who had served in the military part of the conquest, and the three remaining portions would be available to divide among Cortés and all of us, the true conquistadores, and it would be done according to the quality that he felt each one had, and they would be perpetual, because at that time His Majesty had declared that that was the way it would be done, because he had not spent even a penny for carrying out any of those conquests, and he neither knew nor cared about those lands, being at the time in Flandes when we presented to him, for his own possession a goodly portion of the New World that we, as good vassals, had turned over to him, that he should show us his gratitude for all that we had done for him, that was the way we all saw it . . . .[69]

We possess detailed information about the thirty large encomiendas (a surprisingly low number) corresponding to heavily populated areas around Mexico City, which Cortés reserved for himself and his cronies.[70] Only thirty Spaniards ended up controlling a massive number of Indians—a total of 180,000 "tributaries!" This figure probably represents the number of male heads of Indian households, meaning that, if we include women and children, the total number might have approached a half-million Indians. Whereas the "average" among these 30 encomiendas included some 6,000 tributaries, the distribution of Indians was highly skewed: the largest five encomiendas averaged near 11,000 and the smallest twenty about 600. This information implies that the manner according to which Cortés assigned encomiendas ended up reproducing in New Spain a faithful copy of the hierarchical, inegalitarian, social structure that then predominated in the mother country.

The chronist Díaz del Castillo, consistently reliable with the information he imparts, captures the disconformity that many soldiers, including he himself (as a young man) had felt about these criteria for dividing the spoils of victory: First, the soldiers disliked the way in which their leader had carefully studied existing maps, Aztec tribute charts, and his lieutenants' exploratory reports, in order to reserve for himself twenty of the most lucrative of the encomiendas available.

Second, they complained about the implicit class system:[71] receiving encomiendas were six court officials (named specifically by Díaz), recently arriving to New-Spain shores, who had suffered none of the risk, toil, and sufferings of the common soldiers, yet ended up with a giant share of the benefits.

And lastly, Cortés assigned encomiendas to several individuals whom he had known during his childhood days in Medellín. Many of the ex-soldiers, offended by these overt acts of favoritism, began repeating the caustic refrain, "don't divide whatever booty in the cheating way that Cortés did."[72]

The same chronist explains how the distribution of encomiendas occurred in areas far from the Mexican capital such as Oaxaca, Chiapas and Panuco: Cortés empowered his most reliable lieutenants—Sandoval, Alvarado, Olid—to lead combined Spanish-Indian armies to force the submission of new communities; then, these same lieutenants would grant encomiendas to the participating soldiers as a means for maintaining future pacification and stability.

We can assume that Cortés favored the upper class for yet another practical reason: only these would have possessed the literary skills necessary for managing a large agricultural enterprise.

The same chronist explains how the distribution of encomiendas occurre4d in areas far from the Mexican capital: Oaxaca, Chiapas, Panuco, etc. Cortés empowered his most reliable lieutenants—Sandoval, Alvarado, Olid—to lead combined Spanish-Indian armies to enforce the compliance of new communities and then granted new encomiendas to both them and the participating soldiers as a means for maintaining future pacification and stability.

The measures which Cortés took to separate the Spanish from the natives, to control Spanish behaviors, and to distribute encomiendas, are strong evidence that he had come to detest the conduct of many of the common soldiers serving under him. He must have become convinced that in peaceful times their blind ambition for material wealth and their lack of scruples in dealing with the natives would work against another project that some historians believe he (sometimes) promoted: the creation of a new society with humanistic treatment for all.[73] Is this the reason why he prohibited Spaniards from settling in the territories corresponding to the encomiendas which he himself came to control? In this, the historical record is clear with regard the Morelian part of the Marquesado: over the next twenty-five years, the number of Spaniards residing there would rarely exceed a dozen, and those present were either specialized laborers or managers personally selected by Cortés himself.[74]

From the first, Cortés set about constructing a strong civil authority to institutionalize measures designed to control encomenderos' actions with regard to Indian rights. Within a half decade there would emerge another "arm" to control unjust Spanish behaviors: the exceptional team of Franciscan friars that accepted the defense of Indian rights as a top priority of the evangelization campaign they headed. In addition, was it fortuitous that the first two viceroys would demonstrate a continued, and indeed increased, commitment to the same objective?

At the time of the assignments of encomiendas, Cortés could not have predicted any of this. Although he always sought ways to protect the native communities, in the late 1520s, he would briefly resist the new and stronger regulations coming from the viceroy-directed government, as I report further on. After 1532, he would fully embrace the fortified role to this end played by both the Franciscans and the viceregal government.

Within six years, the first viceroy of New Spain, Antonio de Mendoza, would approve of Cortés's closely supervised encomienda institution and would argue before the Crown on behalf of the ex-soldiers, who continued to demand *permanent* ownership of Indian labor. Like Cortés, he and his staff would draw up, print, and distribute an expanded list of ordinances governing encomendero performance; he too would fully support strict governmental action to protect Indian welfare. One new law empowered the Indians, or their representatives, to initiate court proceedings through interpreters and, being illiterate, to have the court accept traditional drawings as acceptable documents in defending their rights in the case of encomendero abuses.[75]

Those controls coming from the newly installed government had an initial effect of moderating the abuses committed against the New Spain Indians. But within a generation, encomenderos would exercise increased control over both land and Indians. Abuses would increase. New Spain would witness, over the next few centuries, extreme exploitation of Indians and their mestizo offspring by a pampered social class whose family power had originated with the original encomienda grants. It is an open question as to whether injustices committed by these differed substantially from those by contemporaneous European princes such as Italy's Medici family who, according to one historian, were "cruel, insecure despots," with lifestyles characterized by luxury and "impressive pomp," and who governed by "craft, cruelty, corruption and quiet murder."[76]

CHAPTER 5

INDIAN SOCIETY

The indigenous communities of New Spain were very diverse, ranging from the well-organized, "urbane" groups in cities such as Tlaxcala and Cuernavaca, and the barbarous, nomadic tribes in the extreme north. There were also "in-between" cases: the materially and culturally impoverished groups in Michoacán and semi-organized communities which the Spanish had first encountered in the coastal areas. This chapter offers perspectives dealing with all three of these vaguely defined groups.

The first part of this chapter focuses on both Spanish and native views with regard to advanced native communities, such as Tlaxcala and Cuernavaca, which exhibited well-policed markets and regulated commerce; serfs and porters enjoyed geographic mobility and were empowered to negotiate the conditions of their own employment; and parents across the social spectrum strictly disciplined their children. An unbiased observer—either then or now—might conclude that these native practices were more constructive or humane than what then existed in Spain.

During the first few post-conquest decades, Spaniards and Indians—in these advanced cities—willingly embraced what contemporary readers might call a "feudal social pact." On the one hand, Spanish leaders believed legitimate and justified their governance in exchange for remuneration in the form of Indian tributes and labor. On the other, Indian society had always lived under the rule of nobles, and the payment of tributes and labor was a customary and inescapable aspect of life. Most native communities celebrated the change from Aztec to Spanish nobles at the top of their social and political pyramids: no longer would they tremble at the arrival to their cities of cruel emissaries from Tenochtitlán. Aztec defeat also meant an end to their forced provision of humans (whether war captives or community members) for their masters' appalling sacrificial altars.

There was—to all appearances—a near-total disconnect between what European leaders believed about the indigenous people in the Americas, in contrast to what Cortés and his army were actually seeing as they began their march toward the Aztec capital.

Debates in Europe would continue well into the century: were the Indians "human beings?" Or were they merely a living species, superior to "animals," but "inferior" to mankind? The "learned" European world would have to wait until 1537, when the sitting pope would issue a *bula* declaring them "rational beings." In Spain the same theoretical debates would continue. What might have been in the head of King Carlos during the whole three-to-four decades of the supposed "Golden Age" of New Spain? Because it was only in 1550-51 when he sponsored the debates of Valladolid to address precisely this issue. Official doubts would be posed—yet once again—and this time by one of the country's most eminent scholars and jurists, Ginés de Sepúlveda (facing off with the famed Dominican monk, Bartolomé de las Casas). Basing his arguments on Aristotle and other classical sources, Sepúlveda would continue arguing that American Indians lacked the ability to govern themselves and were "less than human" on account of their inherited customs of blood sacrifice and idol worship—among other practices.

Jump back to 1519. Cortés and his army, from the first, knew differently. As he and his band of 450 Spanish soldiers left the Mexican coast and began their march toward the Aztec capital, they continually encountered advanced indigenous communities which contrasted enormously with the primitive Caribbean natives they had left behind months before. Cortés, in his first letter to the king, describes the Spaniards' favorable first impressions: they saw "well-proportioned people . . . wearing garments to cover their private parts, and over the body they wore long, fine capes printed much as what the Moors used . . . and the upper-class women dressed in large, well-made cloth shirts, finely decorated with embroidered designs."[77] In treating this same matter, the chronist Bernal Díaz del Castillo provides—as usual—a fairly "unfiltered" (and always detailed) account of a very early encounter: after bestowing upon the Spaniards a welcomed gift of food, a delegation of six Indians escorted them to a community center, a huge plaza surrounded by buildings, opening to spacious patios at the back, and large enough to house a company of soldiers.[78] There they met the Indian *principales*, who generously accommodated the soldiers' immediate needs, while communicating to them an unsettling fear of their tyrannical overlords, the Aztecs.

Seeing signs of the Indians' advanced culture, one can imagine Cortés' initial perplexity: he was obligated to follow the decrees of both his monarchs and his pope who, with very imperfect knowledge, had mandated that the Spaniards, on account of their "cultural superiority," were sanctioned to accept their submission and then govern over them as "inferior" beings[79]—but respecting their rights to "liberty" and "humanitarian treatment." However, if the natives rebelled or offered armed resistance, then he would be allowed to respond in a forceful manner.

Religious considerations also influenced policy. Precedence, for both monarchical and papal authorities, authorized "just war" against not only any Indigenous group resisting his authority, but also against any religious "infidel." Those rules had applied back in Spain to the locals' earlier conflicts with the Moors, and they would also with regard to American natives. The latters' "pagan" belief systems and practices were immediately evident. The chronist Díaz del Castillo points out repeatedly that all the Indian communities, those of the Aztecs as well as the dominated communities, practiced similarly abominable rites. He writes:

> There's a horrible, abominable thing about them that until today we had not seen anywhere else, that in several moments in a given month, and every time they would ask of their idols to accept what they were praying for, and for this to happen they would take many young girls and boys, and even a man or even adult women, and in the presence of those idols they would hold them down alive as they were and they then cut open their chests to pull out the heart and inner organs, all in front of their idols, and they would offer all that as a sacrificial offering.[80]

Cortés was determined to comply with both monarchical and papal authorities with regard to both "religious" and "legal" considerations in determining his preferred course of action.

Almost immediately he must have realized that he was dealing with at least two different Indian groups. First, there were the abominable Aztecs, against whom he would wage a "just war" on both accounts—as stated above. And second, there were the hundreds of native communities over which the Aztecs had imposed their cruel tyranny. With the leaders of these, he would seek submission, accommodation, and then joint governance.

In his successive letters to the king, one looks in vain for Cortés' detailed explanation about the conflictive relationship existing between the Aztec over-class and the submissive Indian communities. But he did anticipate the possible disconnect between what his king would think, and what he himself knew about the Indians he had encountered. On this account, he chose to treat the issue with decidedly careful language: "... certainly Our Lord God would be well pleased if by the hand of Your Royal Highnesses these people were initiated and instructed in our Holy Catholic Faith, and the devotion, trust and hope which they have in these their idols were transferred to the divine power of God; for it is certain that if they were to worship the true God with such fervor, faith and diligence, they would perform many miracles."[81]

In the communities of this second group, the Spaniards found the leaders who were ambiguously friendly. With trepidation they welcomed the Spanish, but at the same time they feared severe reprisals from the Aztecs for doing so. Cortés made known to them—as he would to every native community which the Spanish would encounter—his strict conditions for accepting their submission, and therefore his protection. Bernal Díaz—again:

> Cortés received them with a happy disposition, and he told them that if they submitted peacefully he and his men would receive them as brothers, but that they would have to cease in their devotions to those idols in which they believed and to which they prayed, that the idols represented false gods, and that they should cease altogether their sacrifices to them . . . that in renouncing both idols and their sacrifices we would accept them as brothers, and that those women [possibly prostitutes or female priests] would be baptized as Christians as son as they were willing; and that all of them would have to decease in their sodomy behaviors . . . and that as soon as they cease those offensive practices, if they leave them behind, then on that condition we could accept them as Friends. What's more, that we would see to it that they would become lords of other provinces.[82]

With these dominated native communities Cortés would do all that was possible to form an alliance: the Spanish would offer military assistance in their war against the Aztecs; then, when victory were achieved, he would facilitate their conversion to Christianity. They would become loyal vassals, and in that capacity, they would serve him well as their new master.

He did not provide further details to the King. Nor did he explain the military strategy that was then devising: that if he and his soldiers were to convince the leaders of those subjugated communities about what he proposed, then he and his men would then protect them from future Aztec reprisals, then they would see fit to join the Spaniards to bring about the military defeat their former oppressors. His intuitions about this—as in so many other issues—would prove to be correct. One Indian writer recorded for posterity his elders' remembrances of those early moments: "Captain Cortéz spoke with authority to the *tepanecas*, the *acolhuas*, to those from Xochimilco and Chalco, and this is what he said: "Come here. The Mexicas, with their arrows and shields, took control of your lands, your families, and all that belonged to you. But now, by the power of the swords and shields wielded by my men, I leave you free, and nobody will force you to return to the status as servants of the Mexica. Take back your lands!"[83] An historian, writing in the last half-century, affirms the veracity of this Spanish-Indian alliance: "It's best proof is the facility with which Cortés recruited willing allies the moment he put his feet onto this land. When a whole people joins with foreigners who have come to overthrow the existing government, this demonstratively shows that the citizens living there were eager to end their sufferings." Indeed, on the final march to Tenochtitlán in 1519, his soldiers were accompanied by perhaps 100,000 native allies whose determination matched his own in their shared objective of terminating for once and for all the bloodthirsty threat of Aztec tyranny.[84]

An additional issue about which he was not yet in a position to contemplate—and as a consequence he does not even mention this issue in his letters to the Crown: after the defeat of the Aztecs, how the colonial government under his authority would rule over all these communities? At that early stage he must have already been contemplating the means for simplifying a very large and potentially complex task. Given the very advanced social organization in the natives' major cities, and given these communities' compliance, if not willingness to ally themselves with his own fighting forces, the subsequent task of governing over them might turn out to be fairly straightforward: he would merely have to impose upon this new land the pattern of feudal domination that already existed across Spain back home. Like the reigning marquis in his home district of Extremadura, he would have at his command a whole system of natives experienced in the task of administering or managing large communities—in this case they would be the natives' upper class. The function of the latter would be to continue what they were already doing quite adequately: maintain order in the streets, direct the labor of vassals, and collect the periodic tribute payments which each town or community was required to pay. In many regions, the newly designated Spanish encomendero would simply occupy the place of the vanquished Aztec prince at the apex of the existing social pyramid, and in that position would lord over a whole class of compliant Indian nobles.

Natives' Views

With the Aztecs vanquished, the Spaniards, led by Cortés, put into place the system of domination described above for those indigenous communities which were most advanced: Spanish grandees chose to make few substantial alterations; they replaced the now-vanquished Aztec princes at the top of the governing pyramid and left most affairs associated with local administration in the hands of the experienced *principales*—the natives' upper classes. In ground-breaking studies, historians have provided detailed analysss of this system of joint governance with regard to both the cities of Tlaxcala and Cuernavaca (see Appendix B).

But these recent historians did not have available for their in-depth studies any surviving documents which preserved the "voices" of the Indian chieftains involved. I have located one such testimony, which was written by an elder from the city of Texcoco in which he discusses the leadership of his community before the advent of Aztec tyranny:

> Our leaders always governed following the law . . . They governed with moderation. Those good times lasted only 83 years. They . . . always provided a personal example in their guiding us with upstanding, constructive and fair conduct. The result was a society that functioned well, whether in times of peace or war. . . . They were good examples. They were virtuous citizens who were also brave in moments of combat. On that account they won prizes and recognition, and the people saw fit to elevate them—each time—to ever higher positions of authority. In their roles as leaders they punished those citizens

who demonstrated bad conduct or who strayed from the good path. There were instances when a leader even had to punish his own children. ... We lived in times when the community either lived in peace or had to go to war. Our leaders were, at the same time, both feared and loved."[85]

A second surviving testimony is the interesting letter written to King Felipe II in the year 1560 by the indigenous nobles of the town of Huejotzingo (north of Cholula in the current State of Puebla). With nostalgia they praised the harmonious situation of their community some twenty or so years before, when their encomendero Cortés oversaw the governing actions of their own fathers and grandfathers. However, after the death of Cortés, new Spanish encomenderos undercut the authority of native rulers and abuses grew. So the complaint they register with the King is "the poverty and affliction visited on us who dwell here in New Spain. ... Your pity and compassion do not reach us." They request that the monarch, "May we deserve your pity, may the very greatly compassionate and merciful God enlighten you so that your pity is exercised on us." Before, during the decades of Spanish rule, "not as single town here in New Spain surpassed us . . . we gave ourselves to you." During the struggle to overthrow Aztec tyranny, "we gave [the Spaniards under Cortés] everything they needed; we fed and clothed them, and we would carry in our arms and on our backs those . . . wounded or who were very ill, and we did all the tasks in preparing for war." Then they go on to praise their first encomendero: "your servant don Hernando Cortés, late captain general, the Marqués del Valle, in all the time he lived here with us, always cherished us and kept us happy; he never disturbed or bothered us. Although we gave him tribute, he assigned it to us only with moderation.... He never reprimanded us or afflicted us, because it was evident to him and he understood well how very greatly we served and aided him."[86]

Yet a third surviving document was written by Indian noble, Fernando de Alva Ixtlilxóchitl, who had been educated in the Franciscan Colegio for native youth in Tlatelolco. In this text the contemporary reader finds a history of those earth-shaking events that had transformed the lives of Alva's ancestors—but from the point of view of the natives. In several other works he had harshly criticized the Spaniards under Cortés' leadership for having committed unwarranted violence to the natives during the military conquest. Nevertheless Alva was a devoted Catholic, which accounts, in part, for his expression of "infinite thanks... to God who has removed me from a community of infidels and barbarians ... With his advanced arms and his relatively few companions, [Cortés] conquered this new world, and he converted the natives living here to our Holy Catholic Faith and the evangelical law; his military feat was one of the most difficult every achieved in the history of the world, and the feats of neither Alexander nor Julius Caesar exceed the glory of Cortés.... That leader ... prohibited his men from killing any of the residents of Cortés [de Tizapantzinco] or from raiding their possessions.... With that accomplishment the whole land was freed; the residents were liberated from the former obligation of paying heavy tributes." Because of Cortés' deeds, he writes, all the Indian communities of New Spain were freed from Aztec tyranny. [87]

In further chapters I draw upon yet other sources, newly discovered, that capture the "voices" of Indian leaders from the city of Cuernavaca.[88]

Spanish Views of More "Backward" Indigenous Communities

No Spaniard had more intimate contact with New Spain's native populations during the time period in question than those involved in the historic evangelization campaign. In about 1528, the Segunda Audiencia was experiencing success in bringing to a close the destructive conflict pitting Cortés' supporters against fierce detractors (as I explain further on). That was when the lawyer Vasco de Quiroga, then terminating a two-year term as member of the Segunda Audencia, moved to the State of Michoacán to found both hospitals and mission-communities. Within a decade, New Spain authorities saw fit to name him Michoacán's first bishop.

At the time, Michoacán had few large indigenous communities with advanced social and political structures. Instead, the majority population, with a warlike reputation, resided in rural areas. One recurring theme in Quiroga's memoirs was his realization that the Spaniards' combined evangelization / education efforts would be most effective with those natives residing in close proximity. As such, he advocated and then brought about the exit of many indigenous families from isolated rural areas and their resettlement in centrally located missions. This suggests that natives treated in his hospitals and mission-communities were of a less sophisticated nature than those inhabiting larger cities such as Tlaxcala and Cuernavaca. He wrote: "Treating native people gently . . . we can help them overcome their status as savage beasts, we can make them become tame or meek. We can help them overcome lax sexual behaviors, fears, undue sadness, and the poisoning of the soul. And once we draw them away from their bad habits—in ways that don't launch them into a life of permanent provocation—our methods based on reason make it easier to dominate their spirits."[89]

In another essay he describes typical personality traits of the Michoacán natives he was dealing with:

> It's a people who are simple and have good will; they're very humble and obedient. They have incredible patience. They're free spirited—they enjoy their big fiestas, to which they invite many people. But in having a good time they commit careless acts and they forget their responsibilities. . . . The youth, many of whom are orphans, go about stealing from those selling things in the open markets, or from anybody else. They take the stolen objects to sell to merchants from a nearby village. So you'll find these ragamuffins almost anywhere, living by stealing. It's a problem without an easy solution—because it happens everywhere. And those who are their victims—the honest people—ask in vain for protection. The youths fell into this wayward life because a father, sometimes a mother, and even a relative sold them to another—this happens all the time. [So many of these indigenous] live like savages. Sometimes they inhabit miserable dwellings distant from towns. Truly, they're that way for lack of strong social ties. That's why it's necessary to

have them brought to central locations, as in a city. Because as long as they survive isolated in the countryside, they'll continue in the manner they're currently living. But if they were to reside in a place where they'd be able to learn new habits, they'd not only be able to live in peace, but also, they'd also acquire a sense of humility and obedience. They'd become receptive to changing their ways. They'd come to their teachers walking on their knees and kissing the ground where the Spanish Christians have tread . . . .[90]

Other paragraphs from his writings provide descriptions of the natives which the contemporary reader might regard as "realistic," but hardly flattering:

The majority of them you could call wild and ignorant, living without either lord or law, without science nor discipline. Not living in society, they rarely engaged in conversation with other humans—except with others like themselves. So they were living outside of society, which means they lacked any social order that guides people in the acts of understanding and comprehending, how to use regular implements or tools. Society teaches one to live decently today while saving or planning for tomorrow. Their condition is so different from our own that it would seem "strange" to many. If you don't have the opportunity to observe their way of surviving from day to day, it would be difficult to imagine . . . the misery they live, the tyranny and corruption they suffer—and sometimes even worse than that. May God in his goodness help us to understand them and their way of life, because only then might we be able to raise them from their misery.[91]

Perspectives of Franciscan Friars

The Franciscan friars working in New Spain's central plateau have left portrayals of native populations that contrast starkly with the descriptions left by Quiroga in Michoacán. What stands out is the innate optimism mixed with realism of Friars Motolinía, Pedro de Gante, Mendieta, and Archbishop Zumárraga. The first, in his oft-quoted 1555 letter to the emperor, states:

> Your majesty, when the Marqués del Valle [Cortés] entered this land, God our Lord was very offended with it: people suffered the cruelest of deaths, and our adversary the demon was very pleased with the greatest idolatries and the cruelest homicides there ever were, ... Every day and every hour they offered human blood to the demons, in all the towns and districts of all this country ... [Now with] our holy Catholic faith implanted ... God has brought about a great conversion of people ... and this whole country is in peace and justice ... If your majesty could only see how the church festivals are celebrated all over New Spain and with what devotion the rites of Holy Week are observed, and all the Sundays and holidays, you would give praise and thanks to God a thousand times.... Their mentality is very different from our own. We Spaniards have big hearts that burn with fire, while these Indians are by nature meek. Because of their timidity ... they don't always express their thanks when they should, even when they have benefited a great deal from what we have taught them; and because of their slowness in learning our mentality, some Spaniards find them insufferable. In spite of this, the Indians have achieved aspects of a virtuous life; the majority has been able to learn new vocations or trades; they have good memories and can learn many things. ... The Indians have demonstrated that they have little patience for listening to the Word of God. Many have demonstrated that want only one thing: return to the life of their former vices and sins, participate once again in the sacrifices and fiestas, eat and drink and consume alcoholic beverages in their fiestas, and offer to their idols the blood that they extract from their own ears, tongues, arms, and other parts of their bodies ... [But minutes or an hour later] the fire of religion begins to burn in the hearts of those Indians who have been baptized.[92]

Friar Pedro de Gante, accompanying Motolonía as one of the first 12 Franciscans, offers the same mixture of idealism and realism.[93] For decades, he was the director of the Colegio de Santa Cruz, located in the Central-Valley community of Tlatelolco. About his young male students, whom the Spanish carefully selected from the Indian nobility, he had positive things to say: "in teaching boys of different ages to read, write, preach and sing . . . fair progress has been made; I do not exaggerate when I say that some have become very good scribes and others are now preachers or speakers of great fervor. I should also mention that some of the youth excel to such a degree as singers that they could sing in your majesty's chapel choir; they're so accomplished that perhaps you wouldn't believe it unless you yourself actually saw it." But—in another passage—he documents the sometimes severe difficulties he personally had experienced in attempting to instruct more difficult sectors of the Indian population: "The common people were just above animals without reason, untrainable. For that reason, we could not induce them to even come to the church premises for our workshops or scripture lessons. We failed in teaching them the doctrines; they would not listen to a sermon. Instead, they would flee when given the chance. In one site we persisted for over three years, and I have to admit that we never succeeded in instructing them, because they fled from the friars—and they were even more frightened in the presence of the other Spaniards—they'd flee like frightened animals."[94]

The writings of Friar (and historian) Gerónimo de Mendieta, in a text dating from the 1570s, communicates the optimism that his Franciscan brethren of the previous generation must have felt at the beginning of their evangelization enterprise: "These religious men, in addition to teaching the Indians to read and write and sing, and also the doctrines of the church, . . . went to great efforts so that their students also learned mechanical vocations and other trades according to the technology available at the time. The padres went out of their way to model their own lessons on comparable activities that the natives had practiced even before the arrival of the Spaniards. How the padres sacrificed! This is especially so when we take into account the varying levels of the natives' intelligence, aptitude, and interest in embracing a new religion."[95]

The Archbishop Zumárraga, as expressed in a letter of 1831 addressed to the team of Franciscans heading up the evangelization campaign, describes the Indians whom they would Christianize:

> They are shy people; they act more out of fear than virtue; it's necessary that we protect them and not apply force; it's necessary the us Spanish treat them well, and not in ways that would cause them to lose the reverence and respect they now have for us; they're hard workers if they respect the ones who supervise them; they're good farmers . . . they're fast learners of new trades.... The nobles in their communities are very willing to collaborate with us, they revere us as much as they fear us ... it's a people who will come willingly to our faith. They have a well-ingrained habit of asking for confession; for the most part the majority live lives of many vices, for example their common habit of drunkenness—which means that we have to structure our interventions to impede them from doing so.... The children ... know a lot and learn fast ... they sing with great spirit. Our work among and with them will merit the praise of posterity: it deserves all honor, all glory; these alone will be the payment for our labors.[96]

Posterity should hold in veneration those friars on account of their optimism, their willingness to dedicate their lives, and their relative successes in uplifting a whole population.[97]

Mexico's "Golden Age"?

Chronist Bernal Díaz del Castillo has left for posterity a remarkable description of the most advanced Indian communities functioning under the joint-governance model during the post-conquest period:

In Tlaxcala, in Tezcuco, in Cholula, and in Guaxocingo, and in Tepeaca, and in other large cities, the Indian [nobles] are those constituting the cabildos [local governing bodies]. They parade before their people—they are the governors and mayors holding gold-leafed staff in their hands—just as the Viceroys of New Spain do—and they dispense justice with fairness and authority, just like our own leaders do among us Spaniards. They know their worth; they strive to follow as closely as they can the laws of the Reign each time they pass judgement. What's more, all the Indian chieftains possess horses, they're well off, they mount elegant saddles, they ride through the cities and villages, they travel along the roads to reach distant rural areas, where sometimes they spend the night among the natives living there. And accompanying them are any number of servants to wait on them. Arriving at a new village they play cañas with the locals; they participate in the bull fights, the compete to spear the sortija—and all this is especially festive on the day of Corpus Cristi, or on the Day of San Juan, or the celebration for Santiago, . . . and I can say with authority that all the native Indians of these lands accept and honor the officials from Castilla who live among them. And they now have their own stores where they either service or sell products from all the different vocations you can imagine. Because they live from these; the food on their family table depends on what they can earn. There are skilled silver workers. And those who tool gold. And I assure you that they're ingenious in how they've learned the different trades from their teachers, the Spanish. Among them there are even surgeons and pharmacists. Craftsmen among them even make excellent guitars. Because before we came to New Spain they were workers by nature. Now some of them raise cattle—you see this almost everywhere. Others make bread and biscuits. Some plant their fields and tend to orchards of fruit trees. . . . And each year they participate in elections to choose their community mayors, their judges, their notaries . . . .

(The reader might question why Díaz del Castillo does not include Cuernavaca in his list of cities demonstrating this admirable level of Indian governance. There are two probable explanation: first—as I hypothesized earlier—Cortés was not eager to share information with others about the exceptional visit of that city's chieftains; and second, after his participation in the 1521 military excursion there, "Bernal" had no further contact with that city and region.)

Historian Charles Gibson, exhaustively studying documents of the period, corroborates this description.[98] He writes that 25 years after the conquest, the Indian-run cabildo in Tlaxcala was functioning well due to the "high degree of ... political acculturation" of that region's class of nobles. Across the board, the natives themselves occupied most important positions in the local governments: several judges, four mayors, 12 regidors, administrators for four of the state's different *cabeceras*, a large number of *aguaciles* (police) and *mayordomos* (heads of religious orders). The Spanish King and queen played a major role in having this happen: their edicts promoting the bi-racial governance—Indians and Spaniards—all across the Central Highland, and the relative autonomy of the Indian government in Tlaxcala, which demonstrated "a high degree of independence" in relation to the vice regal authority in Mexico City. (See Appendix B).

Cortés' Benevolent Treatment of Moctezuma's Daughters

Cortés enjoyed a strange type of "friendship" with the Aztec emperor, Moctezuma, during the latter's final months in Tenochtitlán. Unlikely as it might seem, there is no doubt that the two came to respect each other. Contemporary readers might accept at face value what the 16th century historian Gómara writes, that the Aztec prince "mucho amaba a Cortés."[99] But what might have been Cortés' attitude toward the Aztec head of state? Historian José Luis Martínez suggests that Cortés alternated between "sweetness and cruelty."[100] Regardless of his motivations, we know that before Moctezuma's death Cortés promised to protect his two daughters—a commitment which he would fulfill beyond any previous expectation. Even to a perverse degree? Because

Cortés would impregnate each—and each, in turn, would give birth to a mestizo child. However, Cortés was no "womanizer" in the ordinary sense of the term (an added proof: historians have identified no mestizo children fathered by him during his two-plus decades in Cuernavaca). A more convincing is offered by historian Charles C. Mann: he "adopted" the indigenous custom of appropriating power over the Indian masses by "graft[ing] Spanish authority onto native roots" as a means of attaining yet the more important objective of making the Indians "good Spanish subjects [that were to be treated] as equivalent to Spanish elites [who would] mingle on equal terms."[101]

This last explanation also accounts for the subsequent steps he took to empower those three Indian women in social and economic terms. Picture the disillusioned Cortés in 1521, contemplating the problems that he himself was then unleashing upon the future New Spain, when he had no feasible alternative than that of granting encomiendas to hundreds of gold-hungry ex-soldiers. He had no illusions: many of those recipients were greedy and brutal men. Furthermore, he could predict that their heirs, exercising absolute control over the lives and livelihoods of hundreds, if not thousands of Indian lives, would commit terrible abuses. Cortés must have intuited that these or their descendants would seek ways to undo or overturn the measures that he was then taking, that the worst of them—in some future moment—might succeed in reducing Mexico's Indians to life-threatening servitude or slavery. Memories of the Indian genocide that he had witnessed in the Antilles during the past decade must have haunted him every night. How to protect the Indian masses from future savagery?

One idea was to establish a positive example: he could empower Moctezuma's Indian daughters, as well as his translator Doña Marina, by granting to each a large encomienda located near Mexico City. He realized that other recipients of encomiendas in that area, who were in their majority Spanish grandees with racist ideas, might be motivated to obstruct this plan—if not immediately then at some moment in the future. So, Cortés realized that, in addition to the normal paperwork related to encomienda grants, he would also instruct his lawyers to create new, and different layers of legal protection. He had to make sure that none of his enemies, whether now or in the future, would be able to succeed in their challenge to those rights. All this he accomplished. Through both personal influence and his immense monetary resources, he was able to "buy" the necessary favors and "grease" the appropriate bureaucratic wheels. In doing so, he assured the entrance, and then perpetuation, of at least a few Indian princesses (and their mestizo offspring) into the colony's new ruling class.

Historian Charles Gibson, midway through the 20th century, would indicated his "perplexity" upon studying the "special" manner by which Cortés had established those "perpetual holdings," which have continued, generation after generation, to "fascinate[e] the legal minds" [of the country] . . . the abstract quality [of those encomiendas] remote from the ordinary Indian life," and the fact that these were the only encomiendas controlled by Indians—and, in the next generation, by mestizos.[102] My own explanation for what Gibson had accurately observed: the far-minded Cortés, back in 1524, accomplished exactly what he had intended: Marina and Moctezuma's daughters—and the mestizo offspring of each—would come to constitute, metaphorically speaking, an indelible stain on the elegant table cloth of the country's otherwise white ruling class.

Cortés took decisive steps to accomplish all this. He obtained a special dispensation from the Pope that, in effect, legitimized Martín, his bastard son born by Doña Marina (not to be confused with his legitimate heir bearing the same name—whom he fathered with his second wife, Doña Juana Ramírez de Arellano y Zúñiga).[103] He did the same with the Aztec princesses. Furthermore, Cortés saw to it that Marina and each daughter of Moctezuma, in addition to becoming legal recipients of important encomiendas, were married to important Spanish nobles.

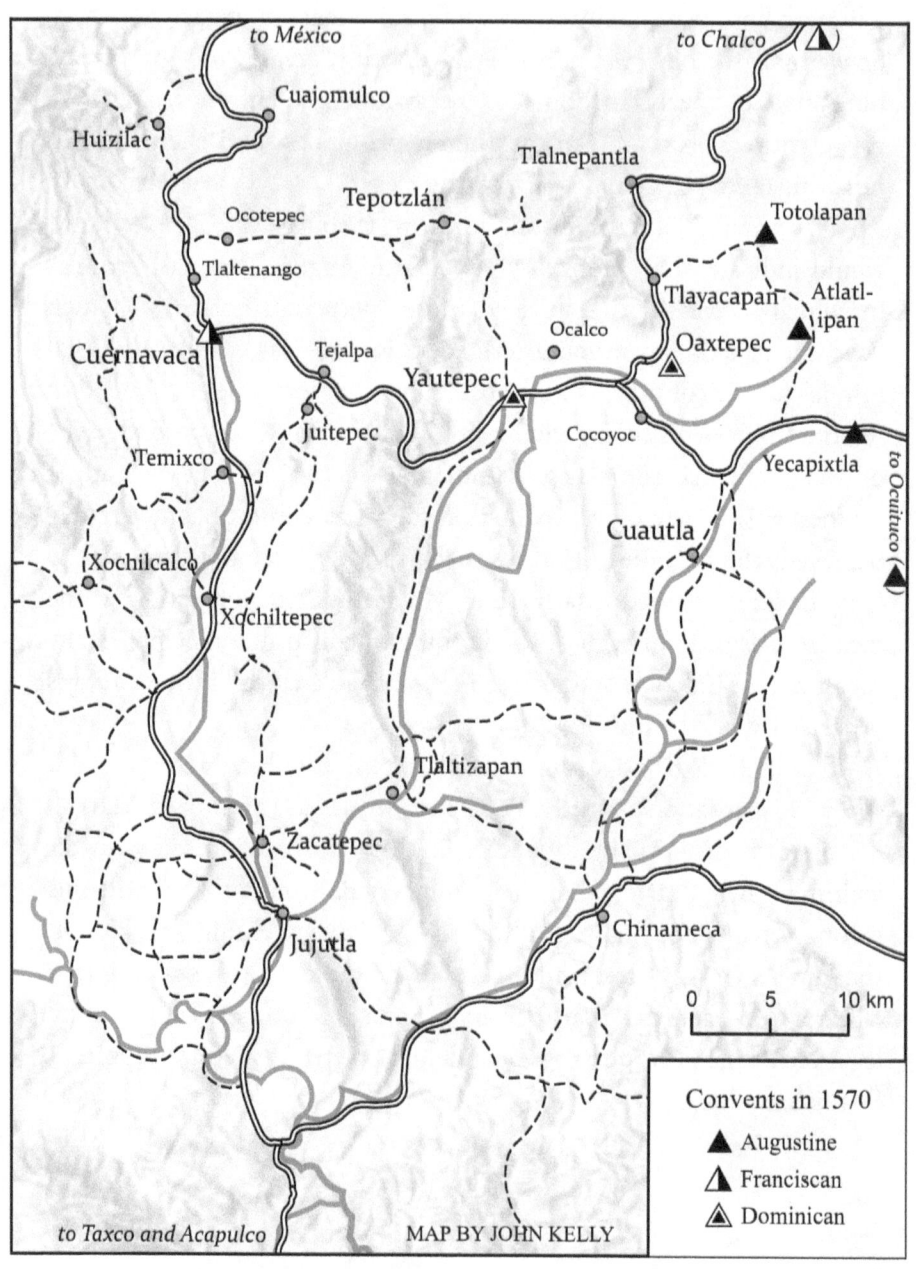

CHAPTER 6

BEGINNINGS IN CUERNAVACA (1521-1524)

With the exception of the tlaxcalteca *ruling class, few other indigenous rulers rivaled Cuernavaca's* principales *in competence and status. The high stature of Tlaxcala's leaders was known to every Spaniard. In contrast, few of the Spaniards must have known about the special nature of Cuernavaca—and it seems to have escaped even the ubiquitous eye of chronist Bernal Díaz del Castillo. Cortés must have decided to inhibit news from circulating about the surprising visit, months before, of that community's leaders to his encampment at Texcoco. He must have decided early on that, when possible, the Cuernavaca encomienda would end up in his own hands.*

The Cuernavaca chieftains would not have objected. On the contrary, they saw him as their "hero," the man who had led the liberation forces against their historical oppressors, the Aztecs. Might they have also felt pride, being that The Malinche would be THEIR feudal lord?

He would now receive their tributes and labor. They expected nothing different; common people, whether in Europe or in their land which the Spaniards now called New Spain, had always tilled the land owned by a lord or baron. It was the latter who gave them

> *a life tenure and military protection as long as they paid an annual rent in products, labor, or money. Indeed, they must have believed: with Cortés as their new Señor, good days lay ahead for themselves, their families, and communities.*

In the weeks after declaring victory over Cuauhtémoc and the Aztec forces at Tenochtitlán, most of the other conquistadors had decided to seek their fortune in those areas of New Spain where, in pre-conquest years, Indian communities had been able to make the richest tributes to the Aztec overlords. Díaz del Castillo writes about his younger self in those weeks:

> I remember that I went to ask permission from Cortés to accompany Sandoval, and he told me: "The way I see things, Mr. Bernal Díaz del Castillo, your perspective on all of this is quite mistaken. First of all, I'd really like it if you stayed here with me; but if it's your desire to go with our friend Sandoval, then go in peace; and I hope that you'll take care in everything that might happen; but I'm almost sure that you'll end up repenting leaving me and the possibilities that right here are offered to you.[104]

An interpretative translation of this passage would have Cortés saying: "Bernal, don't think that your own future would be best provided for in those areas abundant with gold, mines, and blankets; instead, think of other ways to invest your time and energies; I would wager that a decent future can be made in precisely those areas that others from our army mistakenly judge to be 'poorer.'"

These words lead contemporary readers to travel in their imaginations to the area where Cortés had already reserved for his own purposes: Cuernavaca.

Immediately after peace had been secured across the Mexican plateau, Cortés had, among others, several important concerns that drew his attention to Cuernavaca. First, he had to find within the geographical extensions of New Spain the means to become self-sufficient in the production of gunpowder. During his army's final march toward Tenochtitlán, his scarce holdings had caused worrisome nights. Re-supply from Spanish sources in the Antilles had proven difficult, given the obstructive behavior of Cuban governor Velázquez—whom he had alienated—and the jealousy of other rivals who virtually controlled the Caribbean.

Therefore, it was urgent that he locate local supplies of gunpowder's three essential components: charcoal, sulphur, and saltpeter. The first of these offered no problem: in almost any region his men could cut down suitable trees and then oven-bake the wood to produce the desired fuel. To locate the second component, sulphur, took only a few weeks. He relates to the king (in his third "carta" of May 1522) that a few of his men, having braved the walk to the top of the Popocatépetl Volcano, had located sufficient quantities of that substance.[105] But the third essential ingredient, saltpeter? Even before the final rendition of the Aztecs, Cortés had become almost frantic in his search, sending out patrols in every direction. Only months later were his men able to locate a sufficient supply: in the mining areas outside of Taxco. The trip to and from that location would require his men, leading Indian porters –and later horse or mule teams—to pass through that region's primary urban settlement, Cuernavaca.[106]

A second urgent issue was the scarce availability of bronze. His operations—first military, then construction of all types—would depend upon a plentiful supply of this metal. Bronze fittings were especially important in constructing the light sailing vessels that had proven essential for the defeat of the Aztecs. Now, he would need for a steady supply of this same metal, given his rapidly evolving plans to build ocean-going ships to explore the seas to the west. The availability of bronze in the Antilles settlements also proved problematic: in 1524, the ship he commissioned to import bronze from Cuba was shipwrecked in a storm.

Beginning with his army's first excursion to Tenochtitlán, he had taken measures to identify the sources of any and all useful or valuable metals: gold, silver, copper, and tin—this last metal, when smelted with copper, produces bronze. He had interrogated each new allied chieftain about possible mineral deposits, and then had sent out search parties to confirm those leads. But the identification of tin deposits frustrated him for months. Up until about August 1521—that is, the month when the Aztec war machine commanded by Cuauhtémoc had finally submitted to his will—Cortés had nourished the idea that the most promising areas for future metal mines were located in regions corresponding to today's State of Oaxaca. In that month the Spanish party he had sent found deposits of copper. But the search for tin continued frustrating him for months. Historian Martínez:

> First, he requisitioned all the [tin] plates and goblets that were available; but finally [what saved him from that "pickle] was a visit from some Indians from Taxco; they informed him that in that province tin was used to make money pieces and that near their community were located as many mines for tin as there were for iron. This is the story of how—out of military imperatives—the industry of mining had its beginnings in colonial Mexico.[107]

Finally, he located an appropriate source: near Taxco's saltpeter mines. Taxco, located a day's ride to the southwest of Cuernavaca.

In those first few months of the post-conquest period, it became patently obvious to Cortés that Cuernavaca would acquire new importance, being that it was the most important community lying on the shortest road connecting New Spain's capital, Mexico City, with the saltpeter and tin mines of Taxco.

Months later, this would be true for yet another reason: Cortés' search for the most convenient location to establish a Pacific port. He knew about Balboa having crossed the Panamanian isthmus to view from a distance what would become known as the Pacific Ocean (Magellan's passage around the southern tip of South America would not occur for another decade). Cortés lusted to be the person who would first set sail on that new body of water. He would have to hurry—every ambitious adventurer desired the same. But how to access that new body of water?

Months before Cuauhtémoc's epic surrender, Cortés had set himself in action. He had heard vague rumors about a "Mar del Norte" from the messengers sent by the chieftains of Michoacán. But simultaneously he was hearing similar stories about a supposed "Mar del Sur" that lay several leagues to the south of Oaxaca. These "rumors" motivated him to send exploratory expeditions with strict orders to avoid any military encounters and to not head back until that body of water was reached.

He deemed this objective so important that he sent other parties in yet other directions. The best result—initially—was that offered by the group led by Gonzalo de Umbría, in 1522, that passed through yet-to-be "discovered" lands of Toluca (to Mexico City's south-south-west), then travelling for weeks through lands (belonging to today's States of Mexico and Michoacán), and finally arriving at the small Indian village of Zacatula, located on the Pacific coast in the northernmost part of today's State of Guerrero (near today's La Unión). This became Cortés' initial choice for his Pacific port. Immediately, he sent a follow-up expedition, led by Juan Alvarez Chico, accompanied by 122 soldiers, to take possession and to begin the construction of ship-building facilities.[108]

(During his own expedition to Honduras between 1524-1526, those facilities, and his Pacific dreams, would see little action. But immediately upon his return to Mexico, and in spite of the deterioration of his political situation with his arch-enemy Nuño de Guzmán functioning as New Spain's governor, Cortés would see to the completion of those sailing vessels already under construction. By that time he would already be developing similar ship-building facilities at yet another, and even more conveniently located Pacific port: Acapulco.[109] As such, Cuernavaca would acquire even greater importance: thousands of porters—and then, a half-dozen years later, mules and horses—would be coming and going, and passing through Cuernavaca.)

Cortés, more intelligent and farsighted than any of his Spanish peers, recognized the future importance of Cuernavaca as a transportation hub. Within months of the Aztecs' submission, he would be ordering Spanish architects and planners to design bridges and direct Indian laborers to improve roads leading to the south.

Cortés Returns to Cuernavaca

Memories were fresh of the torturous heat that he and his army had experienced only months earlier on that same faint path when they were returning to the Central Valley. His army had just defeated the Indian soldiers defending Yautepec, Jiutepec, and Cuernavaca—events that preceded their successful assault on the Aztec capital by a half year. Now he and his small mounted party were travelling in the opposite direction, traversing the low sierras before the long, southernly descent.

He was now pleasantly surprised by the comfortable temperature—in contrast to the heat of before and the chill he had left behind in Mexico City. The nearby forests now appeared inviting: a hunting playground? Wood for making charcoal or for stoking a sugar-brine fire? Leaving the forests behind, he observed carefully tilled fields to the east. Approaching the densely habited area, he saw cool, spring-fed rivulets flowing down deep gullies.

These first observations communicated future possibilities: where he would want to establish a personal residence in this delightful setting; where could he spend rest days hunting and escaping the chill of Tenochtitlán? Then, an hour later, yet another flash of mental light: in these very fields he could plant sugarcane to produce "coffee-colored gold" for future Mexico-City markets! (He would later realize that those lands to the north and east of Cuernavaca were not sufficiently "tropical" for sugar-cane cultivation. His initial misconception must have been based on memories of his army's exit from that city months before, during an exceptionally hot cycle of Cuernavaca weather). He must have rejoiced upon realizing that the area was ideally situated: close enough to future Mexico City markets, yet far enough to escape the constant conflicts and evil doings of his personal enemies who dominated the politics there. Cuernavaca offered the best of all possible worlds still open to him.

What did he *feel* about the team of *principales*—the Cuernavaca chieftains—who were leading him, as he pulled constantly on the reigns to slow his horse in the descent? The informed imagination can project an answer to this question.

In Texcoco he had met these Cuernavaca chieftains who had made the two-day trip to submit to his authority. They enthusiastically requested their own Christian baptism, and he had obliged by inviting Father Bartolomé to lead the proceedings, with he himself standing in as godfather. Then—over the next year and ending only recently—they had demonstrated their fidelity by leading warriors in the combined forces that he had sent to the far reaches of New Spain to force the submission of other Indian communities.

The *principales* leading him were the object of his curiosity. How might a "friendship" with them further his gigantic dreams? That first night, Cortés' admiration would only grow, as the regional chief led him into a tidy, clean neighborhood of several large, spread-out, well-built houses. Each was a tiny community with a cluster of adjoining rooms on a single level, all with thatched roofs. Many of the rooms used for sleeping were constructed on an elevated base in order that the humidity from the frequent rains would not endanger the health of the inhabitants. Inside the enclosed circle of rooms was an interior patio; hedge-like fences separated the buildings from the green spaces usually located toward the back that featured vegetable gardens and walkways.

Interesting: each chieftain, along with his various wives and dozens of children, occupied a separate housing unit. Although the adult women frequented all these areas in performing their daily tasks, the young girls, under close supervision, were only permitted to leave the housing areas when accompanied by a servant especially assigned to guard them. Rules were similarly strict for the boys and young men: from the age of five they obeyed a routine of walking to the local temple, where they would receive daily instruction about doctrine and service to their revered idols. Cortés saw that boys and girls alike were raised "with constant punishment and discipline."[110]

Most compounds included an adjoining building where there resided the slaves and servants. Among the former he noted—with mixed emotion—that several had foreheads marked with "G" –for *Guerra*, "War"—that his own men must have applied with the branding iron. These were the captives, defeated in battle in Pánuco, Chiapas, and Oaxaca, whom both his Church and his King recognized as legitimate slave material. Mixed emotion, because that practice caused in him a sense of revulsion, and he was already taking measures to do away with the practice all across New Spain. But the sight of those new slaves also was the source of a certain satisfaction, knowing that their presence here constituted yet one more reason for the *principales* to feel indebted to him.

The next day a team of chieftains led him on a tour of the nearby neighborhoods, where the workers and lower classes lived. The houses were positioned haphazardly over the terrain. Most had walls of branches and mud; some roofs were of thatched reeds, others of large cactus (maguey) leaves; they were adequate, at best. These houses were not nearly as large as those of the *principales*; few had the additional rooms for multiple spouses and families. But similar to the families of nobles, the sons and daughters of these Indian commoners were also raised with strict discipline. Cortés personally saw a case of a hard spanking delivered to a boy, along with an angry lecture, because of inattentive behavior.

He was impressed by the orderly domestic life of not only the nobles, but also the lower classes (he had seen the same with regard to the Aztecs, in spite of their bloody, barbaric religious rites). With the exception of the abject poor or those whose families lived in remote areas, they "displayed all the sensitivity of a cultivated nature."—writes an historian who treats this subject with critical detail.[111] Disciplined children translated into safe and orderly neighborhoods, a society where peace reigned. In most cases the boys learned the vocation of their fathers; some were raised to be warriors. But the girls, regardless of their ages, were treated with tenderness and were expected to preserve simplicity in their manners and conversation, neatness in their attire, and modesty before their husbands. All these were attributes of an advanced and cultured society.

(Did any of the Cuernavaca chieftains offer him their daughters in marriage—in accordance with the prevailing Indian custom—in order to assure their continued influence with the new Spanish hierarchy that was in the process of taking control? That is what the nobles of Tlaxcala had done some months earlier upon allying their communities with Cortés' fighting forces. About this, the historical record is silent; to my knowledge no historian has mentioned any personal relationship between Cortés and an Indian female from Cuernavaca.)

In the following days Cortés had the opportunity to ponder critically the status of the Cuernavaca noble class. He realized the exceptional nature of the local revolt that had resulted in the elevation to power of don José Axayacatzin, then the latter's leadership in forcing the obedience of chiefs from all the sujeto communities surrounding Cuernavaca. He recognized the new chief's exceptional leadership attributes. Almost immediately, he had been impressed with how almost all the regional nobles now enthusiastically supported that Indian leader's initiatives.

Furthermore, that chieftain made wise decisions; he gave high priority to the welfare of his class and people. And—after taking all that into consideration—he was offering the full collaboration of his community in the projects that Cortés set before him.

Yet had that visit by several of their leaders months before been the result of a division in their ranks or a power struggle? He would learn shortly that the twenty or so *principales* who had made the trip to Texcoco did not include perhaps the most wealthy and powerful of the region's chieftains. This meant that Cortés' new alliance was clearly on the side of that individual's rivals. In the following months Cortés would act to remove the latter from his former status, while accepting the son under his own wing. After a Christian baptism, this young man would be known to posterity as Don Hernando.[112]

It's a given that there existed gigantic differences between the Spanish and Indian ways of life. But—in those initial moments—Cortés must have realized the parallels between both his and Don José's social positions: both headed hierarchical societies governed, at the top, by a class of nobles. Indeed, seen from this point of view, both he and Don José were peers! Both were *grandes señores*, both believed in the merits of (what we can call) an idealized feudal society where every individual had a prescribed role within the inherited social order. Both believed that their respective Gods had bequeathed to humankind a structured society whose rightful leader was a king who, in turn, commanded over a class of nobles. These, in their turn, followed the dictates of their God in ruling over both the middle leaders, the working poor and a small class of slaves. Both systems resembled each other with their well-defined series of obligations and allegiances running from above to below, but also from below to above. Both systems justified enormous inequalities. In general, both systems "worked," meaning that they were universally accepted as "legitimate." That is to say, neither produced large numbers of dissidents or revolutionaries who rejected the common belief that the existing orders were God's gifts to man. A more critical appraisal might posit that one face of the "Janus" God justified the privileged status of the nobles; while another face assured minimum—but sufficient—rewards for the most humble or miserable of peasants occupying societies" inferior rungs.

At first glance, which Cortés knew was superficial and optimistically positive, he viewed a society that favored its upper-class leaders. In recognizing their services in administering government and dispensing justice, their society bestowed upon them material rewards, beginning with gifts of land ownership or control. Some of these they "rented" out to landless subjects.[113] These accumulated properties were theirs "in perpetuity," constituting each family's "patrimony."

He was gratified to realize that, as different as the Spanish and Indian societies were, both exhibited similar ideologies of land ownership for the noble class. The *principales*, leading him on a tour of the community, must have communicated to him their pride as owners of "lands of *cacicazgo*"—as an elder would later write in the important Cuernavaca codex. He would go on to communicate the sensed obligation of his family to "take care of and maintain" such properties. Another chieftain: "I will leave these parcels to my own sons ... at no future moment will other person have the right to take those properties from my heirs."[114]

In those first strolls through the Cuernavaca neighborhoods, Cortés saw that the most advantageous of terrains were reserved for *los principales*. As in Spain, the social elite kept their own company. In one of the *Cuernavaca códices* we read: In "TEPCAN SAN PEDRO, where the Governor Don Lucas de San Martín y Sandoval lived, in that very house all the *principales* would gather to celebrate their fiestas and where they would dance to the beat of the Teponaztli ...."[115]

Similar to what he had seen in Texcoco and Tlaxcala, the chieftains ran a tight ship. When disorder raised its ugly head, the chieftains in each of these communities took stern measures to enforce the laws and prohibitions against "vices and sins." They applied coercive measures to control dissident or antagonist behaviors on the part of the most difficult or rebellious of its subjects. One elder explains in a Cuernavaca codex: "when a person committing a crime is arrested, then the personnel of the court attempt to convince him to change his behavior. Sometimes they whipped his back in order that he experience fear. In all this the role of the judge is to prescribe the appropriate punishment, but not to personally take the whip in hand, because if he did so he would lose his status as noble and chief."[116] Here,—in contrast to the Aztecs, the nobles rarely recurred to obscene acts of oppression.

In the months following the Aztecs' final defeat, Cortés' trips to the Cuernavaca area increased in frequency. Work on the road linking Cuernavaca with the former Aztec capital was well underway. He had also ordered significant improvements for the most difficult stretches of the path linking Cuernavaca with both Taxco and Acapulco. Another high priority was the construction of shacks that would serve as overnight quarters for the porters who would soon be engaged. Provision of food and water for them was also a concern.

Cuernavaca, as the regional capital for the Acolhua, was the geographical center for the highly populated region; a whole network of roads led off in every direction that united the *sujeto* villages to the city's central plazas. That community was a logical choice for the center of Cortés' future activities.

The only known instance of Cortés appropriating land for his own use occurred during one of those first visits. Some sources identify that terrain as the site of one of Moctezuma's palaces, meaning that Cortés would have been acting legitimately in possessing it. (However, in the months before his death, Cortés would order his people to placate a prominent individual who claimed that the conquistador leader had confiscated that terrain without due compensation—as I explain in the final chapter). He must have been strategizing: his own headquarters should be located as close to the city center as possible. Upon identifying the most suitable terrain, he must have ordered his people to do what was necessary to occupy it in his name.[117] Decision decided and action accomplished. Immediately afterwards, he ordered the leveling of that terrain and the stockpile of rocks that would be used to lay the foundation for what would become his "palace"—and the residence for his future family.[118]

Why did he target for his own use *only* this land parcel? The community must have known that it was owned by the family of Yoatzín, the individual who had served as Cuernavaca's maximum chieftain during the last years of Aztec domination. No existing document explains this. Can we assume that Cortés, in establishing his authority over the Indian communities in and around Cuernavaca, saw fit to minimize the authority of that chieftain when he allied himself with his rivals? Cortés might have calculated that the "confiscation" of this plot would not cause undue hardship for the chieftain involved.

During those first two transitional years, his temporary residence/headquarters was located in the Indigenous community of Tlaltenango—some two kilometers north of Cuernavaca's central plaza. There, his personal staff of twelve resided: several secretaries and managers, a half-dozen paid attendants, and two black slaves to attend to culinary and domestic needs and the care of his horses. In Tlaltenango he would direct both Spanish artisans and Indian laborers in the construction of chapels and churches.

BEGINNINGS IN CUERNAVACA (1521-1524)

This was also where he would also develop sugar-producing facilities similar to what he had already constructed near Veracruz. He had already strategized that the sugar produced on lands bordering the Caribbean would be sold to consumers in Spain and other European ports. In contrast, the sugar coming from Tlaltenango would be destined for the rapidly growing Spanish population in Mexico City. Within months, he would be ordering his team to purchase thousands of sugar cane plants from Hispaniola growers and then their transit from Veracruz to Tlaltenango via Indian porters. Within a year he and those in his employ would begin construction of a *trapiche*—or sugar-cane mill. One of its energy sources would be a steady stream of water rushing down the steep *barranca*, cutting through the village, and separating the barrio of noble residences from those of a worker community.

Meanwhile he would negotiate with the local nobility to rent land for the cultivation of sugar cane. Never during his lifetime would he become an extensive land owner in that immediate area (he would only acquire a few parcels outside of nearby Yautepec to plant vegetables, and later, wheat). Instead, he would rent twenty, perhaps thirty, land parcels, whose noble owners would assist him in directing Indian commoners and a few Black slaves in planting and then cultivating sugar-cane fields. With the legal training he had received a decade-and-a-half before at the University of Salamanca, he was careful to introduce into the community the Spanish custom of documenting any and all such agreements in written form.

Cortés wished to set an important precedent: he would generally respect the pre-existing precedents of land ownership carried over from the period of the Aztec confederacy, whereby native nobles owned and controlled the greater part of Cuernavaca's available land.[119] This was, as he understood, a way of guaranteeing the peaceful collaboration of the "antiguos y naturales señores" in his new area of influence.

Another related project was the improvement of the fresh-water springs just up the hill from Tlaltenango (*los manantiales de Chapultepec*). His engineers offered designs, and Indian laborers, within months, were ferrying loads of rock and calcium (for mortar) and beginning construction. Cortés figured that these water sources would not only supply the needed irrigation for the fertile fields directly to the east. They would also provide a needed water supply for thousands of Indian nobles and workers, whose residences were located nearby.

The region offered yet other benefits. A few kilometers to the north of Tlaltenango and near the road to Mexico City was the community of Quauhxomolco (today's San Buenaventura Coajomulco), which had two points of interest for Cortés. First, this was the area where the huge *agave* plant thrived—the maguey—which the locals harvested to obtain *agua miel* which, when cured, became *pulque*. Early on Cortés must have been impressed with its taste and nutritive value; when mixed with the juices of other regional fruits (the pineapple or guayaba), it became a beverage worthy of a king.

The second attraction of Quauhxomolco were the thick woods, extending to the north for kilometers, where there abounded deer and other game animals. Cortés targeted this area for his own recreational purposes. In those woodsy haunts he would spend an occasional day relaxing or hunting with invited friends. The tall pine trees provided an abundance of shade. One could easily walk or ride through the sparse undergrowth, free of the bothersome spiny plants that thrived at lower altitudes.

Were there lands that did not figure in his immediate plans? He would give attention to the maintenance and security of the roads leading east, passing Yautepec and then on to Oaxtepec and Yecapixtla (the king would wait until 1529 before issuing a Cedula which made official Cortés' control over these nearby communities, in addition to Cuernavaca.) While these smaller cities would continue to administer services over and collect tributes from the surrounding villages, he would not develop any personal enterprise to the east of Yautepec. Within years, he would negotiate the sale of the Oaxtepec and Yecapixtla encomiendas to other Spaniards. (During the early years he also claimed control over Totolapan, but that claim would be disputed and—in a court case—the Audiencia would award it to another Spaniard upon determining its dependency to the *cabecera* community of Chalco to the north.)

The lands to the south of Cuernavaca—in contrast—would prove their utility in Cortés' plans for future development. He would control the silver and saltpeter mines in areas adjacent to Tasco. And the terrains between those two populated areas would serve admirably to produce the agricultural products and animals that he would sell to the exploding population in and around Mexico City, constructed over the foundations of the Aztecs' Tenochtitlán and continuing to function as the urban "heart" of the newly "baptized" New Spain. That was there where the principal markets serving millions of Indians were located. There, also, the majority of newly arriving Spanish settlers were choosing to live. Crown officials, arriving by the dozens, were populating whole neighborhoods. In Cortés' mind, warm bodies meant new demand for building materials, clothing, shoes, wagons, horses, and especially food.

Over the next few years, Cortés would demonstrate his acumen as an entrepreneur with regard to the diet preferred, if not demanded, by the population of that rapidly growing metropolis. He would develop cattle ranches in the Central Valley, and with that beef meat he would establish a near monopoly over Mexico-City markets.[120] He would see similar possibilities about introducing to new white-skinned consumers some of the Indian foods traditionally harvested by communities surrounding Cuernavaca: pulque (the Indians' wine) from Tetela del Monte (near today's Huitzilac), corn and beans from Tepoztlán. Then there were products he would introduce in lands surrounding Cuernavaca that would find ready markets: hides and beef from Yecapitzla, wheat from Oaxtepec, horses and mules from Jojutla, hams from Jiutepec, chicken and eggs from Cuernavaca, sugar (the new "brown gold") produced in Tlaltenango (now a neighborhood in Cuernavaca) and perhaps in other "tierras calientes" located to the south of Yautepec, Huacalco, and Oaxtepec. These possibilities would motivate him to action. Why not? He had the seed money needed to initiate any new enterprise; he had a few capable Spaniards ready and willing to do his bidding; and he had the authority of the king behind his mobilization of Indian labor. Added to that were his entrepreneurial instincts: uncanny was his intuition of future needs as well as practical solutions.

On the occasion of the 1520 visit by the Cuernavaca *principales* to his military encampment near Texcoco, Cortés had engaged the services of one of the religious personnel to organize a suitable ceremony for their baptism. He had been impressed by their fervent desire to do so. The fact that they possessed only a rudimentary understanding of Christian ideas was, for him (as it would be for the Belvís Franciscans) a secondary factor. The natives' willingness, in his eyes, overrode any other consideration.

During one of his early visits to Cuernavaca, he arranged for a similar event, the Christian baptism of scores of the most important nobles from that and the nearby communities. Although they urged him to expedite the Christian conversion for all their vassals, he convinced them that the mass baptism of the majority Indian population could occur only after the arrival of the Belvís Franciscan monks.[121]

Cortés was aware that the matter of Christian baptism was not so simple: there were precedents, rules, and procedures to follow. Permission had to be granted by the appropriate Church authorities. Cortés knew that the state had to be involved (with regard to this issue which a citizen of the twenty-first century might consider an issue of personal consciousness): the Emperor Carlos, at that very moment was waging war in the European sphere over precisely this issue of whether a people, or the citizens of a particular state, had the right to choose a religious practice different from "The True Faith." Furthermore, any circumstances surrounding the baptism of a "pagan" or "infidel" would be carefully scrutinized by the potent Holy Inquisition.

(A few years would pass before the controversy would erupt involving the Franciscan monks' performance of Indian baptisms. The disputes had to do primarily with the question of how much Spanish-language comprehension and doctrinal "proficiency" an Indian subject would be required to demonstrate before his or her baptism would be allowed to occur.[122] That is to say, the Dominican leadership would lead the way in disputing the legitimacy of the Franciscans' practice of favoring rapid baptisms. (See Appendix A.)

The *Cuernavaca códices*, as dictated by chieftains in Náhuatl, make reference to a second baptism ceremony. It occurred in a place that the locals referred to as the "Cruz del Marqués."[123] Unfortunately, no contemporary source preserves a record of this site. In all probability it was a field located near an intersection of two important roads which, following Indian custom, had been marked by the placement of a cross (which had nothing to do with Christian beliefs.) The codex provides some interesting and entertaining details: "When the Marqués (Cortés) came to these lands, he arrived at Huitzilac, where he rested and ate a meal. With him were two companions, one of which had the name Don Pedro Gregorio, and the other Don Antonio Gregorio—they knew how to eat meat (*sabían comer carne*)."[124] Was this barbeque their chosen form of celebration on occasion of the first Christian baptism to take place in Cuernavaca? The Cortés party must have brought with them their own meat—probably a side of hog—that they would have preferred to the chicken or dog meat that the locals might have provided. The quote suggests that the outdoor roasting of that meat was a new—and surprising—event for the local dignitaries, who must have been similarly impressed by the carnivorous appetite of Cortés and his companions.

This baptism ceremony—again—was probably performed by Father Olmedo. One can suppose that the ceremony was conducted in Latin, and that Jerónimo de Aguilar and Doña Marina—or other translators at Cortes's service—communicated to the Indian nobles what was being said. The occasion also involved the symbolic change of personal names; those chosen by the nobles were standard Christian fare: Cristobal, Mateo, Santiago, and Joseph. One can presume that Cortés offered himself as padrino for several notable Indian figures, because several of them would choose to accept "Francisco" as their Christian name and others would decide to drop their Indian family names and replace them with "Cortés."

Following that first baptism ceremony, there probably occurred yet another important ceremony to mark the official change in the community's status, from that of Aztec to Spanish dependency. In the Cuernavaca codex we read:

our new governor, Cortés, assumed power, and we won Nobility and Patrimony, and the authority of our *principales* became official. What we have inherited was recognized by our great Mr. King, and this guarantees that nobody will be forced to go to Tlachco, and we would honor whatever he might require of us, we would receive his orders, as well as those of his soldiers and all the officials of our great Mr. King; that all of these we would receive with respect.

At that moment Cortés initiated the change from Indian law to Spanish law. According to one Indian witness who was there at the time, "In the presence of Cortés Marqués del Valle and all the people of the community, including the elderly men and elderly native women, and before all those who had served before as our mayors, we formally acknowledged this change in authority, in accordance with our ancient customs."[125]

Cuernavaca's Nobles

Beginning in Tlaxcala, Texcocxo, and Coyoacán, and then in Oaxtepec and Cuernavaca, Cortés had acquired considerable experience in dealing with the nobles governing the most advanced of the Indian communities. After initial bellicose encounters, they eagerly allied with the Spanish to overthrow the Aztec tyranny. He had been impressed with their high level of civility. But he also realized that the majority of them shared in the "most hideous vices:" cannibalism, sodomy, idolatry, and human sacrifice.[126] Now, he realize that instructing them to leave behind those abhorrent practices would take time and infinite patience.

In other regions, the Spaniards had been alarmed at observing the sometimes obscene contrast between the wealth and opulent lifestyle of the *principales* and the abject misery of the lowest two-thirds of the total Indian population—the *maceguales*—[127] the poorest of whom subsisted on a daily handful of corn for each adult, and lived in shacks hardly adequate for repelling the seasonal rains. In those other communities, the friars opined that the nobles were no better than "barbarians and tyrants, people beholding to no type of law,"[128] and their sometimes compliant behavior had the objective of undermining the generous assistance offered by the pious Spanish monks. The Spanish queen herself, in summarizing several of the reports received about that low level of noble leadership, had instructed her representatives that "you must accept as a point of departure [in all you attempt] that their leaders force upon the majorities a regime of darkness and subjection."[129]).

Luckily, Cuernavaca offered a welcome contrast. That despicable variant of noble domination did not exist in neither Cuernavaca nor the nearby regions of his Marquesado.[130] Nor did Cortés find here the type of *principales* who ruled without regard for the basic human rights of their most lowly subjects.

However, the local nobility did imitate their Aztec overlords in the age-old practice of owning Indian slaves. Over the first two or so years, and in spite of Cortés' instructions to the contrary, even the most compliant of chieftains continued sending, as part of their required tribute, both young girls (including their own biological daughters) to serve as concubine-slaves for the intimacy-starved Spaniards. That is to say, the *principales* knew that the Catholic king, the Spanish courts and councils, and therefore Cortés himself, approved of the institution of slavery. Aware that they had to fulfill the quota of tributes, many paid part in the form of slaves. The most unscrupulous of Indian *principales* marched with their soldiers to a poor neighborhood under their authority and rounded up a suitable number of workers, branded them according to the accepted custom, and then marched them to the cabecera center to turn them over to the Spaniard in charge of collecting tributes.[131]

Cortés and his advisors had been appalled by such in-grained behavior in other areas, where the Franciscan fathers would instruct and cajole, but with slow results. All across New Spain, including in Cuernavaca, the institution of slavery, in a myriad of forms, was an integral part of the Indians' daily life. The Spaniards' response, at least for the short run, was to prohibit only the most sordid aspects of this practice.

The Indian nobles of Cuernavaca, Oaxtepec, and other nearby communities would demonstrate time and again their gratitude for having been liberated from Aztec tyranny. They would enthusiastically embrace most of the tenants of their new Catholic religion. They would be receptive to Cortés' authority and with honesty and humanity they would carry out the responsibilities of governing over their respective communities.

After Cortés named Don José as acting Indian governor over the network of communities served by the *cabecera* center of Cuernavaca, the two wrote out the list of other nobles who would occupy the different leadership roles for both the *cabecera* city and its twenty-some *sujeto*, or dependent, villages. There would be no significant changes in their duties, except for the cosmetic change of applying Spanish titles for the different municipal positions. The Cuernavaca documents suggest that a standard administrative model was applied for the *repúblicas de indios* across all of New Spain.

In his wisdom, Cortés realized the advantages of not altering in any great way the existing forms of Indian administration and rule; indeed, he would do everything possible to encourage a continuation of Indian government in almost all its forms. Indeed, in and around Cuernavaca—as in at least a dozen of the principal cities of New Spain—the indigenous *cabildo* would provide effective governance for the next three centuries and up to the Independence period.[132]

Meanwhile, Cortés sought out and hired a few capable Spaniards to oversee the nobles engaged in administering the nearby *cabeceras* (principal cities). Cuernavaca's Indian chieftain makes note of this: "It was the 30th of January when our Alcalde Mayor arrived here at Quauhnahuac to establish himself as chieftain of Quauhnahuac, and his name is don Francisco de la Peña ...."[133] (The precise year is not mentioned). De la Peña's job was to oversee the local chieftains of four *cabecera* communities, Cuernavaca, Yautepec, Oaxtepec, and Yecapixtla. (Tepoztlán was then dependent on Cuernavaca.) This individual would guide the local chieftains in making all important decisions, would exercise a critical eye over the activities of the priests and friars, would serve as the top "judge" and "enforcer" for the judicial treatment of Indians violating the law, and would determine the size and frequency and then collect the tributes paid to Cortés' accounts. Within a few years, he would also be in charge of overseeing the Marquez's financial investments, commercial strategies, and ranches producing any number of products (meat and hides from cattle, mules and oxen for transportation, carts, silk, sugar, blankets—*mantas*—and other items of clothing, etc.

In contrast to the broad responsibilities and geographical breadth of de la Peña's responsibilities, Don José's authority would be limited to only the *cabecera* city of Cuernavaca and the smaller *sujeto* communities located within a day's walk. This means that the latter governed perhaps 150,000 subjects (half of whom resided in the area's two largest urban centers, Cuernavaca and Tepotzlán, with—respectively—50,000 and 20,000 inhabitants.)[134]

Cortés also instructed de la Peña to draw up, publicize, and then enforce new rules for commercial transactions in the central markets of all the *cabecera* communities. Reliable measures had to be established for selling quantities of liquids (for example, *agua miel)*, grains, and firewood. As in pre-conquest times, an Indian supervisor was present at each major market center to enforce fair commercial exchanges and to maintain order. As stated in the Cuernavaca codex:

> he began to be present in the marketplace. He would place his chair in the middle of the plaza in order to have within sight all that was being bought and sold, that all products were sold according to the standard measures. He would go around to vendors, checking their measuring stick or weight to make sure it conformed with the official measures he possessed. He would inspect the quality of the chili powder or salt that was being sold. He would be present in the main market place the whole day. Reporting to him was an assistant, who sometimes would be present at his side in the central market, and sometimes would go out to inspect the activity and measures employed in the five other smaller markets of the city.[135]

Reading these Cuernavaca manuscripts, the contemporary reader is impressed by the order, discipline, and communitarian morale of this early post-conquest Indian community.

Another event occurred in or near Cuernavaca which must have been of significance to the Indian community at the time, but to which current-day historians would probably grant little attention. Don Toribio, the codex author, wrote that Cortés, in a return visit to the region, had been accompanied by a personal friend, a Sr. Guzmán. The two made their way to the woods located in today's Municipio de Hatzalah, where Cortés had probably constructed what we today might understand as a vacation shelter. Of interest to the Indian author of said document was the fact that Guzmán chose to not purchase his chosen property, but instead negotiated a yearly rental payment to an Indian neighbor.[136] Why had this "event" been of interest to the Cuernavaca elder—who would remember it decades later? The novelty of that act of "rental tourism" might have become a topic of conversation among the locals over the next several years. Cortés' friend had probably been attracted by Cuernavaca's climate of "eternal springtime" or by the year-long availability of *agua miel*. Or had he been attracted by his host's promise of fruitful hunting—one of Cortés' favorite past-time activities?[137]

Some things would change, but others would remain the same. Contingent upon accepting the Cuernavaca chieftains' submission, Cortés made it clear to them that any and all tributes that they had been paying to the Aztecs would, henceforth, go directly to him. He would neither increase nor decrease the amount of goods or produce constituting those tributes.[138] The Cuernavaca chieftains readily accepted all this as a reasonable condition of their submission. According to one elder: "Fernando Cortés, in the same days that we accepted the Catholic faith, we began paying our tribute to him."[139] In subsequent months, all this would be formalized: Cortés would alter little else in Cuernavaca's pre-conquest tribute system.[140]

Later, he would appoint a second Spaniard to do the same for the *cabecera* communities to the east: Yautepec, Oaxtepec, and Yecapixtla. In future months, taxes would also be levied on commercial activities in the markets. Porters, independently contracted to carry loads to and from Cuernavaca, would pay the same toll fee that they had been paying before—but now to his accounts. Later, Cortés would take measures to increase the transparency of the tribute system: instead of the Indians representing the number and type of their quarterly or yearly payments in the form of objects painted on cloth, he would have that same information recorded on paper in the form of Spanish numbers and word descriptions. He would insist that these documents be printed and distributed, so that the Indians of nearby pueblos could compare their duties with the obligations of every other neighboring community.

Meanwhile, there must have been hundreds of Cuernavaca workers who made their way to Mexico City to participate in one of the most extensive construction projects ever taken in the Americas since the ninth-century construction of the Pirámide del Sol in Teotihuacán: the dismantling of Aztec buildings and temples and the construction in their place of palaces, plazas, and churches for the new Spanish masters. We can suppose that their new encomendero had ordered those workers to make the day-long journey and stay to work for several weeks at a time. Few paragraphs have been written that provide details about this vast enterprise, and very possibly there are written accounts yet to be discovered. Some historians have viewed these massive projects as among the greatest of Spanish achievements in New Spain. However, the Franciscan friar Motolinía would suggest the underside to this glory, that the trials suffered by the Indians participating in these labors constituted "La séptima plaga"—the Seventh Plague—on account of the sufferings involved: "their numbers exceeded those of exploited commoners forced to participate in constructing the Templo de Jerusalem some fourteen-hundred years before."[141]

MEXICO'S "GOLDEN AGE": THE FIRST HALF CENTURY

In sending the thousands of Cuernavaca workers to participate in those vast Mexico City projects, Cortés took advantage of the pliant Indian leadership, requiring them to furnish the number of Indian laborers he demanded. These, in turn, would oblige, neither protesting nor complaining. All of this was unpaid labor. Cortés and other encomenderos simply accepted as a fact of economic life that their servants, slaves, and encomienda workers would follow orders and work long days without compensation or salary. According to historian Gibson (never admitting the positive side to Cortés' actions—see Appendix B), New Spain's Indians had a long tradition of

> providing their own sustenance and ... both local and distant service without pay. ... Indians appeared to be ready to perform, and even to derive satisfaction from ... the Spaniards' demand for labor .... Spaniards quickly took advantage of the Indian attitude .... By controlling the *tlatoque*, Cortés and other Spaniards easily manipulated masses of workers."[142] Indian labor conditions must have resembled those of feudal Europe, where "nine out of ten people spent some time of their life in farming ...[typical workers] were expected... fulfil their contractual obligations ... [paying in the form either of] money and military service [or] labor and produce.... The amount of unpaid labor that an individual had to perform on a lord's estate was an indicator of a person's status in the society.[143]

A curious note: Motolinía, after commenting about the Indians' sufferings while participating in Mexico City's grand transformations, notes that they were *singing* while working. Were their songs comparable to those of African slaves in North America's deep south? Can assume that the Indians labored with child-like acceptance, and even with a sense of celebration, in doing their part to erase from the face of the earth every sign or symbol of their former sufferings under Aztec tyranny?[144]

How many Cuernavaca workers made the trip to Mexico City in the months following the Aztec submission? Did Cortés dispatch specialists to build the special atriums and carpenters to fashion artistic columns or devotional tableaus? We do not know.

Indians under Cortés' authority also worked on projects in and around Cuernavaca. One historian details that during the 1530s the number of workers employed in any one day varied from 2,133 to 2,166.[145] Beyond the vague references I've cited above, there does not survive any document which captures how the Indians themselves might have experienced this required labor.

One codex recounts that a local artisan, Don Melchor de la Cueva, (apparently accompanied by Don Toribio de San Martín Cortés, Don José's successor as Indian governor) spent time performing specialized work in the construction of a cathedral near Altacomulco: "I worked in the Republic, working on the Holy Church until its construction was finished; I resided on the side of a hill called Quauhlotitlán near the entrance to a natural cave... that is what I obtained in a grant from our King at the time of our baptism, the same time when he named us nobles and elevated us to the status of community chiefs, also when I received the faith...."[146]

Don Melchor probably headed the list of several other highly skilled artisans involved. Did the author of the *códice*-document single this worker out on account of his noble pedigree? Or might the latter have been the leader of a whole team of skilled artisans, all hailing from the small community of Tlaltenango?

Other Cuernavaca nobles, in addition to Don Melchor, must have been involved. In another codex, a noble dictates how, years earlier, he had supervised a team of carpenters. It is interesting to note that the children of nobles might have been working alongside common workers: Cortés "ordered wood workers, Quauhxomulco laborers, some of them our own sons, to fashion the wood needed in constructing the church. And our community went out [to the nearby forests to cut down trees and fashion them into construction beams] and we sent him all the lumber that was necessary to bring the work to completion... ."[147]

CHAPTER 7

MEXICO'S EVANGELIZATION CAMPAIGN

"The first forty years after the conquest... were the golden age of Mendicant evangelical enterprise"—thus opines one of the most important historians of this historical period.[148] This remarkable contribution of the mendicant monks in Mexico, led by the Franciscan friars, can be considered the "end result" of a remarkable confluence of events and the actions taken by a few of the age's most outstanding personages.

Spain, geographically situated at the western extreme of the Europe, although hardly a protagonist, nevertheless participated in the intellectual stirrings that, over the past half-century, had dominated in scholarly circles elsewhere. Later historians would call it the beginnings of the "renaissance"—that is, the availability and circulation of texts written by the most prestigious of Greek and Roman thinkers more than a millennium before, which would inevitably come to influence the thought and customs of the time. All of Aristotle's surviving texts had been translated into Latin by the middle of the 1200s. His works were eagerly devoured by a brilliant young nobleman from southern Italy then studying at the University of Paris: Thomas Aquinas (the works of Plato would become similarly available a whole century later). At the dawning of the next century Dante was to call him the "supreme philosopher." In the 1360s Petrarch would be influenced by several classical writers whose works now circulated freely in Latin translation. By the 1440s princes in several city-states (of today's Italy) were sending out their representatives to the abandoned libraries of monasteries to compete in the objective of hosting the most prestigious library of translated classical works. In the most "cultured" of cities, book sellers, hand copying ancient texts, flourished. Then, in the 1450s this love affair with learning exploded with Johannes Gutenberg's invention of the printing press—an apparatus that would come to operate in 19 European cities by 1470 and 255 by 1500, having printed an astounding 12.5 million books.[149]

Hard to believe, but this was the same historical period which another historian has characterized as the "folly of perversity, perhaps the most consequential in Western history, if measured by its result in . . . hostility and fratricidal war [with Catholic] popes adopting as their own the values and style of the piratical princes of the Italian city-states . . . opulent, elegant, unprincipled and endless at odds with each other . . . potentates of discord."[150]

Spain, during this same time period, offered a contrasting scenario. Queen Isabel (queen from 1474 to 1504), with fervent and intense faith, viewed the corrupt practices of the Church with grave concern. Under the supervision of –first—her Jeronymite confessor Hernando de Talavera, an—the—Franciscan Francisco Jiménez de Cisneros, she responded to the deep undercurrents of discontent within the Religious Orders and passionately set about to raise the moral and intellectual levels of her clergy. Change became most evident among the Franciscans, and only later reforms spread to other religious orders. Although Cisneros never embraced openly the humanist objectives then thriving in the Italian states, he did realize the benefits that classical ideas might lend to religious practices in his own country. Under his leadership, the reformers found lessons in the "New Learning" to benefit the work of reform.[151]

Under the guidance of Queen Isabel and Cisneros, there came to exist various "pockets" of progressive religious thought within Franciscan circles—and sometimes in the face of stern opposition. The queen herself did not survive to see realized two of her greatest accomplishments in this realm. First, the promotion of progressive theological issues through the hiring of reformist teachers in established centers of learning such as in the Universities of Salamanca and Alcalá (the latter was founded only in 1508). And second—following in the pattern established by progressive city-states in Italy—she approved and then promoted the publication of the important Complutensian Polyglot Bible, in which the Greek, Hebrew, and Latin texts were printed in parallel columns.[152] For his part, Cisneros—following the pattern of los *hermanos menores reformados* in Italy—promoted the creation of new centers of progressive theological practice within the Franciscan ranks of Spain. There came to exist several geographical areas where these austere and devout Franciscans congregated: Alcarria, Alcalá, Ocaña, Ciofuentes, and Escalona. Efforts were also expended to expand this practice in Portugal, Santiago de Compostela, and Belvís de Monroy in Extremadura (the site from which the future leaders of Mexico's evangelization campaign would be recruited). These reformist practitioners, isolated from the main body of the Spanish Church, generally congregated in "casas de retiro o de recogimiento"—or small monasteries—where they felt free to live in poverty practicing their preferred form of devotion.[153]

The spread of reformist and progressive theological practices was occurring elsewhere in the European theater, but the direction of "influences" would be hard to document. Might Cisneros have had "contact" with booksellers in the Italian city-states, whose business was the publication of classical texts translated for the first time in Latin? Influences also might have been due to monastic travel. For example, we know that some reformist leaders in Spain had traveled to Rome to undergo special training. This was the case of Martín de Valencia—before his initiative in founding the monastery of Sanda Marría del Berrocal in Belvís, Extremadura. Might these individuals have established contacts with printers using the newly available Gutenberg presses to publish and then distribute to ever broadening audiences their new translations of Biblical texts? It is to be assumed that the Franciscan Order nourished its international ties, and that it participated in the spread of ideas, tendencies, and practices from one European setting to another.

Several sources suggest the influence of Erasmus of Rotterdam over the thought of the reformist Franciscans in Spain. This individual would become (along with the German theologian Martin Luther) one of the most important among the advocates for religious reform during the sixteenth century. In the paragraphs below I suggest that his role as tutor of the prince Carlos in the half-decade before the latter's coronation as Spanish king probably had a role in the 1523 selection of the Belvís friars for their important role in Mexico, but that did not translate into an influence over the Spanish church in general. Upon considering the chronology of Erasmus's publications, I am convinced that his thought came to influence the Belvís friars and other progressive Franciscans in Spain only beginning in about 1523—that is, the year when those monks were already preparing to depart for Mexico. After that year, much of Erasmus's international fame, especially in northern Europe, would undoubtedly be due to the new presence of his books coming off that ground-breaking invention, the printing press.

We can therefore assume that a majority of the tomes written by Erasmus which were later found in the personal libraries of Mexican friars Juan de Zumárraga, Pedro de Gante, and others, were in languages other than Spanish and were of tardy acquisition. I embrace the studied opinion of Pérez, that "erasismo" only began to spread in Spain—and therefore in Mexico—toward the latter half of the 1520s. This means that only by coincidence have observers detected similarities between Erasmanian thought and the premises underlying the earliest moments of the evangelization campaign. But—undeniably—there were "*confluencias*" or "*tendencias afines*."[154]

Another clarification is in order here. Yes, there was a significant spread of progressive theological thought in some Spanish circles. But no, this did not have a large impact in other spheres of Spanish society. On the contrary, progressive practitioners met hostile reception on all sides and, within decades, their thought, their advocacies, and they as individuals would be overcome by entrenched interests, whether in government, Church, or society. For a brief period, they with their reformist advocations "simmered" in hidden retreats, generally ignored by mainstream church functionaries who were products and participants in the age's unmovable corruption. before going down to defeat and all but disappearing from public view. After all, this was Europe's brutal, corrupt sixteenth century. Historian Barbara Tuchman states a sad truth which had application as much with the religious order as it did within the social, political, and artistic realms: "To an unusual degree in the Renaissance good walked with evil in a wonderous development of the arts combined with political and moral degradation and vicious behavior."[155] This, in spite of the emergence of progressive thinkers and actors such as Michelangelo, Leonardo, Erasmus, Pope Adrian VI, and—in his youthful years—Charles.

Back to Spain and the initial decades of the new century. Queen Isabel and King Ferdinand had died. When their daughter was declared unfit to rule, the crown—in the year 1509—passed to the six-year-old Carlos (Charles in French and English). Cardinal Cisneros, lucid and active as before, was named to the all-important role of regent in charge of running the now-united kingdom's government, with the additional responsibility of seeing to the care and education of the young prince. Impressed by the competence, intelligence, and progressive views of a young Franciscan priest from Utrecht, Cisneros appointed that man, Adriano, as the prince's head tutor, and shortly thereafter saw to Adriano's promotion to the position of church bishop (this man's future career will be treated below). Historians ignore much about the relationships, associations, and communications between these personages—and their intellectual and theological influences. But it is a matter of historical record that in 1516 Adriano and Cisneros invited none other than Erasmus to share in the tutelage of the young prince and serve as counsellor to the court.[156] At that time Charles must have been about 14, two years shy of his coming of age. To commemorate his appointment, Erasmus wrote a short book, *The Education of a Christian Prince*, which he dedicated to the prince who would soon wear the crowns of both Spain and the Holy Roman Empire.

The background has now been set. Europe's most progressive religious thinker, now added to Spain's most active Franciscan promoters of Church reform, now occupied the highest ranks of Spain's court councilors.

New Spain, 1519 to 1521. Cortés had been repelled from the Aztec capital at a terrible cost. He had collected together the surviving soldiers near the Mexican coast and had recruited new ones from the defeated army of Narváez—as I recount in Chapter One. Then his refurbished force began marching yet a second time toward the Aztec capital. Indian tribes all along his route rushed to either join his forces or demonstrate their allegiance to the new, powerful Spanish army. Defeat of the Aztecs was only months away.

The news from his home country, Spain, couldn't have been encouraging: the monarchy continued to "drift" without firm leadership.[157] Cortés must have realized that it was hardly an opportune moment to seek monarchical orientation for what lay ahead in the soon-to-be conquered American mainland. If not, he still must have realized that he and his men were all alone, that it fell to him alone to make momentous decisions about how to conduct the military conquest and then—months later—how to structure and govern the future Mexican colony.

For Cortés, the lonely tasks of leadership were not a cause for lamentation. On the contrary, he welcomed the power of being able to call all the shots and act according to his own criteria, without undue interference from above. The people surrounding him already sensed that few others matched the young conquistador-leader in intelligence and intuition. That from the start his decisions in directing both Spanish soldiers or submissive Indians were yielding unexpectedly positive results. Slowly, others under his command were beginning to realize what he himself must have felt, that none of the other in his midst equaled him in practical skills and the ability to get things done. Furthermore, none of the potentially rebellious nobles among them rivaled his boldness, sense of destiny, and vision for both their own and that land's future.

Yet he must have sensed apprehension upon hearing reports of how the young king Carlos was already showing signs that he would rule with a stern authority. Only three years before, upon assuming the reins of monarchical authority, he had demonstrated either ignorance or disregard for local sentiment by demanding subsidies from Spain's regional governments (at Valladolid in 1518; and then at Santiago the following year.) Family members back home must have communicated to the young man, eking out a livelihood in the Antilles, that all across Spain people feared that the funds demanded by the young king would not be used for any number of worthy projects or causes within Spain itself; on the contrary, they would fund the campaigns of the king's armies in the Low Countries. (Between 1519 and 1520 the king again would pressure Spanish sources for monies, this time to facilitate, and then celebrate, his assumption of the Holy Roman Empire crown). That perceived "subordination of Spanish to international interests [proved to be] more than the peninsular-minded Spaniards could endure."[158]

Cortés was most probably informed that the newly ascendant king had appointed the two Franciscans, cardinals Cisneros and Adriano, as regents charged with governing the affairs of the country during his anticipated absence to accept the crown of the Holy Roman Empire; that shortly thereafter the aged Cisneros died, leaving Adriano alone to weather the explosion of civic fury that accompanied the revolt of the *comuneros*. Throughout the year 1519, Adriano imposed martial law throughout Spain, and loyalist forces put on trial and then executed over 12,000 rebels. Cortés must have thought: *Was that but a prelude to how the new monarch would begin to intervene in affairs relevant to Spain's new possessions in the Americas?*

Over the previous months Cortés had spent hour upon hour dialoguing with his closest advisor, the Merced monk Bartolomé Olmedo. One important topic was the most desirable way to stabilize Spanish rule over New Spain once victory over the Aztecs was assured. (One historian suggests that Father Olmedo's ideas figured prominently in Cortés's first two letters sent to the king.)[159] These two must have been musing: "Once the Aztecs were subdued, what would the best manner to lead the Mexican people into the Christian fold?" In an early letter to the king he would make an important point that "the natives of these parts are of much greater intelligence" and were far better candidates for "civilized" life than those which the Spaniards had encountered in the Caribbean islands over the previous two decades.[160] Don Vasco de Quiroga and Friar Gerónimo de Mendieta—both writing a generation later—were to add new qualifiers that Cortés would not have rejected: New Spain's Indians were "childlike" (their "Inocencia") and possessed "a naïve nature, so distinct from the corrupt mentality of Europeans" (their "*índole ingenua ..., tan distinta de la mentalidad corrompida de los europeos*").[161] Cortés realized that the Mexicans constituted a new type of Indians, that the considerations and instructions regarding the "treatment" of new-world natives –which had emanated from former monarchs Isabela and Fernando as well as past popes, had been based on old categories and did not necessarily apply to this more advanced native population.

Beginning with these early encounters with Mexican indigenous communities, the intuitive Cortés had begun to contemplate the form of "spiritual conquest" he would direct. According to one inciteful historian:

> On most occasions [in these early encounters] Cortés pays due respect to the natives' traditional places of reverence, because he was able to project the political risk that his Spanish soldiers might provoke if they were to carry out a systematic desecration of them. ... This approach—it behooves us to emphasize—is precisely that adopted by the missionary religious orders that will, within a half-decade, will be charged with heading up the evangelization campaign in New Spain: he consistently chooses the top of the existing pagan temples as the preferred place to implant his own Christian altars and crosses. ... Cortés deliberately chooses the route of inserting the Catholic religion into the context of the pre-existing indigenous cultural context. ...

He does this with full consciousness of its implications. He has understood—from the first moment—that any Christian message would be immediately rejected if it were not presented as an integral part of the natives' age-old pagan practices.[162]

He would have to avoid making the same mistakes made by the Spaniards in the Antilles. Indeed, the monarchy's actions with regard to "infidels" over the previous generation left him fearing the worst. Whereas the Catholic Kings' successful crusade against the Moors had earned the applause of committed Christians everywhere, Queen Isabel's subsequent determination to rid Castile of all remnants of the non-Christian populations—Moors and Jews alike—had translated into "fanatical retaliatory" measures. First, the expulsion, under the threat of death, of 165,000 Jews and perhaps an equal number of Muslims. And second, the restitution of the Holy Inquisition that would execute nearly 9000 "converts" to Christianity and would send yet another 5000 to prison. The greater part of this monarchy-ordered human tragedy had occurred between 1485 and 1498 (under Inquisition head, the Dominican priest, Tomás de Torquemada).[163] That is to say, this occurred during the period spanning the birth of Cortés—in 1485—and his thirteenth year. We can safely assume that the adolescent had been moved by hushed sentiments expressed with regard to these events in the bosom of his childhood home. Is it also possible that a friend of the Cortés family had been one of the Inquisition's unfortunate victims, or that Cortés's accidental presence at a fiery Auto de Fe had left a permanent scar on his budding intelligence? A predictable outcome: Cortés was totally aware that an undesirable form of Spanish imposition over a newly conquered native population would be a prelude to unrepented violence.

He must have been repelled by the crown's blunder of before, that of not promulgating and then enforcing strict rules to govern how the *encomenderos* carried out their charge of evangelizing native serfs and slaves. The result had been disastrous. Yet he also knew that he had no other practical option than elevating his own soldiers to the status of encomenderos, that even the hidalgos serving as officials in his conquistador army were little better than the rank and file of his soldiers, with their corrupt and vice-ridden lifestyles—and their lust for precious metals. So, how could he guarantee the future wellbeing of the natives placed under their charge? He nourished the hope, bordering on the improbable, that if he enacted a strict code of conduct for treating the natives, then his crude soldiers would be transformed into decent, moral landlords accepting the natives as "willing children" and would joyfully offer themselves as positive moral examples. This plan would have to entail the involvement of a dedicated team of Spanish religious individuals to inculcate benign administrative practices in the soldiers; even more important would be their role of initiating a program of native baptism that would incorporate them into the Spanish fold as rapidly as possible.

Another necessary factor: his plan would only be possible through a close collaboration with the natives' chieftains who, after the defeat of the Aztecs, would continue to exercise their authority and govern over their communities. He and Olmedo were witnessing the willingness of friendly chieftains, beginning with those of the powerful state of Tlaxcala, to join with his forces in their campaign against the Aztecs. They were also showing willingness to accept the Spaniards, once the Aztecs were defeated, as their new feudal lords. Aspects of the native culture and religious practices also suggested that, upon the defeat of the Aztecs, there would be widespread willingness among the ruling class as well as the native masses to accept the religion of their new masters.

The future compliance of the native chieftains? This was not assured. From the beginning of their new march toward the Aztec capital, he would have to cultivate their favor. The aged chronicler Bernal Díaz del Castillo recounts what he personally had observed years before as one of the younger members of the conquistador army: In their march toward the Aztec capital, Cortés sought every way to avoid battle with the different native communities. He would not allow any soldier to rob any possession or commit any act that might provoke an angry reaction on the part of the natives: "Our God bestowed His grace upon him, because in every situation [Cortés] acted out of generosity; in every community his objective was to [only] pacify the Indian communities and all their members."[164]

These were not the musings of a "religious fanatic," as an historian incorrectly wrote.[165] I would substitute as more appropriate the adjective "sincere" or "devout." He was not a Pizarro, an Alvarado, a Coronado. In fact, Cortés must be placed, in the moral sense, head-and-shoulders above his generation of Spanish conquistador leaders. He definitely shared certain values and personality features with the others: his lust for conquering and geographical discovery, and the sometimes-brutal behaviors common to his age. But in major ways he differed from them in this one quality: for Cortés, the incipient currents of progressive thought, which intersected with the budding "humanist" inclinations of his age, had touched him and had left their imprint on his values, actions, and beliefs. In this light one must understand the important decisions he was making with regard to the role of religion in the society he would direct after gaining the submission of the Aztecs.

Olmedo and Cortés must have reflected: the traditional bureaucratic procedures of Catholic baptism would not do. Follow mainstream Catholic procedures in requiring the Indians to learn and then demonstrate familiarity with basic Catholic rites *before* their baptism? At best, this would take years and would involve only a small native elite. No. This was not acceptable. Cortés had to seek the means whereby the great majority of the natives of all social classes could be baptized upon demonstrating only their willingness to be baptized. Then these new Christians would have years to learn, whether in Spanish or via lessons translated into their own languages, the necessary liturgies and prayers.

Could this return to a "primitive" form of baptism be possible? What group of religious coming from Spain would accept this special qualification?

In his letter to the king Cortés slyly approached this delicate issue by stating only the basics and avoiding mention of his musings with Olmedo. He wrote that those directing the future campaign affecting the natives should be "religious persons of a good life and character," that they should be that type of "religious personnel ... who would be most zealous in the conversion of these people. They would [live among the Indians themselves,] they would build houses and monasteries in the provinces which we think most appropriate. [They should not be] bishops and other dignitaries who would only ... squander the goods of the Church on pomp and ceremony, and other vices ...."[166] In short, they should be mendicant monks, those who would willingly accept a life of poverty and a simple lifestyle. His words, as quoted here, suggest a further qualification: they should not be the type of monk that favored contemplation and prayer. On the contrary, they had to be healthy, vigorous, and eager to embrace a future of committed activity. He did not state it here, but a further qualification would, in short order, attain enormous importance: they (at least their majority) had to possess a desire and ability to acquire second-language skills; they had to be willing to not only tolerate, but also to assimilate, different cultural practices.

Which denomination of mendicant monks would be most appropriate for this—future—monumental task? In his letter to the king, Cortés diplomatically made no distinction: he wrote that it could be of either Dominican or Franciscan persuasion. That is what he wrote but, truth be told, that is not in all probability what he believed.

By reason of their past actions, Dominicans—he must have thought—could not be trusted. They could not be not be counted on—once the Aztecs were subdued—to place the protection of New-Spain's natives above all else. Would they protect native women before the carnal desires of brutish Spanish soldiers? Or would they stand resolute before powerful Spanish nobles to demand decent working conditions for native males sent to work in the mines and fields?

Historical precedent "told" him: perhaps no. Because by his day the Dominican Order, with a reputation for "rule-bound orthodoxy," was already associated in the public mind with "the Inquisition ... its terrors ... the burning of heretics."[167] Priests wearing that order's habit, over the past generation, had assumed a protagonist role in the hypocritical—if not hateful—politics of the Catholic Kings, who publicly had advocated "Christian piety," but in actual fact had carried out a state policy of intolerance bordering on genocide for the non-Christians then living in their realm. Cortés, early on, had decided that his own group of preferred evangelizers—no questions asked—would be committed to protect the Indians from the Spanish state itself. "Convert" the Mexican natives only to subject them to invasive scrutiny, to public trials by "pious," merciless, religious fanatics, and to a life of fear induced by required attendance at the public burning of their revered community leaders, now condemned as "heretics"? On "his watch," that was not going to happen.

But there did exist a recent, and much more positive, counter-example among Dominican ranks: the priest Antón Montesinos, who still enjoyed the applause of charitable-minded people for having been the first religious figure, only a decade before (in Santo Domingo, 1511), to raise a public voice denouncing the abuses that the Spaniards were committing against native populations in the Antilles. The monarchy's reaction must have been embarrassment, because they had answered with rosy-sounding words and ineffective new policies. Furthermore, Montesino's words of protest had hardly affected the Dominican hierarchy. On the contrary, the latter projected the impression, during those years of monarchical transition, of jockeying to position themselves best in order to cozy up to those individuals who would, within months, emerge as the clerical "powers behind the throne" of the future king. There were indications that even the brethren of Montesino's order had sought ways to ostracize him: after that fiery sermon, he had quickly disappeared from public view.

No. Cortés must have distrusted religious figures professing allegiance to the Dominican Order and must have opposed any Dominican participation in that first moment, when the goals and procedures of the future evangelization campaign would be defined. However, within a decade, once the evangelization campaign were underway, many religious personnel would be needed. Dominican mendicant monks, if they were truly committed to a Christian life of frugality and humility, would make a contribution.

Did Cortés's opposition to a Dominican leadership for the evangelization campaign translate into an out-and-out preference for the Franciscans? Probably not. Not yet anyway. Fresh in his mind were two individuals from that last order who had been integrally involved in the violent, if not hateful, state policies of previous regimes. First, there was Cardinal Jiménez de Cisneros who, under "The Catholic Kings" Fernando and Isabela—only thirty years before—had assumed a leadership role in the country's administration during the Inquisition's fiercest days.

And second, there was the case of the Franciscan Adriano of Utrecht, recently named church cardinal, who was then serving as regent in charge of governmental affairs. How much might Cortés have known about this man? His ascension had been "astronomical." On the one hand, the preponderant influence of yet another foreigner over the new monarch inflamed smoldering passions everywhere. Yet, on the other hand, some court people marveled at Adriano's competence and celebrated the presence of an honest, intelligent, and level-headed man in ruling circles.

Jump ahead a few months. The conquest was complete and Cortés was once again faced with the thorny issue of deciding what form the Spanish domination over New Spain would take.

Makingh news in Cortés's circle was the arrival of Franciscans Francisco de Quiñones—also known as Francisco de los Angeles—and Friar Juan Glapión, both recently authorized by Pope Leo X to visit the newly conquered land, assess future possibilities, and then return to offer their advice to both the Vatican and ruling circles in Spain. The details about those meetings in Mexico City remain enveloped in mystery; to my knowledge no document survives that treats those deliberations between the Franciscan visitors and Cortés, but we can speculate that Cortés found fertile reception in communicating to them the musings of Olmedo and himself over the previous two-to-three years. A further speculation: the two visitors would agree with almost every suggestion made by Cortés and would later experience success in having those suggestions acted upon after their return to Spain. The basis for this assumption? There is no other reasonable explanation for the remarkable meeting of the minds that would come to exist between

Cortés and the Belvís monks once the latter were actually directing the evangelization campaign.

We can only speculate: Cortés must have known about the more benign orientation of that small Franciscan group of "illuminaries" or "alumbrados" living in the monastery of Belvís.[168] Historians today identify this group as the Spanish participants in a continent-wide phenomenon: they were "humanist"-minded individuals who abhorred the corrupt and materialist practices of the religious mainstream and dedicated themselves to a life style of "innocence, simplicity, and profound humility."[169] According to their "illuminary" beliefs, they rejected "orthodox" or "medieval" orientations in favor of "*una estrecha comunión con Dios.*" They preferred o worship their God directly, "*en su forma observante.*"

Their monastery was located in a region under the jurisdiction of the family Monroy, which is the second last name of the conquistador's father, Martín Cortés Monroy. One can speculate that Cortés, as a youth, might have visited that monastery and might have come to know and respect the observant monks' practice. Or another possibility: Cortés, after his meetings with Quiñones and Glapión, wrote urging his father (in correspondence that has not survived) to make personal contact with either Quiñones or with Cardinal Adriano himself.[170] In either case, there must have been some moment or means of contact—whether direct or indirect—between Hernán Cortés and Spain's Franciscan hierarchy.

The Franciscan visitors came and went. Months passed. Cortés and his soldiers, with a predictable delay, were informed about the death of Pope Leo (in mid-1521) and, within months, the election to that position of the Spanish regent—and Franciscan—Cardinal Adriano.[171] (Pope Adriano VI would serve 20 brief months, dying in September 1523). Surviving documents demonstrate conclusively that during his short tenure as pope, Adriano would follow events in New Spain with keen personal interest; that he would issue important decrees supporting the thrust of Cortés' activities and protecting the welfare of New Spain's indigenous population. Most important was his approval of the Spanish Franciscans' selection of the Belvís Franciscans to assume the leadership role in Mexico's evangelization campaign.[172] Equally important—it would turn out—was his issue of the *bula*, bearing the title *Exponi nobis fecisti*, which authorized the Belvís monks to exercise "broad apostolic powers" in carrying out their campaign. We know that Cortés and his soldiers were familiar with those important events given the commemoration by the elderly author of *Verdadera historia*, Bernal Díaz del Castillo (writing in the 1570s) of "*el Papa Adriano.*"[173]

Today's readers must realize the exceptional nature of this series of events. The "illuminary" monks of Belvís constituted a very small minority within the Spanish and European churches and their opponents lurked at every turn in the road.[174] Only a Franciscan pope, and only one receptive to that "illuminary" element, would have approved their selection. Add to that the "accidental" nature of Pope Adriano's election as Pope: as a "compromise" candidate, he was a hated outsider; his premature death after only some 20 months resulted in part from his isolation and the strident opposition he confronted. No other eminent figure occupying that position would have made the same decisions.

The new pope knew that the choice of the Belvís friars would probably trigger instant, strident opposition within the Church, which explains his additional decision of granting them "broad apostolic powers." As such, the Belvís team, in carrying out their mission, would be able to perform baptisms to willing natives and their children. From start to finish the Dominicans would oppose this practice, arguing that it was a violation of standard Church baptismal procedures that required a prior familiarity with scriptures and documented evidence of a lifestyle free of doctrinal sin. However, the preference of the Belvís Franciscans held sway. Their campaign of decades would result in the Church's welcome of millions of New Spain natives, making it one of the most consequential of religious events in the 16th century.[175]

Historians have described that period of European life as one of "frightening vitality ... a hurried and exuberant age." Although a majority of its people harbored "fears and mystic visions," others with "pervasive spiritual overtones" dreamed of fortuitous new beginnings. Many projected that the Franciscan monks were embarking on the crusade of the century! Indeed, in their later writings several of the friars would give every indication that they believed themselves to be *chosen* missionaries, that they had been sent to Earth at that precise moment of time and in that precise geographical place, in order to accomplish an assignment overseen by their Lord in Heaven. The moment was propitious: committed Christian groups everywhere agitated with reformist agendas. Committed youths from several lands glowed in the promise of accepting the mendicant habit with the hope of converting idealistic ideas into fruitful action. People everywhere had been stunned upon learning of the serendipitous discovery of new lands across the Atlantic; at least a few of these embraced a mythological belief that Christendom would soon welcome into its fold a New-World population unspoiled by Old-World corruption.

The "Divine Dozen" Franciscan monks were the first, but within months Europe's major mendicant orders would have no trouble in recruiting other energetic and committed youths. Within a decade several hundred Franciscan, Dominican, and Augustinian monks would follow. They would set sail from a dozen European ports bound for a lifetime of service in Mexico to engage in evangelization activities all across New Spain. It was a dream-come-true opportunity. All had made plans to pass the rest of their lives and careers in the New World.

Accounts differ regarding the geographical trajectory of their sea trip to the New World: Calais, Santander, Belvís, Sevilla? The friars embarked on the 25th of January, 1524, and they suffered two dreary months in crossing the Atlantic Ocean. During their weeks-long recovery in Santo Domingo, they were able to observe firsthand the evolving tragedy of the island Indians. Then they set off to Veracruz—and the rest is well known to history.

Was all this occurring independent of the young monarch's direct action? The eighteen-year-old Carlos, now emperor, finally returned to Spain to oversee the governmental bureaucracy. Soon he would be joined by his enterprising young wife, Queen Isabela (de Portugal). Truth be told, Cortés' activities and initiatives in New Spain, during this whole period, were probably little more than a distraction for the monarch, whose attention and energies would always be focused on the pan-European theatre. Quite possibly he, with Franciscan education and leanings, totally confided in the supervision of such affairs by Spain's Franciscan hierarchy that acted—for a short period of time at least—in conjunction with the Franciscan pope, who was Carlos's ex-tutor and a man enjoying his full trust. Most probably the emperor-king totally ignored the first two letters in which Cortés reported his vanquishing of the Aztecs and his initial acts in establishing the new colony. This might explain, at least in part, the delay in court responses reaching the conquistador-leader.

In the latter days of 1523, or the first days of 1524, Cortés finally received a letter under the name of the young king (with the written date June 26, 1523). The letter stated traditional and expected invocations about the need to Christianize the Indians. But with regard to other aspects of setting up a new Spanish colony, the letter instructed "exactly the opposite, in all aspects, of the political enterprise [Cortés] had already set into motion" during the two years that had elapsed since the Aztecs' submission.[176] Cortés's immediate response: perplexity. He must have asked himself: who, precisely, had penned the responses to his first two letters? Almost for certain it had not been the king. Probably not the (then regent) Cardinal Adriano. Most probably it had been a team of relatively uninformed functionaries following procedures set years before. So, how in the world should he now respond? Then, what would be the response? Perhaps reprimands; perhaps an order to withdraw from the governorship and accept as his replacement another Spanish noble more compliant to ministerial prerogatives.

Cortés' decision was to delay before penning an answer. "Time cures all wounds"—he could only hope. He (most probably) had manipulated events in order that the Belvís monks would head up the all-important evangelization campaign, and now had to do everything possible so that the court bureaucracy would not intervene to alter the situation at hand. He had to make sure that those monks of his choosing would be functioning in this important capacity *before* the bureaucrats found out! With the passage of a few months they, and possibly he king himself, might be reluctant to order any change.

And meanwhile, he would weather the intense personal pressure that this wait entailed. (Indeed, this issue undoubtedly would constitute yet one more cause for the series of crises that Cortés would bring upon himself in the next year.)

Months later, toward the middle of August 1524, the Belvís monks—the "Divine Dozen"—arrived at Mexico City. Their trip had consumed more than two years of time: crossing by mule, by cart, or by foot several European countries, months spent awaiting the departure of an ocean vessel, and two risky months on board to cross the Atlantic, and several weeks visiting the Antilles. Spain's Franciscan leadership must have coordinated with Cortés. Upon the monks' arrival at Veracruz, they eschewed all offers to be carried either by steed or cart; instead, they would march barefoot for the whole two-weeks journey along the road leading to Mexico City. This was designed to impress upon both natives and Spanish soldiers alike that they were charged with no ordinary mission. Daily, crowds of Indians lined the way, offering them food, water, and lodging. One member of the party, Father Toribio de Benavente, was so moved by the pious greetings constantly repeated by the Indians that he decided to transform their words into the name he would henceforth use for himself: *Motolinía*.

Cortés, as New Spain's governor, set about organizing a series of elaborate scenes and ceremonies in order to endow the arriving friars with instant prestige and win the instant devotion of the native population. The number of monks was the symbolic twelve—the same as the disciples of Christ. Cortés had insisted that the *principales* of all the Indian communities within a two-days' distance be present for the friars' arrival at the newly named Mexico City. The Spanish community also turned out in mass, as did thousands of local natives. When the Franciscans reached the causeway leading to the Mexico City Island, Cortés demonstrated a flair for ceremony by throwing himself at their feet. Not only did he wish to publicly honor their arrival. Also, he would demonstrate to the visiting Indian nobles and commoners his total commitment to the evangelization activities in which, from that day on, the Franciscan friars would engage.

Historian López de Gómara recreates this scene.

> Cortés, with a theatrical gesture, removed his hat with a flourish, lowered himself to one knee, and raised the first monk's ground-long habit to his lips to kiss it. He was intent on offering a personal example to all the natives present—those who shortly would become Christians—of his own humility and devotion before the friars. Many of the Indians were highly impressed about the humility he demonstrated before those twelve barefoot friars. Henceforth, they would imitate Cortés in the adoration that he had demonstrated and would show the monks their deep reverence. Cortés instructed them that they should always honor the friars, especially those who would be engaged in baptizing, and that they should always go out of their way to provide the friars with generous donations of food and accommodations.[177]

In addition to this ceremonious welcome at Mexico City, Cortés instructed native leaders everywhere to carry out appropriate celebrations in their respective communities.

For the first few weeks, the party of Franciscans found residence near the old Spanish encampment in the city of Texcoco, where they were housed in one of ex-palaces of the Aztec king Nexzahualcoyotzin. The next day they celebrated their first mass, "with much pomp and ceremony ... for which Cortés and all the Spaniards were present, in addition to [the Mexico-City chieftain] Ixtlilxúchitl with all the Indian princes, his brothers, sisters, and servants. Watching the mass with great attention, the Indians became very emotional—some even cried with contentment knowing that briefly they too would learn the secrets of the mass." In subsequent days "Fray Martín de Valencia ... initiated the evangelization campaign by baptizing the residents of the city of Texcoco—that was the first instance of the fathers implanting among the Indians the evangelical law."[178] Cortés, insisting on his personal involvement, again offered himself as the "baptismal god-father" for several of the Indian princes who participated.

One of the Cuernavaca codices makes note of the celebrations throughout the central highlands that were held to commemorate the arrival of the twelve Franciscan friars. It was no coincidence that the elder—writing decades later—remembered those events so vividly. He, as a boy of eight years of age, and as eldest son of Don José, Cuernavaca's chief, probably made the trip to Mexico City to take part in the welcoming ceremonies for the Franciscan friars. He was baptized by the same friar who would go down in history as the number-one champion of Indian baptisms, Friar Motolinía. To recognize his eternal gratitude for that act of baptism, the young man and future chief—at the moment of his baptism—had been decisive in his choice of a new Christian name: Toribio. Henceforth he would call himself Toribio San Martín. Furthermore, in order to honor that individual who had stood by him at that special moment as his new Christian godfather, he chose to take a second family name. The three Cuernavaca *códices* which he would author decades later display his whole Christian name: Toribio San Martín *Cortés*.[179]

This was the beginning of a life-long alliance between Cortés and the Belvís Franciscans. Within a few years Dominican and Augustinian monks would also arrive to do service.[180] But for Cortés the Belvís Franciscans were special. There was an immediate meeting of the minds. From the start Cortés and the friars agreed on almost every aspect of their now-shared mission. The Franciscans would provide the manpower and Cortés, by reason of being the most influential and richest man in New Spain, would open bureaucratic doors and help finance a great many of the projects that they would carry out.[181]

The monks were pleased to inform Cortés that the leadership of their international order had decided to grant highest priority to this New Spain evangelization project and had already begun efforts all across Europe to recruit additional monks regardless of their order. Within months—they informed him—a second delegation of Franciscan friars would arrive; and within two years they would be joined by mendicant monks from the Dominican and Augustin orders. Meanwhile, the Belvís team would have only months to plan, and then initiate, the evangelization campaign. Then, the future presence of other monks would make it possible to extend their activities to even the most remote corners of New Spain. Indeed, within three decades there would be 380 Franciscan monks working out of 80 different monasteries across New Spain; 210 Dominicans and 212 Augustans, each in 40 "houses."[182]

Immediately needed were living quarters for the twelve monks, which Cortés was happy to provide. Together, they selected appropriate sites for their future centers of operation in both Mexico City and the two nearby communities of Tlatelolco and Coyoacán. Cortés, employing broad powers as the colony's governor, facilitated the requisition of needed land or existing buildings, the acquisition of building materials, and the recruitment of both architects and Indian laborers.

———ooo◦|◦◦◦|◦◦◦◦———

Once the Belvís friars had arrived at Mexico City and plans for the long-anticipated evangelical campaign were well under way—*and not before*—Cortés felt free to answer the king's communication of the previous year. He had waited; and now he would put into writing only vague generalizations and half-truths. He had already decided about his modus operandi with the young, inexperienced—and possibly disinterested—king: "Act first and seek forgiveness later." Full of trepidations, he finally took pen in hand to "explain" his perspective on the evangelization campaign. His words:

> Each time I have written to Your Sacred Majesty, I have told Your Highness of the readiness displayed by some of the natives of these parts to be converted to Our Holy Catholic Faith and to become Christians: and for this purpose I have begged Your Caesarean Majesty to send religious persons of a goodly life and character .... [T]hey would reap great profit. [I] beseech You to send them with all haste ....[183]

The letter carries the date that Cortés must have completed its composition: "the fifteenth day of October in the year 1524." He also saw fit to send a second communication, "*Carta reservada de Hernán Cortés al Emperor Carlos V*"—which bears the same date—in which he elaborated with total frankness his reasons for not having followed the monarchy's previous instructions with regard to encomiendas. But in neither the dated nor the "private" communication did he write a word about the Belvís Franciscans beginning their direction of the evangelical campaign.[184]

The reformist Barefoot Franciscans did not disappoint Cortés; on the contrary, they would prove to be remarkable for their inspired commitment, over decades, in serving Mexico's native populations. Their accomplishments are universally celebrated: heading the list is their baptism of millions of natives and the establishment of more than a hundred monastery/schools all across New Spain. However, historians have been relatively silent with regard to important characteristics of the Belvís friars which account, at least in part, for their astounding achievements.

First, their advanced intellectual formation. They were not "ordinary" mendicant monks. Most of them had pursued advanced studies, which might account—at least in part—for the other characteristics I explain immediately below.

Second, their stubborn doctrinal independence, which undoubtedly contributed to the ways they chose to exercise the "broad apostolic powers" that the sitting pope had granted them. Foremost among the possible issues affected was their decision to forego the use of Latin in their liturgies, readings, and religious activities. It hardly needs be mentioned that Latin—over the past thousand years—had been and continued to be the accepted, indeed mandated, language of ritual for every other Catholic place of worship in the world. Instead of Latin, they almost defiantly chose to favor the vernacular languages in all their activities with New Spain's natives.

Third, the noteworthy results if the above: over thirty years, the members of their order would gain operational fluency in Náhuatl and Otomí (in addition to a few other New Spain languages) and would produce written alphabets and grammars for those new languages; then, they would compose courses to facilitate the second-language acquisition by other monks who were soon to arrive. They would translate the Holy Bible into those languages, prepare hundreds of sermons, and write scores of theatrical scripts and hymns.

Fourth—and very much related—their pragmatism. They accomplished all the above with the foremost objective of facilitating the assimilation of key Christian concepts by native audiences.

Fifth, the Franciscan monks would become pioneers in the study of pre-Hispanic rites, customs, and society. They would become Mexico's first "anthropologists." It is well known that, during the first five-to-six years, their evangelization zeal resulted in the widespread destruction of "pagan" temples and Mexican idols, and the burning of a "mountain" of manuscripts and *códices* in the great plaza of Texcoco. But beginning in about 1559 that emphasis would change; progressively the Franciscan monks would become "archivists of paganism," committed to preserve for future generations the artifacts, legends, and history of both the conquered Aztecs and the compliant tribes.[185] Most noteworthy in this vein is the *Florentine Codex*, treating the customs and beliefs of the Aztecs, which Bernardino de Sahagún composed over a lifetime of painstaking investigation.

Sixth, the progressive nature of their religious convictions—as alluded to above. The Belvís Franciscans carried to Mexico their reform program to combat distasteful materialism in the day-to-day life of their subjects; they would battle against corruption in all forms. They would oppose the sale of "indulgences"—or "works"—to wealthy individuals in exchange for the promise of salvation in the afterlife. Even more noteworthy was their shared "humanist" orientation, whose European protagonists were Erasmus of Rotterdam[186] and Sir Thomas More. One aspect of this was the doctrinal belief that God granted "salvation" to any individual; it was a matter of "grace" that had no material price and could not be bought or sold. This theological issue would assume enormous importance once the barefoot Franciscans began their baptismal activities in New Spain. Also, it would be a central reason—at a later date—for anguished divisions among the Franciscans and the mounting opposition from the Dominicans. These conflicts would lead eventually—some five decades later—to the termination of the Barefoot Franciscans' leadership in the evangelization crusade. (I continue this topic in the book's final chapter.)

And seventh: their "charisma."[187] Well known is the case of Friar Motolinía, whose dedication and personal attributes earned him the devotion of thousands of natives—indeed, his popularity among the Indians was matched only by that of Cortés himself. There is one fact about them that can have no other explanation: the great majority of them "consecrated themselves to Mexico." [*se consagra a México*] That is to say, that land became for the "exiled" monks their truly adopted homeland. The political or religious motivations that fueled their initial commitment to the evangelization campaign slowly became transformed into something much more personal and transcendent (as French scholar, Christian Duverger, has pointed out): "The osmosis between the Mexicans and this breed of religious personnel attained both a spiritual and material dimension: as the Indians became more and more 'Christianized,' the friars became more 'Indianized.'"

In retrospect, Cortés and the Belvís Franciscans fully shared—during those first decades of the post-conquest period—the objective of constructing a new society in which European masters would govern harmoniously over a population of Indian serfs, and in accordance with the humanistic guidelines of a humble Catholic Church. In no other region of Spain's new American possessions would Spanish and Indians embrace with equal enthusiasm a similar project.

Cortés and the Franciscan friars experienced an immediate "meeting of the minds" in their shared conviction they, in their respective roles, would become spiritual "fathers" for the "child-like" natives. Theirs was the mission of channeling the Indians upward on the "scale" of civilization, implanting Christian ideas and practices on *tabula rasa* minds. The monks fully believed that their charges, in time, would become intellectual and spiritual equals; the natives would attain the status of co-participants in the social realm over which the padres themselves would preside. "Thy kingdom come, thy will be done, on Earth as well as Heaven." This would not occur immediately—but they believed (initially) that it was only a matter of time. They were of a singular generation, unique in the history of Humankind, whose sacrifices in the Here and Now would put them on the path leading to this marvelous accomplishment. History would not repeat itself.

In those initial meetings Cortés and the Franciscans outlined, in tentative fashion, the steps that the mass program of evangelization would take over at least the next half century.

First, the Indian communities would be physically separated from the Spanish in and around Mexico City. Cortés had already taken concrete steps to have this occur. The Belvís friars, over two months, had been personal witnesses to the cruel treatment of the natives on the Isle of Hispaniola which, they came to believe, had resulted primarily from the license afforded to all Spaniards with regard to their treatment of the natives. The Cortés-Franciscan team would continue defending this principle for the rest of the country, in spite of the king's orders to the contrary and the new encomenderos' demands for increasing "the social intercourse" between Spanish settlers and Indians in their respective domains of authority.[188]

Second, Cortés and the Franciscans would rely on the services of the Indian nobles for the day-to-day management of Indian communities.

Many of the latter had already demonstrated their willingness, if not enthusiasm to do so.

Third, the Belvís friars would commit themselves to learn the local languages in order to increase their effectiveness in instructing the Indians in civilized behavior and devotional practices. Furthermore—as mentioned above—several of their members would study the history and culture of the Mexican communities and translate key instructional materials, believing that that information could serve as a vehicle to facilitate the Indians' more rapid assimilation of Christian doctrines and practices.

Fourth, the initial idea was that Cortés would facilitate the mendicant orders in acquiring or building simple chapels in the central locations of at least a dozen principle (cabecera) Indian communities. These rudimentary structures would be used by visiting friars for short-term lodging. But—within a few years—that idea grew into the more ambitious plan of building solid, spacious churches, with outdoor atriums large enough for hundreds of Indian participants. Also, the friars soon came to the realization that their mission would best be served by building permanent monasteries at each principal population center. The Indians from each community would provide both the materials and the necessary manpower for construction. Cortés and the monks strategized how a given community would pay for labor, materials, and operation expenses via encomienda tributes, special assessments, or *diezmos*—monthly contributions.

Fifth, most typically two mendicant friars would be assigned to each Indian community. They would live in the monastery and carry out their regular educational and devotional activities either in the adjoining church or the surrounding patios. As Diego Muñoz Camargo, the mestizo author of the *Relación de Tlaxcala* wrote, native education "is the absolute principal work that the friars do ... in all of New Spain."[189] On a regular basis, they would leave their established sites in the principal cities and travel to the surrounding (sujeto) villages in order to perform baptisms or masses for yet other native groups.

Sixth, the friars would place a high priority on destroying those idols still left from the devotions previously practiced under the Aztecs.

This would involve the friars' special study of the role that idols had played and where the locals either kept or hid them from the Catholic friars. Fray Motolinía would dedicate a whole chapter of his *Historia* to this issue, whose title was: "About how the natives hid the idols, in what places they practiced their [pre-conquest] rituals, the objects and procedures involved—about which there were a great many."[190]

Seventh, Cortés urged and the Franciscan friars agreed that from the beginning they would use every possible means to bring to an end widespread Indian practices that were totally unacceptable for any future Christians. This began with rituals involving or resulting in human sacrifice, physical dismemberment, or permanent flesh marking via branding. In this last-mentioned practice, Cortés assumed a protagonist role, because early on he prohibited his own soldiers from copying the Indian nobles in branding the slaves that they, as new encomenderos, were already acquiring. Much related, he and the padres would initiate prohibitions against the Indians' practice of consuming human meat—everywhere across New Spain it was an accepted, and age-old practice, that the victors in any military skirmish would consume parts of the fallen bodies of their enemies. The monks would also take a strong stand—especially as applicable to Indian nobles—against bigamy and the keeping of concubines. Also anathema for these devout Christians was the common Indian practice of sodomy.

After the first half-decade of service, the Belvís friars would become convinced of the need for yet an additional "strategy," and they would seek the means for putting it into practice: they would found a "seminary" to prepare for the priesthood the most apt of the natives' male children; this project would become the very successful Colegio de Santa Cruz in the town of Tlatelolco—about which I present more information below.

Almost simultaneously, the monks would initiate efforts aimed at the education of Indian girls. In 1530 six Spanish nuns arrived at Mexico City, and eight additional nuns would arrive four years later. The future archbishop, fray Juan de Zumárraga, supervised this project that had been funded by none other than the Imperatriz herself—Isabela de Portugal—the wife of King Carlos.[191]

Cortés would continue, long after their initial meetings in Tenochtitlán and Coyoacán, to advise and assist both the Archbishop Zumárraga and the Belvís Franciscans with this evangelization agenda. Historians recount the anecdote that, in the early 1530s, Cortés intervened on behalf of the Franciscan team when he learned of the special abilities of a Spanish child—with the name Alonso de Medina—in speaking and understanding Náhuatl. The son of a deceased soldier, he had grown up among Indian playmates. Cortés obtained permission from the widowed mother for this child to live among the friars. In time, the child would take the vows of a Franciscan monk and would excel in teaching Spanish and Catholic devotions to the New Spain population.[192] One other contribution by Cortés: historian Mendieta recounts that in about 1532 Cortés made a personal visit to his shipyard/port at Teuantepeque to prepare at least two ocean-worthy ships in order to transport eight Franciscans—led by Fray Martín de Valencia—to their chosen site for an (unsuccessful) attempt to "freely preach the Scriptures of Jesus Christ, but to natives who would not have been 'conquered' beforehand by force of arms."[193]

CHAPTER 8

1524-1526: YEARS OF CRISIS, ABSENCE FROM MEXICO

Once Cortés had erased any threat coming from potentially hostile Indian groups or communities within a hundred leagues of his power base in Mexico's Central Valley, and once he had surveyed the possibilities offered to him in Cuernavaca, there awakened in his restless spirit the desire to become, once again, a "conquistador." To the north and south of New Spain were lands yet to be "discovered" and civilizations yet to be vanquished; there were Indians yet to be subdued and transformed into subjects of his Majesty the king. There was also a great body of water: "El Mar del Sur" (the Pacific Ocean) was yet to be explored and whose shores were yet to be claimed in the name of the King of Spain. In short, there was "glory" yet to be won. Perhaps also wealth, honor, and position. What ideas floated in the grey matter of this most competent of leaders? Couldn't he be satisfied with the glory and wealth which were already his?

No. Cortés—perhaps correctly—perceived himself to be the most capable person then alive to carry on with the labors of new exploration. These tasks could not wait: to hesitate would mean yielding this fabulous opportunity to another.[194] At that very moment in time Spain, Portugal, England, France, and the Low Countries did not lack for ambitious, energetic, and well-funded individuals who would seize any opportunity. These could only dream of winning victories similar to what Cortés had accomplished with the Aztecs.

Yet, at the same time, Cortés now had before him the immense task of creating a post-conquest society for New Spain. He lacked neither inspired plans nor energy. Nor did he lack available manpower, because the Indians recognized only him as their leader; he did not lack resources, with a "money machine" of tributes and taxes filling his coffers; nor did he lack the legal authorization to carry out his projects. And lastly, he faced no significant internal opposition: his enemies, challenging him in court, had been stymied; and his internal rivals had been silenced or exiled. It could have been "full steam ahead." But that is not what happened.

This is because Cortés' lust for "glory" was equal to his lust for power. (Some historians have posited that his lust—for gold, land, and possessions—was equally "insatiable," but I would argue that the latter were merely the means for obtaining the former). But those "negative" qualities did not end here. In addition to his greed, he was also an exceedingly "jealous" person. That is to say, if he could not win for himself the new, available, "glory," then he would do anything in his power to obstruct another from obtaining it in his place.

The Honduras Expedition

The above paragraphs suggest what might have been the motivations for Cortes, in 1526, to leave Cuernavaca and New Spain in order to assume leadership of the "discovery" expedition to today's Honduras. He would not return for two years. It was hard for his supporters to understand his reasons for doing so. Did he not understand that his multiple projects—which he himself had inspired and then put into motion—to transform the submissive Indian nation into a New Spain, needed his firm, hands-on direction? His many enemies, temporarily sidelined by his strict leadership, were ready to pounce upon noticing any opening or sign of weakness.

Most historians agree that it was an imprudent decision, that of leaving all behind to undertake a risky expedition to punish a former lieutenant, Cristobal de Olid.

On that expedition, months became years. Far away from New Spain, news would finally reach Cortés about what had transpired in his absence: his appointees Gonzalo de Salazar and Pedro Almindes Cherino had begun jockeying for power. They did not have the leadership skills necessary for the tasks at hand and lacked Cortés' level of prestige and intelligence. Their weakness then invited the aggression of Cortés' enemies, who quickly usurped control. These raided Cortés' dwellings in search of hidden gold which—according to false rumors—he had hidden in the buildings or residences under his control. After their failed search, they confiscated most of his personal properties. Intent upon erasing his influence, they took control of the encomiendas he had assigned for himself—including the Cuernavaca communities of his Marquesado—and turned them over to cronies who would soon demonstrate unprincipled and covetous inclinations. They went on to torture and imprison Cortés' loyalists and even executed a few important individuals. People everywhere across New Spain had accepted as true the malicious rumors his enemies had spread about his own untimely death.

Worse was the tragedy that befell New Spain's Indians. As long as Cortés had been present and potent, mistreatment by the new class of Spanish encomenderos had been minimal. But this changed immediately after his enemies took control. Almost overnight, many encomenderos, now unrestrained by Cortés' strict guidelines, increased the level of Indian tributes and the hours of their required physical labors. Those chieftains, previously honored and rewarded for their loyal service, were insulted and punished. The Indian masses, until then protected by his even-handed policies, would suffer tremendously.

Meanwhile, Cortés' military adventure to Honduras had become a nightmare. One commentator explains that this "tragic, folly expedition" initiated "one of the most turbulent periods that Mexico was to see during the whole history of Spanish domination."[195] Cortes's army spent months attempting to advance through dense jungles. Then, losing their way, they expended enormous energy and resources in building a bridge over swampy terrain that, in the end, led to nowhere. When he learned that certain Indian chieftains accompanying his expedition were planning a revolt, he ordered and then supervised the execution of its ring leader, the Aztec prince Cuauhtémoc. The expedition continued, without accomplishing a great deal. All suffered hunger and hundreds succumbed, with Cortes himself barely surviving. What could have gone wrong did go wrong. This expedition constituted Cortés' major failure as an adventurer, explorer, and conquistador.[196]

While hundreds of Indians and scores of Spaniards accompanying his expedition perished, mainly to hunger, Cortés survived. The Gods, one more time, had smiled down on him. Urgent messages from his associates informed him of the ensuing disorder, the violence they had suffered, and the threats he would face upon his return. Bernal Díaz del Castillo provides a telling paragraph about what he, as a young soldier, had personally observed: the deep sorrow that Cortés demonstrated upon learning of the chaos which had erupted in New Spain due mainly to his own unfortunate decisions: "And the moment Cortés finished reading the message, he felt such deep sadness that he closed himself in his tent and began to cry and he didn't come out again till early the next morning ... and he ordered that before the rising of the sun a mass be said to Our Lady."[197]

Word quickly spread across New Spain that he was indeed alive and would shortly return—information which contradicted the lies fabricated by his enemies. He delayed two extra months in the Caribbean islands in order to recuperate his health, then sailed on to disembark on the shores near Veracruz.

One aspect of this period that must be taken into account is Cortés' immense popularity among both the Indian masses and at least half of the Spanish residents of New Spain. Between 1527 and 1528 most of these two groups had come to believe that Cortés had indeed succumbed either to disease or to the violence of his enemies. These rumors had empowered the latter in New Spain. Then, the dispelling of these false rumors was the cause of unmistakable signs of joy in many

Indian communities. Historian López de Gómara recounts that Cortés, anticipating his return to New Spain after two years of absence,

> sent messengers to all the major cities, and to Mexico City in particular, letting all know of his return in short order. And throughout New Spain, when that was known, people celebrated. The Indians from nearby towns and cities travelled to the coast and were waiting there for his arrival. They had brought turkeys, fruits and chocolate for him to eat; feathers, blankets, silver and gold as presents. They offered their assistance in killing those who had offended him. ... Then, as he made his way along the road leading inland, Indians from more than eighty leagues away came to line the way, bearing presents, offerings, demonstrating their extreme happiness over his return. They swept the road before him, casting down flower petals at his feet, demonstrating their love for him. He listened to their complaints; and many of them cried as they recounted what they had suffered at the hands of his enemies during his absence...[198]

Cortés reached Mexico City in January 1526. Meanwhile, his allies Andrés de Tapia and Gonzalo de Sandoval had jailed the usurpers and assumed governing functions. Cortés, once again present, made plans to resume full authority as governor and captain-general. In the few months that followed, he and his allies set about to reverse the damages done. But their actions were abruptly terminated with the arrival of the individual named to head the Primera Audiencia, who was empowered to remove Cortés from power and administer New Spain in his stead.

The First Audiencia

Cortés' troubles were just beginning. Not only had his enemies usurped, for two brief years, the government and public life in New Spain; they had also controlled the flow of information reaching the king's ear.

MEXICO'S "GOLDEN AGE": THE FIRST HALF CENTURY

In Spain, the crisis of the monarchy, already two decades long, continued. It had been Queen Isabela—the adolescent king's grandmother—who had sponsored the early expeditions to the Americas. When she died, her surviving consort, King Fernando of Aragón, provided continuity to regal authority, but did not exercise jurisdiction over Castilian affairs. Then, upon his death, the governance of Spain's now-united kingdoms passed to their daughter and the undisputed heir to the throne, Juana. But after she was declared mentally incompetent, her son Carlos—still a boy—was declared king, with Cardinal Cisneros governing as regent. A decade would pass. Finally, in 1519 Carlos came of age—the same year that Cortés made first land contact with Mexico. This means that two years later, when the Cortés-led forces were able to force the Aztecs' submission, Spain was being ruled by an extremely young and inexperienced sovereign, not speaking Spanish fluently, whose attention was focused almost entirely on the European military campaigns of his Hapsburg lineage. At no time during this king's long reign did he demonstrate more than a passing interest in the evolving situation, and then the exploding crises, that would affect New Spain's post-conquest society and governance.

During those two years of absence, Cortés' enemies, in control of New Spain's government, had sent reports back to Spain that were designed to malign the conquistador's reputation. Indeed, many of Cortés' actions, in themselves, were bound to raise controversy.

The king's appointees in Spain were hardly prepared to deal with this new flurry of crises: Cortés' questionable legal maneuvers to take control of the conquistador army; the angry letters written by Velázquez, Pánfilo de Narváez and other nobles who felt cheated out of their leadership; the confusing legal status of New Spain's Indians; the legitimacy of Indian slavery[199]; Cortés having awarded encomiendas to his victorious soldiers in violation of royal instructions. Soon enough, they would also have to take a position with regard to the accusations of criminal behavior on the part of Cortés himself with regard to the unexpected deaths of the captive Aztec prince, several crown appointees, and Cortés' first wife.

1524-1528: YEARS OF CRISIS, ABSENCE FROM MEXICO

All of these factors—royal inattention, bureaucratic incompetence, and possibly cronyism—explain, at least in part, the disastrous decisions that the Spanish counselors were to make. They had been operating under the influence of the distorted reports that Cortés' usurpers had provided, and underestimated the bitterness at hand. Admittedly, the Crown was also smitten by a streak of bad luck: at least two of their appointees had died from diseases contracted during the arduous ship voyage to New Spain's shores.

They also had to deal with alarming reports about the mistreatment of New Spain's Indians. Those exercising power during Cortés' absence were, in actual fact, the main perpetrators of those abuses, but they falsely painted Cortés as he who was most responsible. Given the conflicting information about this issue, the court officials did take one action that would turn out to have positive results: they appointed a heretofore little known Franciscan priest, Juan de Zumárraga, as "Protector of the Indians," but in doing so granted him little authority to take significant action.

Zumárraga arrived in New Spain in 1528. Serious conflicts arose when, in fulfilment of his obligations, he publicly criticized those individuals most flagrantly abusing Indian rights. Animosities deepened through 1530, when he began appointing inspectors to visit Indian towns to enforce ordinances designed to lower tribute levels and the hours of Indians' forced labor.

In those months the man demonstrated true heroism in protecting several dozen Indians fleeing from Spanish violence in Huitzozingo by temporarily housing them in Franciscan facilities. Meanwhile, he sought ways to protect Indians all across New Spain from similar abuses committed by the new encomendero class.

Meanwhile, the corrupt Spaniards in charge of the New Spain's government operated a strict control over all communications sent to the mother country. Threatened constantly by authorities, Zumárraga risked his own life in "sneaking" a letter out of New Spain in which he reported to the king the unspeakable abuses being committed to the Indians by colonial authorities. That letter, "possibly the most important ever written from the Indies," was a thorough "indictment" of the regime then in power.²⁰⁰

Unfortunately, the Crown officials could not have made a worse choice in appointing Nuño de Guzmán to head a new governing authority, the Primera Audiencia, which removed Cortés as governor and took control of the New Spain government. Guzmán threatened Cortés with incarceration and exiled him from Mexico City. He and the other officials, interpreting their instructions as a mandate to despoil Cortés' allies and interests, resumed the harsh measures of before and restored several of Cortés' enemies back to power. They and their cronies openly sought the means to enrich themselves by exploiting the Indian communities. They hired sicarios to carry out assassinations and assaults. Armed Spanish thugs took control of the highways. Franciscan friar Sahagún recounts this sad history:

> The Spaniards [who were Cortés' enemies] stationed themselves at turns in the roads and robbed the natives passing by, seizing any money or gold that they carried; they ordered their victims to take off their clothing, which they searched for any hidden valuables. They mainly wanted gold. But they also made off with the good-looking young women—which they used for their pleasure. Also, they rounded up young men and healthy men to be used as slaves, calling them *tlamacazques*, and many of them they marked with branding irons applied to their cheeks.²⁰¹

Meanwhile, Cortés and his allies were powerless to oppose Nuño's abuses. Nor could Zumárraga, who risked his own life by defending Indians threatened by Spanish thugs under Nuñez' orders, and reacted publicly against Nuño's destruction of a leper hospital in Mexico City that Cortés had founded only a few years before.²⁰²

For the time being, Cortés was forced to absent himself from Mexico City. In doing so, he left unprotected the Indian masses who now stood defenseless before the violent and unscrupulous actions of his enemies who would continue in power until the arrival of the Segunda Audienca.

The following chapters treat how, over the next two years, Cortés would reside in Cuernavaca and initiate many projects of lasting value—for himself, the natives, and the entire colony of New Spain. In 1528 he would travel to Spain to meet with the young king.

CHAPTER 9

CORTÉS IN CUERNAVACA, 1526-1528

This chapter draws upon the newly-available sources of information, the Cuernavaca códices, in presenting a sequence of "happenings" in and around Cuernavaca during the period when Hernán Cortés, the Marqués del Valle, governed through a few able Spanish administrators and the Indian chieftains.

A previous chapter outlines the context in which Cortés decided to move to Cuernavaca and where he established both his personal residence and his center of operations.

It was not a period of celebration, on the contrary. The corrupt Primera Audiencia, exercising authority over New Spain, had exiled him from Mexico City. He had suffered "political" defeat. Also, he was suffering from health traumas as a result of the disastrous Honduras expedition, as well as deep disappointment on account of the loss of key friendships.

Also, there is the issue of "dissonance" with the Spanish king. In the immediate aftermath of the conquest, Cortés had had to make momentous decisions that at times conflicted with the sometimes-ill-informed instructions coming from the nearly dysfunctional monarchy. Two such matters were the assignment of encomiendas and the implementation of the evangelization campaign. How would the young king react? Cortés always had his enemies who would not hesitate to report such issues to the king in the way that would cause the most damage to his reputation. Almost every sign, until then, pointed to the possibility that his enemies had, in actual fact, succeeded in winning the support of an inexperienced king who would view in a negative fashion Cortés' most inspired actions. He had to fear the worst.

A second factor: only months before he had looked death in the face. While in Honduras hundreds of Spaniards constituting his army of "discovery" had succumbed to starvation—but he, miraculously, had survived. Again, his body had rallied to resist the Angel of Death and—once again—he had survived. On this and similar occasions, might it have been the hand of God saving him for—perhaps—a larger purpose?[203]

A third issue was the realization that he had stumbled badly. He knew he had an unsurpassed ability to create enemies—this went hand-in-hand with his unique ability to "seize the moment" and "take initiative"—when a different leader would have hesitated. This was the flip side of the coin for his grandiose ambitions and unsurpassed talent. That is to say, his great victories had come at a price: the envy of lesser men. His enemies always occupied the sidelines, waiting eagerly to pounce. That is what had happened when he made the rash, and anger-charged, decision to assume personal leadership of the military expedition to Honduras. New Spain had been safely under his management, and he had put it aside! He saw in the mirror a dangerous gambler, hugely successful at the tables, but willing to risk all with a single throw of the dice. In the future he would have to do better.

And yet a fourth factor: He must have realized that much of the violence directed against him in New Spain had resulted from the inept management of an unconcerned adolescent king and an incompetent, if not dysfunctional, Spanish Court. Cortés must have felt himself suspended in uncertainty. On the one hand, he had every reason for doubting the good will or the fair treatment of his king. Yet—on the other hand—his loyalty to the monarchy would never waiver.

Yet—in those months of forced introspection—Cortés also must have gained energy upon reflecting upon what had gone right. It had been his inspired leadership that had led to the victory over the Aztec overlords. Then, he had done what he could to reward his victorious soldiers with encomienda grants, but at the same time to protect New Spain's Indians from future encomienda abuses. He also rated as superb the measures he had put into gear for erasing the physical traces of Aztec authority and replacing them with new buildings, churches, and plazas. He was confident that those bold decisions would yield positive results.

Meanwhile, the idea was enticing: why not move his center of operations to Cuernavaca? A few years earlier he had taken possession of an ideally-situated plot of land and had set into motion the construction of a building designed to serve the triple function of fortress, palace, and personal residence. His architect and a combination of both Spanish and Indian craftsmen were already at work. Why not make the move—now? The idea was appealing. Cuernavaca had an ideal climate. It was not too far from—yet also not too close to—the madness that would continue to torment him in or near Mexico City. The surrounding lands would offer a whole spectrum of possibilities for crops and livestock. Whereas the threat from his enemies and the ineptitudes of the king would deprive him the position of governing New Spain, he could position himself for assuming a major role in its future economy. It was a good plan.

Furthermore, the king had already granted him control over these and other lands, so he was—relatively speaking—untouchable (the king would delay yet another pair of years before sending the written *merced* to that effect). He would be able to govern as he saw fit and would be answerable to no one. While paying due respect to the Crown's instructions for the treatment of the Indians, he would structure their governance, take advantage of their labor, and impose tributes. With his ideas and these resources, he could put into motion any number of projects, and would multiply a hundred-fold his material wealth. At the same time, he would pursue his idealistic vision of bringing into existence an ideal bi-racial society—along the "utopian" lines articulated in the writings of Saint Augustine, Sir Thomas More, Erasmus, and others.

One sine qua non: he would also exercise complete control over who would—and *not be permitted*—to settle in the domains under his authority: the Spanish. Already, he had founded wholly new pueblos for these in other parts of New Spain: Medellín (now Morelia) and Pueblo de los Angeles (now Puebla). These were communities specifically reserved for both new arrivals and for those Spanish soldiers who wished to retire from their previous warrior life and establish a permanent home in New Spain.[204] But he had already decided: in Cuernavaca and his Marquesado, he would not have to deal with the conduct of the rude Spanish underclass. He would select only a few Spaniards to accompany him. The rest of the Spaniards arriving monthly at New Spain's port of entry at Veracruz would have to go elsewhere. It was his decision: there would be no "República de españoles" in the lands under his guiding hand.[205]

Arriving in Cuernavaca, Cortés was welcomed by the Indian nobility who still recognized him as the legitimate leader. He found temporary housing in the neighborhood reserved for the nobles, and resumed his daily strolls around Cuernavaca. There, he was dealing with perhaps the most advanced and decent of Indian societies that was to be found in any part of New Spain. Thank goodness! Because he had a lot to do. And in order to move ahead on any one of his projects he would need the intelligent and willing collaboration of those local chiefs.

In all this Cortés was a visionary. One could say that he, on account of his projects and subsequent actions, anticipated a new historical age that would come to supplant the feudal institutions of the past. Cortés mused about new ship designs to enable ever longer oceanic voyages. He dreamed of accomplishing new geographical discoveries. He envisioned the creation of a trade empire, with different regions producing goods, a whole social class dedicated to transporting those goods, and a wholly new urban society dependent upon their consumption. Each night, Cortés took to his bed with mental images of new roads, new ship-making factories, new churches and plazas. His days were spent brainstorming with a handful of confidants about raising horses and cattle, growing wheat and vegetables, and producing silk.

All these were the dreams of an entrepreneur—a new word that only then was beginning to circulate in the elite circles of Europe's most advanced cities. Yet Cortés was in Cuernavaca—a city distant from the "renaissance" centers of the civilized world. "Progress" was not a word in common use. "Investments," "profits"? These words would not enter into common usage for decades, if not centuries. Cortés was not surrounded by the "great thinkers"—or the great artists—of his age. Instead, his "community" consisted of a few intimate Spanish-speaking associates and hundreds of Cuernavaca nobles.

Yet his thought process honed in on ideas that predated his own epoch. Only one example: he clearly understood that he could personally "profit" by selling sugar, clothing, bread, hides, and meat to future consumers in Mexico City. He was convinced that these products could successfully be produced in and around Cuernavaca. Then, nobody better than he could organize a system to transport those goods: he would order, the Indian nobles would supervise, and the local *macegual* porters would perform.

Cortés was not one to cast aside the benefits that the encomienda system offered him. If *macegual* labor had been unremunerated in the Aztec-controlled system, then he would be under no constraints to do otherwise. For the next few years he would continue the pre-conquest practice of not paying for those services already required of Indian workers as per encomienda agreements. But times were changing. Beginning about 1530, new legislation coming from Mexico City would establish minimum-wage requirements for encomendero Indians. In response, Cortés at first would protest. Then—after 1532—he would set a positive example of compliance.

As a result of these enterprises, Cortés would become immensely wealthy. But even better: all levels of Cuernavaca society, from the highest of the nobles to the humblest of workers, would benefit.[206] Upon learning new trades, the material circumstances of the Indians' daily lives would improve.

Some historians have portrayed Cortés as a man with oversized ambitions, as a maniac interested in harnessing the labor of thousands of Indian workers to satisfy the cravings of an oversized ego. More correct would be to view him as a hyper-energized dreamer, a leader committed to lifting to the skies not only himself, but also the thousands of human beings surrounding him.

Cortés realized that the founding of new enterprises in the Cuernavaca region would have to parallel his efforts to elevate the material and moral status of the region's Indian inhabitants. For both tasks, the noble class was both willing and compliant. But—how to proceed? The challenges were immense. There might have been 100,000 inhabitants, of all ages and distributed between the urban centers and surrounding rural areas of Cuernavaca, Tepoztlán, Yautepec, Oaxtepec, and Yecapixtla—that is, six of the twenty-four encomiendas granted to him by the Spanish monarchy. Initially, none of the indigenous spoke Spanish and two-thirds of them lived in relative poverty. All of them embraced the beliefs, superstitions, customs, and life styles they had inherited from their Indian ancestors. Most of them continued to practice all but the most heinous of rituals imposed upon them by the now vanquished Aztecs. Cortés harbored few illusions: change would be slow. It would be a process of decades, if not centuries. Yet fate had bestowed upon him the task of beginning the process of transformation.

Now re-established in Cuernavaca, he ordered the resumption of those projects that had languished over the two years of his absence. Indian laborers again took tools in hand to progress with the construction of his "palace."[207] Over the previous two years, individuals supported by his enemies had taken possession of several encomiendas. This meant that in order to regain control, he would have to engage a team of lawyers to initiate lawsuits and undergo lengthy court proceedings. (In short order, the court would rule in his favor with regard to both

Cuernavaca and Tepoztlán. But for Oaxtepec and Yecapixtla, he would never succeed in regaining complete control).

Because the "usurper" would not yield control over the sugarcane project that Cortés had commenced in Tlaltenango, he decided to begin the construction of similar facilities near the central plaza at Altacomulco—only a kilometer to the south, but still two kilometers north of his future palace. He directed work to commence on the masonry surrounding the nearby water source and that the foundation be built for the construction of a mill using a portion of the flow. He negotiated with local nobles for renting several of the surrounding fields. Then, when the sugarcane shoots arrived—which he had ordered months before from the Antilles—he organized Indian brigades to plant them and to begin the construction of irrigation channels.

The Friars at Work in Cuernavaca

Cortés was acutely aware that his Indian communities in and around Cuernavaca—given the effective and humane Indian governments there—would be the ideal proving ground for the Franciscan project of evangelizing all the Indians across New Spain.

After attending to the most urgent issues regarding personnel and construction projects, he decided that the time was ripe for a visit to Cuernavaca by a contingent of Franciscan monks. He assigned an associate to travel to Coyoacán to work out the details: when and how many of the monks would come, and how long they would be able to stay. He arranged for accommodations when they would also pay short visits to the other Indian cabecera communities near Cuernavaca—the issue of Indian baptisms would not wait for any court-case settlement concerning the future control of encomiendas there.

Finally, a delegation of friars made the two-day march from Mexico City to Cuernavaca. Their arrival was cause for a city-wide celebration, as recorded by an Indian elder in the Cuernavaca codex: "Here we put in writing some details of an important event: when El Señor Marqués invited to this community, for the first time, the blessed Monks, who came to baptize us into the Holy Faith. Here are their names: Fray

Ortiz, Fray Luis, Fray Juan de Serva, Fray Franco de Soto, Fray Pedro, Fray Andrés de Córdoba, Fray García de Ceros (Cisneros), Fray Martín de Jesús (Coruña), Fray Juan Juarés, Fray Juan Motolinía ...."[208]

Cortés committed himself to "prepare the terrain" for this first visit by the friar missionaries. He wanted to make sure that his communities would be among the first to benefit from the friars' evangelization efforts. He and a team of committed nobles travelled to the different cabecera communities to choose appropriate locations for the construction of what the Franciscan evangelization plan had indicated as essential: terrain for both a small church and an adjoining structure to house the friars who, within months, would arrive. A few years would pass before plans would be made for expanding the initial residences into monasteries large enough to house an ever-growing number of resident friars.

Two of the Cuernavaca *códices* describe Cortés' activity in selecting appropriate sites for these future churches and neighborhood chapels, which would differ from residential lots.

> The land plots designated for the construction of two churches—Nuestra Señora de la Asunción and Nuestro Padre San Francisco—are not like others in a residential neighborhood. This was made known to us by the officials of the Republic. In those plots there had to be sufficient patio space for celebrating the Day of Nuestra Señora, and also for the surrounding community to assemble to hear masses and sermons from the holy fathers. These areas belong to the Church; no individual can claim them as his private property. Nor are taxes levied on these terrains—that is what the Señor Marqués ordered when we leaders of the community went about designating land plots and measuring the boundaries of all the lands that belong to the community of Quauhnahuac ...."[209]

As a result of these early survey excursions, at least five sites were selected for initiating the evangelization program: Cuernavaca, Tlaltenango, Tlaquiltenango ("six leagues beyond Quanhuanaca"),

Oaxtepec, and Yecapixtla. By 1534, two other communities would be added to this list: Totolapan and Ocuituco.[210]

Friar Motolinía has left a written record of these early visits:

> The first time [a Franciscan friar] went out to visit the provinces of Coyxco [Cuautla?] and Tlaxco [Taxco], he left from Cuauhnauac [Cuernavaca]. This was the place of his residence—it was in his second year here, and that residence was the fifth that we had established. ... The fathers were always well received.... The natives came to receive instruction, to hear the word of God, and to have their children baptized. ... They didn't want to have to return to their homes without having their children baptized first. Indeed, our monks had accepted an immense task: to baptize all the natives, without exception, of the whole region.[211]

In this same period of time, Cortés made sure that yet another team of loyal nobles was employed to accomplish a similar tasks in the 20-30 sujeto communities immediately surrounding Cuernavaca: they began confiscating terrains in order that a new Catholic chapel be constructed within an easy five-minute walk of every residence.

How to fund these projects? This was a question of paramount importance. Cortés had known that the Spanish Crown, although theoretically "responsible" for sponsoring such ventures, was in actual fact, both financially and ideologically committed to other very costly ventures (the young king's priorities were the European wars against both the Turks and a growing Protestant rebellion). Fortunately—a decade hence—Crown officials would finally come around to recognize the need, and then provide funding, for a viceroy and an administrative staff to govern New Spain. At that time, minimal funds would also be designated for promoting Indian education (for both the sons, and then a small number of girls, of the most prominent of Indian noble families) and a few other select projects.

Early on Cortés had realized the extreme unlikelihood that the Crown would want to fund the evangelization project. This was one major reason for his insistence on the participation of mendicant monks: First, their orders would absorb transportation costs. And second, a poor Indian community would be able, through their tributes, to cover the day-to-day expenses of monks committed to a life style of poverty.[212]

Furthermore, a major responsibility of those Spaniards receiving encomiendas was to provide Christian instruction to their Indians. This verbal commitment would include covering the expenses of the religious personnel present on the lands they governed.

For the construction of the new church buildings, Cortés organized teams of Indians to transport materials, level terrains, and lay the foundations. He identified skilled workers to perform the needed masonry work, install the wooden beams, and thatch the roofs. He sought ways to train yet other Indians to produce the devotional items that would beautify church interiors and provide dignity to religious services: wood sculptures, tableau paintings, priest garments, candles, and incense.

Because the Franciscans were in charge, their perspective about the requirements for Indian baptisms prevailed—at least for the first few decades. For them, the only requirement was an Indian's sincere desire to receive the Christian sacraments. Motolinía—here—describes the enthusiasm of some Indians that must have inspired this policy:

> They come to be baptized. Many of the men desire baptism so much that, after hearing our sermon against bigamy, dismiss their concubines and approach us asking that we marry them to their chosen mate. Others come pleading to be baptized, begging us. Some come walking on their knees, others ... approach desperately requesting, amid tears and cries. ... It was, in my judgement, appropriate that we should baptize them in as short a time as possible. And we succeeded: in the period of fifteen years we baptized more than nine million Indians .... In the first years almost all of the friars were in agreement .... But then, the

church missionaries and friars who came later—among them Augustinians, Dominicans, and Franciscans—held different, and sometimes conflicting points of view.[213]

Dominican Friar Domingo de Betanzos took issue with the Franciscans' practice of rapidly baptizing Indians, believing that the latters' easy enthusiasm might be more an indication of their "irrational nature" than religious seriousness. Franciscans—as I explain below—would later come to agree, at least in part, with the skepticism of Betanzos.

Baptism was only the first step, and larger problems still remained: how to instruct the Indian masses in the rites and content of Christian devotion; how to induce them to leave behind a whole belief system founded on indigenous superstitions, idolatrous ceremonies, and devil worship; how to convince them to adopt the practices and customs of Christian subjects. For these, there were no easy answers. The process of cultural transformation would be slow. But Cortés and the fathers realized that their immediate mission was to plan the first steps.

Cortés, from his new vantage-point in Cuernavaca, made periodic trips to Coyoacán to continue advising the Franciscan friars about such issues. All in their order were in agreement that effective communication with the Indians would depend upon they themselves learning the native languages. Already several of the twelve were showing signs of success in deciphering and learning the principal language of Central Mexico, Náhuatl. A few padres had committed themselves to learning other predominant languages—Otomí among them. Several began developing materials for teaching and training the soon-to-arrive religious personnel in the languages of New Spain's Indians.

El Colegio de Tlatelolco

Yet a third group of padres, headed by Friar Pedro de Gante, prioritized the establishment of the Colegio de Santa Cruz—located in Tlatelolco—through which they would instruct the young sons of Indian nobles in both the Spanish language and the essentials of Christian devotion (within decades similar institutions would be founded in Michoacán, Oaxaca, and Mérida[214]). They projected that out of this institution would come key religious personnel, with bilingual skills, who would carry their work into the next generation. This was the first such project initiated by European missionaries in any part of the world. Only Fathers Motolinía, Gante, Mendieta, and Landa—to my knowledge—have left written accounts of the trials, problems, and successes of this and related institutions.

Their first task was to identify those native boys of noble lineage—ideally two from each community—with the greatest promise for excelling in their studies. The students resided within the walls of the colegio and worked to produce their own food. They studied Spanish, Latin, grammar, philosophy, and ecclesiastic theology.

Friar de Gante explains the reasons for the Franciscans' decision to isolate the noble Indian boys completely from their families and communities of origin in order that they not become "corrupted" by the pagan practices of their Indian elders.

> We enclosed the boys in the monastery day and night; we wouldn't permit any communication on their part with their parents—and even less if it involved a mother. The only exception to this was their contact with the Indian servants at the colegio, for example when the latter served them food at the school. All this was so that the Indian boys would forget everything related to the bloody idols and the horrendous human sacrifices that they [might have witnessed during their earliest years], when the Devil had possessed an overwhelming number of Indian souls.[215]

The older students would tutor the younger ones during the hours of in-school instruction; on weekends or festival days, they would go out to instruct Christian doctrine in the different Indian communities and towns. In a typical session, they'd read a sermon, lead the Indians in singing 'Nona de Nuestra Señora,' then they'd cede the floor to Friar Pedro who would continue preaching for about an hour.

Inspiration for founding the Colegio came from Father Pedro de Gante and Archbishop Zumárraga. Gante's written testimony informs us that the teaching faculty included—among others—Fathers Arnaldo de Bassanio (of French origins), Juan Focher, Juan de Gaona, Andrés de Olmos, and Bernardino de Sahagún. Friar Mendieta, writing a generation later in his *Historia eclesiástica*,[216] explains:

> None less than the viceroy himself, Don Antonio de Mendoza, became a substitute father for many of the young Indian nobles. He donated personal funds for the construction the Colegio as well as terrain [so that the students themselves could] provide for their [own provision of meat and grains, in addition to goods that could be sold]; all this so that the Colegio would be self-sustaining. Entering students were between ten and twelve years old; they were the sons of the chiefs and principal families of the largest communities and provinces all across New Spain; the intent was to have two or three of these from every *cabecera* or large community. ... Altogether, there were a hundred boys or young adolescents studying in the Colegio at any one time.

The initial idea of training these children for the priesthood proved to be overly ambitious. For decades Tlatelolco graduates were assigned to different communities with the responsibility of assisting the European-trained priests in administering sacraments, performing masses, and networking with the local Indian officials.

Enthusiastic defenders of the Colegio laud its successes. Twenty years after its founding, Viceroy Mendoza, wishing to counter criticisms of the deficient level of the Indian boys' instruction, published the positive results of the Latin exam he had personally administered, and publicly announced his belief that "these boys would do more for the propagation of the Faith than all the friars in the country." The archbishop Zumárraga, sharing that opinion, requested that the king designate appropriate land parcels in both Oaxaca and Michoacán in order to found similar schools. He also sought out resources to construct a convent in the central valley for the education of Indian girls. (This was at a time when disillusionment was spreading about the failure of both corregimientos and encomiendas in carrying out the crown's priority project of Indian evangelization.)[217]

In his 1555 letter to the king,[218] Friar de Gante provides a personal history of services with Colegio during its earliest years. He calls particular attention to the contributions made by Cortés, who had always gone out of his way to support the Franciscan educational program:

> Hernando Cortés, may he rest in peace, played a huge role in [the labors of all the Franciscan fathers], and posterity should recognize and honor his total dedication in promoting God's Scriptures .... His works in New Spain were of the type that all men should honor—and because of this he surely enjoys eternal Glory in heaven—which I firmly believe to be the case. [In specific reference to the Colegio which I founded and then supervised, he personally took it upon himself to] send instructions [to the Indian princes] residing in communities within twenty-four leagues that all the sons of the noble families and the *principales* had to come to our S. Francisco [monastery] in Mexico City in order to learn the law of God and [upon graduation to return to their own communities] to teach Christian doctrine. [Largely through the initiatives of Cortés, we Franciscans at the Colegio] succeeded in instructing nearly a thousand young [native] men.

On occasion, the older students would receive instructions to search out cases in a specific community where pagan worship was still practiced, and then pass this information on to Padre de Gante. He, in turn, "would send word to the Capítulo in Mexico City, and they would send their own officials to [deal with the problem]. But sometimes it fell to me to go to that elder's house, scold him, and lecture him about proper Christian practices—and hoping that God was guiding me in my actions."

Gante felt it important that the King be aware of that problem of ingrained pagan practices:

> we would threaten them with legal intervention, telling them that they would be punished .... Little by little we went about eliminating those practices and destroying many of their idols. At the very least we were having success with the noble families and the tribal rulers—they were seeing the light, little by little, and embracing the teachings of our Lord. Our objective was to use kind words and praise to get them accustomed to the merciful responsibility [*el yugo suave*] required by our Lord and the Royal Crown. But on occasion we had to resort to harsh scolding, sternly lecturing them about the great difference separating that of serving God and the Royal Crown, and that of living under tyranny and serving the Devil.

Another laudable achievement of the Colegio was that it became the site for outstanding historical and "anthropological" investigations by several of the Franciscan friars. Most noteworthy was Father Bernardino de Sahagún: during the decades residing there, he would prepare 52 sermons in Náhuatl, which were to be used by other clergy throughout New Spain in their doctrinarian efforts. Furthermore, by 1540 he would accomplish the transcription of the Náhuatl language into the Latin alphabet. A third contribution was his transcription of dozens of Indian nobles' testimonies into his acclaimed *Códice Florentino*.[219]

(Decades later—in 1581—Vasco de Quiroga, the respected jurist and later Bishop of Michoacán, would write in praise of the Franciscans: "they are few, they are God's servants, and their work has borne good fruit. They sacrificed a lot ...; their special accomplishment was the instruction of Christian doctrine to the sons of the natives. His own contribution was the founding of "pueblo-missions" in Michoacán based on the experiences of the Colegio de Tlatelolco.[220])

Franciscan persistence was necessary. Their struggle to implant new practices and devotions was tenuous. But, according to Gante, their dedication began to have positive results: "But with God's grace, little by little we learned how to measure their resistances and how to maximize our mild pressure; or what attitude I had to adopt in what situation, in order to persuade them to our Faith while retaining their maximum affection."[221]

The Cuernavaca Church

In one of the Cuernavaca *codices*, Don José Acamapitzin, the acting Indian governor, describes his participation in the construction of the community's first church under the direction of Cortés:

> We, the chiefs of Panchimalco [apparently, the neighborhood where the highest principals lived] received the order coming from el Señor Marqués. He made it directly to us. He ordered us to take measurements of all the land plots on one side of the church. We measured 4,500 varas. That was the total of the seven separate measurements—that is the length of the church grounds—exactly the length that el Señor Marqués had ordered ... that these grounds belong to no one neighborhood ... and that no Spaniard will ever be able to say that they are his, because this terrain belongs to the church, and that is what el Señor Marqués ordered when we made the divisions of all community lands belonging Quauhnahuac. The terrains of the church include no deep gully [barranca]; it's all flat land. But there is a barranca alongside the church terrain, near the entrance facing a Malpaisito. El Sr Marquez saw all this and approved it; indeed, it was he who designated where that entrance to the church would be located ....[222]

In another of the recently discovered Náhuatl documents, the chief of Quauhxomolco (today's San Buenaventura Coajomulco, in the Municipio of Huitzilac—about a league north of Cuernavaca), mentions how the wood used for the beams of the church came from the forests surrounding his own community:

> We are here in our town, whose name is Nuestra Madre Señorita María de la Asunción de la Villa de Cuernavaca. Never will be without the protection of our God and our great masters, Don Carlos V and our master Señor Marqués Don Fernando [Cortés] whose palace is located in this great community, the City of Cuernavaca, whose roof is so large that it measures that arches of its superstructure measure 140 *sombras* .... Following his instructions, the community of Quauhxomulco supplied workers—some of them our own children—who fashioned all the needed timbers out of trees, and raised the wooden supports for the construction of the Church's roof. We supplied all the wooden supports that were needed; that was our donation in building the church. We showed them the limits of our community and the boundary separating our two communities. They asked us, and we sent all the wooden beams needed for the church as well as the palace that are located in the great community that is called the City of Cuernavaca. We supplied all the wood needed for that roof measuring a total of 140 sombras—those two buildings in Panchimalco.[223]

Various community elders took part in the construction of Cuernavaca's church—as they document in the "Códice de la Fundación:

> I, Don Gaspar de San Martín, affirm here that I contributed my labor and completed all my required service to this Republic, that I worked on the Holy Church during its construction; I was there. ... I, Don Felipe Martínez, affirm here that I assisted in the construction of the church and completed my required time serving the Republic .... I, Don Tomás José Axayacatzín, affirm here that I fulfilled my service to the Republic; I personally worked in the construction of the church .... I, Don Jacinto Chilpan, affirm here in this document that I worked on behalf of the Republic, I labored on the Holy church, and I personally was baptized into the Holy Faith. I, Don Melchor de la Cuevas, affirm here that I worked for the Republic, and I labored on

the Holy Church, and I was present when that construction was completed. I, Don Pedro Quauhximatzín, affirm that I served in the Republic; I worked constructing the Holy Church, and it was I who served the Most Holy Sacrament in the ceremony marking our entrance into The Faith.

At least thirteen other Cuernavaca nobles left similar testimonies in this Códice that document not only their personal involvement in the construction of the community's church, but also their baptism into the Catholic Faith.[224]

Within months—as soon as facilities were available—the Franciscans assigned teams of monks to occupy each monastery and begin religious services. In the larger communities—the—there would normally be two monks assigned: "In each one there reside two priests: one administers confessions and gives sermons in either the language of the Indians or that of the Spaniards; the other receives confessions only in the Mexican language."[225] They would reside in the "monastery"—usually a humble two-or-three room dwelling—and would spend a few days each week providing their services to the residents of the immediate neighborhood. But on days of rest or for special religious festivals the monks would travel to nearby communities, which they called "visiting towns". One such team of friars "have under their assignment nine dependent towns. Adding the population of these to that of the primary community, they serve more than three thousand residents."

Monks from the Franciscan Order were the first to arrive at communities outside of Cuernavaca—where for years they would give masses and carry out doctrinal activities. According to Friar Motolinía, it was about 1528—that is, only four years after the New Spain arrival of the Franciscan monks—when

> The Indians from many towns [and in particular Huaxtepec] came in search of the friars and asked them to come and visit ....

In this way Christianity expanded and became deeply rooted ... This was strongly seconded and greatly helped by the governors of these towns, because they were Indians who had left behind vice and had abstained from drinking wine. It was akin to a miracle, for Spaniards as well as natives, to see Indians who did not drink wine; for among adults, men and women too, intoxication was very common .... The first time a friar went to visit the provinces of Coyxco and Tlalco; they traveled there from Cuanhuahuac. The residence here was founded by the friars in the second year after their arrival .... When the friars were not able to visit a particular town, the people came from the nearby villages to the larger town in order to be instructed, hear the word of God, and have their children baptized.[226]

In these same years the friars built a permanent church in Tlaltenango,[227] as well as a primitive monastery and church in Yecapistla[228] (which would be rebuilt and operated by the Augustinians after 1535). Much later, but before the end of the century, the monks from this order would also establish their presence in Xuitepec, Mazatepec and Xochitepec.

Early on, the Dominicans also were present in Cuernavaca. In the 1530s monks from this order built the first church in Oaxtepec, from which their preachers travelled regularly to Yautepec, Tetela del Volcán, Hueyapan, and Tepoztlán. In this last community the friars were said to have encountered stubborn resistance on the part of the locals in accepting new Christian practices.[229] (It is interesting to note Motolinía's opinion/observation that the Indians in many regions preferred the presence of Franciscans over that of the monks from the other two orders.[230])

One historian recounts an interesting anecdote about the Augustinians in the Indigenous community of Ocuituco (probably in the mid 1530s—when Cortés was no longer involved).[231] They had chosen to construct a very elegant church, without taking into account the poverty of the village Indians and—therefore—the latters' meager resources for its edification and maintenance.

Since 1528 New Spain had been governed by a viceroy, who had overseen the implementation of new regulations affecting the financing of the evangelization-educational mission. Each Indian community would continue to make the three or four yearly tribute payments to their respective encomendero—for which the central authority established parameters so that (in theory) the monies or goods involved would not exceed the Indians' economic means. It had also been decided that, in the majority of cases, a given community would not be assessed additional payments to cover the construction costs of a new church or the daily or weekly expenses of religious personnel stationed in the community. Instead, it had been decided that the costs associated with the evangelical mission would be subtracted from the Indians' regular tribute payments, and that these payments would not exceed a third of the total tribute due to the respective encomendero.

In Ocuituco, the financial burden placed on the Indian community for the construction of the church, over a period of months, had been heavy. With that construction project now nearing completion, the Augustinian supervisors, with the approval of the government's inspectors (*los oidores*), had made plans to tax the Indian community in order to cover the new costs of constructing an adjoining monastery. However, Bishop Zumárraga, believed that this new project "made excessive demands on the natives who not only suffered physically, but also became agitated over their lack of time to produce sufficient food to feed their families." The viceroy therefore sent word that the new project should not proceed. The Augustinians chose to ignore this order and continued applying pressure on the Indian leadership, "raining whip blows on them, threatening to enslave them, and all because the natives refused to work according to the schedule that the monks required of them."

The historian continues: "The issue of friars whipping or physically punishing the naturales was not an uncommon affair. We know this because several of the existing written chronicles make mention of this ..., that they did this in the form that a father "corrects" the behavior of his child; it was not done with the intention of harming them, and even less of humiliating them. The friars, regardless of their order, treated the indigenous as children in need of a forceful type of education."

To put an end to this distasteful situation, Zumárraga—acting as New Spain's archbishop—ordered the Augustinians to free all the Indians and to tear down the jail that housed them. Then he named a new priest to oversee all devotional activities in that community and to assure decent treatment by any church official of the local population. The Augustinians, greatly offended, chose to abandon their mission there; they left the town, carrying with them the cast-iron bell and all the church's furnishings—which they then installed in a different service site in the town of Totolapan. Years would pass before they would return to Ocuituco to recommence their religious activities there.

How widespread was this abusive treatment of the Indians on the part of the mendicant friars? Were these abuses typical of the Augustinians? Were they also normal behavior of the monks from the other two orders?

We can assume that news of the abuses recounted above reached the ears of the nobles administering Cuernavaca under the authority of Cortés—only forty-some kilometers separate the two communities. Or did Cortés have a personal hand in educating the Cuernavaca elders about the possibility that Indian exploitation could come from the hands not only of the greedy class of Spanish encomenderos, but also from the Spanish clergy? Unfortunately, there exists no documentation from the period—to my knowledge—that assists the contemporary reader in answering these questions.

But there is no doubt that the Indian nobles, partnering with Cortés in the governance of Cuernavaca, were aware of possible clerical abuse. In the recently "discovered" codex we read the words, translated into Spanish, of the community elder, Don Toribio de San Martín Cortés:

> The order came from the King, our Señor, that we equip ourselves with arms, that we ourselves might have to provide for our own defense, that we might have to free ourselves from the Spaniards, so that for our own defense, so that they do not lose their respect for us, so that they do not attempt to take away from us what is ours, so that our blessed friars do not mistreat us. Our arming, and practice with those arms, is for our own

benefit and protection, because they have entitled us with this right, and we receive it with the Faith we gained through the Holy baptism when Señor Cortés came to these lands, and we received the charge of community leadership and the rights of nobility which we had earned and justly deserved.[232]

That is to say, the Cuernavaca elders wrote of both clerical mistreatment and the threat they felt from other Spaniards entering into their domain and robbing them of their lands and possessions. Is it credible that "the King"—or viceroy—gave them explicit permission to acquire arms and then use those arms against Spaniards? Was it Cortés himself who had instructed them about this very irregular, and perhaps exceptional, privilege? This document states that he instructed the nobles of Cuernavaca that all this was not only their right, but also their responsibility: to protect themselves and their communities from the oppression administered by any Spaniard, whether the latter be a future encomendero or even a minister of the Church.

This surprising quote also demonstrates their sense of "ownership:" they themselves had labored to construct their community's Christian church and now they governed the community. They understood the "vertical" hierarchy involved: orders from the Spanish king passed to their encomendero, Hernán Cortés, then to their priest, then to themselves, the Indian elders. In this codex they honored the memory of the first priest to serve them there: "the first priest who came here to Quauhnahuac. He was our guardian. His name is Fray Pedro García.")[233]

Further Evangelization Activities

The licenciado Juan de Ovando, conducting a formal inspection of religious institutions in New Spain between 1568 and 1571, defined—in his final report to the Crown—the subsequent steps taken by many Church personnel to continue with the evangelization mission.

First, the select group of nobles, who as children had studied in Franciscan schools, would assist the resident friars in all levels of instruction. "The sons of the ruling families—who among them were not only those of noble lineage but also individuals of distinction—received instruction in order to lead their communities and serve in their churches." They would assist Spanish friars or priests in administering masses, baptisms, and sacraments. Also, they would teach the lower-class Indians not only "Christian doctrine" but also lessons so that the "the boys would learn the vocations of their fathers, in order that they, when adults, would be able to provide for themselves and their future families and would be useful for the community. At the same time, they would retain the simplicity of spirit that had characterized their forefathers ...."[234]

A second step was for the friars to enlist the services of an Indian elder, the *merino*, whose responsibility was "call out summons and gather all in their neighborhood, then lead them to the church grounds and maintain order during the service or lesson [from the padre]; at its end, they would lead them back to their houses—all these functions remained almost unchanged from [pre-conquest times]." In those assemblies the friars, assisted by colegio graduates, would teach basic Christian practices, as well as prayers and hymns.

A third step: The friars, assisted by Colegio graduates, would found local schools to teach Christian doctrine and orations to all the other male children from noble families: "In all the communities of New Spain where the religious friars had established a presence (this is true at least for the Franciscan friars) there are several schools, which are within a perimeter where the friars can access easily.... In those schools, the boy children of the *principales* are brought together and are instructed about the Christian doctrine. ... then they are also taught to read and write ...."

Fourth: From among the brightest and most apt of Indian students, the friars would choose about a dozen to participate in the local church's choir. This was not a peripheral concern: choir and instrumental music in the sixteenth century—regardless of country or denomination—constituted an integral part of any religious service. According to the inspector, those Indians selected to participate in the choir committed themselves to spend hours of their time in daily practice: "In these same schools the Indians selected to be choir members (and mass assistants) meet every day to learn the words and practice the music to a number of hymns. They take these lessons seriously; for many singing in the choir will become their vocation; for that reason their diligence is required."

Fifth: The padres understood that the Indian commoners would be engaged in work assignments during the regular days of the week. This meant that on Sunday, the latter would be freed up for special religious instruction. "Every Sunday or day of a special fiesta it is the same: at daybreak the Indians gather in the patio of the church. They're there in a very organized fashion: with each neighborhood group lined up in squads, each with its sergeant or drill master—that is, those whose responsibility was to summon them from their houses and march them to the church grounds. Those neighborhood "sergeants" then count them and "take attendance." Woe be to the Indians who are not present, because it is their obligation. These will later be punished by a half-dozen blows with the end of a rope, because they had not shown up earlier at the church grounds." Assembled, the natives would listen to a sermon and study a new lesson on Christian doctrine before being dismissed for the day.

Sixth. In some Indian churches the religious personnel would select a small number from among the most sincere and devout of the Indian community to assist in specific labors: to receive the church goers and position them either standing or seated before the Altar, to mark the entrance and exit of parishioners with lit candles in their hands, to provide special services to the sick, and to exert pressure so that the most reluctant of neighbors attend masses, even against their will. Many friars and priests believed in the merits of having a *cofradía*—a special order of the devout—in their congregations: "It has been our experience that those Christian communities having cofradías are superior in many ways to those without. It's similar to how an educated individual works with greater diligence and quality than an ordinary small-town worker." The priest or monk saw an additional advantage for the actual participants: "always the communities with confradías enjoy a better society in all respects than those without ... the members there have fewer temptations, because they are kept occupied with religious responsibilities and other virtuous tasks."

And finally, seven. The inspector took special pride in calling attention to the extensive efforts of the Franciscans to publish a number of pamphlets, either in Spanish or in Indian-language translations. These contained the words and/or music of prayers or religious messages that the friars used in their classes. These publications facilitated the Indians' learning of Christian devotions and practices.

There is no doubt that the friars and priests in charge of the churches in and near Cuernavaca practiced most, if not all, of the above evangelization strategies. In the "Códice de la Fundación de Cuernavaca," we read what Don Toribio de San Martín Cortés wrote about his own responsibilities in this regard:

> The first community member named as the overall administrator of the Holy Church was Don Baltasar Valeriano. I myself worked in the Holy Church and served the Most Holy Sacrament to both the members of the community and to the incarnated form of Our Lady of the Assumption. I had the responsibility of preparing the altars. I also supervised the altar boys. With a feather-broom I cleaned those altars. It was up to me to organize all the choir directors, the bell ringers, and door monitors. Every Sunday I was the one who moved the Bible and communion breads to the front altar. And any Sunday that we celebrated conmemorial masses, I had to light the scores of candles that we placed in the nave before Our Holy Christ. Being the person in charge, it was up to me to supervise everything. I had to make sure that the choir singers complied with every single detail of their obligations. All the Sundays during Lent I had to make the examples (nexcuitiles). All this was to encourage every single member of the community to better understand our Catholic rituals and beliefs. I was in charge of all that would happen on days we would celebrate a saint's day. I had to make sure that the never any altar in the church was a loss for flowers. And when someone from the community committed a sin, it was I who accompanied that person to the office of the prosecutor. And after that person received the needed advice to change

his behavior, my responsibility was to order, then oversee, the administration of a number of whip lashes to his posterior or back—enough so that he would fear committing a sin the next time around. The job of the prosecutor was only to sentence the punishment, not to actually take the rope or whip in hand against the one who had sinned, because to do so was against the law and customs that reigned in our City of Cuernavaca; because if the prosecutor were to actually administer the punishment he had ordered, then he would forfeit not only his noble position, but also his high status in the community."[235]

CHAPTER 10

VISITS WITH THE KING, 1528-1529

An unstudied topic is the complex and confusing relationship between Hernán Cortés and the Emperor Carlos V. The year 1519 marks a significant moment in each's chronologies: that was the year when Cortés first landed on Mexican shores to begin his campaign against the Aztecs; that was also the year when the adolescent Carlos, speaking almost no Spanish and never having spent a day in the land he would rule for the next half-century, arrived in Spain to be crowned its new king (the imperial crown of the Holy Roman Empire would follow two years later). Thus began Carlos's reluctant dealings (he always prioritized European issues) with the competent yet idiosyncratic conquistador, his 23 million new Indian subjects, and the problematic administration of New Spain.

Only a few years would pass before the King would fall under the influence of the individual who would emerge in history's eye as Cortés' eternal antagonist, the Dominican friar Bartolomé de las Casas (See Appendix A). One issue which would cause heated conflict over the next century was Las Casas'—and therefore the King's—opposition to the encomienda. Contemporary readers might admire both for taking "idealistic" positions before this difficult issue. But many of their contemporaries, who were more grounded in the harsh realities of organizing New World societies, argued that if the encomienda were eliminated, then what institutions or practices would effectively function—at least in the short run—in its place?

VISITS WITH THE KING, 1528-1529

After returning from his disastrous expedition to Honduras in the middle months of 1526, Cortés spent two years plagued by hostilities and misfortunes. His enemies had usurped almost all his personal possessions and lands, and Crown representatives had, in effect, removed him from all authority in the government of New Spain. Having been exiled from the City of Mexico, he had established residence in Cuernavaca. He wrote letters to the king, requesting assistance on his behalf. But in addition to the expected delays, Court intervention was inexplicably absent. He must have suspected that his enemies, many and well placed, at least in part had captured the attention of the young monarch.

So it was not unexpected that the king, in April 1528, sent instructions for Cortés to travel to Spain. At the same time the king sent instructions that, during the conquistador's absence, court officials would begin a thorough investigation—*the "Juicio de residencia"*—of Cortés' previous years of governance. And, unfortunately for Cortés, it would be his enemies heading the official investigation, and doing everything possible so that it's results would plague him to the end of his life.

In part, the trip back to Spain, after twenty years of absence, was a celebration. Cortés' brilliant conquest of the infidel Aztecs was already the stuff of folklore; if rumors were accurate, he now commanded the personal loyalty and admiration of a whole continent of native subjects. Minstrel singers all across Europe were singing the glories of his incredible feats, and he now enjoyed the support of a score of important Spanish nobles. The royal couple, eager to please the public, sent out proclamations of praise and facilitated the passage of his huge delegation from town to town. But meanwhile, behind the scenes, the actions of the young king took another course.

In that short meeting the king briefly welcomed him, briefly complemented his military successes, and accepted Cortés' two-dozen gifts of New Spain's precious Indian relics and rare animals. Then, he rushed out of the room, hurriedly offering excuses.[236] This left Cortés dumbfounded and confused. "In the following days Cortés suffered on account of what the king's behavior in that short meeting might signify, because he knew that his own future was at stake," wrote Bernal Díaz.[237] Was that royal snub a result of the king siding with his enemies and giving credence to their accusations? Within a week, mounting worries and apprehensions caused in him a mental breakdown. All around him recognized the seriousness of his health crisis. Several regional dignitaries, in addition to the emperor himself, made bedside visits. But the Gods must have decided: Cortés would survive for yet another eighteen years.

Once again restored to health, Cortés had the time to reflect on the monarchy's actions over the previous half-decade that had aimed, to all appearances, at undermining his own initiatives. There is no doubt that Cortés was feeling strong disdain for the young king. It's possible that at this early moment he intuited what would become common knowledge twenty years later among informed individuals, that Carlos was "a loser" and "lacked capacity" for exercising leadership over the realm which by birth he had inherited.[238] Before an aristocratic audience attending mass, the celebrated conquistador led a party of acolytes past the king's family without performing the proper protocol of kneeling and bowing the head; for all observers, this was an obvious act of disrespect that reflected what one historian has labeled the "rude disregard of accepted protocol by a very haughty man."[239]

What might have been the young king's point of view? A familiarity with the respective chronologies of both his and Cortés' actions help to understand a few basic facts. First, that the young Carlos, appearing for the first time in Spain at about the same time as Cortés' final assault on Tenochtitlán, almost certainly had nothing to do with the court's disorganized, if not disastrous, actions vis-à-vis New Spain between 1521 and about 1524. Buy by that last year, many decisions of the new king Carlos took into account deep moral convictions and Christian devoutness (he had been tutored as a child by the most reputable of the reformist Franciscans). This was the king who would meet with Cortés several times during the latter's visit to Spain in 1528.

On the negative side, the king must have been confused by the highly skewed reports he had received about this impetuous subject, his nefarious acts and apparent deceptions.[240] Reputable individuals had accused Cortés of having usurped leadership of the Mexican campaign and "stealing" the arms, horses, and soldiers of his former employer, the Cuban governor Diego de Velázquez. Then, several months later, there were the "questionable events" of the conquistador leading several hundred men to surprise and defeat the much larger army of Spanish noble, Pánfilo de Narváez, and force the incorporation of the latter's soldiers into his own army. Meanwhile, accusations were rife that Cortés, in a domestic squabble, had choked his first wife to death.[241] Then—as far-fetched as it seemed—many people presumed that Cortés had ordered the poisoning of several important officials sent by the court to investigate alleged abuses.[242] Semi-credible accusations also made him out to be a ruthless killer of Indian chiefs, including the defeated Aztec prince who had submitted peacefully to his authority. Even though Cortés, time and again, had been absolved in official investigations with regard to these accusations, his reputation never fully emerged from the shadows.

Another issue which might have influenced the king's wary treatment of his important visitor: accusations that Cortés was laying the framework for assuming the position of renegade king of a savage land—a new Prester John. Had he not assumed a "monarchical" lifestyle, touring in and around Mexico City several times a week in a regal carriage, accompanied by a large entourage of Indian princes and Spanish grandees?[243] If all these were signs of an incipient rebellion, then how could the representatives of the Crown prevent all this from occurring?

Yet, on the positive side, the king and queen must have come to appreciate Cortés' pragmatism as a leader who was capable of brilliant planning, whether it be for a military campaign or the governance of a new and complicated colony. How to explain the loyalty shown to him by a hardened group of soldiers and, in addition, a whole continent of natives? They must have been surprised by recent reports from perhaps the most trustworthy of their own recent appointees, Franciscan monk Juan de Zumárraga, that Cortés, as the colony's governor, was making good decisions that fostered stability among the Spaniards and protection for the millions of new Indian subjects. All that in contrast to other officials appointed by the crown who had ignited turbulence, violence, and inhuman treatment of the Indians! Meeting repeatedly with Cortés over a week, it became patently obvious to them that few individuals on the world stage could equal Cortés' inspired, yet highly controversial, leadership abilities.

Furthermore, they must have been impressed by Cortés' careful planning to carry on further geographical discoveries in the newly discovered Mar del Sur—soon to be called the Pacific Ocean. Any positive results would only enhance their own standing, with new lands under their dominion and new subjects under their authority. (Over the next two decades the king would issue "cédulas" for Cortés to command future voyages of discovery, would offer to reimburse Cortés' expeditions to Pánuco and Honduras, and would encourage new shipbuilding projects on both the Caribbean and Pacific coasts.[244])

Was the royal couple taken aback by his hubris in seeking huge rewards for his services? During one of those face-to-face encounters, Cortés requested as a form of recompense for his "services" the grant of more than twenty encomiendas located all across New Spain. After delaying more than a year, the royal couple made official his new status as Marqués del Valle and their approval of almost all that Cortés had requested. (Whereas they allowed for Cortés and his heirs to enjoy those huge benefits in perpetuity, they would continue to deny that same right to New Spain's other encomenderos).

Other meetings between Cortés and the king were scheduled and some were cancelled at the last minute. The latter was in constant movement, preparing once again to absent himself from Spain to pursue important military objectives in the Low Countries. It was obvious to everybody that he wanted as little to do as possible with the iconoclastic conquistador of New Spain. He must have been—at the very least—extremely irritated that this talented, yet enigmatic, subject had placed upon his own lap a whole new set of complex problems that could not be ignored. One reliable commentator states that whereas the king was publicly obligated to reward Cortés for having led the successful conquest, he was already committed to a course of action that would lead to the removal of Cortés from any official capacity.[245]

The king's actions betrayed his ambivalence: While honoring Cortés publicly, behind the scenes he and his ministers would seek ways to minimize his influence and sideline him from the colony's governance. But the idea might have occurred to them: "Let the *loco* run; set him free to do what he was going to do with no regard for either their permission or instruction." Up until then his acts had produced unanticipated and shockingly huge dividends for themselves. "Let him run."

At the same time, they would keep Cortés under their control. After empowering him as the colony's most potent economic force, they issued secret instructions for auditors, accountants, and inspectors to monitor his actions. With the first sign of a transgression or violation, their appointees controlling the colony's government would be in a position to come down hard.

(After the passage of yet another decade, it would become obvious to all serious investigators that the emperor Carlos showed, at best, little interest in the Americas. Undoubtedly, he regarded the new transoceanic colonies primarily as a source of income to fund his interminable battles in Eastern Europe. But the evolving problems in New Spain would amount to little more than a bother. Cortés' most important biographer writes: "It might be hard to believe, but in the Memoirs that Carlos V would dictate [during his retirement, after passing power off to his son, Philip II], there appears not a single sentence mentioning the New World nor the Indies, nor Mexico, nor Hernán Cortés. Everything he wrote had to do with his European campaigns, his travels, his family, and his paternal lineage [*su gota*]").[246]

La Segunda Audiencia

Had those personal encounters with Cortés produced in the royal couple at least one positive reaction? Because after his departure from Spain they, for the first time, exhibited their willingness to listen to and be influenced by good advice rather than that from self-serving scoundrels. Perhaps this began to occur only after having received Zumárraga's letter. They must have realized their horrid mistake of having appointed Nuño de Guzman as head of the Primera Audiencia.[247] By the time

Cortés had left the peninsula to return to New Spain, they were already on course to select a far superior set of men for the colony's governance.

Only in 1530 would the officials of the Segunda Audiencia assume authority. This new body, constituted by men of integrity such as Bishop Sebastián Ramírez de Fuenleal and respected jurist Vasco de Quiroga, would support not only the evangelical campaign of the Belvís friars, but also the measures recommended by the "Protector de los Indios," Juan de Zumárraga—and have him empowered as the colony's first Bishop. All of these individuals would partner with the powerful Marqués del Valle, Hernán Cortés, in establishing a firm foundation for the colony's governance. They would ably govern New Spain until the arrival, some four years later, of the first viceroy, Antonio de Mendoza.

The Segunda Audiencia appointed Zumárraga to the position as Mexico's first bishop—and later archbishop. In those positions he would offer firm resistance to the clique of men intent on abusing the native population. According to one writer, Zumárraga was

> Inquisition promoter, combattent of Erasmism currents, and as well as medieval enemy to all witches, magic practitioners, and infidels. He was also a protector of the Indians. Zumárraga struggled against encomenderos and corrumpt functionaries in the colonial government. He brought to New Spain the first printing press and he established the first University of the Americas. He was cofounder of the Colegio de Tlatelolco. He believed that the Gospel ought to be taught directly, without any intermediaries. At the same time he organized the priesthood to burn Indian *códices* and "diabolical" objects of Indian worship. He condemned to death by burning one of the chieftains of Texcoco, an act he believed would save the souls of the Indians and would help them escape from the wrath of the Inquisition.[248]

Under Zumárraga, the Inquisition's major targets were "insufficiently orthodox" Spanish priests, and for the most "flagrant cases" it decreed "indulgent" sentences. Only a minority of its cases involved indigenous leaders. When it burned at the stake two such individuals for having continued pagan worship, Crown representatives reacted critically.[249]

From the beginning—and continuing for nearly a half-century—the archbishop provided firm support for the Belvís Franciscan monks in their campaign to baptize the Indian masses. He agreed with their view that clergy would be most effective if they were to learn the language of the Indians to be served.[250] To further both of these ends, he lent his support for the Franciscan Colegio de Tlatelolco which—over a half-century—would play an instrumental role in the preparation for ecclesiastic service of hundreds of Indian youths, primarily the sons of Indian nobles.

Documentary information is scarce with regard to the direct contact or collaboration that Zumárraga might have shared with Cortés, but those moments must have been frequent. In Cortés' last will and testament, he would charge Zumárraga with the task of guiding his son and successor, the second Marqués del Valle, Martín Cortés, during his first years of administering the affairs of the Marquesado.

Vasco de Quiroga would also play an important –but mostly indirect—role in the life and career of Hernán Cortés. Born in 1470, he had served the Spanish monarchy for decades in his capacity as lawyer up to the age of 60 in several important capacities. In 1530, when he was 60 years old, King Carlos named him as one of three inspectors with the responsibilities of travelling to New Spain and bringing to a satisfactory conclusion the civil wars that had erupted between Cortés' enemies and supporters. In New Spain he quickly became convinced about the efficacy of Cortés' early initiatives; he was eager to garner support for the Franciscans in their campaign to convert the Indians to Christianity.

He must have come to respect other aspects of the nation-building work accomplished by Cortés, because the Segunda Audiencia ended up granting reason to almost all of Cortés' contentions. In and around Mexico City, Quiroga's honesty, intelligence, and integrity earned the respect of all parties involved. In 1533 he would move to Michoacán to found—and then direct until the end of his life in 1565—two *hospitals*, in addition to his renown mission-pueblo, the Colegio Seminario de San Nicolás.

The successes of the Segunda Audiencia were several. First, they took adequate measures to restore order to New Spain's governance, to control crime and violence, and to quell the civil war that had arisen between Cortes's enemies and supporters. Second, they implemented effective measures to limit the power of the encomenderos, convert the King's share of Indian communities into *corregimientos* (these were communities under the Crown's—and not the encomenderos' control), and empower a strong central authority to govern all aspects of New Spain society. Third, they enacted measures aimed at limiting the abuses done to the Indians, most important of which was an inspection system to detect tribute or Indian-service abuses and to impose fines for flagrant violations. They made the courts accessible to Indian plaintiffs over possible encomendero violations. Lastly, they enacted measures aimed at increasing the revenue extracted from New Spain and earmarked for the Royal Treasury.[251] They ably governed New Spain until the arrival, some four years later, of the first viceroy, Antonio de Mendoza.[252]

All of these individuals, including Zumárraga and the Franciscan friars, would partner with the powerful Marqués del Valle, Hernán Cortés, in establishing a firm foundation for colonial society and governance. They came together in their belief that the military conquest was "justified" because it rid the sub-continent and the world of the evil Aztec regime. They gave full support to the Franciscan friars in their all-important task of evangelizing the Indian masses. Time and again, they called upon the services of Cortés, the Marqués del Valle, who not only controlled vast resources, but also—second to the Franciscan friars—enjoyed the trust and respect of Indian communities across the colony. As individuals and as a group they supported the role of both the Church and a strong viceregal government in protecting Indian rights and in controlling excessive behavior of both Spanish encomenderos and settlers. And lastly, they firmly embraced the leadership of the Spanish crown in its (at times ill-chosen, but generally) benevolent policies aimed at the construction of a just New Spain society combining both Spanish and Indian citizens.

CHAPTER 11

CORTÉS IN CUERNAVACA, 1530-1536

Might Cuernavaca, with a "cordial" relationship initially existing between Cortés and his native subjects, have experienced even fewer problems than what occurred in Mexico's other favored city, Tlaxcala?[253] *(See Appendix B). During the post-conquest period, there emerged in both of these communities "vigorous, prosperous" civil governments run by noble Indian principales, and the local populations enjoyed "great freedom" in all aspects of life. Spanish leaders there, with sincere "concern," achieved a "remarkably full accord" with the native people they ruled.*

H. J. Elliot, perhaps the most outstanding historian of this period, calls it "the golden age of [the] Mendicant evangelical enterprise. ... [Many friars] were steeped in humanist ideas ... [many of them] were inspired by Erasmus's 'philosophy of Christ' and by Sir Thomas More's Utopia. *[They] saw the American Indians as the ideal material for the realization of the perfect Christian community, ... grouping the Indians into villages, building missions and churches, and imposing a new pattern of civilization on their bewildered charges. The results were remarkable.... Mexican Indians [were assimilating] the superior techniques of their conquerors, and [displaying] a receptivity to European culture which had no parallel in other parts of Spain's colonial empire."*[254]

Yet some tlaxcalteca principales, *in the first years, seemed to have betrayed the initial trust of the Franciscan friars. Four chieftains, taking advantage of the Franciscan monks, publicly accepted new Christian vows while secretly continuing former pagan rituals. Ugly events resulted, which culminated in the Spanish ordering and then carrying out their execution. This "extraordinary measure, unprecedented and never repeated," must have served its purpose in dissuading other natives from attempting the same.*

No such blemish in Spanish-native relations was ever reported as having occurred in Cuernavaca. Yet the natives there would have other problems (it's difficult to assess how "serious"), which would result from the strong feudal values and iconoclastic personality of their señor, Hernán Cortés.

Back in 1526 Cortés had organized the visit of a score of Franciscan monks to carry out the mass baptism of thousands of Indians in and around Cuernavaca. In Mexico City, the Franciscans had been joined by Dominican monks, and those from the Augustinian Order were soon to arrive. Now was the time for the friars to formally begin their evangelization and educational activities in other nearby communities: Oaxtepec, Totolapan, Yecapixtla, and Ocuiculco. Up until now, little had changed in the daily lives of the thousands of Indians residing in these large *cabecera* communities, and less so in the hundreds of *sujeto* villages. All that would change. It would be a vast project of transculturalization that would last decades. Now it was incumbent upon Cortés to oversee the beginnings of that transformation. His designated assistants? The mendicant monks, who prioritized Christian baptism as the first step in the transformation of New Spain's Indians into productive Christian citizens.

In their first group sessions with Cortés, the Franciscan friars had agreed almost immediately with his prioritization of Indian evangelization. Their project of baptizing thousands upon thousands of Indians was well underway. Baptism, as they understood it, would be followed by the Indians' efforts to learn orations and recitations, and then their participation in various Catholic rituals. The Franciscans, as opposed to many Dominicans and other more main-line religious authorities, would not require the Indians' full understanding; they were confident that the comprehension of Catholic rites and concepts would only increase with the passing of the years.

All of this would require time. Some monks moved to *cabecera* cities to direct the construction of churches and monasteries, baptize the surrounding populations, and teach rudimentary prayers and hymns. Others remained in their respective monasteries in or near Mexico City to dedicate their time to either translating the scriptures into Náhuatl (and a few other Indigenous languages of New Spain) or to teaching the children of Indian nobles a minimum level of Spanish and devotional lessons. Meanwhile, all sought ways to further their related objectives: teaching vocational skills in order to lift the Indian masses out of material misery, weaning them from unacceptable practices (such as sodomy, bigamy, human-flesh consumption), and leading them to understand the tenants of the Christian religion.

The Cuernavaca *códices* mention yet another way that Cortés sought to support the evangelization work of the Franciscans within his domain of Cuernavaca: onto his palace/ residence he would build a special "outdoor nave" or chamber on the ground floor that would serve as the meeting place for special community gatherings or Catholic masses. There, the Marqués, when present in Cuernavaca, would host the assembly of Indian nobles for weekly masses. In the codex a Cuernavaca chieftain wrote: "we would send a delegation to the residence of our mayor, accompany him to hear mass at the palace, and then escort him back to his house ...."[255] On festive or ritualistic occasions, Cortés and his family freely mixed with the few Spanish individuals in his employ and the Indian nobility of the city.

The chronist Bernal Díaz del Castillo provides a description of how Catholic devotion became an integral part of daily life:

> They have their Churches with elaborately adorned altars; the different chapels, each dedicated to a holy, divine figure, contain

beautifully decorated crosses and candelabras, candle displays on sliver plates, some of them are huge and others small; you'll also find incense holders, all finely inlaid with silver.... And there are any number of bells for any occasion .... And you'll hear their choirs, all singing with perfectly harmonized voices; they'll have tenors as well as sopranos and bases—all the voices will be represented. While some communities possess organs, in all you'll find Indians playing flutes, sackbuts, *chirimías*, and *dulzainas* ... you'll be impressed by the way the natives help the priest out with singing the Holy mass—this is what the Franciscans and Mercedarios have told me—that they take full charge in maintaining the community's church building ... and they know all the holy prayers and they've correctly learned every part of mass that one would expect them to know.[256]

By the mid 1530s, weekly Catholic rituals were already routine in those Indian communities where the mendicant monks had established their combination church-monastery-schools. A native devotee, called a *merino*, would exercise his responsibility of calling all the members of a barrio to set aside mundane tasks, proceed as a group to the church atrium or terrace, and participate in the activities directed by the priest, assisted by the Christianized noble youth. There would be songs, chants, and prayers. More often than not, the morning would end with a procession, with pious Indians, dressed in religious garb, leading the way and carrying an elaborately decorated cross and effigies of Christian saints.

On these weekly occasions, the *merino* had an additional responsibility, that of taking note of precisely who, from his neighborhood, was not in attendance. Those absent would be punished, sometimes with whip lashings. The folklore of the period records that on one occasion none other than the Marqués chose to subject himself to this form of discipline as a way of setting an example for the indigenous community. Having arrived late for a mass on one occasion, he lined up to receive the appropriate punishment. This was his manner of demonstrating a fundamental precept of the new society that he wished to form: that no individual, regardless of his rank or social position, was above the law.[257]

Over the next twenty years, the construction of chapels and churches—according to the Franciscan plan—would continue apace. The church-monastery of San Francisco, in Cuernavaca, was the fifth site where the Franciscans established a permanent presence. From there, the friars would go out "to visit through the territory of that which is called the Marquesado and they found the people as well-disposed and willing to be Christians as in [Cuernavaca], especially in those [pueblos] called Yacapichtla and Guastepec ...."[258] Another observer reports that, by the 1570s, the Franciscan presence around Cuernavaca had grown considerably:

> Twelve *leguas* from Mexico City—in a site that is located directly in line with the sun at midday, there is another monastery, called la Anunciación de Nuestra Señora. It's in the town of Quanhnanaca, whose master is the Marqués del Valle. Far into the past this community has served as the *cabecera* for a highly populated province. Within it are many—and good—communities. There you'll find monasteries founded by both the Dominican and Augustinian orders. Even though the whole province belongs to what is called the Marquesado—meaning that all the natives are vassals of the Marqués del Valle, they exist fairly independently, meaning you won't find the strict governance over all of them as had existed before, under Aztec rule. Instead, they're administered separately, each community has its own authority, quite independent of the *cabecera* authority in [in Cuernavaca.] Those in control of the latter are the monks of the San Francisco order, who reside there in the monastery. They have eleven separate churches, and each with a related estancia, which they visit. There would be some eight thousand heads of family. In that monastery reside four priests, all of whom speak the natives' language, as well as the general administrator.[259]

By the end of the 1530s, both the Dominicans and the Augustinians had joined the Franciscans for evangelization activities in major centers near Cuernacaca.²⁶⁰ Authorities assigned to the Augustinians the Indian communities in and around Tlayacapan, Totolapan, Yecapixtla, and Ocuituco. The master builders—*alarifes*—engaged by that order to head the construction of monasteries were the following: Juan de la Cruz for the community of Tetela del Volcán, Francisco de Becerra for Tepoztlán and Cuahunáhuac (Cuernavaca), and Jorge de Avila for Tlayacapan. The latter would become part of a "city of God," with 26 interrelated chapels and devotional niches. is admired for its enduring network of religious architecture.²⁶¹

Constructing a Community

During this time period, Cortés decided that formal documents had to be drawn up identifying the boundary lines for any lands considered to be community property. He personally instructed the chieftains from the different neighborhoods in measuring distances with the "vara." The novelty of this operation must have impressed them, because years later the author of a document would describe how, years before, he had participated in measuring his community's boundaries and then dictating to scribes the relevant information. Cortés himself must have preserved the resulting documents, written in Náhuatl, in his own archives.²⁶² That chieftain explains:

> Now listen carefully, all of you, my beloved sons. All of you here are sons of God. You're all natives of this place, Cuernavaca. Listen carefully to these important instructions. Here, today, we are going to mark boundaries and record what we do in a written document. This means that henceforth, no outsider, no other individual, will be able to claim for himself what rightfully belongs to you. No other person will be able to take this community land as his own possession. I give to you these parcels and they will belong to your community until the end of time on this earth. Now, we will record in writing all the

limits to each parcel—we will record the markings for each of the streets forming its outside perimeter; if these have names, we will write them down here. We will draw up this document according to the procedures set forth by the highest laws of the land. What we do is sanctioned by God. Whoever reads this document will know that when we wrote it up, we were following the instructions given to us by God for marking and then documenting the boundaries of this land plot. ... We, the *principales*, ... took in our hands the vara and counted how many varas each boundary measured—we followed faithfully the instructions given to us by el Señor Marqués. The marking and recording of boundaries were performed in our presence.[263]

The last sentences of this quote suggest the trepidation which Cortés might have felt about the hundreds of common Spaniards then arriving at New Spain shores, that those brutish individuals (or even worse: their voracious heirs)—would not hesitate to seek control over Cuernavaca Indians or their possessions. One leader gave signs that the lesson had been learned, that he would be ready to lead his own followers in resistance: "if the day comes when some Spaniard comes along with the intention of presenting false claims, then they will a legal 'hedge' to use against that attempt to rob them of their lands."

It is unknown whether Cortés carried this anti-Spanish crusade to other communities to the east of Cuernavaca—and in particular to the Indian villages of Anaya and Anenecuilco located to the south of the *cabecera* town of Oaxtepec. Because four centuries hence, the followers of Emiliano Zapata would display before the court certain documents that a long succession of village elders had protected and stored since the earliest days of the colony.[264]

Upon assuming authority over Cuernavaca, he chose to not interfere in any great measure with the supervisory function of the Indian nobility, whose members had governed those lands over the previous century.[265] An Indian chieftain had dictated:

Our great master, whose name is Señor King Don Carlos V, has sent us an order, via our local great master Señor Marqués Don Fernando Franco Cortés Marquéz del Valle. The order is that we *principales* of the community of Qaxomulco send carpenters, some of them were our own sons, and they went and labored, raising all the wooden beams needed for the roof of the church. We sent them, and they worked, and they finished their assigned task for the Church. Now, we are documenting the boundaries of the lands belonging to this community and we are doing this in the presence of el Señor Marqués Don Fernando Franco Cortés Marqués del Valle.[266]

Cortés also set into motion several construction projects. Heading the list were the improvements he ordered to be done to the main water sources for both Tlaltenango and Cuernavaca. His enterprises would also benefit, because sugar mill under construction would be powered by a steady stream of water. The same applied to the wheat mill that he ordered built within a stone's throw of the palace. Once the water-source improvements were completed, he imposed rules to govern the community members' water consumption. One *códice* reads: "This is what our great Señor Marqués gifted to us."[267]

Also of note was the construction of two "hospitals" in or near Cuernavaca.[268] First, there was a facility north of the village of Tlaltenango—about which little historical documentation has survived. And second, there was the Hospital de la Santa Cruz in Oaxtepec that treated the incurably sick; it's simple facilities were significantly improved a decade after its founding.

He also placed high priority on the construction of convents for young women. Very little has been written on this subject. In these, Spanish nuns trained young Indian women in the care of sick people treated in the adjoining hospitals.[269]

Although immersed in social and economic activities, Cortés also attended to the comfort of his own family.[270] Now accompanying him was his new wife, Doña Juana de Zúñiga. Construction work had progressed sufficiently on his "palace"—located near the center of Cuernavaca—which would now serve as their personal residence. Did the young *Marquesa* occasionally make a two-day horse ride to Mexico City to visit Spanish peers? No documentation exists. Within months, she gave birth to their first child—and others would follow during the next eight years. To all appearances, Cortés cared for his young wife, and she, in turn, valued their relationship. (After Cortés' definitive departure for Spain in 1538—and after his natural death there in 1547—she would continue residing in the Cuernavaca palace, accompanied by a small Spanish staff, until her own natural death two decades later.) The number of Spanish residents there never numbered more than those personally hired by Cortés to tend to either household tasks or his ever-expanding business interests.

She must have felt herself to be surrounded by decent people. The radius of their daily strolls or play frequently reached as far as Tlaltenango— some two kilometers to the north. Her male children, when sufficiently grown, probably had few restrictions with regard to where they were allowed to play or wander. In one Cuernavaca codex, the Indian author recounts how a supervisor took appropriate measures at the Tlaltenango sugar mill to prevent the occurrence of any accident involving a Cortés child. Mentioned also is how Indian neighbors went out of their way to treat those children as members of a community family.

Although Cuernavaca was nominally his "home" between 1830 and 1838, Cortés would be in constant movement. Sometimes, he would stay for months at one of his three Pacific ports, tending to tasks related to shipbuilding and new-discovery voyages. That, in addition to his diligence in personally overseeing any number of agricultural, cattle, or business ventures between Oaxaca and Michoacán.

In the important *Cuernavaca códices,* the chieftains mention "happenings" that current-day historians might not deem important. Some examples: the labor expended by the Tlatlaltemalpan community to pave their main street with rock;[271] "one day the neighbors came upon the body of a man who had died on the road heading to Texalpan ...;"[272]

an eclipse that occurred in the month of October—with no year given. Yet another "happening: "a married woman with the name María Salomón" was witness to a strange—and miraculous—happening: "she noticed a large opening in a black zapote tree and, upon closer inspection, she found within it a Most Holy Cross." Her retelling of what she had seen set off a whole series of events: she went to "inform the priests in the church; then she found the community treasurer, who followed her to see it; afterwards, the priest himself also went. Then, all the Spaniards in the area went to carry the cross back to the church. The *principales* placed a huge offering on the altar to celebrate its entrance into the church. At the site of the tree, where the cross had appeared, they built a house-like-shrine—its own church—and the priest came to say a mass in honor of the Holy Cross."

Also eternalized in these documents are religious events, for example (what I calculated had happened in the year 1532), the arrival of the statue of "our beloved Virgen of Santa María, our beloved and respected Madre Asunción, which all the *principales* brought from Xochimilco." Another elder makes note of the first performance ever to take place in the Cuernavaca region of two religious comedies: "Re-enactment of Jesus's Passion" and the comedy "The Three Kings" (perhaps in 1535). In a different document, Don Toribio also calls attention to an unfortunate accident that must have occurred in the construction of the local church: "the bell tower above the altar honoring our father Saint Joseph fell down ... and a second time we had to do God's work of reconstructing it according to how we had first built it with the help of the *principales*."

Law Suits: Cortés's Treatment of Cuernavaca Indians

Initially, Cortés and the other newly empowered encomenderos took full advantage of the pre-existing noble-worker relationships in those Indian communities over which they exercised *encomendero* rights: they supervised Indian nobles who, in turn, would order the work to be done and the obedient *maceguales* would obey with their uncompensated labor.

The issue here is Spanish compensation for Indian labor. In a previous chapter I explained how in 1526, when Cortés moved his center of operations to Cuernavaca, he regularly ordered the encomienda Indians under his authority to carry out uncompensated labor. But he also took pains to limit the number of days that Indian laborers from Cuernavaca would be required to work in Taxco mines or other mining areas. Nor would he make excessive demands on unpaid Cuernavaca workers engaged in local tasks: the improvement of roads, the planting of sugarcane, the construction of mills and drinking-water facilities, and the provision of food and firewood for his personal residence.[273] In granting encomiendas between 1521 and 1524, Cortés had also issued strong ordinances to guard against uncontrolled Indian exploitation. Within a decade the Segunda Audencia (and, a few years later, the new viceroy and his appointed officials) would follow Cortés' lead in creating a colonial bureaucracy charged with—among other tasks—increasing the protection of the Indians from new abuses.

Cortés was a protagonist in bringing about these changes. Over the past decade he had leveraged his prestige, both across New Spain and even in the Spanish court, to champion Indians' rights. In actual fact, no other Spaniard—perhaps with the exception of Franciscan friars Zumárraga and Motolinía—enjoyed greater admiration coming from New Spain's Indians. As long as he resided there (he would leave New Spain in the year 1538, and would not return), and regardless of his status vis-à-vis the colonial government, his prestige among the Indians would never waiver. A decade later—and in spite of all the above—he would be called to account for the unjust treatment of the Indians under his care.

In 1524 Cortés had "abandoned" his possessions in Cuernavaca as well as the governorship of New Spain to command the ill-fated expedition to Honduras. Meanwhile, his enemies had taken control of the colony's central government and had distributed among their cronies all the towns previously assigned to him, among which was the town of "Gadnavaca"—Cuernavaca, which they gave to Antonio Serrano. Serrano, acting as new owner, finished construction of the sugar mill that Cortés had begun at Tenaltenango and orchestrated the purchase of nearby land plots from certain Indians.

Cortés, returning to Mexico in 1526, found out that only through court action could he reassume control of the Cuernavaca encomienda and the sugar-producing facilities he had commenced. Therefore, he engaged a team of lawyers to file the required lawsuit against the usurper, Antonio Serrano de Cardona.[274]

He also decided to take direct action, ordering his Indian loyalists to proceed "by foot or by horse ... to lay waste to that sugar mill by cutting down the caña stalks and destroying whatever buildings." His people "would take as prisoners any workers or slaves who are present, they'll seize the oxen and carry away any carts, they'll make sure they're not obtaining firewood by cutting down the trees in the forests surrounding the mill;" they'll also confiscate the axes used by Serrano and his men.

In court, Cortés' representatives defended his own right to the lands in question and pointed out irregularities in Serrano's alleged purchase of Indian properties. They accused Serrano of having imprisoned Indians, perhaps in caves ("en cárceles oscuras"), causing them to suffer hunger, appropriating their lands, and forcing their women and children to perform hard, unpaid labor.

Court officials interviewed the important Cuernavaca chieftain, Don Hernando. Making reference to the figures his people had painted on cloth, he explained the type and quantity of tribute items that Serrano had required, causing "harm to the natives' themselves and destruction to their property." One result was that the latter had had difficulty paying their elevated tributes and lacked the time necessary for cultivating the crops needed to feed their own families. Furthermore:

> Because of these causes we Indians have been under great pressure, we have lacked the time needed to plant for feeding our own families. For these reasons, our town is suffering a population loss because the free workers [*maceguales*] we had formerly employed have fled to other parts, because they have

become frightened over how much the master requires them to pay, over the large tributes he demands that they give ... over the damage he is causing to their inherited possessions in and around Tetela [del Monte]. They don't want to leave, but the master is forcing them to. The Spaniards that he employs in this province contribute to the problem.

The court finally ordered Serrano to reduce the level of Indian tributes. Although it also criticized Cortés for "extortion and bad treatment" of the Indians, it also recognized the legitimacy of his land claim. But in doing so, it still left Serrano in de facto control of the sugar mill. This arrangement satisfied nobody, and heated friction between Cortés and Serrano continued. Several times over the next twenty years, Cortés' representatives would appeal this decision, but to no avail.

A few years later, Cortés initiated another lawsuit in order to regain his control of the encomiendas in Totolapan and Atlatlahuca.[275] In this case, the court ruled against Cortés, leaving the two encomiendas under Crown control. With regard to labor issues, the court ruled that Cortés, while acting as encomendero, had treated the Indians under his charge with fairness and moderation, that they would be obliged to pay him "no more nor less" than what they had paid to their previous overlords.[276]

As the years advanced, regulations coming from both the Crown and the Viceregal government would change. In 1544 the Crown's representatives filed a lawsuit against the Marquesado, accusing both Cortés (then absent in Spain) and his Indian supervisor of raising to an excessive level the tribute amounts for the Indians of Cuernavaca and Acapixtla, and for having seized from them both houses and lands.[277] Other accusations involved wrongful behavior on the part of the Marquesado in both "Guastepeque" and "Yautepeque." This court case must have lasted months—given that its transcription occupies some 44 pages in a recently-published book.

It is interesting to note that Cortés and his people did not deny the substance of the charges made by the Crown's prosecutor. They explained that their collection of tributes followed pre-Hispanic patterns, and that they had been negligent in not changing in order to conform to the new rules imposed by the viceroy so that Spanish encomenderos would grant greater attention to the rights and possessions of the naturales. Another interesting note: several of the Indians, in testifying against the Marquesado, made declarations praising Cortés, saying that Cortés did care for them, and that any harmful treatment was due to the actions of his servant, not Cortés himself. Does this suggest that Cortés unfairly used his charisma to take advantage of the unsophisticated natives? Undoubtedly, he possessed an uncommon skill in dealing with people. The court, with the participation of the viceroy himself, ended the matter by imposing a fine on the Marquesado and set reasonable levels for future tribute and worker-salary levels.

The same transcription records a complaint by Cuernavaca *principal*, Don Hernando that, in the early 1520s, Cortés had confiscated the parcel of land belonging to his family to build the palace-residence. This accusation, although not acted on at that time, would not disappear (I reconsider it in the last chapter). Unfortunately, the transcript records no information about the reaction of other Indians to this accusation—which serious investigators in our own time have believed to be spurious.[278]

Another lawsuit filed in 1847 against Cortés' son, The Marqués Martín Cortés, sheds further light on aspects of New Spain's post-conquest society and the possible role the father, Hernán Cortés, in governing the Marquesado.[279] Functionaries of the state, under the authority of the sitting viceroy Mendoza, accused the young marqués of having violated ordinances dealing with the treatment of encomienda Indians. Local natives gave testimonies—translated from Náhuatl and recorded in Spanish—offering as court "evidence" their cloth paintings. The final judgement stipulated new and lower tribute levels; that the Indians would be required to pay only a single tribute which would cover both the salary payments to local officials as well as normal expenses for the local Monasterio de San Agustín.

Yet another court document treats the issue of whether Cortés routinely treated fairly the Indian porters under his hire.[280] Since the beginning of his residence in Cuernavaca, he had expended considerable energy and resources to improve the road stretching from that city to Acapulco, along which vital materials had to be transported for his shipbuilding activities. Sections featuring steep rises and rock outcroppings offered special problems for the porters he employed. Was Cortés compensating them fairly for their services? Was he following printed guidelines regarding their provision of food?[281]

The law suit might have been initiated by one of Cortés' many enemies with the motivation of causing him legal problems. What resulted were charges filed against Cortés, drawn-out hearings, briefs written by Cortés' lawyers, on-site visits by court officials, and several interviews of porters involved. These proceedings were to occupy Cortés' time and attention for four long years.

In Cortés' defense, his lawyers argued that a number of the porters

> carried high-priority loads: those objects and tools were deemed essential to the outfitting of the ships under construction. They did not carry clothing or anything else. Their loads were of moderate weight and were small. However, other Indian porters—two out of three of the total number—carried the food that was necessary for all the porters. The marqués [Cortés] had ordered that all porters were to be paid for their services: it was a good salary; he paid it before the porters left their homes to make the long trip. Also, he favored them by reducing the tribute they were required to pay. The Indians of Cuernavaca [are free agents]: they charge a daily fee for their services, and the person employing them is required to provide their food.... They are free to go about offering their services; they will choose to work only for those who have a reputation for paying them the agreed-upon wage.

Testifying on Cortés' behalf was Friar Toribio Motolinía, an ally of Cortés over the previous two decades, and at that time serving as supervisor for the Franciscan monastery in Cuernavaca. In the latter's judgement, the road to Acapulco was in very bad condition; along certain stretches, "it was not fit for either loaded horses or hauling carts." He had first-hand knowledge of how Cortés had reduced by half the tributes required of the Indians working that road's hardest stretches, had paid them in advance, and had provided adequate food and provisions.

This must have been a "high profile" case, because the queen herself ordered the New Spain court officials to relay their findings directly to her. After a careful study of all the particulars, and after reading the Indian testimonies as well as the accusations, the queen ended up accepting in full the explanations that Cortés' lawyers had provided. Her written opinion was that Cortés had not taken unfair advantage of the porters and that he had not violated the existing ordinances stipulating maximum weight loads.[282] Instead of ruling against Cortés, she dictated harsh punishment for Cortés' accuser: "Take the accuser as prisoner" because he only wanted to make problems for the Marqués." She ordered that all charges be lifted, that Cortés "has caused no harm to any Indian porter, nor has he violated any of our ordinances ...." She ordered a summary end to all related inquiries: "Put an end to all these accusations. Consider this as the final word on the matter." Both the queen and the king now realized—in contrast to five years before—the immense rewards that might be reaped by supporting the activities of their difficult and unpredictable vassal, Hernán Cortés. The queen's pointed words: Cortés "works on our behalf."

Chapter Conclusion

By the mid-1530s a "consensus" was emerging among the Franciscan leadership, the officials of the Segunda Audiencia, and then the newly installed viceroy and archbishop: all were in tacit agreement that stability in New Spain depended upon not only the material strength of the encomendero class, but also upon a thriving Indian community. One way to achieve this was to have in place laws to protect the Indians from encomendero abuses and then to strictly enforce them.

The court cases treated above help the contemporary reader to understand Hernán Cortés' legacy in not only Cuernavaca, but also in the whole of New Spain. He had been removed from power over New Spain affairs in 1526, but after that he had continued, from his palace-residence in Cuernavaca, to direct a multitude of projects all across New Spain. While he consistently required reasonable tribute levels from the Indian communities under his authority, he initially resisted the new legislation dictating minimum salaries for the labor of his encomendero workers. According to reliable documentation, Cortés did not pay for Indian services up to 1532. As a result, several fair-minded Spaniards, including religious personnel, stepped forward to defend Cuernavaca natives; one result was that after that last year he would make full, regular payments.[283] What emerges is the portrait of a man with gigantic ego, head-strong disposition, and iconoclastic personality.

Also evident in these court-case transcripts are changes in the Indian—and Mestizo—leadership after a generation of Spanish rule. These were now aware of the power granted by Spanish authorities for them to engage in court cases. Indian empowerment was an obvious and positive result. But there were also negative consequences. According to the Crown inspector Alonso de Zorita, writing in the 1550s, a whole group of "ambitious bilingual Indians spent their time launching lawsuits. It was 'law-suit fever' ... or 'anarchy.'"[284]

Meanwhile, Cortés—in his actions administering encomiendas and Indian communities in both Cuernavaca and elsewhere—had many defenders, among whom were important, principled, individuals. Indian leaders throughout the viceroyalty continued to admire and respect him, and the queen herself had intervened on his behalf. In Chapter 5 I have already quoted from the important letter, written in the year 1560 to King Felipe II by the indigenous nobles of the town of Huejotzingo (north of Cholula in the current State of Puebla) which, like the communities surrounding Cuernavaca, were administered by Cortés. With nostalgia they praised the harmonious situation of their community some twenty or so years before, when Cortés, as their encomendero, oversaw the governing actions of their own fathers and grandfathers. Forty years before, during the struggle to overthrow Aztec tyranny, "we gave [the Spaniards under Cortés] everything they needed; we fed and clothed them, and we would carry in our arms and on our backs those... wounded or who were very ill, and we did all the tasks in preparing for war." They had nothing but praise their first encomendero in the years that followed: "your servant don Hernando Cortés, late captain general, the Marqués del Valle, in all the time he lived here with us, always cherished us and kept us happy; he never disturbed or bothered us. Although we gave him tribute, he assigned it to us only with moderation.... He never reprimanded us or afflicted us, because it was evident to him and he understood well how very greatly we served and aided him."[285]

Similar praise for the acts of Cortés—some decades before—also came from three of the most important Franciscan monks, Motolinía, Zumárraga, and Gante, who could not have ignored the court cases treated above—which seem to cast Cortés' actions in bad light—yet nevertheless chose to leave for posterity very positive testimonies regarded the positive contributions to New Spain society of their erstwhile friend and collaborator.

Motolinía's position with regard to the iconoclastic Cortés is particularly telling. Over three decades both had enjoyed friendship and close association. On multiple occasions the two had joined together in seeking ways to defend New Spain's Indians against persistent abuse perpetuated by not only other Spaniards, but also by crown officials themselves. Then, during as few key years, when Motolinía was serving as prior for the Franciscan monastery in Cuernavaca, he personally had witnessed how the courts served the interest of his friend's enemies in defaming both the contributions and the legacy of that superior man (as I explain in a previous chapter)

In 1555—a decade after Cortés's death—Motolinía would write to the young king Felipe II that Cortés, in spite of accusations to the contrary, had been a devout Christian, that "whenever he travelled, he carried a cross. It was so wonderful to see how God worked through him to topple and destroy the idols that [the Aztecs] had raised in honor of their pagan gods."[286] He defended Cortés' command of Spanish troops during the conquest, always seeking ways to minimize the number of Indian deaths. He also said a positive word about the conduct of Cortés during the 1530s in supervising the Cuernavaca Indians, never ordering them to perform services that might cause physical harm. In periods of crop failures during dry spells, Cortés had demonstrated his generosity by supplying them with corn and other foods. In spite of the continuous attempts by his enemies to discredit his name, Cortés never became embittered. On the contrary—according to the testimony of Motolinía—throughout his life Cortés set the highest standard for personal honesty: "He worked hard, continuously, to speak the truth and to be a man of his word. This, in turn, made so that the Indians under his care were the most fortunate in all of New Spain."

Motolinía's general conclusion about Cortés: "Who cared for and defended the Indians in this New World more than Cortés? ... I believe that he is the Son of Salvation who, in Heaven, wears a better crown than any of those who, in life, sought to discredit his acts. And he himself had written that in [bringing Indian multitudes into the Christian fold as a result of the] conquest of Mexico, he was a messenger of the Sacred Monarchy. It was God who chose, in our times, to enable this singular captain to perform his great acts in our Occidental lands."

The reader finds similar praise or the legacy of Cortés in the angry 1885 letters which two other important, and now aged, personages— the bishop Juan de Zumárraga and the Franciscan educator, Pedro de Gante—wrote to king, Felipe II. Both denounced the most recent Las Casas publications for its offensive distortions but—more important here—they stridently complained about Las Casas' intent to discrediting the legacy of Cortés, now decades after the latter's natural some death decades. Both wrote strong words praising Cortés' inspired leadership which had done so much, in those early post-conquest decades, to put New Spain on a stable, constructive path.

Especially relevant is the letter by Zumárraga, in which he wrote that throughout the years of the post-conquest period, Cortés always had enjoyed the "affectionate respect" of all natives. "Because he enjoyed unquestioned authority and such a high opinion among the Indians that, if it came to a necessary punishment, they would insist it come from no other hand other than his own. In the same fashion, it was for them the highest honor that they receive whatever reward only from him."[287] That in spite of the libels and criticisms constantly circulating, "I have never demonstrated my partiality to the Marqués (in spite of accusations to the contrary; ... I have held him to be a friend ... because ... he is a true and sincere servant of Your Majesty ... and every day I give special thanks to Our God that both I myself and the religious serving in these parts enjoy the good will of the Marqués in his protagonist role and instrument for the objectives of Your Majesty, that so many souls have been saved and because he has always supported the friars' efforts to convert them and in all the latters' activities to further the service of God and of Your Majesty." And all that in spite of the fact that Cortés' enemies had "blamed [him] and [demonstrated] hostility to those very objectives." This was the case of even some emissaries "sent by Your Majesty to carry out thorough and supposedly impartial investigations on your behalf."

In a similar communication send by the now elderly Friar Pedro de Gante—written in the same time frame—we find relatively the same sentiment: "Fernán Cortés, may he rest in peace, his contributions were the main cause for the spread of God's Word [among the Indians of New Spain], who embrace it with such reverence; for [the Indians] honoring to such a high degree the Church's ministers and following their guidance. He is worthy of praise for so much that we in this world deem worthy of Honor; for so much that God in heaven would praise with Glory; for surely Cortés, there, has earned both Honor and Glory."[288] Gante detailed the contributions of Cortés in the education of Indian youth and in the founding of hospitals for sick or diseased native and Spanish alike. He recounted that when Cortés would parade through their communities, accompanied by the local chiefs, they would kneel down to demonstrate their respect: for them he was the *Malinche*—which for them signified "Law Giver."

CHAPTER 12

CUERNAVACA: AGRICULTURE, MINING, CATTLE, INDUSTRY

An economic historian might describe the situation as thus: In the 35 years following the Aztecs' submission—when feudal institutions continued to predominate across the world—Cortés, ahead of his time with keen "entrepreneurial" instincts, experienced unparalleled success in founding new enterprises in Cuernavaca lands. There, he was the first "Mexican" to produce sugar, silk, and European vegetables, and to breed and raise horses, oxen, beef and dairy cattle. The "capital" necessary for those "investments" originated as "feudal" tributes received from the native communities of his Marquesado. He would pay independent taimanes for transporting these products to the outlets he had established in Mexico City, which enjoyed a near monopoly over these and other products.

As such, Cortés appears as a pre-renaissance prototype: he was a businessman skilled at grafting "capitalist" ("super structural") institutions onto a pre-existing "feudal" base.

Between 1532 and 1538—his Cuernavaca years—Cortés continued demonstrating to all that he was a man of intense passions, uncanny vision, and incessant action. Historians analyzing the stirrings of a "capitalist" spirit in the dominant countries of the time might find

MEXICO'S "GOLDEN AGE": THE FIRST HALF CENTURY

a telling example here. Cortés, free from the "rigid hierarchies" that dominated Old Spain, let loose his imagination and energies, both of which aimed at the modernization of New Spain.[289]

He guided the reconstruction of Tenochtitlán, now rebaptized Mexico City. He founded new cities for the thousands of Spaniards arriving every year at the Caribbean ports of New Spain. He was the first and most important of a new entrepreneurial group that imported hogs, wheat, grapes, silkworms, horses, mules, etc.—precisely those things that a new Spanish population would need. He provided leadership for improving the infrastructure all across New Spain: the construction of new roads, bridges, and sources of potable water. The man was a true genius in social and city planning. Nobody else, in the old country, was accomplishing even a tenth of what Cortés was achieving on America's side of the Atlantic.

Radiating energy in every direction, knew what he needed most to continue in this path of accelerated transformation of New Spain: money. And thankfully for him, the feudal institutions of the day, along with the king's (first reluctant, then willing) compliance, made that possible: the monarchy obliged his requests by granting him dozens of encomiendas all across New Spain, meaning that the Indian tributes of 24,000 vassals (or might it have been 30,000 or even 50,000?) would go directly to him.

Second, he needed to create a whole network of capable Spanish administrators, loyal to him alone, who would manage the enterprises he kept on founding.

Third, he devised the means to manufacture necessary products: smelter facilities for producing the bronze required for his ships and cannons; local facilities to manufacture gunpowder, carts, carriages, and house-construction materials. He organized whole communities to engage in the preparation of lumber, bricks, stone, and limestone (for making mortar). The list could go on.

Fourth, he organized resources to improve the road infrastructure needed to transport products from their place of origin to their site of use.

And fifth: he organized the means for transporting all those goods along the new roads. To this end he imported mares and stallions, oxen and donkeys. He created ranches to breed those animals which would carry goods to the desired locations. Within years, he would also establish facilities specializing in the manufacture of carts and wagons.

Ship building and discovery activities. A most intense passion was that of continuing to play a protagonist role in discovery and conquest activities. This objective kept him in constant movement between Cuernavaca and the three sites of his ship-building activities: Zacatula (in the current State of Jalisco), Acapulco (Guerrero), and Tehuantepec (Oaxaca). He ambitioned discovering, exploring and then claiming for his monarchs the lands bathed by the Pacific Ocean—both to the north and south of New Spain. He knew it to be a tight race: the royal houses of the Netherlands, France, England and Portugal were already committing significant monies and recruiting the best navigators for this purpose. His pursuit of this objective enjoyed the blessings of both the king and queen, who also knew that vast material awards would benefit that country whose navigator flew their banner. There was gold to be discovered. And spices—their century's premier commercial good. Or per chance there were sedentary native people—as in the Antilles, and then in Mexico and Brazil—who would become exploitable workers producing lucrative crops for new and expanding world markets.

Advancing in age, he continued to be a man of "grit," rising at dawn, indefatigable in constant movement, and passing nights in crude dwellings near the ship yards. His unceasing goal was to hasten the preparation of his ships. On a few occasions he himself boarded the command ship to spend months sailing to unnamed lands.

But he always returned to his palace-residence in Cuernavaca, which continued to be the hub of regional commerce, transportation, and communication.

Mining. Cortés, from start to finish, shared with other conquistadors the passion for gold—although there were instances when he attempted to argue otherwise. Even before the final submission of the Aztecs, he was sending out expeditions to all corners of the future New Spain in search of gold or any other metal that would prove to be either useful or profitable. Then, when the administration of the colony was firmly in his hands, he dedicated significant resources and energy to establish mining enterprises in dozens of locations. He differed little from other prominent Spaniards (including Mexico's first Viceroy, Antonio de Mendoza) in purchasing and then employing African slaves to perform the most hazardous of tasks.

The lands over which he would exercise control in and around Cuernavaca would never become important mining sites. However, in the nearby areas surrounding Taxco, he was a leader in developing mining enterprises for the extraction of silver, tin, and saltpeter.

Sugar. "Cortés' passion for planting, refining, and selling sugar—is a well-established fact."[290] In New Spain, Cortés was the first investor to plant sugarcane and then produce sugar. By 1524, he was already turning a profit selling the sugar produced in a small mill near Veracruz, a location that facilitated the commercialization of sugar to European consumers.

Little has been written about one important aspect of Cortés' sugar-producing enterprises in the Cuernavaca region: how he partnered with Indian nobles in the development of his sugar-producing enterprises. His activities to this end began at Tlaltenango; a decade later he would establish a second *ingenio* in the nearby Hacienda de Altacomulco.[291] Within his lifetime, he would develop yet other sugar-producing facilities between Oaxtepec and Cuautla—an area which would later emerge as the country's prime sugar-producing region (he also developed facilities to produce sugar in Oaxaca, Tehuantepec, and Toluca).

Inventories taken in the months after his death indicate that Cortés' sugar operations employed more than 250 slaves—whether Indian or African in origin. 165 of these worked in the Tlaltenango mill, with tasks ranging from tending boilers, household, or livery services. Another 80 belonged to families engaged in agriculture or skilled trades (we know that a quarter of these were under the age of nine, but we have no knowledge about the Marquesado's practices related to child labor.)

The mill also required the paid, daily services of over 2000 Indians coming from Cortés' encomienda communities. After 1547—that is,

CUERNAVACA: AGRICULTURE, MINING, CATTLE, INDUSTRY

a year after Hernán Cortés' death—that number dipped considerably, due to the high mortality rate caused by measles and other epidemics.[292]

Spanish employees, generally few in number, were paid generously; to all appearances the Cortés family sincerely demonstrated their gratitude for their services.

From the beginning, sugar operations relied heavily on Indian labor under the supervision of Cuernavaca chieftains. Most workers would arrive in groups headed by an Indian noble or the Cortés-appointed native governor. Marquesado payments would be made directly to the *principales* involved—not to the individual laborers.[293] It is possible that this arrangement gave rise to the Viceroyalty's accusations—about the year 1531—that Indians were working without due compensation. After that year, documentation shows conclusively that Cortés and the Marquesado administrators faithfully complied with the crown's guidelines in paying regular wages.

When functioning regularly, Cortés' sugar operations depended on the labor of specialized or semi-specialized *naboria* workers who were free agents, received regular salary, and chose to reside on the plantation grounds. The operation complied with viceroyalty guidelines that regulated salaries and work conditions according to the type and duration of the natives' required services. Owners were allowed to use encomienda Indians in planting and harvesting the cane, but not for the more dangerous tasks of servicing the mill or the sugar boilers. This would explain, at least in part, the presence of African slaves, for whom the regulations coming from the Viceroyalty did not apply. As a result—as records show—very few indigenous workers in the Marquesado's history died as a result of injuries received from working with or near the boiling cauldrons of sugar fluids.[294]

Wheat. Between 1530 and 1540 Cortés planted wheat on over 250 acres that he either owned or rented near Yautepec, and a Marquesado mill grounded the grains to flour. While some of this production was sold in Mexico City markets, most of it was used to feed his servants and slaves in the Cuernavaca area.[295]

Mulberry trees to produce silk. This was one of the least successful of Cortés' enterprises in the Cuernavaca area. As early as 1523 he obtained cuttings for the planting of mulberry bushes—the main food source for the worms that produce silk. After 1530 he raised silkworms on land near Yautepec, but with little success. After his departure for Spain in 1538, his nephew and head administrator, the Licenciado Altamirano, would plant some 32,000 mulberry trees, an effort that—again—would bear less-than-desirable results.[296]

Cattle. Cortés expended considerable time, energy, and resources in establishing ranches south of Cuernavaca for raising both *ganado mayor* (beef cattle and mules) and *menor* (goats, sheep, pigs), all of which proved to be a major source of productive wealth. He developed other cattle estancias near Toluca, Oaxaca, Tuxtla, and Mexico City. At the time of his passing, his cattle enterprises, when considered altogether, housed more than 40,000 animals—an extraordinary number for those times.

He established a relatively large cattle ranch approximately 25 km. to the southwest of Cuernavaca. An inventory taken a few years after his death describes its location as "between the two towns that the locals call Mazatepeque and Micatan"—an area later known as the sugar plantation of San Salvador Miacatlán or Mazatepec. The ranch, bordering on a shallow lake then known as Guatetelcxo, featured swampy flat areas and rich pastures on a gentle hillside. The meat produced there was primarily for feeding workers in the Taxco mines and his growing labor force in Cuernavaca, Tlaltenango, and Atlacomulco.[297]

Cotton clothing. Cortés collected a large quantity of Indian-made shirts and blankets (*mantas*) as part of the tribute payments coming from his encomienda communities. With these, he established a commercial network: woven in and around Cuernavaca, he transported them to sell in Mexico City through an elaborate system of retail outlets. His near monopoly provoked the opposition of local vendors, who would seek damages against him via the courts.[298]

As a fitting conclusion to this chapter, I copy the words of one of the region's most important historians: "Those who see Fernando

Cortés merely as symbol for the hateful right of conquest will feel only sentiments of hatred and aversion; but those who judge him according to a more serene and less passionate criterion, will also see him—in spite of his huge errors—as a gifted military leader, wise in his civil leadership, a skilled administrator, and a courageous discoverer; in other words, an extraordinary man."[299]

CHAPTER 13

AFTERMATH OF MEXICO'S "EDAD DORADA"

Franciscan historian Friar Gerónimo de Mendieta, writing in the latter decades of the Sixteenth Century, called it Mexico's "Edad Dorada" or "Golden Age," a period beginning with the submission of the Aztecs and lasting more than a half-century.[300] Few of the historical actors, and therefore even fewer historians, over the centuries, have left us concrete information about this period. Indeed, the greater part of any information that has survived comes from the pens of three Franciscan friars, important leaders in that special society: Toribio Benavente Motolonía, Joaquín de Mendieta, and Bernardino de Sahagún—each writing in a successive generation. All three survived to an old age; each wrote his respective "memorial" in the autumn of his years. According to Mendieta, the best days were those up to about 1564, the year marked by the passing of Mexico's second viceroy, Luis de Velasco. But the memorials written by all three also treat events after that year. Indeed, one can read in the texts written by Sahagún—composed a generation after that of Motolonía—about happenings near the end of the sixteenth century.

According to all three of these friar-historians, good times in New Spain were experienced across the social spectrum. First, there were the victorious Spanish soldiers. To reward their contributions, Cortés (contrary to the initial instructions of the Crown) followed the respected

Spanish tradition of granting them encomiendas and important administrative jobs which—in effect—elevated them to the status of New Spain's ruling class. On a page written by the conquistador-turned-chronist, Bernal Díaz del Castillo, one reads of his pride in accepting the honors and also the responsibilities associated with this elevated status:

> We, the true Conquistadores, freed the Indians [from the Aztecs], put them on a positive path for a new life, and we've taught them the Hold doctrine. [Then, a few years later] when all these lands were at peace, the good Religious Franciscans came to New Spain and continued their good personal example and teaching the holy doctrine, and three or four years later they were joined by other religious individuals of the Mr. Saint Domingo order who have also done the same, accomplishing good acts in teaching the holy doctrine. We the true Conquistadores—we who discovered and conquered these natives—for the start we [assisted the Fathers] in taking from the Indians their idols, assisted in having them understand the holy doctrine—and in this we encomenderos are owed the most gratitude, more than any other group: our actions in all this outweigh those of any others, including the [mendicant monks] because we the encomenderos were the first in accomplishing [these good acts] and for that alone we deserve the praises of posterity. Any Reader could learn about our contributions to the New-Spain society, especially our actions taken on behalf of promoting Christianity among the natives, and their just treatment. In conclusion, these have been our contributions—and God himself is the final judge of the honesty of my words that without us having arrived here and accomplished all that I've detailed here, the naturals of New Spain would not have enjoyed any of these positive benefits. And here, I'll leave for now this topic.[301]

Throughout his long life, Bernal Díaz took pride in his encomendero status, the role he played as a leading citizen of a well-governed colony, and his class's fair treatment of the Indians. His admirable personal qualities were not exceptional; perhaps they were typical for his time. Over his long life, he felt pride as a subject of his king, and believed that the quality of the Spanish realm was unequaled in the world. The repeated praise in his history for both the character and acts of his former Captain, Hernán Cortés, was sincere. Similarly, throughout a long life Díaz' Catholic faith remained strong; in thought and writings he honored the actions of Pope Adrian VI who, in the months immediately following the 1521 submission of the Aztecs, set the stage for the remarkable Golden Age that would follow. Readers today, although holding different values, still recognize that Díaz del Castillo's affirmation of institutions such as the encomienda, "colonialism," "conquest," and white superiority, were embraced and honored by the most respectable and honored leaders of his preterit times.[302]

It is important to underline a related fact, that the leaders of New Spain, during this period, came together in embracing not only the general views expressed by Bernal Díaz, but also the significant decisions made by Cortés, the Crown, and the Pope in the decades following the Aztecs' submission. In administration, there were the members of the Segunda Audiencia, Sebastián Ramírez de Fuenleal and Vasco de Quiroga, as well as the colony's first two viceroys, Antonio de Mendoza and Luis de Velasco. In New Spain's church, there was the colony's first bishop and archbishop, Juan de Zumárraga. Also embracing this consensus were the Franciscan leaders: Martín de Valencia, Pedro de Gante, Motolonía, Mendieta, and Sahagún. This shared consensus that would last nearly a half-century, also included the most important leaders in the Indian communities—in several chapters I have singled out the optimism and collaboration of Cuernavaca's Indian chieftains.

Undoubtedly, much of the "good" that characterizes this Golden Age is due to the wise decisions taken, in the initial months, by Hernán Cortés, the conquistador-turned-nation builder. With unequaled intuition and practicality, he imposed strict regulations to contain aberrant Spanish behavior and encourage their permanent residence; to have done otherwise would have led to the new colony's material impoverishment, similar to what was happening in the Spanish settlements across the

Antilles. Historian William Prescott writes that Cortés "devised a system of government for the motley and antagonist races, [bringing them] under a common dominion; repairing the mischiefs of war; and employing his efforts to [develop] the latent resources of the country, and to stimulate it to its highest power of production. The narrative may seem tame, [when we consider his leadership in the military conquest of the Aztecs], as bold and adventurous as those of a paladin of romance. But only by the perusal of [these accomplishments of him as civic leader] we can form adequate conception of the acute and comprehensive genius" of the man.

This was also a "golden" period for the great majority of Mexico's Indian population. In one of the Cuernavaca codices, an Indian chieftain communicates that in 1521, scores, if not hundreds, of native communities had enthusiastically sent their warriors to join with Cortés' army in order to bring about the defeat of the hated Aztecs who had tyrannized their daily lives for over a century. Then, in the next moment, hundreds of thousands of natives would come to love and emulate the monks who resided in their communities and would celebrate the opportunity to be baptized into the Catholic faith. Mexico's first and most accomplished historian, William Prescott, writes that although the Mexican natives could have "comprehended little of the dogmas . . . and vital spirit . . . of their new faith . . . the cause of humanity and good morals must have gained by the substitution of these unsullied rites for the brutal abominations of the Aztecs."[303] In this book I have quoted from those codices, as well as from pages written by Bernal Díaz, that describe what would come about over the next half-century: the natives' enthusiastic participation in choirs, *cofradías* or church-related service groups, and other religious activities. The natives also benefitted in the "institutional" sense: most were able to continue, almost uninterrupted, their former lifestyles, but now freed from the cruel imposition of their former Aztec rulers. This is because, with the exception of a period when Cortés was absent from New Spain, the colony's leaders sought ways to protect them from the type or severity of abuses that natives had suffered in other Spain-controlled American lands. There, the Spaniards—as long as this type of progressive leadership existed, the Spanish leaders respected the natives' pre-existing governmental structures according to which Indian nobles ruled over Indian masses. Furthermore, the natives benefitted from the Spaniards' teaching of new trades, introduction of new foods, mules and horses to upgrade transport systems, and other possibilities for economic advancement.

The natives' upper classes would continue residing in separate neighborhoods or nearby cities, and would come to enjoy a higher level of life-style, "each with their horses, and they're rich, mounted on jeweled saddles, and they pass through cities, towns, and along rural roads . . . accompanied by Indian servants who accompany them"—according to the chronist Bernal Díaz. [304] The lot of New Spain's common Indians would also see dramatic improvements: the Indians of "these lands have taken upon themselves in an admirable manner all the vocations that exist in Castilla among us [Spaniards], and they have their own stores where they practice those skills, and they earn their own money to feed their families, and there are fine artisans tooling gold and silver, they finely shape their pieces with the soft pounding of their hammers, they even make fine pieces for official occasions; there are, at the same time, skilled specialists making fine artistic works in precious stones and decorative paintings."

The idea of a "golden" period also pertains to the experiences of members of the Franciscan Order—as I explain in Chapter 7. For over fifty years, as long as the Evangelization Campaign remained in force, those participating monks were singled out by both the Spanish monarchy and the pope for providing leadership in the most important religious events of their century: that campaign which, over a half-century, involved the conversion of 23 million Mexican Indians into the Catholic fold. Whereas more than eight hundred Franciscan monks led the way, they were joined in this venture by hundreds of Dominicans and Augustinians. With regard to the national origins of these individuals, Spain led the way, but similarly committed individuals from a dozen other countries would also participate. For all of them, it was the calling of a lifetime; no other cause or issue would capture to such a degree both their imagination, and then their commitment.

AFTERMATH OF MEXICO'S "EDAD DORADA"

The basis for Mexico's Golden Age had been set, at the outset, by Hernán Cortés, whose wise decisions in the days following the final submission of the Aztecs—a topic treated in Chapter 3—set the stage for the peaceful decades that would follow. One such accomplishment was the demolition of the Aztec capital and then the construction, in its place, of Mexico City. There, the Spaniards constructed elegant houses and palaces, each with impressive patios. In addition, the conquistador leader had his specialists design, and his builders erect elegant public buildings, thoroughfares, and plazas. An attractive church, chapel, or monastery was constructed on almost every block. In one writing Friar Motolonía pointed out the negative side to this issue: the Indians' uncompensated labor to dismantle the buildings and sacrificial pyramids of the former Aztec capital constituted the "seventh plague" of the new Spanish colony. But learned observers give more credit to the positive side of these happenings: there would arise, within months, the outlines of what would be constructed over Tenochtitlán's foundations: a new Mexico City which admirers, both then and today, have praised as one of the most formidable cities in the world.

Was it a quirk of history that this period in Mexico coincided with Spain's own short-lived openness to "Renaissance Europe's alluring cosmopolitan character"?[305] Perhaps nowhere else in the world did two distinct races and ethnicities share governance with a greater degree of harmony.

End of the Golden Age

New Spain's Golden Age would prosper for several decades before showing signs of increasing disorder. In the following paragraphs I treat the key moments of this decline, for which the exit from the scene of New Spain's masterful first leader, Hernán Cortés, marks the first chapter.

In 1538 Cortés sailed off to Spain, never to return (he would die there six years later). His encomendero lands in the Cuernavaca region continued to function under the supervision of trusted lawyer and nephew, Diego Altamirano. Present were only a few dozen Spanish employees, whose functions ranged from domestic servants to enterprise supervisors.

In 1547, a petition was filed with the Viceroyalty by "The Indians of Cuernavaca against Juan de Carasa, about the personal services required of them by [Cortés,] the Marqués del Valle."[306] With the master absent, activity had declined year by year at the family's palace-residence, just a block away from Cuernavaca's central plaza. Upon leaving for Spain, the Marqués had insisted that his two youngest male children accompany him. But the Marquesa stayed. Speaking Spanish with only a half-dozen maids in waiting, she continued supervising the education and activities of her daughters. Weekly masses with the Indians' noble families were discontinued. No longer did the sounds of the blacksmith, the horse trainers, or the shouts of the livery attendants fill the air. A stillness set in. Only infrequently did the delegation of natives arrive to fill the firewood bin and larder. Many of the Indian women formerly attending the mansion's large ovens had been dismissed. Only a fraction of the former household staff—that before had numbered hundreds—still remained. Yet some daily rituals continued. Less and less frequently did the slaves, assigned to domestic labors, catch a glimpse of the Marquesa venturing outside. And the consensus was: all this was for the better, what with her cantankerous personality. Truth be told: the natural joy of the servants quickly vanished when she came into the room to complain of corporal ailments and the noncompliance of the Indians assigned to carry out the manor's daily tasks.

Years before, the Marqués, when present, had been the center of things; it was he who had supervised the many attendants in carrying out a multitude of orders.

But now, in his absence, silence filled the void. The palace-mansion—in the minds of the *principales* residing nearby—was slipping into irrelevance. From the street a passer-by would seldom hear the bark of orders from a Spanish administrator. It was almost as if the Marqués' family had ceased to exist.

Yet the multiple enterprises associated with the Marquesado continued to function. Routine now ruled, not the Marqués' orders for yet another task to be undertaken. Indian subjects continued paying their quarterly or semi-yearly tributes, but that was to administrators and those transactions never involved the isolated residents in the *palacio*. Kilometers away, the huge crews of Indians and slaves continued complying with their daily tasks of tilling the sugar-cane fields, stoking fires underneath the vats of boiling sugar-brine, whipping the backs of the oxen turning the mill, or corralling the animals at the Marqués' mule, mare, hog, and horse ranches. All had become routine.

Some Indians did have complaints, and a sympathetic Franciscan friar stationed in the Cuernavaca monastery helped them to write the petition and deliver it to the appropriate authorities in Mexico City. The main issue was that the Spanish foreman's insistence that they continue to supply the firewood to be burned in the palace kitchen and the necessary meat, chicken, and vegetables for the Marquesa's table. Is it that Cortés, before his departure for Spain, had made no provision to pay the natives for these regular services?

In short, the functionaries of the Marquesado continued using the personal services of the Indians in the customary way. This, in spite of the fact that the new public authority now insisted that Spaniards throughout New Spain pay encomendero Indians for any labor "freely and voluntarily offered." The lawsuit called the Marquesado to account, that they "had demonstrated their unwillingness to comply with the Audiencia's orders by making just payments to the Indians."

There was, in addition, a less serious complaint, which had to do with whether a small public roadside shrine—*un humilladero*.[307] The Indians argued that it was not "a public work," and therefore they were not obligated to provide uncompensated labor. Furthermore, they requested that Court authorities prohibit the Spaniards from imprisoning Indians who protested the lack of pay. The document is silent about what might have ensued as a result of these complaints.

Things—obviously—had changed considerably in comparison to the New Spain society immediately following the Aztec's definitive defeat. The colony now had a strong, functioning government with authority to enforce labor laws protecting the Indians. The latter were not the passive, child-like beings that the Spanish had first encountered. Now, in contrast to only a few decades before, they were well informed of their rights and how New Spain's legal system functioned. They knew that if they were to find a translator and present in written form a legitimate complaint about an encomendero's abuse, then sympathetic ears, beginning with the Viceroy himself, would give their case a sympathetic examination and, if warranted, would act to pressure any offending Spaniard to comply with the existing laws.[308]

After the first two decades, there was also evident a change in the previously cordial relationship that the Marqués had enjoyed with his former allies, the Franciscan friars. Cortés' trusted friends in that order, with whom decades before he had initiated the continent-wide evangelization campaign, had aged. Some had retired, a few had died, yet others had moved to new locations to continue offering their pastoral services. The new generation of Franciscan monks embraced a different sense of social justice. Most ignored what, decades before, had been the close collaboration of colony's most powerful encomendero, Cortés, with the now-crusty Franciscan veterans. The Marquesado's supervisory team, perhaps surprised,

> pinpointed the friars of San Francisco as instigators of the disconformity and new flood of complaints on the part of the local Indians. . . . . . They knew that it had been a religious figure in the community's monastery who had induced the Indians to refuse complying [with the Marquesado's order] to labor in maintaining the *humilladero* and other similar tasks such as providing firewood or other services for the Marqués' household, without adequate compensation. And if the Marquesado staff continued insisting, then the friar himself would carry to the appropriate authorities a written accusation.[309]

In October 1547, in Sevilla, Spain, the aged and now sickly Hernan Cortés would dictate and then attach his signature to a new document: a last will and testament. Anxious about his approaching death, he had written this document with the desire of settling earthly concerns "with the will of God—who shortly will take me away." He instructed that the executors of his estate fulfil certain conditions so that he might die "with a calmed soul, and with total assurance that I am at peace with my conscience."[310]

Guilt? Qualms about his past acts? Doubts about his final legacy with regard to his accomplishments over the past fifty-some years in New Spain? Some historians have proposed that this, atypical, aspect of his multifaceted personality might have surfaced after long conversations months earlier with the man who would emerge for posterity as his eternal antagonist, the Dominican friar Bartolomé de las Casas.

On the 2nd of December, 1547, Hernán Cortés, the first Marqués del Valle, died in Castilleja de la Cuesta, near Sevilla.

The powerful Marqués del Valle was no more. From beyond the grave, the words from that testament instructed the executors of his estate:

> That within a reasonable time they expend the necessary resources and time in order to learn specifically: whether, in any moment of my life and activities [in New Spain] I might have taken for my own use any land or property that legitimately belonged to any other person—these might be instances or cases—or complaints about the same—that I might not have been aware of. I therefore order [that the executors of my estate] return said property or make due compensation, whether it be to the person affected or his heirs or descendants. The executors should seek out any other type of complaint against either my person or my estate and make—in their judgement—due compensation to the injured party.

On the first day of October, 1549, the *principales* of Cuernavaca (don Hernando, don Gabriel, don Pedro, don Toribio y Estevan), representing themselves and the other property owners and *naturales* from that community and the surrounding villages, met with the lawyer Diego Altamirano, who was the legal representative of the new Marqués del Valle, Martín Cortés. The issue at hand was to carry out provisions concerning Cuernavaca's Indian community, as per the instructions left by the deceased Hernán Cortés in his last will and testament. A Franciscan friar was present to translate and defend the Indians' interests. The judge, Doctor Bartolomé Melgarejo, had made the trip from Mexico City to preside over this unique meeting, to mediate over all negotiations having to do with fulfilling the conditions of the last will and testament, and to certify all the signatures that were to be affixed to the resulting accord.[311]

All present were aware of the animosities that had existed between the officials of the Marquesado and the Indians over the previous few years. In the preceding days, all the individuals named above had heard testimonies and had examined relevant documentation with regard to the first Marqués' activities during the previous 28 years. At issue were the region's three sugar mills, a wheat mill, the different terrains used for the planting of sugarcane and other agricultural products, the construction of corrals and buildings for the Marqués' ranches, and the construction, and then use, of various *acequias* (fresh-water sources). Those assembled discussed Don Hernando's allegation that the first Marqués had confiscated from his family the land parcel where the palace now stood.[312] A few of the *principales* from the neighboring communities of Acatequipaque and Xivtepeque made similar claims (again, it is difficult if not impossible to identify these places with currently existing places). The last paragraphs of the final agreement between the parties involved read:

> After having explained to all present the different clauses of the negotiated agreement [between the Marquesado and] the Indians, all participated in an open discussion about its implications. They called attention to its positive features. All understood that the written agreement placed obligations on all parties signing it, that the agreement had to do with both the private property of some present, and the community property of the larger community, its neighborhoods, and its surrounding areas. The lawyer Altamirano, representing the new marqués, congratulated all for having come to this friendly resolution to long-standing complaints. He promised that the new marqués and his heirs would fulfill all the promises and commitments in said agreement, and in particular those having to do with

property and rent levels. Both parties [—the representatives of the Marquesado and the assembly of Indians] accepted the agreement in full knowledge that it was now sanctioned by the state as official and that all of its conditions would be legally binding on all parties. . . . All parties agreed that the agreement was fair and good.

The Deadly Epidemics

Two years before Cortés' definitive exit, all corners of Mexico were struck by the first of several horrific plagues that would cause the death of perhaps 85% of the Indian population before the end of the century.[313] Unfortunately we totally lack accounts of the inevitable suffering of individuals from the Indian communities—from those who perished but also from the terrified survivors.[314] We can assume that Indian survivors were daily witnesses to the extreme suffering ending in the premature death of children, spouses, family members and neighbors. They must have reacted in ways similar to Europeans, two centuries earlier, before the Black Death epidemic of 1348. Indeed, perhaps the perspectives and emotions of Indian leaders became even more "twisted," given their 85% death rate between 1545 and 1600, in comparison to only 50% for all of Europe—or 85% for the people of Florence (between 1348-49).

The Florentine writer, Giovanni Boccaccio, has left a personal testimony of how the massive number of plague deaths caused "mental alterations" in thousands of the survivors.[315] Some individuals—according to his account, "shut themselves up" to avoid any contact with the afflicted; and yet others did the opposite, "drinking too much" and giving themselves over to carnal pleasures. . . . Almost no one cared for his neighbor . . . [many] became careless in their ways." One can predict that a whole generation of responsible leaders disappeared, leaving in their place a new set whose characters had been formed in those terrible times. Historians have speculated that on account of that terrible epidemic, Europe's somewhat noble "medieval period" came crashing to a close, only to be replaced by "The Dark Ages." One could suppose that much the same applies equally to the latter half of Mexico's sixteenth century.

Whereas Mendiota hardly touched upon the topic of the social and psychological sufferings experienced by New Spain's Indians, the Franciscan historians provide many clues as to how those same horrid events affected both themselves and their brethren. From beginning to end, the evangelization project, such as it came to be played out in New Spain, had involved an intimate association between the friars and the native population. Their role was that of both "corporeal as well as spiritual physicians" of the Indians."[316] Mendieta, writing toward the end of the 1570s—after serving three years as guardian of the monastery of Xochimilco, realized that the two epidemic waves over a decade had claimed the lives of nearly a million Indian victims! The future of New Spain assumed for him bleak proportions: "Once the Indians are exterminated, I do not know what is going to happen in this land except that the Spaniards will then rob and kill each other." This pessimistic assessment carried a providential meaning of apocalyptical gloom—well in tune with his medieval imagination: "doubtless our God is filling up the throne-chairs of Heaven with Indians, so as soon to end the world." These words suggest the deep depression which was to color the views and imagination of all the mendicant monks from that time forward.

Other Causes

In addition to the periodic epidemics, commencing toward the end of the 1540s, Friar Mendieta listed other—related—causes for the Golden Age coming to a close. It was inevitable that, with the passing of the decades, older, trusted Indian leaders in the communities would retire; and the massive number of deaths due to the successive epidemics, only hastened this leadership turn-over. Unfortunately, the new generation of Indian nobles, in general, demonstrated less commitment to the tasks of effective leadership; many were more prone to corruption, debauchery, and dishonorable behavior. especially blame this new generation of Indian leaders for the failure of the friars' pet projects such as the Colegio de Santa Cruz and the hospitals for treating native indigents.

A third cause was much related: the proliferation of corrupt practices which undermined the colony's institutions.

Mendieta also singled out for strong criticism the new class of Spanish leaders who were replacing the tried and trusted conquistadors. Many demonstrated less respectful for New Spain's regulations having to do with public conduct and official responsibility. A result was the breakdown of law and order in many cities. Similarly troubling was the increasing number of cases where Spanish land or mine owners sought ways to sidestep official regulations, force the Indians to perform longer and longer hours of labor, and abuse them in any way possible. In Mendiota's words, "ranchers and encomenderos would pay thugs to rob Indians' possessions, to kidnap their small children—especially the girls—; these thugs, with near total impunity, would descend upon an unsuspecting Indian community in the middle of the night to do their evil—and not a one has been punished by the colony's government."[317]

Yet a further, troubling cause for the disintegration of social peace was the rise of a new mestizo class. These individuals, the sons and daughters of marriages uniting Spanish conquistadors or settlers with Indian women, were the object of scorn of both the pure-blooded Spaniards and many in the Indian communities. Existing laws and traditions excluded them from inheritance and prohibited their acceptance into many sectors of the workforce. An added slap was their ostracism by the Crown, the Church, and the Viceregal administration, none of which recognized their legal status nor provided for their employment. The mestizos' exclusion from proper society motivated rebellious behavior. With nothing to lose, they rebelled. Many demonstrated destructive behavior, with New Spain society as their primary target.

The Eroding Situation of the Encomenderos

New Spain's encomenderos, always supported by Cortés and his New Spain leadership team, found themselves in a tenuous situation from beginning to end; after twenty-five years most were thoroughly demoralized; a few had reached the point of rebellion. The same could be said about Cortés himself, whom the king had forcibly detained in Spain during his final six years, and who would die in 1547 as a frustrated and de-spirited man.

We remember that even before the final surrender of the Aztecs, Cortés had been concerned about the difficult decision he would have to make about rewarding his soldiers once victory was assured. He as well as his soldiers were familiar with the age-old Spanish tradition of awarding encomiendas to such individuals for their exceptional service; his soldiers had every expectation that their captain would follow suit. But the encomienda? On the one hand, he had reservations: he thoroughly abhorred the Indian genocide resulting from the way the encomienda had been established only fifteen short years before in the Antilles. But—on the other hand—he knew that if he did not reward his brave warriors with significant benefits, then he could possibly face their armed rebellion. It was also an issue, important to him, of fulfilling a commitment to them: at that important Veracruz gathering in 1521, only weeks after arriving on Mexican shores, he won their vote to usurp army leadership from the former commander (and his former employer) the Cuban governor Velázquez, only upon promising a fair distribution of "booty" or prizes if and when a final victory over the still-unknown Indian empire were achieved. Now, in those weeks preceding the final victory, he harbored a related preoccupation: his form of "reward" had to induce their continued and hopefully permanent presence in New Spain to guarantee social stability and protect the new colony against revolt attempts by dissident groups among the soon-to-be-defeated enemy. In short, he had few options. It took little time for him to become converted to the encomienda in principle, but in modified form. His solution—as explained in an earlier chapter—was to impose upon every new encomienda recipient a strict set of regulations "to guarantee the friendship and good will of the Indians"—as he had written in his letter to the king—regulations that would go way beyond those stipulated in the Laws of Burgos written up by crown officials a decade before.[318] This is what he did.

During the following decades and years, the leadership in New Spain would come to embrace the system for which Cortés—over and above, and at times in direct contradiction to Crown mandates—had laid the foundation. Policies emanating from Spain during this time period were first inspired by ignorance and at times bad judgement. Then, beginning in the 1530s, when the royalty came increasingly under the influence of Dominican friar Bartolomé de las Casas, new edicts and policies revealed the royalty's contradictory position: its commitment to terminate all encomiendas while at the same time recognizing that institution's fundamental role in providing stability to New Spain society. During the first half-century, New Spain's leaders, with diverse backgrounds, would regard favorably Cortés' earliest decisions and accept his assistance in their continuing governance. These individuals included the first two viceroys, the members of the Segunda Audiencia, the Franciscan leadership of the impressive evangelization campaign, and the Indian chieftains who would continue governing their respective communities. All these came together in embracing in good faith the tenants of the New Spain system whose economic base was the class of regulated, compliant encomenderos.

In the beginning, the king had tolerated Cortés' disregard for royal instructions against the encomienda system because he and his young queen had the good sense of recognizing the pragmatism, and possibly genius, of the conquistador-leader now transformed into civic leader. That being said, the royal couple continued embracing an established state policy of choosing as colonial governors from a group of eligible contenders that excluded military leaders. And in spite of their admiration for some of the doings of Cortés, they could not put aside his act of insubordination—that of distributing encomiendas when court officials had instructed him not to do so. Added to all that the troubling idiosyncrasies of Cortés' character, but especially his unequaled ability to create enemies! With all this in mind, they crafted a Janus-like policy in their treatment of Cortés, which they would continue to practice up to, and even after his death: while bestowing honor upon honor upon the man in the public forum, through secret channels they would work to undermine his prestige and undo many of the policies he had enacted. How should posterity judge all this? On the one hand, moralists might condemn their deviousness as an early—and obvious—instance of inmoral "Maquiavellian" politics (*avant la lettre*).

But, on the other, should posterity consider their long-term objective as a positive march for humanity, that is to say, their uncanny intuition of the need for an enlightened leadership to recognize the need for going beyond defects of an anachronistic feudalism—such as the New Spain system based on the encomienda entailed, and usher into reality a better alternative?

It was inevitable that the monarchy's politics became an issue of heated public debate. First, the crown ordered New Spain officials to "declare null and void" any newly granted encomiendas. Second, it decreed that any encomienda that Cortés had created during those first formative months would cease to exist after the death of a conquistador-turned-encomendero's first heir. And meanwhile, the Crown would issue an ever-greater number of measures aimed at controlling encomenderos' actions, especially with regard to abuses of the native population. Eventually, the encomienda would cease to exist; in its stead, court officials would place Indian communities directly under the Crown in a centralized Crown-controlled system of Indian government called the *corregimiento*. These measures pleased few in New Spain. As the number of corregimientos grew, so did the colonial bureaucracy; increasing on par were appointments based on cronyism and instances of corruption. Indians found themselves less and less protected. And the number of angry ex-encomenderos multiplied, with predictable results.

As years extended into decades, this time-bomb continued ticking: each encomendero knew that his family fortune would disappear in the near future. His immediate heir might live in comfort, inheriting what he himself had legitimately earned. But there would come a time when the family legacy and the material benefits derived from his family's governance over their encomienda would end. This would probably result in the sudden fall in social standing, and very possibly the financial ruin, of his descendants. The mere thought of this happening in the not-too-distant future was, for many encomenderos, too horrifying to contemplate. Cortés, initially, had made promises to pressure the Crown on their behalf, to bring about a correction for what they considered an injustice. Yet the encomenderos knew that the remedy was beyond his powers, that only the king could grant to any ex-soldier the permanent right to encomienda governance. As the years passed by, they continued to support their former captain and celebrated his prominence in the new society that had come to exist. On a few occasions, when Indian rebellions threatened, they had rallied to his call to arms, eager to serve yet one more time under his command. They closely followed Cortés' successive, yet failed, attempts to convince the officials serving the Crown, that it was in New Spain's interest to *permanently* empower their class of encomenderos which Cortés himself had created. It was predictable: as his frustrations increased, theirs did also.

Crown activism in this direction hardened with its issue of the New Laws of 1542, which ordered viceregal officials to implement giant measures aimed at expediting the elimination of the encomienda. Anger exploded. In Peru, encomenderos and other locals took arms in revolt; with their bloody rebellion aimed at gaining full independence from Spanish rule. A more prudent leadership in Mexico simply refused to implement those unpopular policies. Informed citizens everywhere interpreted the New Laws to be the Crown's unscrupulous means to achieve a "transfer of power;" to "usurp the lands that had been awarded in compensation for the conquistadors' remarkable service." Whispered rumors became public shouts: the king was seizing from them what they considered their "rightful" privilege. Detractors viewed all this as one more example of emperor Carlos's incompetence and incapacity for leadership. In short order he would renounce his reign and pass the governance of the monarchy on to his child son. Regardless of the supposed "idealism" inspiring them, detractors saw the New Laws as one more tactic chosen by a desperate monarch, at the twilight of his reign, to finance yet one more il-conceived military venture in the European theater.[319]

The individuals exercising leadership in New Spain saw all this as yet one more explanation for their diminishing faith in the ruling capacity of the Crown and the court. Cynicism, already rampant, corroded motivations everywhere. Among leaders as well as followers, self-interest trumped civic duty. Civility progressively disappeared. Even the now-elderly Franciscan leaders began to despair. Their optimism and sense of rarified mission waned. Problems in every domain of public life now outweighed invigored action.

Tensions Affecting the Franciscan Order

The Franciscan monk-historian Mendiota would indicate yet different causes contributing to the "waning" of New Spain's Golden Age.[320] He labeled some "interior" causes—meaning that they had to do with the growing discord within the Franciscan Order itself; and others he called "exterior"—where tensions confronting the mendicant orders would increase due to their waning stature vis-à-vis the Crown and before the increasing power exercised by the bishops and the secular clergy in New Spain.

The "inner" conflicts were several. First, there were the ongoing disputes—especially with the Dominicans, regarding the original Franciscan practice of baptizing natives "at their request," and without their first having assimilated basic Church doctrine; many Franciscans, especially those having arrived at New Spain in recent years, viewed with alarm the undisputable evidence that many among the older generation of Indians accepting Catholic vows years before, continued practicing worship to older, pre-conquest idols. The "inner disputes" also touched upon practical considerations related to the Colegio for natives at Tlateloco and other sites of Indian education: within Franciscan ranks there emerged a significant division between those who held, and those who denied, whether the most studious of males from Indian families succeeded in learning sufficient Latin in order to qualify for acceptance as full priests. Then, there emerged yet another split separating those Franciscans who believed that their "civilizing" activities aimed at the total assimilation of Indians into a new bi-racial and multi-ethnic society, and those who argued, on the basis of an emerging "mystical theology," that their mission was to construct and administer "on the eve of the end of the world, a terrestrial paradise where the whole race of [Mexican Indians] would be consecrated to evangelical poverty."[321] And lastly, Mendieta was becoming increasingly alarmed over the diminished enthusiasm of the newer generation of monks, that included individuals less committed than their forerunners to a life of poverty, selfless service, and moral incorruptibility.

Then there were the "external" reasons fueling Mendieta's increasing sense of alarm. Since the beginning of the Spanish presence there had simmered a rivalry between the mendicant monks and the regular clergy. During their first decades in New Spain, the authority of the Franciscans was nearly uncontested in their direction of the evangelization campaign and in their supervision of the different Indian communities. This had been due—in large part—to the high regard held by the young king for Franciscan priorities, and the special powers granted in 1522 to the original Franciscan twelve by Pope Adrian VI. In addition, during this early period, they enjoyed the firm support from other influential individuals who proudly supported them: Cortés, the first two viceroys, archbishop Zumárraga, and other civic and religious leaders—and with the implicit support of the Emperor Charles V. But things would change considerably, due at least to two reasons. First, the exit of Cortés from the scene: he had left for Spain in 1542, never to return to New Spain; he would die in Spain of natural causes in 1547. And second, the exit of Emperor Charles V from power in the year 1556: tired and frustrated by his endless, and largely unsuccessful campaigns against the rising tide of Protestantism, that was the year he retired from public life and handed over the realms of both Spain and the Holy Roman Empire to his less-capable son, Felipe II.

The times were changing, and what was happening all across Europe came to effect life and governance in New Spain: the "lenient Catholicism of the Renaissance [disappeared before] the rigid orthodoxy of the Church after the Council of Trent" (1545-63). "The urbane Catholicism of Erasmus gave way to the militant orthodoxy of Ignacious Loyola."[322] Undoubtedly, much of this interlinked with the increasing religious intolerance all across Europe.[323] The reputation and writings of the humanist religious thinker, Erasmus of Rotterdam, came under increasing attack. Humanist-minded individuals were purged from power circles. Throughout his reigns, the Inquisition expanded its fierce pursuit of heretics and witches; Jesuit priests began usurping religious authority in religious circles. As Northern Europe's embrace of Martin

Luther's doctrines deepened, Felipe II continued not only his father's belligerent confrontations, but also the path of defeat. All this, in its turn, accompanied dramatic changes adopted by the Crown in the administration of its up-to-then most prosperous colony, New Spain.

With the new reign, Phillip's advisors favored the existence of a single Church of the Indies and saw as an anomaly the concentration of power which the mendicants had exercised in episcopal, governmental, and economic matters during the reign of his father, the emperor Charles. The plan adopted by Phillip and his advisors was to diminish and then terminate the authority that the Franciscan monks had held over the New Spain Church since the military defeat of the Aztecs.

The Belvís Friars came under attack, with official support waning for their baptismal procedures and charitable activities. Their close association with Cortés could have only worsened tensions—both in New Spain and in the mother country. Accusations going back to 1529 were renewed—that the long-range plan of the Franciscans was to expel all Spaniards and take control of New Spain's government.[324] This and other accusations, although not acted upon at the time, provided motivation for increased scrutiny by their opponents.

Different contemporaneous accounts call attention to the revered status which the Franciscan monks, even a half-century after the initiation of the evangelization campaign, continued to enjoy among the Indians. Predictably, this constituted yet one more factor accounting for the increasing opposition of Spaniards who stood to gain if the friars' zeal in protecting Indians against exploitative labor conditions were to lessen. These factors caused a great increase in the animosity [on the part of those Spaniards whose lives were characterized by] disorder and unchristian conduct, who launched infamous libel suits and many ceased to attend masses. Their goal was to sideline the friars, get the government in their own hands, and themselves enjoy all the things that the friars had struggled to deprive them of."[325]

The new king's advisors lost few opportunities to encourage the growth of the episcopacy and the secular clergy at the expense of the mendicants[326]—which led, inevitably, to growing disputes between mendicant orders and the secular Church. In the early 1570s Mendieta, acting as spokesman for the Franciscans, wrote a letter to Juan de Ovando, soon to be installed as President of the Council of the Indies, to express the growing concerns of his order. Heading the list were their disagreements with the newly arrived bishops who were jealous not only of the special ecumenical powers enjoyed by the mendicant monks, but also of the favor the Franciscan monks enjoyed in New Spain's Indian communities. One can imagine that the Franciscans wished to hold on, and sometimes jealously, to both their doctrinal leadership, but also their prestige and control over Indian communities. Even their special "theology," as it evolved, reflected this preference: their theological beliefs placed themselves at the center. As penniless and selfless friars, they were those "servants of God" especially selected to lead the Indian church—in keeping with their interpretation of certain scriptural passages—that elevated to a holy status its resemblance to a Primitive Apostolic Church –which had dominated before the emergence of the post-Constantine Church presided over by the bishops. They argued that "the natives should have a separate ecclesiastical regime administered by penniless and selfless friars, for avaricious bishops and worldly secular priests would only demoralize the faith of the neophytes."[327]

The Mexican Church councils of 1555, 1565, and 1585 were dominated by the bishops, which gradually but remorselessly enforced the decree of the Council of Trent that undermined the jurisdiction which mendicant friars had previously monopolized over Indian communities. Over the 1560s the secular clergy increased in numbers, training, and religious favor. In 1574 a cedula placed the mendicants under viceregal and diocesan supervision. A new cedula of 1583 gave the secular clergy preferential treatment in several important administrative matters. "By the time the century ended, the friars were left with but two alternatives: to retire peacefully . . . or to transfer their missionary enthusiasm to the colonial frontiers among the less civilized natives."[328]

Las Casas Demoralizes the Franciscans

By the early 1530s, it became apparent that many of the policies emanating from Spain with regard to any and all aspects of Indian life in Spain's American domains revealed the growing influence over Crown policies of the Dominican monk Bartolomé Las Casas (I discuss this in greater detail in Appendix A.) This was especially apparent in the Crown's continued dissatisfaction with Cortés' early distribution to his soldiers of lands held as encomiendas. After his 1536 visit to Mexico, Las Casas added to the animosity already existing between Dominicans and Franciscans by denouncing the latters' practice of prioritizing the Indians' mass conversions. Whereas the Franciscans took immense pride in achieving the willing and enthusiastic baptism of millions of natives, Las Casas and other Dominicans insisted on individual converts thoroughly mastering church doctrine before any conversion was possible. Then, there were the "New Laws of 1542," which New Spain leaders had the good sense to literally "ignore"—knowing that their enactment would bring about a rebellion similar to what did happen in Peru. Jump to the 1550s, when Las Casas criticized the conquistadors' previous actions by arguing that Indian bloodshed could have been avoided if peaceful means had been employed to Christianize the Indians. Beginning in 1553, his views turned even more "radical." He began to condemn all individuals and parties who had either performed or facilitated the conquests of the previous half-century: the pope, the emperor, the nobles advising the Crown and formulating colonial policies, viceregal authorities, and the whole colonial bureaucracy. New Spain's leaders, with the exception of the Dominicans, condemned these views which, they correctly interpreted, was a frontal attack on the product of their shared life's work: the construction of Mexico in the post-conquest period.

Three of the now-aged Franciscans—Motolinía, Zumárraga, and Pedro de Gante—were so incensed that they took pen in hand to write angry letters to the new king, Felipe II.[329] All denounced Las Casas for his distortions and intellectual dishonesty. In a previous chapter I quote those letters to document their anger over how Las Casas intentionally distorted the legacy of Cortés—who had died in the mid-1540s—by creating a false "black legend" about his acts and completely ignoring the conquistador's inspired early leadership that had done so much to put New Spain on a stable, constructive path.

How to explain these angry reactions felt independently by three of New Spain's foremost leaders, now in the autumn of their years? One can suppose that each was alarmed by the growing chaos of New Spain society; each must have suffered over the disappearance of so many Indian friends due to the ravages of periodic epidemics. Each must have been saddened by the growing attacks coming from bishops and secular clergy who now outnumbered the mendicant friars. And lastly, they must have experienced increasing disillusionment upon seeing signs of that new monarch, Felipe II, was bent upon terminating the favoritism which the previous emperor, his father Carlos V, had (inconsistently) shown for the Franciscan monks.

But signs continued to emanate from the home country that revealed the vacillation of Crown policies affecting the American colonies. The Valladolid debates of 1555 suggested that the Crown's policies in a number of areas—especially with regard to the encomienda and Indian slavery—were still open for debate. Meaning that of prime importance was the question of who, among scores of individuals, would "win the ear" of an indecisive monarch and his principal advisors. And—given the recent publications of Las Casas and their broad circulation—the Franciscan friars must have been frightened to death that that their own previous influence was waning. That what they considered their positive, God-sanctioned, legacy in the construction of Mexico's unique bi-racial society, would at best be "blackened," and worse would be excised from the history books to be read by future generations.

This went hand-in-hand with the Franciscans' realization that a gap was widening between their own positive evaluation of their lives' work in New Spain and what others—primarily the Spanish Church and monarchy—were more and more likely to condemn.

The conflicts between New Spain's secular and mendicant leaders would only deepen in subsequent decades. By the mid 1580s a new figure would emerge as the spokesperson for the beleaguered Franciscans, Friar Bernardino de Sahagún—whom posterity would recognize as Mexico's first, and perhaps most important, "anthropologist" on account of the significant body of Indian testimonies and texts that he would compile and transcribe over decades as a "resident scholar" at the Tlateloco school for Indian youth. Sahagún, three decades younger than the Franciscan initiators of the evangelization campaign—Valencia, de Gante, Motolonía, etc.—had been born in Spain in 1499, induced into the Franciscan order at an early age, and completed the passage to New Spain in 1529. In 1884, the greater part of his intellectual labors were already in the past when he, a vigorous and intellectually sharp octogenarian, took the initiative of writing at least three important letters to Crown officials, in which he ably defended the order's sixty years of service and their notable accomplishments.[330]

Over the next three years conflicts within the New Spain church became open and heated; there was a growing division between the "seraphics" and the secular clergy; that is, between the Franciscans' veteran "criollos" and the growing number of "peninsulares."[331] Events were precipitated by the arrival of one of the latter, Fray Alonso Ponce, who had recently been named to supervise Church affairs across New Spain. The lines of conflict were clear: the Franciscans, supported by the viceroy, were pitted against the growing number of bishops and secular priests who were emerging dominant in the New Spain church; an additional factor was the growing opposition to the friars on the part of land and mine owners who stood to gain if the previous protections afforded to the Indian communities were to be lessened. The seraphics accused the secular church officials of wanting to condemn sixty years of Franciscan work in New Spain; the latter, supported by the king and Spain's church hierarchy, accused the former of maneuvering to create an Indian church in Mexico that would be independent of any Spanish authority.

Tensions continued to mount as the years advanced. Franciscan authority over Indians and their communities would be increasingly undermined, and newly arrived Dominicans and Jesuits supplanted Franciscans in important positions. Franciscans complained that members of those other two religious orders enjoyed a more collaborative relationship with New Spain's landed elite—many of whom were succeeding in extracting greater profits through the increase in tributes and uncompensated Indian labor. And, unfortunately, their hardened perspectives were more and more favored by the king, Emperor Carlos' ultra-devout son Felipe II. At the beginning of the 1570s, the acting archbishop of Mexico, don Pedro Moya de Contreras, wrote a letter to the young King arguing for the repeal of what Pope Adriano had granted some half-century before: the Franciscans' broad ecumenical powers. Commentators have speculated that Contreras' major complaint was the "mysterious" attraction that the Franciscans exercised over the Indians, which made it difficult for other Spaniards to enter into their communities.[332] With less Franciscan presence, encomenderos, mine owners, and other speculators operated with greater freedom; the strict state guidelines previously enacted to protect the Indians from abuses of any type were removed. Finally—in 1572—Pope Gregory XIII, obviously under pressure from the Spanish emperor, retracted the "broad apostolic powers" previously granted to the Franciscans, and brought to an end that orders' influence over Indian communities and the Mexican church.[333]

Other commentators have suggested that for all the above reasons the *entusiasmo religioso* of Franciscan leadership, after several decades of energetic labors and successes, disappeared.[334] A major cause was undoubtedly their anguish upon witnessing close up the extreme suffering of Indian communities smitten by the now-frequent waves of epidemics. They were saddened upon witnessing the rise of racist attitudes and an increasingly rigid class system that favored "pure-blooded" creoles over natives, mixed-blood mestizos, and mulattos.[335] Previous enthusiasm over the emergence of a racially hybrid society had faded before fearful accusations about a supposed *contaminación moral*.[336] And among their own ranks, Franciscan veterans anguished upon seeing that so many of the new generation of mendicant monks lacked the humanist values and idealistic sense of mission of the original Belvís friars.

There is so much we don't know for sure—and never will.

For all the above reasons, New Spain—the future Mexico—stumbled into a new, and no longer glorious, historical epoch.

APPENDIX A

BARTOLOMÉ DE LAS CASAS AND THE DISPUTES BETWEEN FRANCISCANS AND DOMINICANS

No informed reader harbors the minimum doubt as to the immense contributions of Bartolomé de Las Casas in Latin America's struggles for justice. However, the great majority of existing histories and biographies treating this historical personage totally ignore, or skip over, the conflictive relationship he had with the Belvís Franciscan friars—and por ende Hernán Cortés—who made such an outstanding contribution to New Spain in the first decades following the submission of the Aztecs to Spanish authority. The world still awaits an honest history of the events leading up to that situation—events I only allude to in the abbreviated paragraphs below.

Las Casas shared an early history with Cortés: both were from families of Spain's minor nobility, both were *secundones*—that is, they would not inherit any title or family land in their native Spain; both coursed university studies, and both possessed strong Christian values. And then, both had remarkably similar beginnings in the newly-discovered Americas. Although Las Casas was Cortés' senior by about eleven years, both arrived at the Antilles at about the same time: 1502 vs. 1504. Both received "repartimientos" of natives—first in Hispaniola, then in Cuba. That is to say, both participated in the accepted practice of the time, that in exchange for the "gift" of Indian laborers, they would provide them with a Christian education. The record is abundantly clear that both were horrified by what they—independently—observed: the extremely cruel treatment afforded to the natives by almost all the other Spaniards in that Brave New World, which led to a rapid disappearance of native people.

At the same time, the Spanish crown was similarly outraged by what was happening. Years earlier, the Catholic Kings, Fernando and Isabel, had accepted the charge from the Pope to evangelize and protect the native peoples that their discoverers had and would encounter. In her earliest instructions, Queen Isabela urged a humane treatment for the natives, her new subjects. She was naively convinced that the Indians would learn from the Spaniards' "good example" about not only the True Faith, but also about those behaviors conducive to a decent and proper life. Was she aware that the very opposite to her admonition was then occurring?—that the great majority of the Spaniards already occupying *Las islas* exercised few moral scruples in their insatiable thirst for instant wealth, and that no laws or authority could stop them: they imposed inhuman conditions on the native workers assigned to them in order to extract gold and pearls. Their acts had a nefarious result: due to forced labor and starvation, the natives died at an appalling rate; many committed suicide. And then, almost immediately, a new class of traders arose who realized that profits could be made from raiding other Caribbean islands in order to enslave and then sell fresh native bodies as human fodder for the Spaniards' mines. For the latter, simple economics ruled: the cost to purchase new Indian workers was less than the food to feed the old.

The searing sermon by the Dominican Fray Antonio Montesinos in 1511 pushed courtly authorities back in Spain to take new steps for the natives' protection. Thus began nearly a century of philosophical, and then legal, deliberations about the nature and status of the New World's native population.

In 1512, King Fernando issued new ordinances that incorporated the perspectives of the recently deceased Queen for the protection of the natives. According to "natural law" (which was held to be a derivation of "divine law"), he held the natives to be "rational beings" (unlike the "infidel" Moors) and, as such, were intellectually capable of receiving instruction in the True Faith. Consequently, American Indians had a right to liberty and humanitarian treatment and, unless they rebelled, should not be reduced to slavery. But Fernando, and therefore The Crown, also embraced the views that natives were "naturally lazy with a tendency to given in to their vices," and that they had a tendency to forget rapidly what they once learned. One remedy—in their thinking—was that the Indians, if living "close to the residences or towns occupied by the Spanish," would have *converrssacion contynua* to facilitate their learning of things relevant to faith and civilization.

However, it was one thing to publish a set of idealistic laws and another to have the crude soldiers and *conquistadores* obey them. In actual fact, King Fernando had little interest—indeed, he had little actual power (being that he exercised only the authority of regent, after the death of his wife the Castilian queen)—to enforce those ordinances governing those Castilian subjects. And so, the Spaniards in the Antilles continued their inhumane practices, paying no heed to those stricter laws. Little in *Las islas* changed; the Spaniards' savage exploitation of the natives continued apace.

Meanwhile Las Casas, exercising the rights and responsibilities as yet one more Spanish encomendero (in charge of several dozen Indian slaves) in *Las islas,* was entering a new chapter of his life. Arriving in 1502, he had been granted an encomienda—a share of native laborers—for his labors to extract gold and farm. He was ordained a priest in 1507, but he didn't celebrate his first mass until 1510. About then he began spending time with Dominican—and later Franciscan—priests who only then were beginning to arrive. In 1512 he, as *capellán*—or chaplain—accompanied Diego Velazquez in the conquest of Cuba, and—like Hernán Cortés—received his second *repartimiento* of native laborers. But it was the fortuitous visit of Friar Antonio Montesinos and then the Franciscans which finally caused Las Casas to leave behind his previous life and totally embrace the new cause of defending the natives against Spanish abuses.

APPENDIX A: BARTOLOMÉ DE LAS CASAS AND THE DISPUTES BETWEEN FRANCISCANS AND DOMINICANS

In 1515 Las Casas traveled to Spain with that expressed purpose. In a personal meeting, his arguments reputedly impressed the aged King Fernando, who died shortly thereafter. The next year Las Casas, with "extraordinary political talent,"[337] impressed the regent, Cardinal Cisneros, who issued orders to abolish all encomiendas in the new territories and free the Indians. Cisneros ordered that the natives be consolidated in agricultural communities dependent upon the Crown and under the guidance of Spanish colonists.

The next year Las Casas returned to *Las islas*, eager to see firsthand the implementation of these new guidelines. He now carried the presumptuous, but in reality totally meaningless, title of "Universal Protector of all the Indians." In the succeeding months, his own life was threatened as he witnessed the total failure of the Crown's plan: everywhere the colonists violently resisted, realizing that the abolition of the encomienda would mean their economic ruin. They mocked Las Casas and his utopian views of the natives; they successfully argued before the Crown's representatives that the Indians were incapable of self-government and, if freed from their servitude to the Spaniards, they would flee to the mountains causing economic ruin in the Crown's new colonies.

In 1517 Las Casas returned to Spain and, through talent and persistence, became an advisor on Indian affairs before the Flemish advisors of the new young king, Carlos I (of Spain, within months crowned Carlos V of the Holy Roman Empire). He wrote his first memorial, "Remedio para La Tierra Firme," in which he continued to argue for the suppression of the encomienda.

The king and his new-world advisors closely followed the skewed advice of Las Casas in formulating and then promulgating the Burgos Laws, which signaled a short infatuation of policy makers with what they, within a decade, would regard as utopian fantasies. Las Casas argued, and then won official approval, for his Indian baptismal program that would occur without the prior military domination of new Indian groups (the Belvís Franciscans, a decade later, would also fall under the persuasive power of this myth). The idealistic Las Casas had a plan that he and a select group would be peacefully received by an indigenous community of a yet-to-be-explored region of northern

South America, would guide the latter in adapting his norms about proper dress and personal conduct, and they would joyfully convert to Catholicism.

In 1520 he finally won Crown approval to carry out this plan near the coast of today's Venezuela. But while making preparations in Las Islas, his problems began almost immediately: ruthless Spanish slave traders had provoked a violent rebellion among the natives in the very coastal areas designated for Las Casas' colonies, and now the Audiencia was at the point of sending soldiers to punish and "pacify" the rebellious natives. Other obstacles to Las Casas' venture presented themselves: colonial authorities, in addition to the Caribbean settlers, saw his venture as a threat to their continued ownership of encomiendas, and did everything possible to obstruct Las Casas' plans. The farmers he recruited also proved to be unwilling: once arriving in the New World, several turned their backs on the settlement venture to join the raiders seeking new native slaves; an even greater number jumped at the opportunity to sail off toward Florida on a crazy—and, as it resulted, tragic—venture at conquest. All that could go wrong did; within two years, Las Casas witnessed the total failure of this project. Shortly thereafter he took the fateful decision of entering into the Dominican Order, and spent the next ten years in monastic study.

In 1521 Cortés, leading his combined Spanish-Mexican army to win the submission of the Aztecs, earned near-universal acclaim across both Spain and Europe. Those capable of a "just estimate" realized that his "remarkable [conquest] placed him on a level with the greatest captains of his age"—in the words of the brilliant historian, William Prescott.[338]

But this was not the opinion of Casas, still morally bruised by his failed settlement project. He continued to harbor the same negative impressions of Cortés that he had formed during their earlier Santo Domingo and Cuban years: ambitious, arrogant, solicitous of his superiors' favor, immersed in personal and legal problems resulting from a lust for women. But the future bishop also must have seen a "crafty," but nevertheless very competent, individual who had become relatively wealthy through his economic activities and who enjoyed widespread respect on account of his administrative skills as mayor of the Cuban town which had served as the colony's nerve center. Las Casas, in his subsequent writings, would continually credit Cortés' military successes to undeserved luck and "calculated ruthlessness." Whereas few if any European opinion leaders questioned the legitimacy of that conquest, Las Casas did. He denounced as "inhumane" the procedures practiced by the Cortés-led conquistador army with regard to the Indians encountered, that—according to his somewhat distorted perspective—after inviting peaceful submission Cortés' men brutally executed Indian leaders. This means that Las Casas chose to ignore the fact that Cortés was able to win to his side the great majority of New Spain's subjugated Indian groups by promising them liberation from the frightful domination of the Aztecs. Nor did he grant great importance to the fact that through that conquest Cortés and the Spanish *conquistadores* set into motion the process of evangelization which, in effect, "saved the souls" of millions of New Spain Indians and brought them into the folds of "The True Religion."

Between 1524 and 1540 Las Casas made two, and possibly three, trips to New Spain. New Spain's foremost public figures celebrated (after 1528 or so) Cortés' wise leadership in bringing into existence (again in the words of Prescott) a fairly harmonious "system of government for the motley and antagonist races ... now first brought under a common dominion; repairing the mischiefs of war; and employing his efforts to detect the latent resources of the country, and to stimulate it to its highest power of production."[339] Did Las Casas not witness the peaceful relations then enjoyed by the Indians and the efficient means whereby the latter benefited from the measures taken by the administration of Viceroy Mendoza to protect their interests? It therefore remains a mystery as to why, subsequently, Las Casas would choose to exaggerate the problems and condemn that system which until then had offered a positive model for inter-racial governance. There is further evidence of Las Casas' intellectual dishonesty: the harmonious relations which he must have observed as existing between the Spanish regime and the Indian masses in New Spain probably served as the model for the measures he would later urge for a colonial governance protecting the rights and welfare of the indigenous masses, as described in his own publication—published decades later—*Del único modo de atraer a todas las gentes a la religión verdadera.*[340]

Meanwhile, Las Casas continued to exercise immense influence over the policies emanating from Spain with regard to the treatment of the American Indians. Under his influence, the New Laws of 1541 were written and then propagated. The Crown's attempt to implement those laws ignited a civil war in Peru that almost culminated in a successful rebellion against Spanish rule. In Mexico, more serene individuals were in power; while the latter saw the idealism behind those New Laws, they also realized that the implementation of those laws would cause undue social turbulence.

The aura of "saintliness" conferred on Las Casas by the historical establishment might lead current-day readers to ignore the controversies surrounding him during his lifetime. Many of these had to do with his association with the Dominican Order. (Ethelia Ruiz Medrano in *Gobierno y Sociedad*, 48ff, provides information for the following two paragraphs).

In spite of the Crown's good intentions, its decisions and acts continued to fuel the inhuman treatment of American natives by ruthless and greedy Spanish soldiers and settlers. Finally, in about 1528, its leadership in Spain sought remedy for their terrible blunder of empowering Nuño de Guzmán and his cronies of *La primera audiencia*. Such is the origin of the Segunda Audiencia, constituted by outstanding individuals—foremost among them were Fuenreal and Vasco de Quiroga—who would succeed in reestablishing an upright governing authority in New Spain. The Segunda Audiencia members recognized the wisdom and worthiness of the Belvís Franciscan monks, who in previous months had commenced their evangelization campaign. And the Franciscans, in turn, became their firm and reliable advisors. The Segunda Audiencia also elevated the status of Juan de Zumárraga—the Franciscan who until then had occupied the relatively powerless position of "Protector de los Indios" –and permitted the Franciscans to exercise broad authority over aspects of Indian life all across New Spain.

APPENDIX A: BARTOLOMÉ DE LAS CASAS AND THE DISPUTES BETWEEN FRANCISCANS AND DOMINICANS

The Dominican Order, during this period, did not enjoy equal favor, on the contrary. In 1531 the Segunda Audiencia strongly reacted against the "excessively ornate" convent being constructed by the Dominicans, that required excessive labor on the part of the indigenous workers. Then, two years later, the Audiencia, as well as the Franciscan monks, rejected outright the opinion of the leading Dominican in New Spain, Friar Domingo de Betanzos, that the Spaniards should exercise complete control over Indian society on account of the latters' "irrationality." Even the queen became involved: she criticized the implicit linkages of the Dominicans with the First Audiencia, and expressed "her surprise" that the Dominicans had challenged the authority of the Crown's representatives.

Within a year New Spain's first viceroy, Antonio de Mendoza, would begin his governance.[341] A strong and principled leader, he quickly realized the wisdom of supporting the Franciscans in their saintly activities on behalf of New Spain's native communities—as would Vasco de Quiroga. All these figures came to constitute the solid leadership cadre of New Spain over the next few decades—those who oversaw the region during its "Golden Age."

At times, these leaders had cause to heatedly oppose the Dominican influence—as they would later oppose Las Casas' positions and views. At this time the dispute between the Dominicans and the Franciscans was open and public.

Yet Crown politics were changing. A hidden topic—to my knowledge untreated by historians—is the decline of Franciscan influence in the Spanish court. Would the Crown's new preoccupations with the chaotic politics in post-conquest Peru (beginning about a decade after its initiation in New Spain) be a reflection or result of this? Because in Peru the Franciscans played almost no role in the early Spanish leadership—in stark contrast to their preponderant role in Mexico.

Very apparent in the 1530s was the immense influence that Las Casas, and the Dominicans, began to exercise over the policies emanating from the Crown with regard to the Americas. Under their influence, the Crown mandated the "New Laws of 1541," which brought the American colonies to the verge of rebellion.

In 1533 the Spanish court reversed its previous position and allowed Indian slavery in the Americas—a position supported by the Dominicans and heatedly opposed by the Franciscans. This change provoked fervid activity among almost all religious leaders in the Americas who organized, wrote letters, and delivered sermons condemning the new position.

After his 1536 visit to Mexico to meet with church officials, Las Casas added to the animosity already existing between Dominicans and Franciscans by denouncing the latters' practice of prioritizing the Indians' mass conversions. Whereas the latter took immense pride in achieving the willing and enthusiastic baptism of millions of natives, Las Casas and other Dominicans insisted on individual converts thoroughly mastering church doctrine before any conversion was possible. Las Casas would misrepresent what was happening in New Spain by insisting on "the futility of these forced conversions, by which it is proposed in a few days to wean men from the idolatry which they had been taught to reverence from the cradle." In Las Casas's words, "The only way of doing this is by long, assiduous, and faithful preaching, until the heathen shall gather some ideas of the true nature of the Deity and of the doctrines they are to embrace."[342]

Another decade would pass. The Dominicans, following Las Casas' lead, continued their silent war with the Franciscans. Friar Gerónimo de Mendieta's long *Historia eclesiástica indiana*[343]—written in about 1600—provides a written testament to the bitterness of this feud between the two orders.

Much has been made by subsequent historians about the 1550 convocation in Valladolid, called by the Emperor Carlos, in order for specialists to advise the Council of the Indias about key colonial issues—and especially the debates between "Indian defender," Bartolomé de las Casas, and philosopher Ginés de Sepúlveda, arguing in favor of slavery for the less-that-human American natives. Whereas many idealistic readers have embraced the general tenants of Las Casas's positions in those debates, the perspective of American historian Louis Hanke is more persuasive: "To practical *conquistadores* and administrators ... Las Casas' reiteration [of Spaniards' need to forego military measures to Christianize] Indians by peaceful means alone must have seemed dangerous nonsense."[344] But it must also be emphasized that the arguments Sepúlveda also carried little weight with at least two of the most notable opponents of Las Casas who were present: the ex-conquistador and future chronist, Bernal Díaz del Castillo and the universally revered Vasco de Quiroga.[345]

Another decade would pass. The new king Felipe II (son of Carlos) was not blind to the fact that principled individuals heading New Spain's colonial government deeply resented Las Casas' court influence, and that the implementation policies recommended by him had caused nothing but turbulence. Nor could he have been pleased by Las Casas's writings that condemned both Spanish colonial policy and governance in the Americas.

Las Casas, in his writings, continued expressing his extreme position with regard to Spain's American conquests, the treatment of the natives, and that country's post-conquest reconstruction. He condemned everyone involved: the pope, the emperor, the nobles advising the Crown and formulating colonial policies, viceregal authorities, and the whole colonial bureaucracy. He publicly denounced "the sins of many and the blindness of others."[346] This explains, at least in part, why the Crown acted to ban the publication or circulation of all writings by the Dominican leader.

Refusing to be silenced, Las Casas found foreign presses willing to publish his *Brevísima Historia*, written in 1553—some seven after Cortés' natural death—which was translated and published across Europe. Almost all clerics in New Spain, with the exception of the Dominicans, condemned this last work which, they correctly interpreted, was a frontal attack on the product of their shared life work: the construction of Mexico in the post-conquest period.

Rivals of both Spain and its activist king, in addition to the newly potent Protestants, found in this work the justification for their fierce ideological war against not only Spain, but also the Catholic Church.

The now aged Franciscans—Motolinía, Zumárraga, and Pedro de Gante, among others—who had been key leaders in the foundation of New Spain's post-conquest society, were so incensed by Las Casas' publications that they took pen in hand to write angry letters to the new king, Felipe II. All denounced the most recent Las Casas publication for its offensive distortions. They were all angered over Las Casas's lies, that were aimed at discrediting the legacy of Hernán Cortés and they wrote strong words praising Cortés for his inspired early leadership that had done so much to put New Spain on a stable, constructive path. On a more personal level, they saw in Las Casas's words a frontal attack on their shared life work: the construction of Mexico in the post-conquest period.

In 1555 Motolinía coined a long letter to King Felipe II to express the collective sentiments of the New Spain Franciscans, whom he now headed. He lambasted Las Casas for his intellectual dishonesty, and felt it necessary to correct the historical record: "[I felt it necessary that] your majesty ... be informed of the truth and might know about the services that Captain don Hernando Cortés and his companions have performed, and the great loyalty, surely worthy of reward, that New Spain has always shown your majesty. And your majesty may be sure that the Indians of New Spain are well treated, and that they pay less tribute and tax than the farmers of old Spain .... May God pardon Las Casas for so gravely dishonoring and defaming, so terribly insulting and affronting the ... communities [of New Spain] and the Spanish nation, its prince, councils, and all those who administer justice in your majesty's name in these realms. ... I was unhappy with the royal council for allowing such a thing to be printed. . ."[347]

Also surviving into old age, the ex-archbishop Juan de Zumárraga wrote essentially the same: Throughout the years of the post-conquest period, Cortés always had enjoyed the "affectionate respect" of all natives. "Because he enjoyed unquestioned authority and such a high opinion among the Indians that, if it came to a necessary punishment, they would insist it come from no other hand other than his own. In the same fashion, it was for them the highest honor that they receive whatever reward only from him."[348] That in spite of the libels and criticisms constantly circulating, "I have never demonstrated my partiality to the Marqués (in spite of accusations to the contrary; ... I have held him to be a friend ... because ... he is a true and sincere servant of Your Majesty ... and every day I give special thanks to Our God that both I myself and the religious serving in these parts enjoy the good will of the Marqués in his protagonist role and instrument for the objectives of Your Majesty, that so many souls have been saved and because he has always supported the friars' efforts to convert them and in all the latters' activities to further the service of God and of Your Majesty." And all that in spite of the fact that he has been "blamed and judged hostile to those very objectives" –even by some of the best emissaries sent by Your Majesty to carry out thorough and supposedly impartial investigations on your behalf."

The octogenarian Friar Pedro de Gante echoed the same sentiment. In 1588, some 40 years after Cortés' death and toward the end of his own life, de Gante wrote to King Phillip II to present a summary of his life-long services in New Spain in baptizing and educating the region's native population. "Fernán Cortés, may he rest in peace, his contributions were the main cause for the spread of God's Word [among the Indians of New Spain], who embrace it with such reverence; for [the Indians] honoring to such a high degree the Church's ministers and following their guidance. He is worthy of praise for so much that we in this world deem worthy of Honor; for so much that God in heaven would praise with Glory; for surely Cortés, there, has earned both Honor and Glory."[349] He detailed the contributions of Cortés in the education of Indian youth and in the founding of hospitals for sick or diseased native and Spanish alike. He recounted that when Cortés would parade through their communities, accompanied by the local chiefs, they would kneel down to demonstrate their respect: for them he was the *Malinche*—which for them signified "Law Giver."

This unambiguous, posthumous praise, coming from trustworthy, venerable witnesses, is bound to confuse the contemporary reader.

On the one hand, if new readers choose to respect the opinions of Cortés' contemporaries, then they will disregard or grant relatively little importance to much of the surviving documentation that paints Cortés in a negative light.

But on the other hand, informed contemporary readers know of the immense contribution of Las Casas in defending the status of the American Indians. But does this mean that we should join Las Casas in condemning not only Cortés (and his apologist, the chronist Díaz del Castillo), but also Zumárraga, Mendoza, Motolinía, de Gante, Martín de Valencia, Mendieta, Vasco de Quiroga, the Emperor Carlos, Pope Adriano VI, etc.? Does this mean our recognition that the fiery Dominican propagandist, in spite of his questionable methods, embraced a higher, and more worthy objective? That he was right to condemn all those participants, who were the most important historical actors of his age? Following the lead of Las Casas, should we condemn what this latter group of New Spain leaders, during the first decades of the post-conquest period attempted and accomplished, and should we hold in contempt rather than praise what Father Mendieta believed was Mexico's "Golden Age"?

May the debate continue.

APPENDIX B

TLAXCALA: THE IDEAL INDIAN COMMUNITY AND CHARLES GIBSON

The case of Tlaxcala offers exemplary examples in at least three domains. First, no other New-Spain community or region in the sixteenth century can compare with its high level of organization and cultural attainments. Second, the state, during this "golden age" of postconquest history, produced New Spain's most notable and accomplished intellectual, writer and historian, the mestizo Diego Muñoz Camargo. And third, the accomplished American historian, Charles Gibson, has written an exhaustively documented account of Tlaxcala's exceptional history: *Tlaxcala in the Sixteenth Century.*

An abundance of information from the immediate postconquest years have been preserved for both Tlaxcala and Cuernavaca. Whereas historian Charles Gibson focused his exceptional research energies to study the former, no individualof comparable research skills has yet appearedto do the same for Cuernavaca. To all appearances, the Spaniards found in those two cities and surrounding areas the most organized, respected, and trustworthy nobles in all of New Spain. There, Spanish leaders formed strong alliances with Indian leaders; politico-religious transformation was most complete, welcomed, and consequential. In those two cities, the Spanish left fairly intact the pre-existing Indian hierarches –in their role of local governors and administrators—with the least interference for the next two centuries.

Whether due to implicit policies enacted by Cortés or overt policies enforced by the viceroyalty, the influx of Spanish settlers, merchants, or adventurers was minimal. Relevant to both Tlaxcala and Cuernavaca, historian James Lockhart writes: "indigenous structures and patterns survived the conquest on a much more massive scale and for a longer period of time than had seemed the case when we had to judge by the reports of Spaniards alone. [Impressive in these two cases was the Indians'] social and cultural autonomy."[350]

Out of Tlaxcala came the early Indian historian, Diego Muñoz Camargo. He was a "notable mestizo tlaxqueño,"[351] born in the first years of the post-conquest period, and his writings expound about many issues relevant to the economy, daily life, society, and politics of his home state of Tlaxcala. The chronicler Juan de Torquemada (*Monarquía Indiana*), residing in that city, incorporated many of Muñoz's writings into his own detailed accounts. Other chroniclers also provide information about Tlaxcala, whereas they are relatively silent about Cuernavaca. In the text of this book, I have speculated that this "silence" is due to Cortes's efforts to "reserve" Cuernavaca for his own purposes. Because other early Spanish leaders were involved with the grandiose promise of Tlaxcala, they appreciated the formidable role of that community in the Spaniards' dual projects: the conquest of the Aztecs and the construction of a "utopian" post-conquest society. For that reason, one historian argues that, in reference to Mexico, we should talk not so much about a "conquest," rather a successful *rebelión generalizada* that was led by the Spanish-Tlaxcala alliance.[352]

If the Spanish—but especially the Franciscan friars—experienced difficulties in overcoming undesirable practices and forms of worship inherited from the years of Aztec domination, American historian Charles Gibson (perhaps the best historian writing in English about these matters in *Tlaxcala in the Sixteenth Century*) explains that this was not their experience in Tlaxcala. There, Christian baptism, doctrines and practices experienced an enthusiastic, "thorough [and] striking reception" (37). There, between 1536 and 1537, an astounding 500 Indian youth studied and then assisted the friars in "close collaboration" (40).

APPENDIX B: TLAXCALA: THE IDEAL INDIAN COMMUNITY AND CHARLES GIBSON

But it took a harsh measure to achieve such a seamless alliance: at the orders of Cortés, the Spaniards executed four local chieftains in 1527—an "extraordinary measure, unprecedented and never repeated" (35). Writings by Motolinía (*Memoriales*) and Muñoz Camargo (*Historia de Tlaxcala*) explain some details: Spanish authorities offered exemplary punishment to one chieftain (perhaps figuratively representing other *principales*) who, although accepting Christian baptism, dogmatically continued his idol worship. This, in spite of the exhortations of his own Christianized son, Cristobal, whom he ended up killing.

This was also the case with regard to governance. Gibson provides an excellent explanation about how the Spaniards, during the first decades of the post-conquest period, adopted "practical and economical" measures to partner with the local chieftains. Good thing, because if the friars' evangelization campaign was well organized and administered, Spanish civic authorities were "disorganized," and generally sought "spoil for private gain." (64). Cortés and other "good" Spanish administrators wisely decided to leave relatively intact the pre-existing Indian hierarchies in the inferior levels of administration, which adopted well to new Spanish guidelines. This included the system of justice, policing (*aguaciles*), collection of tributes, and neighborhood institutions (mayordomos de la ciudad), that were almost entirely (at least in Tlaxcala) administered by natives (107-21). "Hispanization [never reached] the lowest rung of government." (122) As such, Indian governance "preserved local order, handled all details of tribute extractments; it came rarely into conflict with Spanish authority. . . Nothing in Spanish government after 1530 or before the last quarter of the century prevented them from creating a vigorous, prosperous society." (123, 145)

Perhaps special to New-Spain colonization was its "remarkable . . . concern for the welfare of native peoples. [They stressed the successful] incorporation of local native governments as in Spanish municipalities. . . . [I]n the 1530s and 1540s conditions were favorable for the peaceful Indian adoption of Spanish ways" (191). By midcentury, the Spaniards and the Indians governed in "a remarkably full accord." (192)

Posterity has to applaud Gibson's thorough search through dozens of archives between Mexico, Spain, and France in order to locate the multiple documents that made possible this ground-breaking work. His Appendices V and VI provide long lists of those natives participating in "cabecera successions" or serving as governors for each of Tlaxcala's four cabecera-cities between the years 1519 and 1608!

Historians will logically question why similar research has not been done for other Mexican cities or regions.

Largely missing in Gibson's important study of the post-conquest period of Tlaxcala is an acknowledgement that much of the positive that occurred was due to the solid governance and inspired decisions of New Spain's first leader, Hernán Cortés. (I find no special merit in the biography that Gibson believes to be the best in existence about Cortés, Henry R. Wagner's *The Rise of Fernando Cortés*—Los Angeles: Fox & The Cortes Society, 1944). In Chapter 4 I call attention to Gibson's similarly excellent research, published in a different book, *The Aztecs Under Spanish Rule*, in which he occasionally refers to Cortés's actions in the communities near Mexico City during that same time period. However Gibson, similar to several other historians writing in the twentieth century, would not have known about the letters to the king sent by Friars Motolinía, de Gante and Zumárraga and that by the indigenous nobles of the town of Huejotzingo. Nor would he have read the not-yet-"rediscovered" *códices* of Cuernavaca. If Gibson had been familiar with these documents, his perspectives about Cortés might have been more positive.

Early on, Tlaxcala was placed directly under crown control. This was in contrast to Cuernavaca and a few other urban areas in today's State of Morelos, which Cortés had requested from the king and had received in the form of encomiendas that became part of his Marquesado. I surmise that, beginning with his military excursion to Oaxtepec and Cuernavaca in 1520 (as I recount in Chapter One), he realized the exceptional nature of the Indian societies existing there—which were only comparable to what he had found earlier in Tlaxcala. The superior nature of the Tlaxcalan nobles became known to everybody in his army—including the king's representatives incorporated into its ranks. But few others in his army knew about the special visit of the Cuernavaca chieftains to meet with him later that same year (as I present in Chapter Two).

APPENDIX C

CÓDICES DE CUERNAVACA

The 1992 work of Juan Dubernard ed. y introd., *Códices de Cuernavaca y unos títulos de sus pueblos* (Morelos: Gobierno del Estado 1991) is perhaps the most important of those funded by *the Mexican government in commemoration of the 500th anniversary of Columbus's 1492 voyage of discovery*. It contains photo copies, along with Spanish translations, of several documents written in Náhuatl during the first half of the sixteenth century. Untold, for the majority of the included documents, are the respective histories of who, how, and when they were removed from Mexico and carried to Europe. Several had remained totally undetected for hundreds of years in the National Library of Paris!

Unfortunately, the readers of this valuable book will be inconvenienced by the lack of an index and the confusing page numbers, as listed in the Contents pages at the book's end. It measures 23 X 31 cm. It's 396 pages present 1. full-page photos of 30+ documents in Náhuatl, maps, and a few historical buildings; 2. translations into Spanish of most of those texts; 3. and short pages of "commentary," written by Mr. Chauveau himself, about several of the documents.

The origin of these documents? Many of them were dictated in Náhuatl by Indian chieftains to scribes writing in Náhuatl. Upon reading them, it becomes apparent that these chieftains were operating under the direct orders of none other than Hernán Cortés, their encomendero, with whom they enjoyed a constructive relationship in governing their respective communities.

How original are these documents? Gibson, in *Tlaxcala*, provides perhaps the most complete catalogue of written materials surviving from that city and time period. (The world awaits a researcher willing to expend the same time, energy and care to treat the documentary history of Cuernavaca as Gibson has done for Tlaxcala!). He mentions several sixteenth-century documents written in Náhuatl which—in my opinion—do not resemble what I have encountered in the Dubernard book. The chieftains of Cuernavaca wrote these documents in their somewhat simple and naïve language during the same time period that their peers in Tlaxcala were recording, in Náhuatl, the minutes of the cabildo meetings that they themselves were running!

Interestingly, Robert Haskett, in *Indigenous Rulers*, p. 4, suggests that there exists a "rich documentary record [consisting of] thousands of pages" written in Náhuatl by Cuernavaca Indian nobles and currently held in the Hospital de Jesús section of Mexico's Archivo General de la Nación. So, the obvious, nagging, question: how exceptional are the documents included in the Chauveau book? Any possible answer must come from future researchers.

For the purposes of this book, I have occupied myself with only the first four documents, all dating from the sixteenth century, whose Náhuatl originals were discovered (and still exist) in the Biblioteca Nacional de París (pp. 29-214). Of interest to other scholars are documents, also included (along with photo-copies and Spanish translations) from the Colección Juan Dubernard Chauveau; from La Diócesis de Cuernavaca; from the Archivo de Indias, Sevilla; and from the Archivo General de la Nación, México.

About the documents stored in Paris: even though the Spanish translation of the most important one has been known to assiduous researchers over the past century, most historians and the public at large ignore its existence.

In several of these documents the native chieftains, dictating to scribes writing in Náhuatl, explain their primary motivation: their new authority, the Marqués Hernán Cortés, guides them in the (Spanish)

APPENDIX C: CÓDICES DE CUERNAVACA

process measuring the boundaries of land plots, dictating those measurements to scribes, and therefore creating official "documents" that are to be stored in a public archive. These chieftains accomplish precisely these operations, and the documents they create are precisely those surviving to this day. They perform these labors in order that (in their own words, which supposedly copy those of Cortés): "no Spaniard in the future will succeed in usurping said lands" from either them or their descendants. Several of the documents name as their primary "relator" the long-serving governor of Cuernavaca (serving from 1529 to 1574—p. 377), don Toribio de San Martín Cortés.

In the introductory essay, editor Chauveau (confusingly) explains how these documents have survived to the present day. 1. Some of them existed "hasta poco después de 1855 en el archivo de la Comuna de la ciudad de Cuernavaca." (29). 2. Sometime at the beginning of the eighteenth century, Lorenzo Boturini united a disperse collection of said documents and donated them to the Biblioteca Nacional de París. 3. Sometime toward the end of that century, the Cuernavaca priest José Antonio Pichardo (born in 1748 to two Indian parents and distinguished as linguist and historian, translated a few of these documents to Spanish (and we assume that he deposited them in the archives of the Comuna de la ciudad de Cuernavaca. 5. In about 1885 it was reported that those documents were no longer to be found in said archives. 6. In about 1891 a Spanish translation of said document was published by the historian Fredericka Martin. 7. In 1901 a Monseñor Plancarte y Navarrete again published a Spanish copy. 8. Other publications subsequently followed, but without wide dissemination. 9. Chauveau—around 1985—obtained Náhuatl copies, in addition to a Spanish translation of one of them, from the same archive where they are currently stored. 10. In 1973 Riley, *Fernando Cortes* (pp. 100-109), published a Spanish translation in the form of an appendix, although he gave little consideration to it in the body of his study.

The years given by the different documents create confusions for the contemporary reader. Several state an impossible year for their production: 1574. We remember that Hernán Cortés had died some thirty years earlier. My explanation for this date: it could be the year that the long-time governor of Cuernavaca, Don Toribio de San Martin, submitted them to the archives of the city's *Comuna*. I therefore assume that this, the surviving document, might be based on a previously existing one written in the 1530s—that is, during the decade when Cortés was present in and around Cuernavaca. Some of its details suggest to me that its authors had, fresh in their minds, the terrible disorder that their communities had suffered at the hands of Cortés' enemies while the latter was engaged in the expedition to Honduras between 1524 and 1526. Also referred to are abuses the natives had suffered at the hands of some religious personnel—events that probably occurred after the natural death of Hernán Cortés in 1846.

For the purposes of this book, I refer to the four initial documents—those directly relevant to Cuernavaca—with capital letters, A, B, C, and D. The editor provides photos of the Náhuatl originals (as well as the surviving Spanish translation for document A), and then provides legible scripts for all in both Náhuatl and his own Spanish translations.

The first two documents present different Spanish translations of the same Náhuatl document, for which translators have bestowed the Spanish title, "Códice de la fundación de Cuernavaca, llamado también Municipal" (A: pp. 23-90; B: pp. 93-101), a work known to scholars since the eighteenth century. The author identifies himself as Dn. Toribio de San Martín Cortés. I speculate that Don Toribio wrote it in about the year 1575, and then saw its preservation in the Comuna (archives) of the city (might Cortés have preserved a copy in his own archives?).

Before this 1992 printing, Documents C and D had never before been either published or translated to Spanish. The title given for document C is "Códice de la reedificación de Cuernavaca" (pp. 103-144). Author: Indian noble Don Joseph Axayacátzin. Translation to Spanish: J. A. Pichardo—early in the twentieth century. On the basis of its contents, I would retitle it: "Indian noble measures and provides detailed descriptions for the outer limits of Cuernavaca's Five Barrios—as ordered (and in moments personally accompanied) by 'el Señor Marqués don Fernando Francisco Cortés Marqués del Valle.'"

The title given for document D is "Títulos del pueblo de Quauhxomulco" (pp. 159-83). The version in Náhuatl was corrected by Chauveau, and Pichardo produced the Spanish translation. The present-day name of this town is San Buenaventura Coajomulco, which is located in the Municipio of Huitzilac. This town—about four kilometers to the north of his palace in Cuernavaca—is probably where Cortés had constructed a small house which he used for rest and recreation. The document is complicated: the author, again the Gran Noble, Don José Axayacátzin, writes that he was present when Cortés instructed him and the other Indian leaders to measure the said lands and create a document recording his descriptions—in Náhuatl—of those boundaries. He quotes Cortés explaining the reason for this document: so that "las tierras que ninguna persona se lo coja, ni se lo quite esta tierra que les doy por todo tiempo del mundo." Don José's boundary-measurement activities might have taken place in the decade of the 1530s.

BIBLIOGRAPHY

Acosta, Joseph de. Prol. Edmundo O'Gorman. *Vida religiosa y civil de los indios (Historia natural y moral de los Indios)*. México: UNAM, 1995.

Adorno, Rolena. "Bernal Díaz del Castillo: Soldier, Eyewitness, Polemicist," in Bernal Díaz del Castillo, *The History of the Conquest of New Spain . . .*, ed. & introd. David Carrasco. Alberquerque: New Mexico University Press, 2008.

Aguilar de la Parra, Octavio. "Hernán Cortés y la Hacienda de San Antonio Atlacomulco," in Patronato, *Cortés*, Pp.155-66.

Alberro, Solange. "El imperial Colegio de Santa Cruz y las aves de rapiña: Una modesta contribución a la microfísica del poder a mediados del siglo XVI," en *Historia Mexicana*, lxiv, no. 1. Mexico: El Colegio de México, 2014. Pp. 7-63.

Albornoz, Rodrigo de. "[Letter] to Charles V, December 15, 1525," in Simpson, *The Encomienda*. Pp. 205-13.

Alva Ixtlilxóchitl, Fernando de. Introd. Edmundo O'Gorman. *Obras históricas: . . . Historia de la Nación Chichimeca*. México: UNAM, 1985. Vol. II.

Angulo, Jorge & Chappie Angulo. *El museo cuauhnahuac en el Palacio de Cortés: Recopilación histórico-arqueológica del proceso de cambio en el Edo. De Morelos*. México: Instituto Nacional de Antropología e Historia, 1979.

Anderson, Arthur J. O., Frances Berdan & James Lockhart. Trans. & introd. Ronald W. Langacker. "29. Letter of the Council of Huejotzingo to the King, 1560," in *Beyond the Codices: The Nahua View of Colonial Mexico*. Berkeley & Los Angeles: Univ. of California Press, 1976. Pp. 176-90.

Antín, Felipe. *Vida y muerte de la inquisición en México*. Mexico: Posada, 1973.

Archivo General de la Nación, Secretaria de Gobernación, Introd. R. L. [Rafael López]. *Documentos inéditos relativos a Hernán Cortés y su familia*. México: Talleres Gráficos de la Nación, 1935.

Archivo General de la Nación, UNAM. *Nuevos documentos relativos a los bienes de Hernán Cortés, 1547-1949*. Mexico: Imprenta Universitaria, 1946.

Barlow, R. H. *The Extent of the Empire of the Culhua Mixica*. Berkeley and Los Angeles: University of California Press, 1949.

Barrett, Ward. Trad. Stella Mastrangtel., *La hacienda azucarera de los Marqueses del Valle (1535-1910)*. México: Siglo XXI, 1977.

Basalenque, Diego de. Introd. Heriberto Moreno. *Los agustinods, aquellos misioneros hacendados: Historia de las provincial de San Nicolás de Tolentino de Michoacán, escrita por fray Diego de Badsalenque (selección)*. Mexico: SEP & Consejo Nacional de Fomento Educativo, 1985.

Bataillon, Marcel. *Erasmo y España: Estudios sobre la historia spiritual del siglo xvi*, 2nda ed. Revisada. Mexico: Fondo de Cultura Económica, 1966 [el original en francés: 1937].

Baudot, Georges. "The Last Years of Fray Berdardino de Sahagún (1585-90): The Rescue of the Confiscated Work and the Seraphic Conflicts. New Unpublished Documents." In Munroe S. Edmonson, ed., *Sixteenth Century Mexico: The Work of Sahagún* (Albuquerque: University of New Mexico Press, 1994).

Boccaccio, Giovanni. Trans and ed., Mark Musa and Peter E. Bondanella. *The Decameron: A New Translation* . . . New York: W. W. Norton, 1977.

Bornemann, Margarita Menegus. *Del señorio indígena a la república de indios: El caso de Toluca, 1500-1600*. Mexico: Consejo Nacional para la Cultura y las Artes, 1991.

Broda, Johanna. "La expansion imperial mexica y los sacrificios del Templo Mayor," in Jesús Monjarás-Ruiz, Rosa Brambila, Emma Pérez-Rocha, eds. *Mesoamérica y el centro de México: Una antología*. México: INAH, 1976. Pp. 433-76.

Brown, Chris. *King and Outlaw: The Real Robert the Bruce.*Stroud, Gloucestershire: The History Press, 2018...

Benítez, Fernando. *Historia de la Ciudad de México, II (Siglo XVI)*. México: Salvat, 1984.

Biermann, Benno O. P. "Don Vasco de Quiroga y su tratado *De Debellandis indis (II)*," in Zavala, *Recuerdo de Vasco de Quiroga*. Pp. 191-7.

Bustamante, Carlos María. "Notas a la primera edición de la *Historia general de las cosas de la Nueva España*, de Fr. Bernardino de Sahagún, publicada en México en 1829-1830." En Sahagún, *Historia general*. Pp. 965-1057.

Camara, Amalia Iniesta. "Los coloquios de Sahagún," in Patricia Nettel Díaz, ed., *La utopía franciscana en la Nueva España (1554-1604). El apostolado de Fray Gerónimo de Mendieta*. Mexico: Universidad Autónoma Metropolitana, 2010. Pp. 647-60.

Carrasco, David. "The Exaggerations of Human Sacrifice," in Bernal Díaz del Castillo, *The History of the Conquest of New Spain* . . ., ed. & introd. David Carrasco. Alberquerque: New Mexico University Press, 2008. Pp. 327-44.

"Carta del Consejo de Huexotzingo al Rey Felipe II, 30 de julio de 1560," in Miguel León-Portilla, ed. *Visión de los vencidos: Relacines indígenas de la conquista*. México: UNAM, 2004. Pp. 169-74.

Calderón Quintero, Francisco R. "Causas y efectos inmediatos de la conquista," in Patronato Mexicano, *Cortés*. Pp. 27-52.

Campos Rebollo, Marco Ramón. *La casa de los franciscanos en la Ciudad de México: Reseña de los cambios que sufrió el convent de San Francisco, de los siglos XVI al XIX*. México: Desarrollo Social Socicultur, 1986.

Cervantes de Salazar, Francisco. *Crónica de la Nueva España._. México en 1554 y Tumulto Imperial*. Prol. Edmundo O'Gorman. México: Porrúa, 1975.

Chauveau, Juan Dubernard, ed. y prol. *Códices de Cuernavaca y unos títulos de sus pueblos*. Cuernavaca: Gobierno del Estado, 1991.

Chimalpain Cuauhtlehuanitzin. "La relación de Chimalpain: lo que siguió a la toma de la ciudad." En Miguel León-Portilla, ed., *Literaturas indígenas . . .* México: Ediciones patria, 1991.

Chauvet, Fray Fidel de Jesús O.F.M. *Franciscanos memorables en México (1523-1982): Ensayo histórico*. Mexico: Centro de Estudios Bernardino de Sahagún, 1983.

Clendinnen, Inga. *Ambivalent Conquests: Maya and Spaniard in Yucatan, 1517-1570*, 2nd ed. New York: Cambridge University Press, 1967.

Cliff, Nigel. *Holy War: How Vasco da Gama's Epic Voyages Turned the Tide in a Centuries-Old Clash of Civiliations*. New York: Harper-Collins, 2011.

Cline, Sarah, "The Spiritual Conquest Reexmined: Baptism and Christian Marriage in Early Sixteenth-Century Mexico," *Hispanic American Historical Review* (1993): 73 (3): 453-480,

Cohen, J. M. Introduction" to Bernal Díaz, *The Conquest of New Spain*, trans. J.M.C. England: Penguin Books, 1963. Pp. 7-12.

Conrad, Geoffrey W. & Arthur A. Demarest. Trans. Miguel Rivera Dorado. *Religión e imperio: Dinámica del expansionismo azteca e inca*. México: Alianza, 1988.

Cope, R. Douglas. *The Limits of Racial Domination: Plebian Society in Colonial Mexico City, 1660-1720*. Madison: University of Wisconsin Press, 1994.

Cortés, Hernán. Introd. Manuel Alcalá. *Cartas de relación*. México: Porrúa, 1988.

_____ Ed. José Luis Martínez. *Documentos cortesianos*. México: UNAM, 1991. Threre volumes.

_____ Trans. & Ed. Anthony Padge. Introd. J. H. Elliott. *Letters from Mexico*. New Haven: Yale Univ. Press, 1971.

Díaz, Patricia Nettel, ed., *La utopía franciscana en la Nueva España (1554-1604). El apostolado de Fray Gerónimo de Mendieta*. Mexico: Universidad Autónoma Metropolitana, 2010.

Díaz Migoyo, Gonzalo y Germán Vázquez Chamorro, "Introducción." Hernando de Alvaerado Texzozomac, *Crónica Mexicana*. Madrid: Dastín, 2003. Pp. 5-51.

Díaz del Castillo, Bernal. Prol. Carlos Pereyra, *Historia verdadera de la conquista de la Nueva España*, 3era ed. Madrid: Espasa-Calpe, 1975.

Duffy, Eamon. "The World Split in Two," *New York Review of Books*. April 18, 2019. Pp. 65 64-67.

Durant, Will. *The Story of Civilization. The Age of Faith: A History of Medieval Civilization—Christian, Islamic, and Judaic—from Constantine to Dante: a.d. 325-1300.* New York: Simon and Schuster, 1950.

Duverger, Christian. *La conversión de los indios de Nueva España. Con el texto de los "Coloquios de los Doce" de Bernardino de Sahagún (1564).* Mexico: FCE, 1993 [French: 1987]. .

_____. *Cortés.* France: Fayard, 2001.

_____. *Crónica de la eteridad: ¿Quién escribió la Historia Verdadera de la conquista de la Nueva España?* México: Debolsillo, 2015.

_____. "La idealización del mestizaje," *Nexos.*, May 2019. Pp. 50-55.

Edmonson, Munroe S. ed.. *Sixteenth Century Mexico: The Work of Sahagún.* Albuquerque: University of New Mexico Press, 1994.

Elliot, J. H. *Imperial Spain: 1469-1716.* London: Penguin Books, 2002.

[Erasmus, Desiderio], Erika Rummel, ed., *The Erasmus Reader.* Toronto: University of Toronto Press, 1990.

Escandon, Patricia. "La provincial franciscana de Mexico (1530-1590)," in Jesus Paniagua Perez & Maria Isabel Marinas, Viforcos, ed. *Fray Bernardino de Sahagún y su tiempo.* Spain: Universidad de Leon e Instituto Leones de Cultura, 2000. Pp. 403-12.

Fernández Buey, Francisco. *La gran perturbación: Discurso del indio metropolitano.* Mexico: Ensayos/Destino 26, n.d.

Fernández Ramírez, José. Prol. Antonio Castro Leal, 3era ed. *Fray Toribio de Motolinia y otros estudios.* México: Porrúa, 1986.

_____. Prol. Ernesto de la Torre Villar. *Relatos históricos.* México: UNAM, 1987.

Fernández, Rafael Diego. *Antonio de Mendoza.* Mexico: Planeta DeAgostini, 2002.

Fuentes, Carlos. *El espejo enrterrado.* Mexico: Taurus, 2007 [1998].

Gante, Pedro de. "Carta de Fr. Pedro de Gante al Rey D. Felipe II." In García Icazbalceta, *Nueva colección.* Pp. 220-7.

García Icazbalceta, Joaquín. *Fray Juan de Zumárraga: Primer Obispo y Arzobispo de Méjico.* México: Espasa-Calpe, 1952.

_____, ed. *Nueva colección de documentos para la historia de México. II: Códice franciscano, Siglo XVI.* Mexico: Francisco Díaz de León, 1889.

Gibson, Charles. *The Aztecs Under Spanish Rule: A History of the Indians of the Valley of Mexico, 1519-1810.* Stanford: Stanford University Press, 1964.

_____. *Tlaxcala in the Sixteenth Century.* Stanford: Stanford University Press, 1952.

Giménez Fernández. Manuel. *Bartolomé de las Casas, Capellán de Carlos V, poblador de Cumaná.* Sevilla: Consejo Superior, 1982.

Gómez Canedo, Lino. *Evangelización, Cultura y promoción social: Ensayos . . . sobre la contribución franciscana a los orígenes cristianos de México (Siglos XVI-XVIII)*, José Luis Soto Pérez, ed. México: Porrúa, 1993.

Gómez Serafín, Susana. *Altepetl de Huaxtepec: Modificaciones territoriales desde el siglo XVI*. Mexico: Instituto Nacional de Antropología e Historia, 2011.

Google, "Zacatula."

Greenleaf, Richard E. *Zumarraga and the Mexican Inquisition, 1536-1543*. Washington: Academy of American Franciscan History, 1961.

Grijalda, Juan de. *Crónica de la orden Augustin en las provincias de la Nueva España . . . 1533 hasta 1592* [1624]. Mexico: Victoria, 1924.

Hanke, Lewis. *Bartolomé de Las Casas: Bookman, Scholar and Propagandist*. Philadelfia: University of Pennsylvania, 1952.

Hemming, John. *The Conquest of the Incas*. San Diego et al: Harvest Books, 1970.

Hojacastro, Fray Martin de. "Letter of 1544 to the king," in *Nueva Coleccion . . . Códice franciscano*, Pp. 187-93.

Kellogg, Michael K. *The Wisdom of the Renaissance*. New York: Prometheus Books, 2019.

Kelly, Joseph. *Marooned: Jamestown, Shipwreck, and a New History of America's Origins*. New York: Bloomsbury, 2018.

Land México: Atlas de carreteras. México: Guía Roji, 1995.

Las Casas, Bartolomé. *Brevísima relación de la destrucción de Las Indias*. Prol. Nelson Martínez Díaz. Barcelona: Orbis, 1986.

León-Portilla, Miguel, *Broken Spears: The Aztec Account of the Conquest of Mexico*, ed. & introd. ML-P, trans. Lysander Kemp. Boston: Beacon Press, 1962.

_____, ed. *Literaturas indígenas . . .* México: Editorial Patria, 1991.

_____. "Hernán Cortés y el Mar Bermejo." In Patronato Mexicano, *Cortés*. Pp. 259-76.

_____. *Visión de los vencidos: Relaciones indígenas de la conquista*. Mexico: UNAM, 2004.

"Relación de Tezcoco dispuesta por Juan Bautista Poman." In León-Portilla, *Literaturas indígenas . . . .* Pp. 641-82.

Leonard, Irving A. "Introduction." In *Bernal Díaz del Castillo*. Trans. A. P. Maudslay. *The Discovery and Conquest of Mexico, 1517-1521*. Kingsport, TN: Farrar, Straus and Cudahy, 1956. Pp. xi-xviii.

Lockhart, James & Enrique Otte, eds.& trans., *Letters and People of the Spanish Indies: Sixteenth Century*. New York: Cambridge University Press: 2010 [1976].

[López, R.], "Introducción." In *Documentos inéditos relativos a Hernán Cortés y su familia*. México: Talleres Gráficos de la Nación, 1935. Pp. vii-ix.

López de Gómara, Francisco. Introd. Juan Miralles Ostos. 3era ed. *Historia de la conquista de México*. México: Porrúa, 1997.

Madariaga, Salvador de. *Hernán Cortés: Conquistador de México*. London: Hollis & Carter, 1954.
Mann, Charles C. *1493: Uncovering the New World Columbus Created*. New York: Alfred A. Knopf, 2011.
Martínez, José Luis. *Hernán Cortés* (México: UNAM & FCE, 2003 [1990])
Martínez, María Elena. *Genealogical Fictions: Limpieza de Sangre, Religions and Gender in Colonial Mexico*. Stanford: Stanford University Press, 2008.
McAlister, Lyle N. *Spain and Portugal in the New World, 1492-1700*. Minneapolis: The University of Minnesota, 1984.
Mendieta, Fray Gerónimo de. *Historia eclesiástica Indiana*. Prol. Joaquín García Icazbalceta & Antonio Rubial García. Mexico: Consejo Naciobnal para la Cultura y las Artes, 1997.
Miranda, Jose. *El tributo indígena en La Nueva Espana durante el siglo XVI*. México: Colegio de México, 1972.
Monjarás-Ruiz, Jesús, Rosa Brambila, Emma Pérez-Rocha, eds. *Mesoamérica y el centro de México: Una antología*. México: INAH, 1976.
Monterrosa, Mariano. "La evangelización." In *Historia de México*, eds. Juan Salvat y José Luis Rosas. México: Salvat Editores, 1986. Vol, 7, pp. 1073-1136.
Montya de la Rica, Eduard. *Hernán Cortés*. Madrid: Dastin Export, 2004.
Motolinía, Fray Toribio de Benavente. "In Tlaxcala, México, to the Emperor, 1555. In Lockhart, *Letters and People*. Pp. 218-47.
_____. *Memoriales. Manuscrito de la colección del Señor Don Joaquín García Icazbalceta. Publícalo por primera vez su hijo Luis García Pimentel*. Méjico: Casa del Editor, 1903,
_____. Introd. Edmundo O'Gorman, *Historia de los indios de la Nueva España: Relación de los ritos antiguos . . .*, México: Porrúa, 2014,
Muñoz Camargo, Diego. *Relaciones geográficas del siglo XVI*. México: UNAM, Instituto de Investigaciones Antropológicas, 1981-88.
Muñoz Camargo, Diego, Alfredo Chavero & Edmundfo Aviña Levy. *Historia de Tlaxcala*. México: Oficina del Secretario de Fomento, 1892 (Facsimile 1966).
Nettel Díaz, Patricia, ed. *La utopía franciscana en la Nueva España (1554-1604). El apostolado de Fray Gerónimo de Mendieta*. Mexico: Universidad Autónoma Metropolitana, 2010. Pp. 647-60.
Ocaranza, Fernando. *Capítulos de la historia franciscana [primera serie]*. Mexico: s.e., 1933.
Orendáin, Claudio Favier. *Ruinas de utopía: San Juan de Tlayacapan (espacio y tiempo en el encuengtro de dos culturas)*. Mexico: Gobierno del Estado de Morelos, 1998.
Patronato Mexicano del V Centenario de Cortés. *Cortés: Navegante, político, arquitecto, economista y literato*. México: Diana, 1992. .

Pérez, Joseph. "El erasmo y las corrientes espirituales afines." In Revuelta Sañudo, *El erasmismo en España*. Pp. 323-38.
Phelan, John Leddy. The *Millennial Kingdom of the Franciscans in the New World*. Berkeley: University of California Press, 1970.
Prescott, William H. Trad. José María González de la Vega. Ed. Lucas Alamán. Prol. Juan A. Ortega y Medina, *Historia de la conquista de México* . . . México: Porrúa, 1976.
_____. *History of the Conquest of Mexico and History of the Conquest of Peru*. New York: The Modern Library, n.d.
_____. *Mexico and the Life of the Conqueror, Fernando Cortés. In Two Volumes*. New York: Peter Fenelon Collier, 1896. . (Cover title: *History of the Conquest of Peru with a preliminary view of the civilization of the Incas*).
"Un pueblo indio se dirige al rey: el Ayuntamiento de Huejotzingo, México, al rey Felipe, 1560. In Anderson, *Beyond the Codices*. Pp.176-90.
Quiroga, Vasco de. Ed. Paz Serrano Gassent. *La utopia en América: Cronistas de América. México en tres tiempos: Virreinato. No. 33*. Monterrey: APP, s.f.
_____. "Informacion en Derecho." En *La utopia*. Pp. 242-97.
Reséndez, Andrés. *The Other Slavery: The Uncovered Story of Indiabn Enslavement in America*. Boston & New York: Houghton Mifflin Harcourt, 2016.
Revuelta Sañudo, Manuel, et al, eds.. *El erasismo en España: Ponencias*. Santander: Sociedad Menéndez Pelayo, 1986.
Ricard, Robert. *The Spiritual Conquest of Mexico*. Berkeley: University of California Press, 1966.
Rand Parish, Helen and Harold E. Weidman. *Las Casas en México: Historia y obra desconocidas*. México: FCE, 1996 [1992].
Riley, G. Micheal. *Fernando Cortes and the Marquesado in Morelos, 1522-1547: A Case Study in the Socioeconomic Development of Sixteenth-Century Mexico*. Albuquerque: University of New Mexico Press, 1973.
Roberts, J. M. and Odd Arne Westad, *The History of the World*, 6th ed. New York: Oxford University Press, 2013.
Rodríguez-Sala, María Luisa et al.. *El Hospital Real de los Naturales . . . (1531-1764 . . .* Mexico: UNAM, 2005.
Romero Galván, José Rubén & Pilar Maynez, eds. *El universio de Sahagun: pasado y presente. Coloquio 2005*. Mexico: UNAM, 2007.
Romero Reséndiz, Alonso. *Lo de Tlaxcala: Análisis imparcial de los sucesos acaecidos en época de la conquista*. México: B. Costa-Amic, 1974.
Ruiz Medrano, Ethelia. Trans. Julia Constantino & Pauline Marmasse. *Reshaping New Spain: Government and Private Interests in the Colonial Bureaucracy, 1531-1550*. Boulder: University Press of Colorado, 1987.
_____. *Gobierno y sociedad en Nueva España: Segunda Audiencia y Antonio de Mendoza*. Michoacán: Gobierno del Estado y Colegio de Michoacán, 1991.

Rummel, Erika. "Introduction," in [Erasmus], *The Erasmus Reader*. Pp. 3-13.

Sahagún, Fr. Bernardino de. Introd. Angel María Garibay K. *Historia general, de las cosas de Nueva España*, 8 ed. Mexico: Porrúa, 1992.

Salinas, Miguel. *Historia y paisajes morelenses*. México: Ernesta Salinas, 1981.

Seaver, Henry Latimer. *The Great Revolt in Castille: A Study of the Comunero Movement of 1520-1521*. New York: Octagon Boooks, 1966.

Secretaría de Educación Pública (SEP). *Morelos: nieve en la cima, fuego en el cañaveral*. México: SEP, 1992.

Sigüenza y Góngora, Carlos de. Introd. Jaime Delgado. *Piedad heroyca de Don Fernando Cortés*. Madrid: José Porrúa Turanzas, 1960 [1663?].

Simpson, Lesley Byrd. *The Encomienda of Spanish Mexico*. Berkeley and Los Angeles: University of California Press, 1966.

Smith, Rhea Marsh. *Spain, A Modern History*. Ann Arbor: University of Michigan Press, 1965.

Tuchman, Barbara W. *The March of Folly: From Troy to Vietnam*. New York: Ballentine Books, 1984.

Warner, Henry Raupand Helen Rand Perish. *The Life and Writings of Bartolomé de Las Casas*. Alburqueque: University of N.M. Press, 1967.

Womak, John Jr. Trans. Francisco González Aramburo. *Zapata y la Revolución mexicana*. Mexico: Siglo Veintiuno, 1985.

Zavala, Silvio. *De encomiendas y propiedad territorial en algunas regiones de la América Española*. México: Robredo & Porrúa, 1940.

_____. *Estudios indianos*. México: El Colegio Nacional, 1948.

_____. "Ideario de Vasco de Quiroga." In *Recuerdo de Vasco de Quiroga*, 4er ed. (México: Porrúa, 2007. Pp. 35-62.

_____. *Las instituciones jurídicas en la conquista de América*. Mexico: Porrúa, 1971.

_____. *Tributos y servicios personales de indios para Hernán Cortés y su familia (Extractos de documentos del siglo XVI)*. México: Archivos de la Nación, 1999.

Zorita, Alonso de. *Los señores de la Nueva España*. Prol. Joaquín Ramírez Cabañas. Mexico: UNAM, 1993.

NOTES ABOUT SOURCES

The writing of this book has entailed scholarly encounters with distinct bodies of sources that can be grouped imperfectly in the following categories.

Part I.

I list here those documents and studies relevant to the topic of this book that were known to serious researchers up to about the first few decades of the nineteenth century. Then, at that time—which coincided with Mexico's struggle for independence from Spain—the authors of these sources of information either fell into disfavor or were progressively ignored.

1. Heading this list are the only two texts written by actual participants in the Mexican "conquest." First, there are the important letters that the conquistador-turned-governor Hernán Cortés wrote to King Carlos I (of Spain, later known as Emperor Carlos V of the Holy Roman Empire) that have been collected under the Spanish title *Cartas de relación*, or, in English, *Letters to the King*. As stated in the introduction, I suspect that readers or observers—then, now, or at any moment in between—will never come to agreement about whether the positive ever outweighed the negative in Cortés's character and acts, even though all informed observers continue to marvel at his unsurpassed leadership skills and the exceptional nature of his contributions.

2. The second work from the pen of a soldier accompanying Cortés during the whole historical period under study is Bernal Díaz del Castillo's *Historia verdadera de la conquista de México*. Perhaps it's sheer length and difficult, chaotic style have discouraged investigators from giving it serious consideration. Unfortunately, many of the prejudices that have led investigators to devalue many of the positive contributions of Hernán Cortés—as I've explained in the section immediately above—have also affected their appraisal of the Díaz del Castillo book. Indeed, there exist very few studies over the past two centuries by researchers from Mexico, Europe, or the United States which have gone beyond

praising its precursor status for contemporary novels of the "magical realism" style. In contrast—after extensive investigations—I recognize the veracity of a greater part of the history that Bernal Díaz presents!

Consequently, the Bernal Díaz work constitutes the primary source for much of the information that I communicate throughout this book. Let there be no doubt: this work, written by an octogenarian focusing his astounding powers of memory to reconstruct a thousand small details of his youthful past, constitutes one of the most fascinating and impressive works ever written by an American.

Bernal Díaz del Castillo, as a youth, participated alongside Cortés in the Mexican conquest, but waited over a half-century to put into writing this lengthy, and in some places astounding, commentary. About his text, mysteries abound. Inviting is the bold hypothesis of Christian Duverger (in his *Crónica de la eternidad*) that Cortés, in the last half-decade of his life while residing in Spain, secretly wrote the Díaz del Castillo text. Arguments supporting this thesis: (A) A historical Díaz del Castillo did exist and was an encomendero in Guatemala. But the author by that same name could have been an invention by a sly-minded Cortés. Indeed, aspects of Díaz's biography simply do not square with known historical information. Leading the list: this name does not appear in any of the surviving documents that Cortés had preserved from the early conquest months, and especially on the 1519 petition that Cortés was careful to draw up and have more than 350 Spanish soldiers sign in order to justify his assumption as leader of the Spanish army. (B) It stretches the credibility of the reader to believe that "Bernal" (I write the name in this way in reference to the young soldier), as a green youth, had gained Cortés's confidence to such a degree that the latter allowed his presence in so many important and intimate occasions. Can we believe that Cortés singled "Bernal" out in 1526 to show him important correspondence from the king? (C) Or that in 1540 Cortés invited him, and he accepted, to accompany Cortés to the court of Carlos V in 1540, and there "witnessed" firsthand the presence of Vasco de Quiroga and others in important hearings? (D) More likely, the devious writer, Cortés, wished to add authority to the resulting text, made his creation, the author Díaz del Castillo, into a credible witness for communicating important (and self-serving) information. (E) No learned reader has come across a single significant error in Díaz's detailed rendering of the 500+ names of both Mexican places and Spanish soldiers. It is hard to believe that an 84-year-old man was able to remember with such accuracy the individuals and events of 55 years earlier? More persuasive is the explanation that the true writer of *Historia verdadera* was able to make use of Cortés's extensive archives in order to record exact names from itineraries and documents written within days of the actual events in the 1520s. (F) Although Díaz provides substantial criticisms of Cortés in the narration, "he does ample justice to his great and heroic qualities"—in the words of the perhaps the best historian who treats the ideas and actions of Cortés, William Prescott. To this I can add: Bernal Díaz's most important opinions—and indeed his world view—do not differ substantially from those of Cortés. (G) The aged Cortés must have known that the issue of Viceroy Mendoza taking a personal role in the count of the Marquesado's vassals (during the 1530s) constituted an authenticated view of Cortés's flawed moral values, so Cortés has his invented author dedicate a whole page of rambling sentences to partially defuse or justify that conduct. (cxcix) (H) An authenticated document exists in which the historical man, Bernal Díaz del Castillo, asserts that he was "not a man of letters"—and perhaps posterity should take him at his word. And finally, (I) The Díaz del Castillo narration displays erudite allusions and a masterfully crafted, "spontaneous recital of adventures, spirited anecdotes, and the invented speeches and dialogues" which only a learned and skilled narrator—such as Hernán Cortés himself—could have produced. Duverger's thesis is inviting.

Notwithstanding the convincing arguments of Duverger, I choose to follow convention here and continue recognizing Bernal Díaz del Castillo as the true author of *Historia verdadera*. Well into the future, mysteries will continue to surround this fascinating and perplexing work.

A note about the two of the English translations which I have consulted: Bernal Díaz del Castillo, trans. A. P. Maudslay, introd. Irving A. Leonard, *The Discovery and Conquest of Mexico, 1517-1521* (Kingsport, TN: Farrar, Straus and Cudahy, 1956); and Bernal Díaz del Castillo, trans. J. M. Cohen, *The Conquest of New Spain* (London: Penguin), 1963. Being that neither of these two works include in their selections for translation the passages that I treat in this book, I have decided to provide my own English translations throughout—which I document according to their chapter numbers—as given in the 1975 edition (see bibliography).

3. After the important texts authored by Cortés and Bernal Díaz del Castillo, the sources most important for writing this book were authored by a handful of Spaniards, mainly religious, who worked intimately with Indian communities throughout the half-century following the 1521 submission of the Aztecs. In this book—for the first time ever in English—I quote from their most important writings in English translation.

   (A) Heading this list is the lawyer Vasco de Quiroga, born in 1565 and arriving in Mexico to serve in the Segunda Audiencia, and moved to Michoacán in 1533 to begin 32 years of devoted service to the natives Michoacán; he was named bishop of that area by King Carlos in 1537. In several writings he provided details of the missions he founded and his successes in "pacificar [a los nativos], sin necesidad de las armas, sino con afecto y propuestas de mejoras en su organización" (Wikipedia). In several chapters I quote from his *Información de derecho*.

(B) Three Franciscans who spent a lifetime living among Indian communities in New Spain's central plateau have left important writings that touch upon both the aspect and culture of native populations and their different responses to the friars' Christianizing activities: Friars Toribio Benavente "Motolinía," Pedro de Gante, and Archbishop José de Zumárraga. In this book I quote from their descriptions of the Indian groups they worked with. I also provide quotations from the letters written by each, in the autumn of their years, to the sitting king. Perhaps because each, in his own words, saw fit to praise the life and works of Cortés—at the time of their writing, the death of Cortés was already two decades in the past—an unappreciative public, over the past two centuries, has not accorded to these men the praise that they deserve.

(C) A similar fate has suffered the writings of Indian noble, Fernando de Alva Ixtlilxóchitl, who had been educated in the Franciscan Colegio for native youth in Tlatelolco. He, an Indian historian and devoted Catholic, held the accomplishments of Cortés among the greatest of feats in the history of the West.

(D) Rounding out the list of sources originating in the first half-century after the 1521 submission of the Aztecs are important histories by two important writer/historians who were protagonists in the Evangelization Campaign, Franciscans Gerónimo de Mendieta and Bernardino de Sahagún. The "humanist" orientation of these two (in addition to Vasco de Quiroga, Juan de Zumárraga and others) contrasted with the fierce nationalist conflicts and religious intolerance of their age. Most important for this book are Mendieta's *Historia eclesiástica Indiana* and Sahagún's *Historia general de las cosas de Nueva España* (more popularly known as *Códice Florentino*).

After passing consideration given by the prodigious Prescott, the writings by these important activist/writers have been largely ignored by subsequent researchers.

About Mendieta: He was born in Spain in 1525, took the Franciscan habit at an early age, and arrived in New Spain in 1554 (some thirty years after the commencement of the evangelical campaign) and, with the exception of one trip to Spain—1570-1573—he devoted the rest of his long life to missionary labors among the Indians. His important writings pay homage to his Franciscan predecessors and their devotion to New Spain's native population. In the latter years of his life (coinciding with the last decades of New Spain's sixteenth century), Mendieta' suffering upon witnessing the severe demographic and economic crises affecting Mexico's indigenous communities.

About Sahagún: Born in 1499, he took vows in the Franciscan Order before arriving in Mexico in 1529 to assume responsibilities in the Colegio de Santa Cruz instructing native youth. Attaining a mastery of the Aztec language, he took upon himself the life-long project of interviewing native subjects to record for posterity things related to Aztec history and customs. Ageing well, by the 1570s he was recognized as the leader and spokesperson for all the Franciscans still active in the Evangelical Campaign.

4. One must make a temporal jump toward the middle of the eighteenth century to arrive at the next *opus magnus* treating this book's chosen topic: English historian William Prescott's *History of the Conquest of Mexico*. Beginning in 1838, this tireless polyglot spent years between Spain and Mexico studying a vast body of materials located in important archives and public, private, and monastic libraries, many of which had been overlooked by even the most accomplished of his predecessors. The informed reader today can only marvel at how Prescott preceded by at least a century the trajectory embraced by serious researchers in any number of fields of inquiry in order to bring to fruition a serious piece of research.

    In the preface to his singular history, Prescott "asks the reader's indulgence" for continuing his history in order to treat events even after the military conquest: "I cannot regret that I have adopted this course; since, whatever luster the Conquest may reflect on Cortés as a military achievement, it gives but an imperfect idea of his enlightened spirit, and of his comprehensive and versatile genius."[353] Thus wrote Prescott, the most accomplished of Cortés's biographers, in words reflecting the values and mentality of his pre-Victorian age.

    Even after two-and-a-half centuries, this work by Prescott remains unsurpassed. It still offers the most detailed, balanced, and documented commentary available. Indeed, this is especially the case for the long chapter he dedicated to the life, time, and character of Cortés himself, with its unequaled treatment of both the latter's defects but also his glory. As to be expected, Prescott's text became a predominant influence for the most important leaders of his preterit age: Otto van Bismarck (constructive conquest), England's Queen Victoria (benign empire), Charles Darwin (with his "social-Darwin" followers), and Rudyard Kipling (poet of "the White man's burden").

5. Against the backdrop of Mexico's struggle for independence in the early decades of the nineteenth century, all the works mentioned above would suffer an abrupt fall in the estimation of Mexico's writers, readers, and historians. Early

writers, previously honored, were now discredited.[354] One unfortunate result: the protagonists of the early postconquest period, who had previously been considered as national "heroes," fell into disfavor.

What are the possible reasons for this movement to maim the country's early post-conquest history? There are several reasons: (A) The period of benign colonialism that I treat in this book was of relatively short duration. (B) Some forty years after the Aztecs' submission, all of Mexico was smitten by recurring plagues that decimated the native population. (C) The plagues, the termination of Franciscan authority, and other factors ushered in a new period typified by injustice and extreme cruelty in Spaniards' treatment of the native population. (D) The hostile nationalism of opinion leaders, beginning during the independence period at the beginning of the 19th century, motivated their intentional distortion of the historical past. (E) Everywhere learned individuals came to honor the opinions and biases of Dominican friar Bartolomé de las Casas and discredit those of his antagonist, Hernán Cortés (see Appendix A). And (F) All across the West, terrible plagues, vicious wars between the power-hungry heads of different city-states, and incorrigible abuses on the part of princes and church officials contribute to learned readers' "difficulty of empathy" with regard to events and people of the Sixteenth Century.[355]

6. Jumping ahead, these same causes contributed to the biases, sometimes conscious, sometimes unconscious and institutionalized, came to flavor a great many of the important historical studies undertaken in the mid-twentieth century. A handful of dedicated historians, hailing from both Mexico and the United States, expended enormous time and energy to visit existing archives, locate relevant documents, and present careful analyses of new and important information. Some of their research areas were relatively new: "anthropological" studies of "folk" communities, statistical balances of different types of agricultural production, charts documenting the uninterrupted Indian administration of Mexico's most important colonial cities, etc. Two names head the list of these important researchers: Silvio Zavala (Mexican) ; and Charles Gibson (the United States).

This dedicated generation of scholars shared a few important deficiencies: first, they discounted the importance of Prescott's work (add to that the writings of Prescott-disciple Salvador de Maradiaga), undoubtedly because of their own generation's biases against common and accepted sixteenth-century practices; and second, their (apparent) disdain for (and derivative silence about) things accomplished or written by Mexico's two most important White "conquerors" and "colonialists:" Hernán Cortés and Bernal Díaz.

7. Unfortunately, the same applies to the most significant works of that outstanding generation of scholars that focus specifically on the geographical area as well as the time period that I treat in this book: Charles Gibson's *Tlaxcala in the Sixteenth Century (1952)* and *The Aztecs Under Spanish Rule (1966)*; G. Micheal Riley's *Fernando Cortes and the Marquesado in Morelos* (1973); Arturo Warman's *"We Come to Object:" The Peasants of Morelos* (1976); Ward Barrett's *La hacienda azucarera de los Marqueses del Valle* (1977); Cheryl English Martin's *Rural Society in Colonial Morelos* (1985); and Robert Haskett's *Indigenous Rulers . . . in Colonial Cuernavaca* (1991). None of these researchers had access to the recently "rediscovered" documents mentioned in Part II or (obviously) Part III—below. Surprisingly, none of them provide detailed information about the acts or motivations of ex-conquistador-turned-civic- leader Hernán Cortés in either Morelos or Cuernavaca.

What are the reasons for explaining their relative silence? First, it was a period when there were few Spaniards residing in Mexico, and most of them were men of "action" not overly interested or concerned about leaving written documentation of their own activities or of the society that was emerging as a result of their efforts. A second reason: it was a period when archives or libraries did not exist, when paper and printing presses, only beginning to appear in European cities, were strikingly absent. And third, for a myriad of reasons, the great majority of Mexico's population—that is to say, the Indian chieftains and the millions of their subjects—ignored the Spanish language, lacked literary skills in any language, and had no access to channels of written information. Consequently, little information concerning that time period's demographics and society would have been recorded, and even less would have survived to the present day.

Related is the near silence in works written—whether four centuries ago or during the current age—about the work, thought, and deeds of the exconquistador leader Hernán Cortés during his twenty-five years of prominence in that "golden age" of Mexican history—that is to say, during the period of his life spanning the time between 1521—when the Aztecs were forced to submission- and Cortés' natural death in 1546. Given his control over extensive lands, immense wealth, and his unequaled prestige among Spaniards and Indians alike, he ended up leaving his "stamp" of influence over almost every aspect of Mexican life. Yet in study after study accomplished over the past century, the name Hernán Cortés is hardly mentioned. Undoubtedly, many of the same reasons I've enumerated in the previous paragraph help to explain this notable absence. Add to these the possibility that officialdom (most notably the king, in addition to Mexico's first two viceroys) sought ways to sideline his influence and public profile. Add to all this his decision, and then subsequent acts, to exclude any Spaniard not specifically under his employ from either residing or exercising any type of activity in the Morelos area[356] of his Marquesado—that is to say, in the locality where he chose to construct his personal residence, house his Spanish wife, and raise his children. It is predictable that these decisions went hand in hand with his discouragement of writers, minstrels, secretaries, historians, and other types of commentators from focusing their discursive energies on his person, acts, and legacy.

PART II

I now turn to the second body of sources, those that have been known to the world only since the last decades of the twentieth century. These materials were totally unknown to Prescott, writing his histories in the eighteenth century. Similarly, they were unavailable to the able historians and anthropologists publishing up through the 1970s—this includes Charles Gibson, Silverio Zavala, and the dozens of historians and anthropologists, teaching and carrying out important research while employed by the major universities of United States, Mexico, and Europe.

1. Most important in the writing of this book are documents that, beginning in the 1970s, were "stumbled upon" in the national archives of a half-dozen countries, having been left untouched for centuries, probably because they were written in Náhuatl, the lingua franca of upper-class Mexicans at time of the Conquest. Most important for writing this book were texts dictated and archived by a handful of Cuernavaca chieftains under the supervision of their encomendero, the ex-conquistador Hernán Cortés (the how, why and when of these documents' transit from Mexico to important archives in Los Angeles, Paris, and Berlin remains a mystery!) Under the sponsorship of the Mexican government, these documents were translated, photocopied, and published by Juan Dubernard in his groundbreaking book of 1991, *Códices de Cuernavaca* (as treated in Chapters 6, 7 and 9, and in further detail in Appendix C).

2. Other documents, similarly written in Nahuatl, appeared and were published by Arthur Anderson and James Lockhart respectively, in *Beyond the Códices* and *Letters and People* (both in 1976; I provide more information about the documents' sources in the endnotes of Chapters 5 and 11). Heading this list is the letter, "*Un pueblo indio . . .*" (translated title: "An Indian Town Addresses the King") written to King Felipe II in the year 1560 by the indigenous nobles of the town of Huejotzingo (north of Cholula in the current State of Puebla). In that letter of protest, the Indians of that community praise the harmonious situation that their community

had enjoyed some twenty years earlier when their first encomendero, Hernán Cortés, supervised their own fathers and grandfathers in governing their city.

3. Also reappearing, only in recent decades, were letters written in Spanish to King Felipe II during the 1560s by three Franciscan friars who had been protagonists in the groundbreaking Evangelization Campaign: Toribio de Benevente "Motolinía", Pedro de Gante, and Juan de Zumárraga. It is significant that, in their respective letters, each offer unrepented praise for the contributions of Cortés more than two decades after his natural death (I quote from these three letters in chapters 5, 11, 13, and Appendix A).

4. An additional "recently discovered" sixteenth-century document, which could be added to the list of information unavailable to previous researchers, is referred to by Sylvanus G. Morley, rev. ed. George W. Brainerd, *The Ancient Maya*, 3rd ed. (Stanford: Stanford University Press, 1956 [1946]), 115. Morley located (and confirmed to himself its authenticity) a document written by the grandson of the sixteen-century Mayan chieftain (in today's Guatemala near the Honduran border), along with a drawing of the decapitated Cuauhtémoc, which explains how the latter had approached his grandfather, inviting him to join the conspiracy against the Spaniards led by Cortés. The chieftain, instead, chose to inform Cortés who, facing "no idle fear," took legitimate action, according to Morley, in immediately executing the Aztec leader.

Part III
Materials developed and published since the 1970s.

1. Heading this list are the recent ground-breaking studies by Christian Duverger, and in particular his *Crónica de la eternidad*. Given the material offered by Duverger in this book, the reader will give serious consideration to his first thesis, that Hernán Cortez was the real author of the book normally accredited to Bernal Díaz del Castillo, *Historia Verdadera de la Conquista de Nueva España*. and will never again question his second thesis, that the greater part of the historical information provided in that same book is accurate and reliable.

2. On the occasion of the five hundredth anniversary of Christopher Columbus's "voyage of discovery," the Mexican government stepped in to provide financial support for the country's most distinguished researcher

Silvio Zavala to unite a collection of important sixteenth-century documents that had not enjoyed broad circulation during the previous centuries. The result is *Tributos y servicios* (1999), parts of which I discuss in chapters 9 and 11.

3. Also important to include in this list of recent studies is the (perhaps definitive) biography of Hernán Cortés, written by José Luis Martínez: *Hernán Cortés* (1990), accompanied by the three volumes of *Documentos cortesianos* (1991).

ABOUT THE AUTHOR

William H. (Bill) Katra, an independent scholar, resides primarily in La Crosse, Wisconsin, but also spends time in both Uruguay and Mexico. He served in the Peace Corps in Uruguay from 1966 to 1968. With degrees from University of California-Berkeley (B.A. 1970) and the University of Michigan-Ann Arbor (Ph.D. 1977), his most important writings treat historical topics. Most noteworthy are: *José Artigas and the Federal League in Uruguay's and Argentina's War of Independence (1810-1820)* (2014; in Spanish 2024); and *The Argentine Generation of 1837: Esteban Echeverría, Juan B. Alberdi, Domingo F. Sarmiento, Bartolomé Mitre*—(1996; published in Argentina as *Los que hicieron el país*—2000 and 2024). These were preceded by three other book-length studies which offer the most authoritative treatment available about key literary and political figures in Argentina's 19th century. The Library of Congress named him contributing editor for its *Handbook of Latin American Studies: Humanities* (1990, 1992, 1994). *The Literary Review* (Fairleigh Dickinson University) invited his services as guest editor for its issue treating "Argentine Writing in the Eighties" (Summer 1989). He has also published highly regarded articles or book chapters treating: a history of liberation theology in Latin America; the *Facundo* as historical novel; Sarmiento's travels to the United States; an ideological history of Uruguayan literature; the narrative of Mexican writer, Juan Rulfo; a Mexican liberation-theology hymnal; and the poetic tradition of the gaucho. In a different tone, his *Mountain Climber: A Memoir* was published in 2020. (Google his name to find out information about other books; copies of reviews are also available there.)

ENDNOTES

INTRODUCTION

1   Fray Gerónimo de Mendieta, *Historia eclesiástica Indiana*, prol. Joaquín García Icazbalceta & Antonio Rubial García (México: Consejo Nacional para la Cultura y Las Artes, 1997), II, 65. In this work I focus primarily on the *historical* aspects of the "Golden Age" and provide only passing mention to the "mystical" or "theological" importance which Mendieta, and to a lesser degree other Franciscan monks, held for the term.

2   Bernal Díaz del Castillo, *Historia verdadera de la Conquista de la Nueva España*, prol. Carlos Pereyra, 3er ed. (Madrid: Espasa-Calpe, 1975), ccvii. Given the various editions of this important work, I will only designate chapter numbers for my own translations.

3   Although Cortés signed documents and commonly used the Christian name "Fernando," posterity has come to know him as "Hernán," a "convention" that I honor here.

4   Sylvanus G. Morley, rev. ed. George W. Brainerd, *The Ancient Maya*, 3rd ed. (Stanford: Stanford University Press, 1956 [1946]), 115. A document "discovered" by Morley convinces me that Cortés, during his expedition to Honduras, took legitimate action in executing Cuauhtémoc, the Aztec leader.

5   Here I follow the convention of using throughout this book the "nonsensical" Hispanicized name for this city, "Cuernavaca." Some early texts provide a more phonetically faithful Spanish rendition of what must have been its Indian name, "Quauhnahuac." Early writers were hardly consistent in Hispanicizing its name: "Cuedlavaaca," "Cornavaca," "Coadlabaca," etc.

6   The positive comment made by Tuchman, *Distant Mirror*, 57, is in reference to two outstanding contemporaries in the European theatre, Leonardo da Vinci and Michelangelo. I might add two names from the previous generation, Thomas More and Desiderius Erasmus, and one from the following generation, Michel de Montaigne.

7   Only one Spanish-reading historian, to my knowledge, has given critical attention to this episode from the Bernal Díaz history (but not with the extended

treatment it deserves): Salvador de Madariaga, *Hernán Cortés: Conqueror of Mexico* (London: Hollis & Carter, 1954), 396-7. With the publication of the recent ground-breaking study by Christian Duverger, *Crónica de la eteridad: ¿Quién escribió la Historia Verdadera de la conquista de la Nueva España* (México: Debolsillo, 2015), critical readers in the future will grant to the Bernal Díaz work the esteem it deserves.

8   The areas constituting today's State of Morelos were separated from the State of Mexico (which surrounds Mexico City and the Federal District) early in the twentieth century. In Morelos, Cortés exercised control over five of his (original) twenty-four encomiendas: Cuernavaca, Oaxtepec, Tepoztlán, Yecapixtla, and Ocuitulco.

9   Charles Gibson's *Tlaxcala in the Sixteenth Century* (Stanford: Stanford University Press, 1952) is a thorough study of the centuries-long indigenous leadership in that city (see Appendix B). Riley, *Fernando Cortes,* 136-7, suggests that other documents in Mexican archives, to date still unidentified and unstudied, might provide additional relevant information to the indigenous chieftains of Cuernavaca.

CHAPTER 1

10 Sources for this section are two early and excellent biographies: William H. Prescott, trad. José María González de la Vega, ed. Don Lucas Alamán, prol. Juan A. Ortega y Medina, *Historia de la conquista de México ...* (México: Porrúa, 1976); and Salvador de Madariaga, *Hernán Cortés: Conqueror of Mexico* (London: Hollis & Carter, 1954).

11 Will Durant, *The Story of Civilization. The Age of Faith: A History of Medieval Civilization—Christian, Islamic, and Judaic—from Constantine to Dante: a.d. 325-1300* (New York: Simon and Schuster, 1950), 555-7. Bernal Díaz del Castillo, prol. Carlos Pereyra, *Historia verdadera de la conquista de la Nueva España*, 3era ed. (Madrid: Espasa-Calpe, 1975), ccvii.

12 Hernán Cortés, *Cartas de relación,* Introd. Manuel Alcalá (México: Porrúa, 1988), I, 12. (This work unites the official reports Cortés wrote to the Spanish court over the decisions, and their results, that he had made in his official capacity of Capitan-General of the Spanish conquistador army.) The English translation I have used is *Letters from Mexico,* trans. & ed. Anthony Padge. Introd. J. H. Elliott (New Haven: Yale Univ. Press, 1971), which unfortunately and inexcusably leaves out the important "secret communication."

13 Prescott, *Historia,* 187.

14 Díaz del Castillo, *Historia verdadera,* cxlii-cxlv.

15 José Castro Seoane, O. de M., *El P. Olmedo en la formación espiritual del ejército de Cortés* (México: Editorial Jus, 1992).

16 Hemming, *Conquest of the Incas*, 262, labels Cortés "a religious fanatic," but this exaggeration suggests an important truth: that the religious beliefs of the Mexican conqueror were sincere and deep—in great contrast to other conquistador leaders of his generation.
17 Díaz del Castillo, *Historia verdadera*, xl.
18 Castro Seoane, *P. Olmedo*, 70.
19 A most interesting document, whose composition dates as early as 1544 [I would personally date the events it refers to as occurring two decades earlier, given the assumed presence of Cortés' right-hand lieutenant, Pedro de Alvarado], attests to the fact that virtually the same manner of "benign conquest" continued to be practiced by armies under Cortés even after the submission of the Aztecs. There is no mention of other, the extremely cruel acts reputedly ordered by Alvarado during that campaign. See "Título de caciques," in *El título de Yax y otros documentos quichés de Totonicapán, Guatemala: Edición facsimilar*, trad. y ed. Robert M. Carmack and James L. Mondloch (México: UNAM, 1989), pp. 211-14, which treats the submission of Indian communities in rural areas to the south and east of today's Guatemala City.
20 Cortés, *Cartas de relación*, 1, 12.
21 Castro Seoame, *P. Olmedo*, 67; also 66, where this author quotes from Cortés.
22 Prescott, *History*, 379.
23 Information for this section is taken from the only two participants who wrote accounts of the events treated: Cortés, in *Cartas de relación*, and Bernal Díaz del Castillo, in *Historia verdadera*, cxlii-cxlv.
24 Díaz del Castillo, *Historia verdadera*, cxlii—from which come all other quotes in this section,
25 *Ibid.*, cxlii.
26 Existing maps of these "peñoles" are by William H. Katra (currently posted at the entrance of the building housing the offices of the Municipio de Tlayacapan) and Orendáin, *Ruinas de utopía*, 80-4.
27 Díaz del Castillo, *Historia verdadera*, cxliv.
28 Much later in his written account Díaz del Castillo provides further information about the battles that Cortés led a few weeks later near communities located in (today's) Morelos: "There were two other battles in the place that Cortés refers to as "los peñoles," where the Mexicans killed nine [of our] soldiers, and many of us came out wounded—all because of the faulty judgement of Cortés in those skirmishes." Here is one section where the aged chronist obviously falls into confusion over distant memories: he seems to confuse events that had happened at Tlayacapcan with those at Yecapixtla and/or Cuernavaca," because all three of these places sport topographical features that one might consider to be "peñoles."
29 Cortés, *Letters*, 186.

30   Prescott, *History*, 550-64, details the participation of 818 Spanish foot soldiers and another 150 Spaniards manning the *bergantines*. This, in contrast to the 50,000 warriors from Tlaxcala, an equal number from Tezcuco, multitudes from both Xochimilco and the nearby communities whose warriors collected at Chalco (which probably included those hailing from the Cuernavaca area).

31   Rolena Adorno et al., "El mito de la Conquista: Una ronda revisionista." In *Nexos* (August 2021), 21-8. The opinions quoted are from, respectively, Federico Narvarrete (author of *Quién conquistó México*), Camilla Townsend (author of *Fifth Sun: A New History of the Aztecs*) and Mauricio Tenorio (author of *Clio's Laws: On History and Language*). After this solid assertion embraced—apparently—by all the colloquium participants, a few of them argue unsupportable fictions. First, that the "technological and social differential" existing between Cortés' Mexican Indian allies and his own men was "primarily invisible." And second, that the alliance forged between the two attacking groups was "largely due to initiatives" taken by the mesoamericans.

32   Leslie Byrd Simpson, *Many Mexicos* (Berkeley and Los Angeles: University of California Press, 1959), 22—an exception for the period, offers reliable information about Cortés and Mexico.

CHAPTER 2

33   Chauveau, *Códices de Cuernavaca*, 166.

34   Chauveau, in his editoral "commentaries" throughout the book, provides an interesting accounting of how the different place names mentioned in these documents correspond to current-day neighborhoods and towns. I surmise that the Cuernavaca chieftains' range of influence included the whole western part of the current State of Morelos (from Huizilac in the north to near Taxco in the south), but did not extend any further east than Jautepec.

35   Sarah Cline, in "The Spiritual Conquest Reexamined: Baptism and Christian Marriage in Early Sixteenth-Century Mexico," *Hispanic American Historical Review* (1993): 73 (3): 453-480, researches important folios dating from 1535 to 1540 that are currently held in Mexico's national archives, that list what we can assume as a few important communities located near Cuernavaca: Huitzillan, Quauhchichinollan, Tepozlan, Molotlan, Tepetenchic, and Panchimalco. The first and third of these bear resemblance to the names of current communities; the last is mentioned in the Cuernavaca codex that I've quoted in the text.

36   Chauveau, *Códices*, names this place Yoalcuixtli, and the Cuernavaca elder, as quoted in document, calls it Ahuehuexotla.

37   Riley, *Fernando Cortés*, 58.

38   Díaz del Castillo captures well this detail: "Y desque llegaron donde Cortés estaba, le hicieron mucho acato y le presentaron ciertas joyas de oro, y le dijeron que les perdonase porque no salieron de paz, quell señor de Méjico les envió a

mandar que, pues estaban en Fortaleza, que desde allí nos diesen guerra, e que les envió un buen edscuadrón de mejicanos para que les ayudasen, e que a lo que agora han visto, que no habrá cosas, por fuerte que sea, no la combatamos y señoremos, e que le piden por merced que los reciba de paz." (cxliv)

39 Especially helpful for this section is R. H. Barlow, *The Extent of the Empire of the Culhua Mixica* (Berkeley and Los Angeles: University of California Press, 1949), 73-82. Some Mexican studies refer to the Indigenous groups occupying Morelos in the immediate pre-conquest period as the Tepanecas.

40 Secretaría de Educación Pública, *Morelos: nieve en la cima, fuego en el cañaveral* (Mexico: 1992), 53.

41 Johanna Broda, "La expansion imperial mexica y los sacrificios del Templo Mayor," en Jesús Monjarás-Ruiz, Rosa Brambila, Emma Pérez-Rocha, eds. *Mesoamérica y el centro de México: Una antología* (México: INAH, 1976), 488 [433-76], quotes the chronist Durán.

42 Geoffrey W. Conrad & Arthur A. Demarest, trans. Miguel Rivera Dorado, *Religión e imperio: Dinámica del expansionismo azteca e inca* (México: Alianza, 1988), 75.

43 With the benefit of retrospective knowledge, it becomes apparent that nowhere else in the Americas did Spanish conquistadores encounter such a high standard of native leadership as they did in Tlaxcala and Cuernavaca. Not even it Peru. There—according to the most authoritative historian treating this issue, Hemming, *Conquest of the Incas*, some native-ruled communities . . . became successful" but in perhaps the majority of communities "[native] alcaldes were not obeyed or respected by the Indians [and in others the chieftains] treated their own natives with more cruelty than any Spaniard." (360, 403)

44 Díaz del Castillo, *Historia verdadera*, cxlii.

45 *Sahagún, Historia general*, 844, captured well the regard that the Franciscans held for Cortés: they condoned his military conquest of the Aztecs and praised his efforts to destroy vestiges of the latters' idolatrous religious practices and blood human sacrifices. Then, they would partner with him to carry out the mass baptisms of the Indians and found institutions aimed at the latters' material betterment and assimilation of Christian beliefs and practices. However, they contemned Cortés's initial role in creating the new class of encomenderos whose greed would lead to terrible abuses imposed upon the defenseless Indian population. Sahagún, with a prophetic voice, states in his 1579 prologue (p. 18): "Esta gente [los españoles] os destruirá a vosotros y a vuestras mujeres e hijos, y todo cuanto poseéis, y destruirá todos vuestros pueblos y edificios. Esto a la letra ha acontecido a estos indios con los españoles: fueron tan atropellados y destruidos ellos y todas sus cosas, que ninguna apariencia les quedó de lo que eran antes."

46 Chaveau, *Códices*, 120: "porq luego recibi la ley de Dios y el Sto bautismo, y haverle dado lo necesario pa el y su gente, y haver andado con el pr todas parte a su vista, y haviendo vuelto aca lefui a dexar hasta aonde comio con autoridad y regocijo . . . ." [sic]

CHAPTER 3

47 Díaz del Castillo, *Historia verdadera*, clvii. Given what I consider to be significant deficiencies in the two English translations in my hands, all English translations included in this book are of my own.

48 According to the usually reliable memory of Bernal: "basta que diga que pocos días después de ganado Méjico, y preso Guatemuz, y desde ahí a otros dos meses envió Cortés a otros capitanes a otras provincias. Dejémoslo agora de hablar de Cortés . . ." (clvii) Two months of changes which would become perhaps the most important two months in the history of Mexico.

49 "[Cortés] mandó hacer unas atarazanas y fortaleza en questuviesen los bergantines, y nombró alcaide que estuviese en ella, parésceme que fue a Pedro de Alvarado, hasta que vino de Castilla un Salazar de la Pedrada, nombrado por Su Majestad . . . ." (clvii)

50 Cortés and his soldiers—by August 1521, that is in the weeks subsequent to the Aztecs' submission—already had nearly two years of experience with young Indian concubines (in chapter lxxvi Díaz de Castillo relates how, in October 1519, the chieftains of Tlascala made presents to the Spanish soldiers of their nieces and daughters). We can assume that, subsequently, the most brutish of the Spaniards treated the native girls as mere female carnage for masculine lust. But we can also suppose that other soldiers treated the young females with tenderness and respect—and even as respected "spouses." Bernal highlights a major division within Spanish ranks with regard to this issue in chapter cxlv: apparently many of the common soldiers had been offended by the cruelty to native women, as demonstrated by "los oficiales del Rey" assigned to accompany the conquistador army. The animosity between those "officials of the king" and Cortés was apparent to all. In the previous few months—in both Tepeaca and Tezacuco—those officials who "tenían cargo de ellas [the young female native captives], hacían lo que querían, por manera, que si mal se hizo una vez, esta vez peor" (cxliii). In reaction to that cruelty, the more humaine-minded soldiers sought ways to secretly protect (at least the most "desirable" of) the young female captives: "y desde allí adelante muchos soldados que tomábamos algunas buenas Indias, porque no nos las tomasen como las pasadas las escondíamos, y no las llevábamos a errar, y decíamos que se habían huido . . . (cxliii) [S]i mal lo habían hecho antes, muy peor se hizo esta vez, que después de sacado el Real quinto, sacaba Cortés el suyo, y otras treinta sacaliñas para Capitanes; y si eran hermosas y buenas Indias las íque metíamos a herrar las hurtaban de noche del

montón, que no parecían hasta de ahí a buenos días, y por esta causa se dejaban de herrar muchas piezas, que después teníamos por Naborías." (cxlvi)

Díaz del Castillo makes clear that an important group of soldiers stood firmly behind Cortés in whatever dispute: "cuando Cortés estuviese sentado a la mesa comiendo con sus Capitanes y soldados, que entre aquellas personas que tenían hecho el concierto, , que trajesen una carta muy cerrada y sellada, como que venía de Castilla . . . y que cuando la estuviese leyendo le diesen de puñaladas, así al Cortés, como a todos los Capitanes y soldados que cerca de Cortés nos hallasemos en su defensa. . . . y luego acordó Cortes de tener guarda para su persona . . . y le velaban de dia y de noche, y a nosotros de los que sentía que éramos de su banda, nos rogaba que mirásemos por su persona y desde allí adelante, aunque mostraba gran voluntad a las personas que eran en la conjuración [the pact he had signed with rival groups in Veracruz], siempre se recelaba de ellos" (cxlvi).

51 The animosity between some sectors of the conquistador army was very high. Cortés's most complete biographer, José Luis Martínez, *Hernán Cortés* (México: UNAM & FCE, 2003 [1990]), 258ff, recounts that in May of 1520, "Cuando parecía que la conquista . . . se iba consolidando sin violencia mayor," Pánfilo de Narváez, hired by and obedient to the aggrieved Cuban governor Diego de Velázquez, arrived at Veracruz with an army of 800 soldiers, intent upon overthrowing Cortés and seizing leadership of the campaign against the Aztecs. Díaz del Castillo, *Historia verdadera*, in chapters cxx to cxxii, recounts how Cortés dealt masterfully with this threat to his leadership. The positive result was the (unwilful) incorporation of Narváez and his men into the conquistador army directed by Cortés. But the negative result was the incessant activity on the part of Narváez and other followers of Velázquez to undermine Cortés's leadership. Martínez, *Hernan Cortes*, 296: "Cortés tuvo noticia de que un grupo se soldados -amigos de Veláquez planeaban asesinarlo." And Díaz del Castillo, *Historia verdadera*, cxxi, makes continual mention of the "espías" –"siempre espiaba sobre nosotros" at makes continual mention of the "espías" –"siempre espiaba sobre nosotros" at the orders of Narváez, continually seeking ways to cause problems for Cortés.

52 Díaz del Castillo, *Historia verdadera*, cxliii.

53 Díaz del Castillo, *Historia verdadera*, clvii.

54 Díaz del Castillo highlights the firm support that Cortés always enjoyed with a considerable number of soldiers (perhaps the majority of whom had accompanied him since the beginning of the Mexican campaign in 1519), and how they joined together to confront the threat to Cortés's authority that both Velázquez and his hireling Narváez represented: "cuando Cortés estuviese sentado a la mesa comiendo con sus Capitanes y soldados, que entre aquellas personas que tenían hecho el concierto, que trajesen una carta muy cerrada y

sellada, como que venía de Castilla . . . y que cuando la estuviese leyendo le diesen de puñaladas, así al Cortés, como a todos los Capitanes y soldados que cerca de Cortés nos hallasemos en su defensa. . . . y luego acordó Cortes de tener guarda para su persona . . . y le velaban de dia y de noche, y a nosotros de los que sentía que éramos de su banda, nos rogaba que mirásemos por su persona y desde allí adelante, aunque mostraba gran voluntad a las personas que eran en la conjuración [the pact he had signed with rival groups in Veracruz], siempre se recelaba de ellos" (cxlvi). In the moments before he led his soldiers of confidence in the May 1520 confrontation with Narváez, Bernal has Cortés saying: "no tengo más que pediros por merced, ni traer a la memoria, sino que en esto está el toque de nuestras honras y famas para siempre jamás; y más vale morir por buenos, que vivir afrentados." And with the successful outcome of that bellicose encounter, "muchos amigos de nuestro Capitán, y así como venían, iban a besar las manos a Cortés . . . Pues ver la gracia con que les hablaba, y abrazaba, y las palabras de tantos cumplimientos que les decía . . . y tenía mucha razón de verse en aquel punto tan señor, y pujante." (cxxii). These were the soldiers who would stand by their leader and support his initiatives up to his final days.

55   I differ with Madariaga, *Hernán Cortés*, 396, who writes that the low number of *naborias* deciding to return to their Mexican spouses and/or families is hardly credible.

56   It is interesting to note how, during these first two months of the post-conquest period, the soldiers belonging to the "band" of Cortés perceived the "representatives of the king" as a threat (but perhaps not as great a one as that offered by the soldiers loyal to Narvaez). And the quote from Bernal suggests that the common soldiers supporting Cortes associate the name of the king with what they considered to be the new, unjust, division of spoils in order that the king receive "his fifth" again. Martinez, *Hernan Cortes*, 183, explains that "procuradores"—that is personnel charged with the responsibility of assuring that the monarch receives the first "fifth" of any booty—were already present and involved: "El premier regio presente que Cortes enviaba al rey Carlos fue inventariado . . . el 10 de julio de 1519." We can suppose that, after that date, "procuradores" were ever present and accompanied every new military excursion to every newly encountered Indian village.

57   Eduard Montya de la Rica, *Hernán Cortés* (Madrid: Dastin Export, 2004), 202: "los cambios en su personaldad: Cortés [ya] no aparece como un conquistador arriesgado y sobrio, sino como un monarca . . . ."

58   Chronicler Peter Martyr reports that he was given a cypher in order to send his letters, in one of which he wrote: "From that time we were not without suspicion of [Cortés's intentions [animus]]. These [letters] were written against Cortés's mad designs, consuming avarice and partially revealed tyranny" (*De Orabe Novo*, fol. CXV. trans. II, 406. Quoted from Hernán Cortés: *Letters from Mexico*, Trans. & Ed. Anthony Padgen, Introd. J. H. Elliott (New Haven:

Yale Univ. Press, 1971), 509 n.63. Archivo General de la Nación, Secretaria de Gobernación, R. L. [Rafael López], "Introducción," *Documentos inéditos relativos a Hernán Cortés y su familia* (México: Talleres Gráficos de la Nación, 1935), vii [vii-ix] makes reference to "la codicia proverbial" of Cortés.

59 Eduardo Montoya de la Rica, *Hernán Cortés (Madrid: Dastin Export, 2004)*, 202, who adds that this was "la representación de un poder al estilo de un rey absoluto."

60 Díaz del Castillo, *Historia verdadera,* clviii. The quotations for the rest of this chapter have the same source.

CHAPTER 4

61 Hernán Cortés, "Carta reservada . . . al Emperador Carlos V," in José Luis Martínez, ed, *Documentos cortesianos* (México: Univ. Nacional Autónima de México, FCE, 1991*)*, I, 286. [285-95]. Several Franciscans will repeat this idea of the behavior of the common Spaniards corrupting the Indians. See, for example, Fray Toribio de Motolinía: *Memoriales. Manuscrito de la colección del Señor Don Joaquín García Icazbalceta. Publícalo por primera vez su hijo Luis García Pimentel* (Méjico: Casa del Editor, 1903), 253.

62 Some biographers suggest that Cortés (born in 1485) should be considered yet one more actor in the Europe-wide humanism movement, whose main protagonists/influences were Erasmus of Rotterdam (born in 1466) and Sir Thomas More (1478)—the latter became a combination of disciple-intimate friend-co-collaborator of the former. More probably, Erasmus-like "humanism" was a common thought-tendency of the time among religious progressives.

63 Martínez, *Documentos,* "Carta reservada . . .", I, 289.

64 J. H. Elliot, *Imperial Spain: 1469-1716* (London: Penguin Books, 2002), 70.

65 Díaz del Castillo, *Historia verdadera,* clxix.

66 *Ibid.,* cciv, ccx.

67 Charles Gibson, "Spanish Exploitation of Indians in Central Mexico," in Lewis Hanke, ed. *Latin America: A Historical Reader* (Boston: Little, Brown and Co., 1974), 80.

68 Díaz del Castillo, *Historia verdadera,* clxvi, clxxxv, cxci, cxciii, ccvii, ccx, clxix, cxci, etc.

69 Díaz del Castillo, *Historia verdadera,* clxix.

70 Gibson, *Aztecs,* 61.

71 In another passage Díaz calls all the conquistadors "hijosdalgo," (quiere decir, *hijos de algo*—or "authors of valient acts—the origin for the word "hidalgo," or lower nobility. He explains that there would always be social differences and differences with regard to each's level of "generosity or virtues," even though all are born as "equals." (ccvii)

72 Díaz del Castillo, *Historia verdadera,* cciv ccvii, ccix.

73 Sorely lacking are studies comparing Mexico's early colonial years with—for example—England's earliest colonization efforts in Virginia a century later. Joseph Kelly, *Marooned: Jamestown, Shipwreck, and a New History of America's Origins* (New York, etc.: Bloomsbury, 2018), 115, writes that third of the initial Virginia settlers were "gentlemen," or "principal men," meaning that only these were entitled to serve as "soldiers," and later (we presume) land owners. This stark division between classes in the English colonization experience would become a cause of deadly conflict when they faced difficult times, because "England did not allow the rich much room to maneuver. A gentleman could do little without losing dignity. He might manage his lands, lead soldiers, captain soldiers, hold government or church office, but that was about it. Most types of work shamed a gentleman in the eyes of his peers.

74 Riley, *Fernando Cortés*, 55: "The Spanish laborers employed by Cortés in the Morelos area numbered but a few until 1531; thereafter, their number averaged about twelve. They filled skilled and personal or household service positions in the Morelos labor force."

75 Almost all of these features of post-conquest Mexican society—during the first half-century contrast starkly with the comparable period in Peru. See Hemming, *Conquest of the Incas*, who argues that although "disease was . . . important, [the]main cause of the sharp decline during the first forty years of Spanish rule . . . resulted more from profound cultural shock and chaotic administration" (350).

76 Will Durant, *The Story of Civilization. Part V. The Renaissance* . . . (New York: Simon and Schuster, 1953), 175.

CHAPTER 5

77 Cortés, *Cartas de relación*, 21.
78 Díaz del Castillo, *Historia verdadera*, li, lxi.
79 Silvio Zavala, *Las instituciones jurídicas en la conquista de América* (México: Porrúa, 1971), 213-4, copies from "Bula Inter Caetera," issued by Pope Alejandro VI in 1493: "todo hombre tiene alma, supuesta superioridad de los españoles sobre indígenas . . . tienen derecho a conquistar y a dominar a los indígenas. La superior a la inferior. ...Los indios . . . son hombrecillos, homúnculos menores que hombres, carentes de la palabra, la razón y el entendimiento . . . ."
80 Cortés, *Cartas de relación*, 22. A new tendency among younger critics: to salvage the historical reputation of the Aztecs. See David Carrasco, en "The Exaggerations of Human Sacrifice," en Bernal Díaz del Castillo, *The History of the Conquest of New Spain* . . ., ed. & introd. David Carrasco (Albuquerque: New Mexico University Press, 2008), 327-44.
81 Cortes, *Letters from Mexico*, 279.
82 Díaz del Castillo, *Historia verdadera*, li.

83 "La relación de Chimalpain: lo que siguió a la toma de la ciudad," in Miguel León-Portilla, *Literaturas indígenas* ...(México: Ediciones Patria, 1991), 301.
84 Francisco López de Gómara, *Historia de la conquista de México* (México: Porrúa, 1997), 195.
85 "Relación de Texcoco dispuesta por Juan Bautista Poman," 645-6, in León-Portilla, ed. & introd., *Literaturas indígenas* . . . . The editor gives no indication as to the identity of this text, except his suggestion that it belongs to "La tradición indígena puesta en castellano en el siglo XVI." (xix).
86 Huejotzingo, City Council of, "An Indian Town Addresses the King," in Lockhart, *Letters and People*, 166, 167, 169. In Spanish: "Carta del Consejo de Huexotzingo al Rey Felipe II, 30 de julio de 1560," in Miguel León-Portilla, ed. *Visión de los vencidos: Relaciones indígenas de la conquista*. México: UNAM, 2004), pp. 169-74. Both Lockhart and León Portilla state in footnotes that this letter first appeared, both in Spanish and in English translation, in Anderson, *Beyond the Códices*, 176-90. Although Lockhart and León-Portilla state that this document was "rediscovered" (I have been unable to locate information about this specific "rediscovery") in the Archivo Histórico Nacional, Madrid, Anderson in his Preface identifies both Mexico's Archivo General de la Nación and the McAfee Collection of UCLA's Research Library as the "two main sources of our selections" which include "Náhuatl wills, land translations, municipal council minutes, local tax records, and a rich variety of petitions and correspondence" (v).
87 Fernando de Alva Ixtlilxóchitl, *Obras históricas: ...Historia de la Nación Chichimeca,* Introd. Edmundo O'Gorman (México: UNAM, 1985), II, 195, 198, 205. Fr. Bernardino de Sahagún, introd. Angel María Garibay K., *Historia general, de las cosas de Nueva España*, 8 ed. (México: Porrúa, 1992), 873" "Gran cosas por cierto había hecho Cortés y los demás conquistadores en plantar la luz evangélica en este nuevo mundo, si no hubieran hecho las crueldades y las cosas referidas en esta historia . . . ."
88 Chauveau, *Códices de Cuernavaca.*
89 Quiroga, "Información en derecho," traduce una carta (originalmente en griego) escrito por Guilleromo Vudeo al "gran Basilio," 175-6.
90 Ibid., 209, 152, 106, 118.
91 Ibid., 156.
92 The first part of this quote comes from Lockhart, *Letters and People,* 222; the second part is my own translation of Fray Toribio de Benavente o Motolinía, introd. Edmundo O'Gorman, *Historia de los indios de la Nueva España: Relación de los ritos antiguos* (México: Porrúa, 2014), 296.
93 Robert Ricard, *La conquista espiritual de México: Ensayo sobre el apostolado y los métodos misioneros* . . . . In some circles, the Ricard book is regarded as perhaps the most important source of information about "evangelization" in

New Spain/Mexico. It almost totally ignores the role of Hernán Cortés. I view the book as flawed, given the author's strong (almost hidden) biases leading him minimize the achievements of the Franciscan fathers' (and especially Motolonía's) accomplishments (most visible on pp. 459-64). That is, he chooses to ignore fifty years of evangelization successes and bases his final judgements on the admittedly difficult situations presented to the original padres toward the end of their careers. This is akin to calling Hemingway a failed writer on the basis of his last flawed work! Could it be that Ricard, at the dawning of the 20th century, sought to renew the anti-Franciscan vendetta of the 16th century Dominicans (explained in Appendix A)?

94 The first part of this quote comes from Lockhart, *Letters and People*, 213; the second part is my own translation of Gante, "Carta," 223.
95 Mendieta, *Historia eclesiástica*, II, 65.
96 Zumárraga, *Don Fray Juan de Zumárraga*, II, 269-70.
97 Readers should therefore question the opinions of a writer such as Elliot, *Imperial Spain*, 72, who misunderstands the context and accomplishments of the friars by characterizing their labor as "the destruction of . . . a native civilization . . . ; [the friars'] were much less successful in eradicating old pagan beliefs . . . [they] overestimated the Indians' spiritual aptitude . . . [and they] became disillusioned by [their] lack of progress and began to change their views. In the end the majority probably disdained the natives." This view ignores the significant changes that occurred over a half-century to Mexican society and the day-to-night ideological shift of the Spanish monarchy, as represented by the passing of authority from the cosmopolitan Carlos V to his ultra-reactionary son, Felipe II.
98 Gibson, *Tlaxcala*, 103, 115. See Appendix B.
99 Gómara, *Historia*, 151.
100 Martínez, *Hernán Cortés*, 822.
101 Charles C. Mann, *1493: Uncovering the New World Columbus Created* (New York: Alfred A. Knopf, 2011), 304.
102 Gibson, *Aztecs*, 61, 74, 76. Gibson ignored essential aspects of Cortés' career when he wrote his important book on Tlaxcala—as I explain in the Introduction.
103 Martínez, *Hernán Cortés*, 515. A copy of Cortés' important 1523 letter to the king is found in Cortés, *Documentos*, I, 265-71.

CHAPTER 6
104 Díaz del Castillo, *Historia verdadera*, clvii.
105 Cortés, *Cartas de relación*, III, 171.
106 Martínez, *Hernán Cortés*, 399-400.
107 *Ibid.*, 399-400,
108 Google, "Zacatula."

109 "Carta ... a Francisco Cortés," in Martínez, *Documentos,* I, 316 fn3 [316-18].
110 Motolinía, *Memorias,* 248-9.
111 William H. Prescott, *Mexico and the Life of the Conqueror, Fernando Cortés. In Two Volumes* (New York: Peter Fenelon Collier,1896), I, 120ff. After five lucid pages on this topic of the central-valley Mexicans' domestic and affective lives, Prescott concludes: "In this remarkable picture of manners, which I have copied faithfully from the records of earliest date after the Conquest, we find no resemblance to the other races of North American Indians. ... The Aztec character was perfectly original and unique." (125)
112 Silvio Zavala, *Tributos y servicios personales de indios para Hernán Cortés y su familia (Extractos de documentos del siglo XVI)* (México: Archivos de la Nación, 1999). From chapter 18: "Cuernavaca y sujetos, tributos y servicios al marqués del Valle, 1544."
113 Don Toribio unabashedly listed the numerous properties that he either controlled or owned outright—Chauveau, *Códices de Cuernavaca,* 98, 87.
114 *Ibid.,* 72.
115 *Ibid.,* 73.
116 *Ibid.,* 78.
117 In my own close reading of court-case transcripts, I have concluded that Riley, *Fernando Cortes,* 58, with anti-Cortés biases, exaggerated in asserting that Cortés appropriated other land areas as well.
118 Riley, *Fernando Cortes,* 60-1, provides an alternative narrative of this affair and gives 1533 as the year when Cortés took possession of this land.
119 Martin, *Rural Society,* 15—repeating information communicated by Riley, *Fernando Cortes,* communicates that even though the day-to-day lives of the indigenous communities in and around Cuernavaca during the first few post-conquest decades underwent "pervasive change," this did not involve either the exploitation of Indian labor nor the pre-existing land-tenure system. In spite of the fact that Cortés's "ambitious economic enterprises and ubiquitous tribute-collectors and other agents"—he acquired a modest amount of personal property.Via the similar Indian-Spanish land-selling conventions, the end result was that at the time of his death in 1546, only "a relatively small amount of land [had passed from Indian owners to Spaniards."
120 Martínez, *Documentos* II, 279. Some historians suggest that another reason for the high priority Cortés gave to cattle production was to motivate Indians to choose this source of "animal protein" the bodies of fallen warriors. "Bernal"—unlike the more "discrete" Cortés in his letters to the king, or the friar López de Gómara—makes frequent mention of this alimentary benefit of pre-conquest societies.
121 Riley, *Fernando Cortes,* 119 fn. 54.

122 These were two of the most heated issues in the acrimonious feud between Franciscans and Dominicans (see Appendix A).
123 Chauveau, *Códices de Cuernavaca*, 162, 166.
124 *Ibid.*, 70.
125 *Ibid.*, 93, 166,
126 Lesley Byrd Simpson, *The Encomienda of Spanish Mexico* (Berkeley and Los Angeles: University of California Press, 1966), 56.
127 Vasco de Quiroga, "Información en Derecho," Introd. Paz Serrano Gassent, *La utopía en América: Cronistas de América. México en tres tiempos. Virreinato.* 33 (Monterrey: App Editorial, n.d.), 155.
128 Quiroga, "Información," 151.
129 José Miranda, El tributo indígena en La Nueva España durante el siglo XVI (México: Colegio de México, 1972), 74.
130 In reward for his leadership in the successful conquest, Cortés requested control over 22 separate encomientas, an immense jurisdiction located all across Mexico. Crown officials, perhaps ignoring the scale of his request, ended up awarding to him the Marquesado, which included nearly all the areas he had requested. Three of the 22 towns were Cuernavaca (which included Tepoztlán), Oaxtepec, and Acapixtla—which are located in today's State of Morelos. Bernardo García Martínez, *El Marquesado del Valle: Tres siglos de regimen señorial en Nueva España* (México: El Colegio de México, 1969), treats legal aspects of the Marquesado, arguing (without explaining in depth) that it should be considered a "señorío jurisdiccional" (with the Cortés family exercising perpetual rights to unoccupied lands and broad authority over the "vassal" inhabitants) instead of an encomienda—which Cortés granted to many of his soldiers (who only enjoyed temporary rights limited to collecting Indian tributes and employing their labor). Like other studies accomplished by members of his generation, García excels in archival research, but offers paltry information about the personal activities or character of Hernán Cortés himself or the Indian communities involved.
131 Rodrigo de Albornoz, "[Letter] to Charles V, December 15, 1525," in Simpson, *Encomienda*, 209.
132 Haskett, *Indigenous Rulers*, 4.
133 Chauveau, *Códices de Cuernavaca*, 94.
134 Secretaría de Educación Pública (SEP), *Morelos: nieve en la cima, fuego en el cañaveral* (México: SEP, 1992), 53. This source also gives population estimates for Oaxtepec, 50,000; Totolapan, 20,000; 12,000 for each of Tlayacapan, Tetela [del Volcán?], Yecapixtla, and Ocuituco (53).
135 Chauveau, *Códices de Cuernavaca*, 94.
136 *Ibid.*, 122.
137 [R.López], *Documentos inéditos ... familia,*" 5.

138 Archivo, *Nuevos documentos*, 153. Gibson, *The Aztecs*, 196, affirms the same on the basis of his careful studies of surviving records from Texcoco, Xaltocan, Coyoacán, Tlalmanalco, and other communities.
139 Chauveau, *Códices de Cuernavaca*, 203
140 Martin, *Rural Society in Colonial Morelos*, 15-17, remarks—on the basis of her reading of the 1580 *Relación de Oaxtepec*—that as the process of transculturalization progressed, the tributes required of the different indigenous communities near Cuernavaca progressively favored new products—European fruits, beef, and service animals such as horses and oxen—which the Cortés establishment would use in its commercial dealings with consumers in Mexico City and elsewhere.
141 Benítez, *Historia de la Ciudad de México*, II, 10.
142 Gibson, *Aztecs*, 220.
143 Chris Brown, *King and Outlaw: The Real Robert the Bruce* (Stroud, Gloucestershire: The History Press, 2018), 145-7.
144 We lack information (and I distrust that which we do possess) about the forms of "compulsion" applied to New Spain Indians during the first few decades after the Aztecs'submission. But I feel confident in rejecting the message communicated via the pictorial interpretations by Diego Rivera inside the Palacio de Cortés (in Cuernavaca) that depict a cruel, mounted, Spanish mayordomo, with whip in hand, threatening bodily punishment if the Indian commoners did not work in the sugarcane fields.
145 Manuel Fernández de Velasco, "Cortés y el inicio de la ganadería," en Patronato mexicano, *Cortés*, 90.
146 Chauveau, *Códices de Cuernavaca*, 80.
147 *Ibid.*, 166.

CHAPTER 7

148 Elliot, *Imperial Spain*, 71.
149 Ross King, *The Bookseller of Florence: The Story of the Manuscripts that Illuminated the Renaissance* (New York: Atlantic Monthly Press, 2021), 394.
150 Tuchman, *March of Folly*, 53.
151 Elliot, *Imperial Spain*, 103-5. On p.161: the Erasmian invasion of Spain is "one of the most remarkable events" of the century, with a widespread diffusion of works and "a natural bond of sympathy" among leading Spanish intellectuals and Carlos's regime—which inspired their hopes for a universal peace. Later, Elliot treats the falling from favor of these ideas under the leadership of Carlos's son and heir, Felipe II.
152 *Ibid*, 105.
153 Pérez, "El Erasmo," 392, 331. I've taken the liberty to add the name of the San Gabriel or Belvís de Monroy monastery to the list provided by Pérez. The

primary and secondary literature is almost silent with regard to the religious thought of the monks in this enclave. It is my impression that almost all that posterity knows about these comes from the information provided by Motolinía in his *Memoriales*.

154 *Ibid.*, 326. A few of these affinities: First, both Erasmus and the Mexican Franciscans embraced the apostles' commitment to "free" baptism; both implicitly rejected Scholastic formations in favor of "interior" or personal "faith"; both shared reference for the life of the "spirit" over materiality; and both shared a commitment to humility and poverty.
155 Tuchman, *March of Folly*, 57.
156 Erasmus, "Catalogue of his Works," in Rummel, "Introduction" to *The Erasmus Reader*, 35.
157 Cortés must have been totally informed about the relatively "empty" status of regal authority in Spain during the first years of his activities in Mexico—from 1519 to 1521—when the young king, Carlos was just initiating his reign.
158 Rhea Marsh Smith, *Spain, A Modern History* (Ann Arbor: University of Michigan Press, 1965), 142. Henry Latimer Seaver, *The Great Revolt in Castille: A Study of the Comunero Movement of 1520-1521* (New York: Octagon Books, 1966), depicts Adriano as "a saint" urging clemency, conciliation and gentleness (155) when as regent, the Crown administered "unsparing justice [and] exemplary punishments" (351).
159 Castro Seoane, *P. Olmedo*, 75-6. The same could be said about "Ordenanzas para Tlaxcala," because the ideas contained in both were "worthy of a theologian; only a theologian [such as Olmedo] would have been able to redact them." This fragmentary documentation leads to a persuasive supposition that Father Olmedo played a huge role in helping Cortés think through the options, at this early stage, for the Mexicans' future conversion to Christianity.
160 Cortés, *Letters frorm Mexico*, 332-3.
161 Marcel Bataillon, *Erasmo y España: Estudios sobre la historia espiritual del siglo xvi*, 2da ed. revisada (Mexico: Fondo de Cultura Económica, 1966 [original in French: 1937]), 821, 824fn.72.
162 Christian Duverger, *La conversión de los indios de Nueva España. Con el texto de los "Coloquios de los Doce" de Bernardino de Sahagún (1564)* (México: FCE, 1993 [French: 1987]), 20-1.
163 Marsh Smith, *Spain*, 121-5.
164 Díaz del Castillo, *Historia verdadera*, xxv.
165 Hemming, *Conquest of the Incas*, 262.
166 Cortes, *Letters from Mexico*, 332-3.
167 Will Durant, *The Story of Civilization. The Age of Faith: A History of Medieval Civilization—Christian, Islamic, and Judaic—from Constantine to Dante: a.d. 325-1300* (New York: Simon and Schuster, 1950), 802-3. See also Duverger,

Conversión de los indios, 189-91; *Cortés* (France: Fayard, 2001), 371-2; and Gibson, *The Aztecs,* 117, writes that "Punishment and force played a larger role in Mexican conversion that is customarily recognized," that the Christian pedagogy included "routine beatings and imprisonments."

168 According to Fernando Ocaranza, *Capítulos de la historia franciscana [primera serie]* (México: s.e., 1933), 16ff, the Monastery of Belvís was also known as that of Belvis or Berrrocal, and belonged to the Provincia de San Gabriel (in Seville?), and that Martín de Valencia, the Belvís leader, had a reputation as "heir" to the recently deceased Juan de Guadalupe, leader of the Barefoot Franciscan reform movement in Spain (el Orden de los Hermanos Menores Descalzos de la Estricta Observancia—also known as the Guadalupian movement of Extremadura). He had formerly resided in the convent of Santa María de los Angeles, in the province of los Angeles.

169 Michael K. Kellogg, *The Wisdom of the Renaissance* (New York: Prometheus Books, 2019), 66.

170 Duverger, "Idealización de mestizaje," 55, proposes (without documenting his source) that Fernán's father, Martín Cortés, played an essential role in the communications with the new pope, that the elder Cortés had earned the pope's eternal gratitude when, on a military campaign years earlier, he had performed an important service to the latter's son.

171 Durant, *Renaissance,* explains that in 1515 the Franciscan Adriano of Utrecht so impressed King Fernando of his administrative ability and moral integrity that the latter appointed him bishop of Tortosa and then assistant to Cardinal Cisneros in governing Spain in the absence of the young Carlos. In Spain, Adriano "lived simply and pursued heretics with a zeal that endeared him to the people. ... The reputation of his virtues reached Rome, and Leo made him a cardenal." (622) Upon Leo's death in 1521, the cardinals elected him pope—in a very unpopular decision. Adriano VI's 14 months in that position were marked by conflict and controversy. His attempts at reform met solid resistance. He was "an anomaly in Renaissance Rome: a Pope who was resolved at all costs to be a Christian." (621) According to Tuchman, *March of Folly,* 118-19, Adriano's two frustrating years as the Catholic Pope might be taken as an epitome for the short "golden age" of post-conquest Mexico. He was a "reform-minded ... person .... Reformers ... encouraged by Adriano's reputation, were hopeful at last.... [Assuming his functions as Pope in 1519, he] made his intent clear at once ... imploring the Cardinals to banish corruption and luxury from their lives and ... set a good example to the world by joining him in the cause of reform. [But he ended up] alienating the papal court. ... Adrian found the system too entrenched for him to dislodge. 'How much,' he sorrowfully acknowledged, 'does a man's efforts depend on the age in which his work is

cast!' Utterly frustrated, the outsider died unmourned ... after a year and two weeks in active office."

172 On the 9th of May, 1522 the Franciscan leadership, in the name of the king, appointed the Belvís Franciscans to head up the Evangelization Campaign in New Spain.

173 Díaz del Castillo, *Verdadera historia*, cxcv.

174 Many might consider that the more "typical" religious life and thought in the Spain of that epoch is represented in the figures of the greedy cleric, the Friar of the Merced, and the Church pardoner, as depicted in the groundbreaking picaresque novel, *Lazarillo de Tormes*, first published in 1554. See the excellent introduction offered by editor Chad M. Gasta, [anonymous], *Lazarillo de Tormes y de sus fortunas y adversidades* (Long Grove, IL: Waveland, 2013).

175 In spite of the importance of her essay, Cline, in "The Spiritual Conquest," does not state a fundamental fact, that it was the Belvís Franciscans, in opposition to the Dominicans, who "seem to have returned to the ideals of the early church, stressing personal commitment" for the baptism of a native to occur (in contrast to the Dominicans' emphasis on prior knowledge of scriptures, etc.) in "the hope of baptis[ing] as many as possible as soon as possible [and therefore believing that] continued instruction in the catechism after baptism as the most practical next step."

176 Duverger, *Cortés*, 273, provides most of the information for this paragraph. The 1523 letter from the king is reproduced in Martínez, *Documentos*, I: 265-71.

177 Díaz del Castillo, *Historia verdadera*, clxxi.

178 Sahagún, *Historia general*, 860.

179 Chauveau, *Códices de Cuernavaca*, 100, 76.

180 Juan de Grijalda, *Crónica de la orden Augustín en las provincias de la Nueva España ... 1533 hasta 1592* [1624] (México: Victoria, 1924), p. 66, mentions early Augustian presence in Totolapan, Yecapixtla, and Tlayacapan. On p. 14, the author depicts the heroic dimensions of the "valeroso" Cortés in one important aspect of the Evangelization Campaign: the values/cultural changes of New Spain's Indians.

181 Mendieta, *Historia eclesiástica*, 55-61, recounts the attempts by Franciscans to carry out missionary activities in areas other than New Spain.

182 Lyle N. McAlister, *Spain and Portugal in the New World, 1492-1700* (Minneapolis: The University of Minnesota, 1984), 168.

183 Cortes, *Letters from Mexico*, 332-3.

184 Martínez, *Documentos*, I, 285-95, reproduces this "Carta reservada." While the editors of Cortés, *Cartas de relación* include this "carta reservada" (207-18), they fail to mention its presence in the "contents." Unfortunately, the editors of English translation, Cortes, *Letters from Mexico*, exclude it entirely.

185 Duverger, *Conversión de los indios*, 153ff.

186 Surprisingly, Marcel de Bataillon, in his renown and detailed *Erasmo en España: Estudios sobre la historia espiritual del siglo xvi*, 2nd ed. rev. (Mexico: FCE, 1966 [First French edition: 1937]), does not mention the Franciscan "Orden de los hermanos menores descalzos de la estricta observancia;" nor the latter's founder Juan de Guadelupe; nor the monastery at Belvís; nor the Custodia de San Gabriel de Extremadura. But in the twelve pages before the long book's conclusion (pp. 819-20) he does mention Franciscans Martín de Valencia and Juan de Zumárraga.

187 Duverger, *Conversión de los indios*, 132; he dedicates a whole chapter to this topic.

188 The only writing by Friar Martín de Valencia which I have been able to locate is "Carta de Fray Martín de Valencia y otros misioneros al emperador," included in García Icazbalceta, *Nueva colección*. Valencia wrote this letter in Tenochtitlán in 1526. In it he repeats many of the arguments made by Cortés in his 1524 letter to the king: the Franciscans' important task of converting the natives and their disaccord with the crown's opposition to the encomienda. Current-day readers must understand that Valencia and the Franciscan friars (as well as Bernal Díaz del Castillo and Vasco de Quiroga—both present in Valladolid toward 1550) defended the encomienda only with regard to its practice in the early New Spain regime, where encomendero excesses were largely contained via the Franciscan friars' intervention on behalf of Indian rights and the strong executive authority (as it existed under the first two viceroys) which proved resolute in defending those rights. Another issue: in contrast to the position of Cortés, Valencia embraces the Court's position about the desirably of mixing Spaniards and Indians.

189 Diego Muñoz Camargo, *Relaciones geográficas del siglo XVI* (México: UNAM, Instituto de Investigaciones Antropológicas, 1981-88), 4: 52.

190 Motolinía, *Memoriales*, 33.

191 Mariano Monterrosa, "Evangelización," in *Historia de México*, eds. Juan Salvat y José Luis Rosas (México: Salvat Editores, 1986), vol, 7, 1132. In this outstanding essay, the author suggests that New Spain's "edad dorada" might appropriately be called "The Zumárraga Period"—an idea ignored by the great majority of historians, including Silvio Zavala in his *The Political Philosophy of the Conquest of America*, trans. *Teener* Hall (México: Editorial Cultura, 1953).

192 Monterrosa, "Evangelización," 1105-6, who cites Mendiota.

193 Mendieta, *Historia eclesiástica*, 55.

CHAPTER 8

194 Martínez, *Hernán Cortés*, 359, 420, explains the reasons for why Cortés, in 1523, made the "decisión arrebatada" to embark on the Honduras expedition.

195 Quotes from this and the following paragraphs come from Martínez, *Hernán Cortés*, 417, 386, 449, 417.

196 Morley, *Ancient Maya*, 114-7, offers a description of Cortés' Honduras route, which is followed by a surprising opinion (which readers must treat seriously, given Morley's reputation as one of the most distinguished of American reseachers over Latin American topics): "This formidable undertaking constitutes one of the most sustailed efforts in military history. ... When it is remembered that this expedition was undertaken in the early years of the sixteenth century, Cortez' outstanding qwualities of leadership are magnified to almost unbelievable proportions" (114).

197 Díaz del Castillo, *Historia verdadera*, clxxxi.

198 López de Gómara, *Historia*, 264.

199 Silvio Zavala, "Ideario de Vasco de Quiroga," in *Recuerdo de Vasco de Quiroga*, 35-62. In this and other sources Zavala provides good explanations for the debates about slavery in New Spain: At the dawning of the Sixteenth Century, the Catholic Kings had issued ordinances prohibiting any form of Indian slavery, which the Spanish encomenderos in the Antilles largely ignored in practice. Cortés, upon beginning his governance of New Spain after the Aztecs' military defeat, gave a deaf ear to existing prohibitions in light of the very widespread practice of the institution among almost all of New Spain's Indian communities. It was a complex issue. In brief, the Indians allied with the Spanish practiced a benign type of "slavery" and were reluctant to give it up. They handed slaves over to Spanish as a form of tribute. Furthermore, many Spaniards, who had participated in the defeat of hostile Indian groups, argued that Spanish precedent should allow them, by law, to enslave the defeated warriors. The King, under enormous pressure, decided in 1534 to overturn existing prohibitions. But two of the three members of the Segundo Audiencia then administering New Spain demonstrated strong opposition to the King's recent ruling: the lawyer Vasco de Quiroga and the Audiencia's chairman and ex-bishop, Ramírez de Fuenleal. These two, independently, wrote well-researched rebuttals. Debates in official circles would continue into the 1550s. Cortés, as well as the viceroy, Antonio de Mendoza, owned hundreds of both African and Indian slaves. Even the Dominican monk and defender of the Indians, Bartolomé de las Casas, would come to promote the slavery of Africans as one of his solutions to save the American Indians from extreme exploitation and early death at the hands of the cruelest of Spanish settlers in the Americas.

200 Simpson, *Encomienda*, 177.

201 Sahagún, *Historia general*, 755.

202 Zumárraga mentions this in his 1525 letter to the king, as translated and published by Simpson, *Encomienda*, 217.

CHAPTER 9

203 Madariaga, *Hernán Cortés*, 485, quotes from the letter that Cortés was to write to the emperor three years before his death: "This work which God did through me is so great and marvelous . . ."

204 Cortés, *Cartas de relación*, III, 165. In this third letter to the king (1522), he gave evidence of having founded two new cities (today we know them as Puebla and Moreilia) in which the Spanish, separated from the Indians, would reside.

205 Cortés, in one document, declared that "nunca pobló villa alguna en Oaxaca." Martínez, *Documentos*, II, 260.

206 Riley, *Fernando Cortes*: "Even before the viceregal order of 1535-36, Cortés evidently paid wages to some of these *macehuales*, particularly those tending livestock and working either with silkworms or in mulberry groves …. In later years, Cortés paid wages to most and probably all of his encomienda workers. Conclusive data as to the value of these wages, unfortunately, are not available for either period. It does appear that payments were made on a job rather than a time basis." (50) "Cortés used large numbers of his Morelos Indians as *tamames*, paying wages initially only to those who made long trips but eventually to all of them." (51) "The Indian laborers provided by these towns were, as a rule, paid wages after 1534-35, and together with his Indian slaves they constituted the greater part of his labor force." (91)

207 Two existing sources treating Cortés' palace provide little or no information about its initial years: Jorge Angulo & Chappie Angulo, *El museo cuauhnahuac en el Palacio de Cortés: Recopilación histórico-arqueológica del proceso de cambio en el Edo. de Morelos* (México: Instituto Nacional de Antropología e Historia, 1979) y Miguel Salinas, "El Palacio de Cortés," en *Historia y paisajes morelenses* (México: Ernesta Salinas, 1981), pp. 40-56.

208 Chauveaux, *Códices de Cuernavaca*, 76. See also Riley, *Fernando Cortes*, 119, n.54.

209 Chauveau, *Códices de Cuernavaca*, 124, 132.

210 Monterrosa, "Evangelización," indicates that in 1528 the Dominicans began construction of both a convent and hospital in Oaxtepec (p. 1092). In 1534 the Agustinians founded parishes in Totolapan and Ocuituco; and in 1535, they began evangelization activities in Yecapixtla and Zacualpan (p. 1096).

211 Motolinía, *Historia*, 116.

212 The Franciscans' early activities in New Spain are discussed in Duverger, *Cortés*, 275-6; McAlister, *Spain and Portugal*, 170; Monterrosa, "Evangelización;" Ruiz Medrano, *Reshaping New Spain*, 27.

213 Motolinía, *Historia*, I, 4 & 117. Other Franciscan monks, even 30 years later, would experience the same (sometime frantic) willingness of Indians to be baptized. For example, Monterrosa, "Evangelización," 1126, quotes Friar Mendieta: "the Indians [living in isolated areas] are so frightened and full of dread if a child of theirs dies without having been baptized. I've seen mothers, trembling as they remove a suckling baby from their breasts and hold it out—whether in desperation or joy—for us to baptize it; some think that without that baptism the child will fall sick and die."

214 Friar Diego de Landa, *Yucatan Before and After the Conquest, with Other Related Documents, Maps and Illustrations*, William Gates, trans. (New York: Dover, 1978), 28. (Landa's landmark history, *Relación de las cosas del Yucatán*, was based on decades of personal experience, beginning in 1542, among the Mayas in New Spain's region of the Yucatán Peninsula.)
Yucatan, 29-31, has left a description of a similar colegio for noble Indian youth that the Franciscan friars founded in Mérida.

215 Gante, "Carta" [1558], 223.

216 Mendiata, *Historia eclesiástica*, 78-9.

217 Simpson, *Encomienda*, 120. While different Spanish individuals received tributes via the encomiendas assigned to them, the King would receive his "fifth" via the corregimiento, that rarely functioned well under government-appointed administrators.

218 [Fray] Pedro de Gante, "Carta de Fr. Pedro de Gante al Rey D. Felipe II," In García Icazbalceta, *Nueva colección ...; Códice franciscano*, 220-27. De Gante's birth name was Pierre de Gand, and he is considered one of the "Divine Dozen"—but in actual fact he arrived at New Spain in 1523—that is, a year before the others. The letter, written in the 1550—toward the end of de Gante's life—is in actual fact a reminiscence of the role he himself had played some thirty years before in the Franciscan experiment in Indian education—that is, before the advent of a new generation of native chieftains intent upon causing chaos.

219 Jose Ruben Romero Galván & Pilar Maynez, eds. *El universio de Sahagún: pasado y presente. Coloquio 2005* (México: UNAM, 2007), 9-11. The Lic. Juan de Ovando, visiting New Spain between 1568 and 1570, had good words to say about the operation of the Colegio in the report he later submitted to the Consejo de las Indias. He calls attention to the dedicated service of its founder, Friar Pedro de Gante, who was "el primero que enseñó a los indios a cantar y la música que ahora tañen, y les ha hecho aprender el pintar y otros oficios en que se igualan y exceden a los españoles, y ha perseverado en instruirlos y aprovecharlos hasta el día de hoy, que vive de edad de noventa años." (Ovando, "Informe," 6)

220 Quiroga, *Utopía*, 67.

221 The Colegio de Santa Cruz in Tlatelolco: From its beginnings the Franciscans suffered incessant criticisms and opposition, mainly from the Dominicans and then from a growing group of Spaniards. Ricard, *Conquista espiritual*, pp. 391-419, unjustly criticizes the Franciscans of "excesiva audacia" (415) because he earlier explains that important leaders (among them Fuenleal and Antonio de Mendoza supported it. It is undeniable that the aging Franciscan fathers, after two or three decades of the Colegio's successful functioning, began to lose "fe en su obra" (410) upon seeing its growing problems and the rising opposition to it among Spaniards. But I cannot agree with Ricard's apparent reasoning, that

this was sufficient reason to call the original Colegio a failure. (410) Solange Alberro, in "El imperial Colegio de Santa Cruz y las aves de rapiña: Una modesta contribución a la microfísica del poder a mediados del siglo XVI," en *Historia Mexicana* lxiv, no. 1 (México: El Colegio de México, 2014), 7-63, 17, explains that "entre 1546 y 1566 ... los franciscanos de Santa Cruz dejaron en manos de sus exalumnos y conciliarios el gobierno del Colegio, y ... se cayó todo el regimiento y buen concierto del Colegio a causa de[l fraude] del mayordomo, la negligenia y descuido del rector y conciliarios, y también por el descuido de los frailes."

222 Chauveau, *Códices de Cuernavaca*, 124, 132.
223 Ibid., 164, 167-8.
224 Ibid., 78-80.
225 Garcia Icazbalceta, , *Nueva Colección ...; Códice franciscano*, 20.
226 Motolinia, *Motolinia's History*, 178, does not mention his possible residence in Cuernavaca in the 1530s, when he gave positive court testimony about Cortés' treatment of the Indian porters.
227 Susana Gómez Serafín, *Altepetl de Huaxtepec: Modificaciones territoriales desde el siglo xvi* (Mexico: Instituto Nacional de Antropología e Historia, 2011), 59. See also Riley, *Fernando Cortés*, 15-17.
228 Riley, *Hernando Cortes*, 119, n. 57, 59.
229 Ibid., 17.
230 Motolinía, *Historia*, II,4.
231 Monterrosa, "Evangelización," 1097.
232 Chauveau, *Códices de Cuernavaca*, 68.
233 Ibid., 93. Neither Mendieta nor Monterrosa mention by name Friar Pedro García.
234 Ovando, "Informe," 55, 56, 57, 59, 77.
235 Chauveau, *Códices de Cuernavaca*, 78.

CHAPTER 10

236 Martínez, *Hernán Cortés*, 503. Cortés' enemies accused him of the same: grandious plans to rebel and base a wholly independent New Spain regime on the unquestioned adhesion to him of the Indian masses. However, no conclusive evidence about this exists—to my knowledge. Another source: Ethelia Ruiz Medrano, trans. Julia Constantino & Pauline Marmasse, *Reshaping New Spain: Government and Private Interests in the Colonial Bureaucracy, 1531-1550* (Boulder: University Press of Colorado, 2014), 24.
237 Díaz del Castillo, *Historia verdadera*, cxcv.
238 Duverger, *Crónica de la eternidad,* 136. See also: 49, 61, 137-9, 262, 268.
239 Martínez, *Hernán Cortés*, 503: la "jactanciosa malacrianza [de un] hombre tan ensoberbecido."

240 While many individuals—Indians and Spanish alike—benefitted from Cortés' actions, some biographers state—wrongly, in my opinion—that a few closest to him were the brunt of an unforgivable ingratitude. Printed documents from the Juicio de Residencia—that is, the official court investigation into Cortés' actions between 1518 and 1526—demonstrate beyond any doubt that a large number of respected individuals, most of whom had served under him, offered public support. This, in spite of the weighty accusations made by his many enemies. That court, after 21 years of hearings, never offered a significant ruling against him. Finally, in 1545 (that is, months before his death), all charges were dismissed: "se desiste ... en dicho juicio en vista de sus notorios servicios." -words of Cortés, *Documentos*, II, 12.

241 A Cortés ally, Juan de Salcedo, testified in the Juicio de Residencia what must have been Cortés' own explanation for that sudden death of his wife: she had died of cardiac arrest. Cortés, *Documetos*, II, 380. Summary documents for the drawn-out trials resulting from the accusations of Catalina Suárez's mother, Doña María de Marcyda, can be found in [R.López], *Documentos inéditos*, II, 34-178.

242 According to Martínez, *Hernán Cortés,* 370, 463, the nebulous circumstances surrounding the deaths in Mexico City of crown-appointed officials Garray and Ponce de Leon caused rumors to fly about Cortés' nefarious motivations and will to commit evil acts.

243 Díaz del Castillo, *Verdadera historia*, clxxiv: The army was led by fifteen prominent Spaniards—"and many others whose names I can't now remember. These were followed by twenty of the most powerful Indian chieftains from the Central Valley, as well as a collection of other individuals: a priest and two Franciscan friars, a chief assistant, a bottler, a dessert baker, huge vases of gold and silver . . a table servant, a surgeon ... many common servants, two assistants in charge of the soldiers' lances and eight others to carry spurs, two hunters with their hawks, five *chirimías* and *sacabuches*—species of trumpets—, an acrobatic dancer and a tumbler, and all of these came with the chieftains who I said were followed by three thousand Indian warriors with their weapons."

244 Martínez, *Hernán Cortés*, 504, who cites Díaz del Castillo, *Historia verdadera*, cxcv, as a source treating Cortés' ship-building activities on the Caribbean. Cortés, *Documentos*, I, publishes a few dozen documents about some of Cortés' activities, between 1522 and 1527, involving discovery expeditions sent from Mexican shores, to Brazil, Argentina, Paraguay (?); also to Maluco (today's Indonesia) or Islas Especies.

245 Duverger, *Crónica de la eternidad*, 61, " . . . Carlos V intentó destruirlo . . . ."

246 Martínez, *Hernán Cortés*, 74. Duverger, *Crónica de la eternidad*, 134ff, provides an analysis of Carlos V's acts, which help us to understand his harsh treatment of not only Cortés, but also many subjects during his long reign. "Llevado por quién sabe qué deseo de venganza, ... ordena una espantosa matanza"—not

only of Spain's Medina del Campo in 1520, but also of his home town of Ghent in 1540. (49, 134) Then, Cortés himself suffered from interminable court investigations and unresolved accusations in the late 1520s, due largely to Carlos's "espíritu inquisional y con una finalidad exclusivamente fiscal y que fue [su] arma permanente." (61) Was it jealousy or some other perverse motivation that led Carlos to order the burning of all Cortés' writings in 1527—and to impose a lifelong prohibition against writing and publishing? (94) In 1541 Cortés was aboard the same war ship to witness the emperor's embarrassing loss of half his navy off the shores of Algiers. "Al ceder ante la intemperie ... Carlos V se pone en ridículo. [E]s un perdedor .... Ese fracaso, inconscientemente deseado, es un preludio a su retiro de la escena Española: su descrédito le sirve de pretexto." (136). Before abandoning the crown and deserting Spain ("solo tiene una idea en la mente: acabar con las responsabilidades") , he approved of the Nuevas Leyes de 1542, which were simply the last of his money-grabbing schemes, "son en realidad leyes de despojo de los encomenderos." (137) A result: the imposition of "el absolutismo" over New Spain, the end Cortés' life-long efforts to preserve indigenous institutions and promote electoral democracy; and the final reduction of the latter's power over New Spain governance.

247 Simpson, *Encomienda*, Appendix 3, 214-29, provides an English translation of this important letter.
248 Benítez, *Historia de la ciudad de México*, II, 9.
249 Greenleaf, *Zumárraga and the ... Inquisition, 77;* Francisco Fernández Buey, *La gran perturbación: Discurso del indio metropolitano* (México: Ensayos/Destino 26, n.d.), 132.
250 García Icazbalceta, *Zumárraga*, 195.
251 Greenleaf, *Zumarraga and the ... Inquisition,* 13-14.
252 I know of no authoritative bibliograpy of Viceroy Antonio de Mendoza. (The only "useful" part of the work by Rafael Diego Fernández, *Antonio de Mendoza* [Mexico: Planeta DeAgostini, 2002] is the chronology offered in its final pages, 145-51). Ruiz Medrano, *Gobierno y Sociedad*, provides a valuable treatment of some of Mendoza's economic activities while serving as New Spain's first viceroy. Born in 1477, Mendoza spent 40 years serving the monarch in various capacities before accepting the positions as New Spain's first viceroy, governor, and president of the Audiencia de México. It was in November of 1535 when he finally arrived at Mexico City to commence serving in those positions; that service would end 15 years later, when he would be reassigned to similar positions in the new viceroyalty of Peru. Arriving in 1535, he found peace largely restored to New Spain's government and society. During the previous seven years the Segunda Audiencia, under the direction of Bishop Fuenleal (and with the participation of the lawyer Vasco de Quiroga), had succeeded in reestablishing a respectable level of justice and respect for the governance of the new colony. The violent rivalry between the allies and enemies of Cortés had been silenced,

and the flagrant abuses against the Indians in encomiendas and corregimientos had been minimized. (Simpson, *The Encomienda,* 109) Mendoza copied the model already established by Cortés: he became investor and founder of a variety of economic enterprises: cattle ranches, clothing shops, and sugar mills. Toward the end of his decade-and-a-half in New Spain, he and Cortés enjoyed the renown as the principal owners of both land and slaves, and the most prosperous entrepreneurs in mining, agriculture, and cattle. (Ruiz Medrano, *Reshaping New Spain,* 186). Cortés shared important orientations with not only Mendoza, but also with Vasco de Quiroga and the Franciscan friars, including Zumárraga: their firm belief in the beneficial role of the conquest and the evangelization campaign, the positive role of the viceregal government, their shared support for both the institution of the encomienda and its practice; the necessity for the state to enforce strict codes of conduct in order to protect the Indians, and their shared support for the institution of African slavery. During Mendoza's first two years as New Spain's viceroy, he enjoyed as cordial, but tense relationship with Cortés. Riley, *Fernando Cortés,* 44-5, documents how Mendoza ordered viceregal authorities to initiate investigations—which ended in law suits in a few instances—in order that Cortés fulfill to the letter the the Crown's regulations stipulating the máximum levels of tribute and labor that encomenderos such as he were requiring of the Indians under their jurisdiction. Mendoza, as viceroy, also assumed an active role against the obstinate, and at times unscrupulous, actions of Cortés—in particular the latter's self-interested interpretation of the Crown's stipulation that he, through his Marquesado, would control no more than 23,000 Indians—or heads of Indian families. (Martínez, *Hernán Cortés,* 639-47.) In spite of the friction between the two, they—as the richest and most powerful men in New Spain—collaborated in sponsoring an elaborate celebration in Mexico City on the occasion of the peace negotiations between Emperor Carlos and the King of France in 1538. (Díaz del Castillo, *Historia verdadera,* cci, offers a splendid description of these celebrations.) After 1538, communications between the two desintegrated, and their relationship became that of rivals, if not enemies. Duverger, *Cortés,* 363ff, explains the reasons for that "rivalry:" the envy of Mendoza, and his support for the Inquisition versus the passionate opposition of Cortés. León-Portillo writes about their "permanent rivalry" in each's endeavors to discover and claim for the Crown new geographical areas (Miguel León-Portilla, "Hernán Cortés y el Mar Bermejo," in Patronato Mexicano, *Cortés,* 259-76. See also Martínez, *Hernán Cortés,* 713-21). It was during his mandate that New Spain—in 1545—was stricken with the first of several deadly epidemics (which during the next century would carry 80-90% of the Indigenous population to an early grave.) In 1550 Mendoza was replaced by Don Luis de Velasco as New Spain's second vicroy—when Mendoza accepted the role of heading the new viceroy in Peru.

CHAPTER 11

253 All the quotes in this introduction come from the impressive work by Charles Gibson, *Tlaxcala*.
254 Elliot, *Imperial Spain*, 71.
255 Chauveau, *Códices de Cuernavaca*, 84.
256 Díaz del Castillo, *Historia verdadera*, ccix.
257 Monterrosa, *Evangelización*, 1125, recounts that "De este hecho deja testimonio la pintura que se conserva en la portería del convento de Ozumba."
258 Riley, *Hernando Cortes*, 15, quotes Mendieta.
259 Ibid, 21.
260 Cline, "Spiritual Conquest," studies "a corpus of six Nahuatl-language household censuses" to provide a unique perspective about the patterns of baptism in different native families and communities near Cuernavaca.
261 Orendáin, *Ruinas de utopía*, 80-4, 80 fn., 99, 128, 179. Unfortunately, this author provides insufficient documentation for the sources of his interesting information. Diego de Basalenque, Introd. Heriberto Moreno, *Los agustinos, aquellos misioneros hacendados: Historia de las provinciales de San Nicolás de Tolentino de Michoacán, escrita por fray Diego de Basalenque (selección)* (México: SEP & Consejo Nacional de Fomento Educativo, 1985), provides information about the early presence of the Augustine Order in Mexico.
262 A reading of García Martínez, Marquesado, 95ff, suggests how Cortés himself might have benefitted from the Indians' descriptions of communal lands: according to the conditions of the Marquesado, he himself could assume ownership over any forest, field, or stream not thus included.
263 Chauveau, *Códices de Cuernavaca*, 162, 124.
264 John Womak, Jr., in the second chapter of his groundbreaking study, *Zapata y la Revolución mexicana* (México: Siglo Veintiuno, 1985), traces his protagonist's rise to regional, and then national, prominence—primarily through his activity in the rural areas near the campesino villages of Anaya y Anenecuilco, near the city of Cuautla—State of Morelos. There and elsewhere, between 1880 and 1910, robust national and international sugar markets were motivating unscrupulous investors to acquire new lands. To obtain these, they would employ any means at hand, violence, manipulation of the courts, etc. At issue were lands traditionally controlled by campesino communities. This struggle for the land played out in the face of two different legal systems: one that was "historical," which recognized historical precedent (that is, who in the past was actually working the land in question); and the "modern" legal system, which recognized the validity of real estate titles certified by the government—which in practice favored the petitions of a new class of landowners. Campesinos became infuriated before violent siezures of land performed by this new landowning class. But a few of these traditional communities were led by leaders who did not hesitate to take their complaints to court. Womak afirms, but he

does not offer details, that many communities would lose in court in spite of the fact that their elders presented before the judges written land titles dating as far back as viceregal times (44). And thus, the insurrection of Zapata and his followers. How to explain the existence of these centuries-old land titles, originating in small communities formerly belonging to Cortés' Marquesado? The Chauveau book—*Códices*—presents only documents relative to the Indigenous land in or near Cuernavaca and the nearby Quauhxomulco (today called San Buenaventura Coajomlco—in the Municipio of Huitzilac). I believe it improbable that Cortés himself, or his representatives, ever visited these very communities belonging to his Marquesado—but who knows? So, how to explain the sixteenth-century origin of these documents? Warman, *We Come to Object*, pp. 29-30, provides a posible explanation. He suggests that in the year 1567 (we remember that Cortés had died some 22 before) the acting viceroy of New Spain, el Marqués de Falces, carried out the instructions coming from the Crown to measureand provide written documentation—a "fundo legal"—for each village's common or community land. In 1687 a new law stipulated the expansion of each community's land to 600 "varas" extending in every direction (as measured from the former parcel's exterior perimeter). All this was intended to arrest what officials had noticed as the near total "disappearance of native population;" it was the Crown's attempt to "vaguely declare its respect for the territorial integrity of the native population"Todo ello destinado a detener la casi "desaparición total de la indigenous población" (29). Even though this bit of information does not establish a link between the land policies of Cortés and Zapata, it does suggest an important inspiration for the agrarian laws of Mexico's early twentieth century.

265 As far as I know, there is no existing documentation regarding Indian governance as it applied to Cuernavaca—in contrast to the plentiful information coming from Tlaxcala. See Appendix B.

266 Chauveau, *Códices de Cuernavaca*, 162, 164.

267 Ibid., 94.

268 A careful reading of the documents of the time reveals a confusion between what contemporary readers would consider two distinct institutions: "hospitals" to treat the sick and infirm, and "missions" to house, instruct, provide gainful employment, and evangelize the Indian masses. Other sources suggest that a "hospital" in those days served also as a hospice or guest-house for transients and for persons otherwise in need of board and lodging.

Historians have treated one hospital in particular: that which Cortés, in conjunction with the Franciscan friars, founded in Coyoacán: the Hospital de San Lázaro for lepers that Cortés' enemy and the acting head of the Primera Audiencia, Nuño de Guzmán, destroyed in 1524, and which Cortés later ordered to be rebuilt. (María Luisa Rodríguez-Sala, et al., *El Hospital Real de los Naturales ... (1531-1764)* ... (Mexico: UNAM, 2005). See Carlos de Sigüenza y

Góngora, prol. Jaime Delgado, *Piedad heroyca de Don Fernando Cortés* (Madrid: José Porrúa Turenzas, 1960 [1663?], 1.

269 Cheryl English Martin, *Rural Society in Colonial Morelos* (Albuquerque: University of New Mexico Press, 1985), 17-20, provides valuable information about the subsequent history of the hospital located in or near Oaxtepec, information which she learned from the *Relación de Oaxtepec*"—apparently prepared in 1580 by the Indian leaders of that community—which is stored in the Joaquín García Icazbalceta Collection, University of Texas Library, Austin Texas.

270 Martínez, *Hernán Cortés*, 625, heads a mini chapter: "En Cuernavaca. Supuesta pacificación de indios." If these "supposed" events did occur in the latter months of 1530, there is no existing document that links them with the Indians of Cuernavaca.

271 Chauveau, *Códices de Cuernavaca*, 132.

272 Ibid. Here and in the next paragraph I quote from pp. 128, 70, 99-100, 95, 215, 99.

273 Charles Gibson, in *Aztecs*, offers an alternative explanation: "It is clear that the early demands made by Cortés ... strained to the full the native capacity to pay." (196) "The Spanish recipients of Indian labor depended upon town organizations, profiting from the authority of each community's tlatoani ... and from the *macegual* classes accustomed to orderly direction." (222) But, "By many means in the sixteenth century the crown sought to create a working force that would be free to choose its own tasks and adequately recompensed in wages. Such a working force never came into being in the colonial period, but [one cannot deny] royal efforts to implement it ...." (223)

274 "Cuernavaca, servicios de encomienda, 1531," in Zavala, *Tributos y servicios*, 17-33.

275 "Tributos de Totolapa y Atlatlahuca," in Ibid, 109-14.

276 "Cortés contra el Fiscal licenciado Benavente, sobre los pueblos de Totolapa e Atlatlahuca," in *Archivo General de la Nación, UNAM, Nuevos documentos relativos a los bienes de Hernán Cortés, 1547-1949* (Mexico: Imprenta Universitaria, 1946), 121-70.

277 The law case, "Cuernavaca y sujetos, tributos y servicios al marqués del Valle, 1544," in Zavala, *Tributos y servicios*, 145-71. Paragraphs further on quote from material from pp. 154, 168.

278 Zavala, *Estudios indianos*, 273.

279 "Visita, Tasación y cuenta de la Villa de Yecapixtla, Mor., una petición de Don Martín Cortés, Marqués del Valle, Año de 1561," in Archivo, *Nuevos documentos*, 171-267.

280 "Hernán Cortés, servicios de tamenes de Cuernavaca, 1532," in Zavala, *Tributos y servicios*, pp. 85-106. Background information essential for understanding many of these documents is contained in several of Zavala's earliest of publications,

most notably *Estudios Indianos*. Unfortunately, the sparse commentary in this recent book sometimes provides distorted information.

281 Zavala, "Hernán Cortés, servicios de tamenes de Cuernavaca, 1532," in Zavala, *Tributos y servicios,* 85-106. See also "Quejas de los tributaries de Cuernavaca, 1533," in *Ibid.*, 107-8.

282 "La reina," in Archivo, *Documentos inéditos relativos a Hernán Cortés y su familia* (México: Talleres gráficos de la nación, 1935), 23-5.

283 Gibson, *Aztecs,* 220, etc.

284 Díaz Migoyo and Vázquez Chamorro, "Introducción," 34, quotes Zorita.

285 Huejotzingo, City Council of, "An Indian Town Addresses the King," in Lockhart, *Letters and People,* 166, 167, 169. In Spanish: "Carta del Consejo de Huexotzingo al Rey Felipe II, 30 de julio de 1560," in Miguel León-Portilla, ed. *Visión de los vencidos: Relaciones indígenas de la conquista.* México: UNAM, 2004), pp. 169-74. Both Lockhart and León Portilla state in footnotes that this letter first appeared, both in Spanish and in English translation, in Anderson, *Beyond the Códices,* 176-90. Although Lockhart and León-Portilla state that this document was "rediscovered" (I have been unable to locate information about this specific "rediscovery") in the Archivo Histórico Nacional, Madrid, Anderson, in his Preface, identifies both Mexico's Archivo General de la Nación and the McAfee Collection of UCLA's Research Library as the "two main sources of our selections" which include "Náhuatl wills, land translations, municipal council minutes, local tax records, and a rich variety of petitions and correspondence" (v).

286 O'Gorman, *Historia,* 315-6. See Appendix A.

287 Zumárraga, "Carta al rey, 1533, "in García Icazbalceta, *Fray Juan de Zumárraga, III, 36-8; the letter, according to the editor,* was written after a personal visitation to Cuernavaca (the center for Cortés' Marquesado) and was also based on the reports coming from reliable sources (III, 36-8). The Archbishop wrote both positive comments about Cortés—for example II, 173—and negative—see II, 171.

288 Pedro de Gante, "Carta de Fr. Pedro de Gante al Rey D. Felipe II," in Joaquín García Icazbalceta, ed. *Nueva colección de documentos para la historia de México. II: Códice franciscano, Siglo XVI* (México: Francisco Díaz de León, 1889), 221.

CHAPTER 12

289 In Kelly, *Marooned,* pp. 186-95, I find an English equivalent (but nearly a century later) in the figure of Sir Francis Drake, also a precursor in a "new partially meritocratic society ... [in which] capitalism was walking on the lanky, jointy, and clumsy limbs of its adolescence ...."

290 Octavio Aguilar de la Parra, "Hernán Cortés y la Hacienda de San Antonio Atlacomulco," in Patronato, *Cortés,* 156. Also treating Cortés' earliest

sugar-producing facilities: Martin, *Rural Society in Colonial Morelos*, 8-13; and Salinas, *Historias y paisajes morelenses,* II, 15-22.

291 Sources: Riley, *Hernando Cortes*, 64-5; Barrett, *Hacienda azucarera*; Alejandro García García, "Hernán Cortés y la agricultura; la caña de azúcar, la industria azucarera y sus proyecciones," en Patronato, *Cortés*, 71—80; Aguilar de la Parra, "Hernán Cortés," 155-65; and Salinas, *Historias y paisajes morelenses,* II, 21.

292 Fernández de Velasco, "Cortés ... y la ganadería," 90.

293 Barrett, *Hacienda azucarera,* 201,

294 Ibid., 211.

295 Riley, *Fernando Cortes,* 66.

296 Ibid., 63.

297 Barrett, *Hicienda azucarera,* 79-80. Information about Cortés' ranches can also be found in Salinas, *Historias y paisajes morelenses,* II, 71ff.

298 See "Precios de la ropa de Cuernavaca, 1535, in Zavala, *Tributos y servicios,* 115-20, in which the reader learns of Cortés' entrepreneurial acumen in organizing a near monopoly on the supply and retail sale of cotton clothing (obtained as tribute items from Morelos communities) in and around Mexico City.

299 Salinas, *Historias y paisajes morelenses,* II, 76.

CHAPTER 13

300 Mendieta, *Historia eclesiástica,* 79, 178, 181.

301 Díaz del Castillo, *Historia verdadera,* ccvii.

302 One signature example: Díaz del Castillo, *Historia verdadera,* ccxi, recounts how in the year 1550 he, alongside the venerated Vasco de Quiroga—in addition other respected citizens from Peru and New Spain—were present for the Court hearings at Valladolid in order to argue (again!) the case for American encomenderos to permanently enjoy the "rights" previously granted to them over land management and Indian labor.

303 Prescott, *History of the Conquest,* 641-2.

304 Díaz del Castillo, *Historia verdadera,* ccviii.

305 Elliot, *Imperial Spain*, explains the confusion and hostility with which conservative elements in Spain received Carlos (1516-20), who viewed him as "an alien Emperor" surrounded by courtiers and advisers who embraced the ideas of their doctrinal enemy, Erasmus (and other religious progressives—215-6, etc.). During Carlos's reign, Spain's leaders in Court, universities, and religion flirted with "the humanist culture of the Renaissance, the "idealized vision of an earthly paradise ... the idealism of Renaissance culture and ... its anthropocentric emphasis ... and to fuse them with the reinvigorated Roman Catholicism of the post-Tridentine age" (245-6). In other Spanish circles, there smoldered the "perennial struggle between two Spains ... intensively fought from the 1520s to the 1560s" (216).

306 "Convenio del marqués del Valle con indios de Cuernavaca, 1549," in Zavala, *Tributos y servicios*, 199-205.

307 Salinas, *Historias y paisajes*, 21, informs us that this *humilladero*, later called Ermita del Calvario, was located "al sur del pueblo ... en un punto de la Avenida de Morelos ... lugar donde concurren cinco vías públicas."

308 Zavala's *Tributos y servicios* republishes the court transcripts of several of these trials in which Indians successfully sued Spanish encomenderos—Cortés included—for abuses suffered.

309 *Ibid.*, 199.

310 Cortés, "Cláusulas del testament de Hernán Cortés, 1547," in Zavala, *Tributos y servicios*, 197-8.

311 Zavala, *Tributos y servicios*, 199.

312 "Declaración de los tributaries de Cuyernavaca contra el marqués del Valle," in Zavala, *Tributos y servicios*, 105-6, which is a transcription of a formal complaint filed in 1533 by a group of disgruntled Cuernavaca *principales*, headed by Don Hernando, that never acquired the status of a law suit nor resulted in a formal investigation of Cortés' or Marquesado officials' actions. It's difficult to assess the validity of the Indians' charges. Obviously, they had learned that officials in Mexico City would give serious consideration to any of their accusations, and they obviously wanted to create problems for the Marqués. But the fact that the 1549 proceedings ended up satisfying all the Cuernavaca *principales*, and in particular Don Hernando, leads one to suppose that the 1533 accusations might have been less than serious.

313 Gibson, *The Aztecs*, "Appendix IV: Epidemics," 448-51, provides details about the series of epidemics that killed so many natives in New Spain. Not to be ignored is the fact that Spaniards were not the only carriers of deadly diseases. During that same time period, according to Wikipedia, "The Black Death is estimated to have killed 30% to 60% of Europe's population in the 14th century ... and repeatedly returned to haunt Europe and the Mediterranean throughout the 14th to 17th centuries."

314 The issue of deaths due to epidemics was hardly treated by the Franciscan intellectuals/ writers. Barbara Tuchman, *A Distant Mirror*, 105, calls attention to a similar absence in the writings of, Chaucer and other Europeans. Her explanation: "Divine anger [aiming at the] extermination of man did not bear close examination."

315 Giovanni Boccaccio, "Introduction," trans and ed., Mark Musa and Peter E. Bondanella, *The Decameron: A New Translation* ... (New York: W. W. Norton, 1977), 5-11.

316 Phelan, *Millennial Kingdom*, 93-4.

317 Mendieta, *Historia eclesiástica*, 79, 178, 192. Gibson, *Tlaxcala*, points to other reasons accounting for Tlaxcala's decline in about the same time period: in the

1540s white colonists, originally excluded, progressively "infiltrated" and settled on nearby lands, a factor which contributed to the progressive loss of Indian prosperity and about which the viceregal administration "was inadequate to the task of regulation." (79-84). Then—decades later, "In all four of the [Tlaxcala] cabeceras, dynastic failure was characteristic of the last decades of the century." (99) Díaz Migoyo, "Introducción," pp. 34-5, is the source for information about the "continuos pleitos" that caused "el caos judicial," leading to "la más absoluta de la anarquía."

318 Simpson, *The Encomienda*, 67.
319 Duverger, *Crónica de la eternidad*, 61, 136.
320 Phelan, *Millennial Kingdom*, 55, mention the letter Mendieta penned in the early 1570s to the important Spanish noble, Juan de Ovando on the occasion of the latter being named the new President of the Council of the Indies.
321 Phelan, *Millennial Kingdom*, 58.
322 Durant, *Renaissance*, 689.
323 The fate of Erasmus's "humanist" teachings in Spain and all across Europe parallels more or less what happened, during the same time span in New Spain. In short, the Belvís Franciscans, as individuals, came under increased attack by more conservative voices within the Church. The same could be said about their baptismal activities with New Spain natives, their charitable works with regard to missions and hospitals, and the strong relationships they had formed with indigenous community leaders. Is it a quirk of fate that the false appraisals made by Bartolomé de las Casas about the Spanish treatment of natives in New Spain during the first post-conquest decades turned out to be prophetic for what was to follow? Because Las Casas's "Black Legend" has induced hundreds of readers over the past several centuries to ignore whatever positive might have occurred during (what Franciscan historian Mendieta called) Mexico's "edad dorada"—that is, the four-to-six decades which followed the overthrow of Aztec tyranny.
324 Díaz, *Utopía franciscana*, 15.
325 Landa, *Yucatan*, 28.
326 Phelan, *Millennial Kingdom*, 55.
327 *Ibid.*, 55-8.
328 *Ibid.*, 54.
329 Fray Toribio Motolinía, "Carta al rey, 1555," in Edmundo O'Gorman, ed. & intro., *Historia de los indios de la Nueva España: Relación de los ritos antiguos ...* (México: Porrúa, 2014), 295-316; Juan de Zumárraga, "Carta al rey, 1533," in García Icazbalceta, *Fray Juan de Zumárraga, III*, 36-8; and Pedro de Gante, "Carta de Fr. Pedro de Gante al Rey D. Felipe II," in Joaquín García Icazbalceta, ed. *Nueva colección de documentos para la historia de México. II: Códice franciscano, Siglo XVI* (México: Francisco Díaz de León, 1889), 221.

330 An important part of Sahagún's famed history (sometimes called *Codex Florentino*) are the "literary texts" which Sahagún transcribed from select Aztec elders a half-century after the 1521 submission of their past warriors. It is unfortunate that neither he nor another "friar-anthropologist" preserved similar stories or poems recited by surviving elders from either Tlaxcala or Cuernavaca—that is, from communities that had suffered under Aztec rule. Unfortunately, what Mendieta did preserve has given rise in the 20th century to a mistaken nostalgia for the Aztec regime—see, for example, works by Miguel León-Portilla, *Visión de los vencidos: Relaciones indígenas de la conquista* (Mexico: UNAM, 2004), and the latter's English translator, Lysander Kemp, in *Broken Spears: The Aztec Account of the Conquest of Mexico*, ed. & introd. Miguel León-Portilla (Boston: Beacon Press, 1962).

The elderly Sahagún's defense of the Franciscans' New Spain accomplishments was not without its contradictions. During those painful years of conflict—1884-87—he would come to criticize the early decisions of his order in baptizing natives not fully embracing Catholic dogma; his depression would grow upon realizing the wide, continued practice of idol worship among many Indians who had embraced Catholicism only in name. As a culmination, he would come to question the final legacy of the "Divine Twelve" who had sorely underestimated the gigantic task of leading Mexico's Indigenous masses into the Christian fold: should they be considered less as (perhaps naïve) heroes and more as "the fathers of disillusionment and disappointment"? (Georges Baudot, "The Last Years of Fray Bernardino de Sahagún (1585-90): The Rescue of the Confiscated Work and the Seraphic Conflicts. New Unpublished Documents," in Munro S. Edmonson, ed. *Sixteenth-Century Mexico: The Work of Sahagún*) Albuquerque: University of New Mexico Press, 1974), 187.

331 Baudot, "Fray Bernardino de Sahagún, 174-87.
332 Díaz, *Utopía franciscana*, 16.
333 Duverger, *Conversión de los indios*, 209.
334 Gibson, *Tlaxcala*, 41.
335 María Elena Martínez, *Genealogical Fictions: Limpieza de Sangre, Religious, and Gender in Colonial Mexico* (Stanford: Stanford University Press, 2008), 141-2.
336 Mann, *1493*, 312.

APPENDIX A

337 Manuel Giménez Fernández, *Bartolomé de las Casas, Capellán de Carlos V, poblador de Cumaná* (Sevilla: Consejo Superior, 1984), 1.
338 William H. Prescott, *History of the Conquest of Mexico and History of the Conquest of Peru* (New York: The Modern Library, n.d.), 641.
339 *Ibid.*, 642.

340 This is the implication of Henry Raup Warner, with Helen Rand Perish, *The Life and Writings of Bartolomé de Las Casas* (Albuquerque: Univ of N.M. Press, 1967), p. 101, who conclude that Las Casas began writing this important work during an extended stay in Mexico City between 1837 and 1840.
341 Helen-Rand Parish y Harold E. Weidman, *Las Casas en México: Historia y obra desconocidas* (México: FCE, 1996 [1992]), 23.
342 Prescott, *Mexico*, 194, fn5.
343 The bibliographic reference is: Fray Gerónimo de Mendieta, prol. Joaquín García Icazbalceta; introd. Antonio Rubial García, *Historia eclesiástica indiana* (Mexico: Consejo Nacional para la Cultura y las Artes, 1997).
344 Hanke, *Latin America*, 82.
345 Díaz del Castillo, *Historia verdadera*, ccxi.
346 Parish & Wiedman, Las Casas en México.
347 Motolinía, "In Tlaxcala," 236, 238-9. Although Motolinía wrote his "célebre carta" some seven years after Cortés' death, it was first published—according to a footnote written by Lockhart (p. 247; see bibliography 258)—in 1884. My Spanish-language copy: Fray Toribio Motolinía, "Carta al rey, 1555," in Edmundo O'Gorman, ed. & intro., *Historia de los indios de la Nueva España: Relación de los ritos antiguos ...* (México: Porrúa, 2014), 295-316. Much of my information about Motolinía comes from these two sources, in addition to Prescott, *History of the Conquest of Mexico*, pp. 309-11. I have not found in the publications of either Charles Gibson or Silvio Zavala (the most accomplished researchers on this and related topics), any indication of their familiarity with this important letter. The same can be said about the respective letters—treated in the next few paragraphs of the text—written by friars Juan de Zumárraga and Pedro de Gante. Evidence is strong that among all the Franciscan monks, Cortés enjoyed the strongest friendship ties with Motolonía. In 1532, the latter—while serving as "guardian del monasterio de la Villa de Guernabvaca de la orden de San Francisco"—provided testimony favorable to Cortés before the courts in a case treating the alleged abuses to Indian porters ferrying loads between Cuernavaca and the ship-building facilities in Acapulco. He provided personal observations about Cortés' good treatment, that the porters were well provided for and "muy contentos" in carrying out their orders from Cortés. This testimony, coming from he who enjoyed near universal respect, must have played a significant part in the favorable court results for Cortés.
348 Zumárraga, "Carta," 37; *the letter, according to the editor,* was written after a personal visitation to Cuernavaca (the center for Cortés' Marquesado) and was also based on the reports coming from reliable sources (III, 36-8). The Archbishop also did not hesitate to criticize some of Cortés' activities—for example II, 173—and negative—see II, 171.
349 Gante, "Carta," 221.

APPENDIX B
350 Quoted in R. Douglas Cope, *The Limits of Racial Domination: Plebian Society in Colonial Mexico City, 1660-1720* (Madison: University of Wisconsin Press, 1994), 4.
351 Diego Muñoz Camargo, Alfredo Chavero & Edmundo Aviña Levy, *Historia de Tlaxcala* (México: Oficina del Secretario de Fomento, 1892) (Ed. Facsimile 1966), ix.
352 Alonso Romero Reséndiz, *Lo de Tlaxcala: Análisis imparcial de los sucesos acaecidos en época de la conquista* (México: B. Costa-Amic, 1974), 168.

Notes About Sources
353 William H. Prescott, *Mexico and the Life of the Conqueror Fernando Cortés... in Two Volumes* (New York: Peter Fenelon Collier, 1898), 5.
354 Julio Jímenez Rueda, "La historia de México y Don Joaquín García Icazbalceta," in Joaquín García Icazbalceta, *Opúsculos y biografías*, introd. Julio Jiménez Rueda (México: UNAM, 1994), xii, xiv.
355 Barbara W. Tuchman, *A Distant Mirror: The Calamitous 14th Century* (New York: Ballantine Books, 1978), xix.

INDEX

A

Acamapitzin, José, 155, 248-9
Acapulco, town of, 81
Acolhuas, 87.
    See Mixtecas
Adriano de Utrecht, n171
    cardinal (became Pope Adriano VI), 106, 115-7, 220
    Carlos's tutor, 106-107
    selecting Belvís monks, 115-7
Aguilar, Jerónimo de, 9
Acolhuas, 18-20
Altacomulco, town of, 145
Alva Ixtlilxóchitl, Fernando de, 57-8, 65-8, 262
Alvarado, Pedro de, 3, 11, n19
Anderson, Arthur, 266
Antilles, 110, 146
Augustian Order, 76
    in Ocuituco, 158
    punish Indians, 159-60
    in Morelos, 176, n180
Axayacátzin, José, 22, 84, 95-6
Aztecs, xii, xiii
    fear-inspiring, 6, 26-7
    idol worship, 24, 94
    savage customs, 94
    researchers romanticize, n80, n330
    tiranny with concubines, 36

B

baptism, 22, 92
    Franciscans only require Indians' willingness, 149
    Franciscan practices criticized, 222
Barrett, Ward, 265
Belvís, town of, 107
    monastery, 104, 116-8, n168
    and baptisms, 117
    defend Indians, 56, 171
    optimism, 66
    progressive beliefs, 104-6, 124ff
    origins in Belvís, 104
    Erasmus influence, 147-8
    linguistic aptitudes, 111-12
    from Spain to Mexico City, 118, 120-23
    outstanding characteristics, 124-7
    first visit to Cuernavaca, 147-8
    strict discipline, 159-60
    1550s routine, 164-66
Benevente. See Motolinía
Betanzos, Friar Domingo de (Dominican Order), 149-50
bronze, 79-80

C

Carlos I (of Spain, also Carlos V), xv, 37, n305
    and Cortés, 140-1, 168-72, n246

on slavery, 49
on Indians, 59
passes crown, 206, 220-1
role in choosing Belvís friars, 108-10, 118-9
favors Europe, 166, 168
and Las Casas, 166, 230-2
praised by chieftains, 181
stern authority, 124-5
"*Carta reservada.*" See Cortés
Cartas de relación. See Cortés
Casas, B. *See* Las Casas
Catholic Church, 102-3
  in Spain, 103-4
  in Morelos, 176-9
  1560s opposition to Franciscans, 223-4
Chalco, city of, 13
Charles I. See Carlos
chieftains. *See* Cuernavaca chieftains
Cisneros, Cardinal Jiménez, 103, 114-5
  as regent, 106-8
clerical abuse, 160-1
Códice Florentino. See Mendieta
Códices de Cuernavaca (see also Dubernard), 95-100, 140-9, 245-50
  sites for churches, 146-7
Colegio de Santa Cruz (also de Tlatelolco), 70, 129, 150-53, n219
  student routines, 151
  according to Gante, 151-2
  principal friars, 151
  successes, 152-3
  decline, 214, n221
concubines, 31-5
conquest?, xi, 19-20, 55, n79
  praised, 202
  benign, n19, n31, 125-6
conquistadors, vii, xii
  types, 1-2
  Cortés different, 113

and Las Casas, 236-7
Cortés, Hernán, viii
  his palace, x, xiv, 87, 177, n3
  Life: conquistador, xii, 1
  his type of conquest, 7-9
  godfather in baptisms, 82
  not womanizer, 84
  university studies, 89
  hunting recreation, 89
  chronology in Mexico, 21
  origins in Extremadura, 48
  governs Morelos, 140-53
  his encomiendas, n130
  wife, the Marquesa, 182-3
  exit from New Spain, 207-8
  death and last testament, 210-13
  name, n3; visits with king, 166-202
  Beliefs or impressions: religious not fanatic, 7
  good mind for commerce, 82
  on Cuernavaca *principales,* 83
  respects Indian land, 89
  detests Spanish settlers, 56
  about Aztecs, 61
  first impressions of Mexican Indians 108-9
  Cuernavaca and friars, 146-54
  commitment to modernization, 195-204
  lust for exploration; and Dominicans, 114
  Character: humor, 3
  led by example, 3
  superior leadership, 4-5
  religiosity, 5-7, 9, 52, n16
  charisma, 2-4
  cruelty, 15
  intuition, 34, 62
  pragmatism, 48
  humanist, 48-9
  lust for glory, 131

greed, 40, 142-3, n58
entrepreneur, 90-1
hyperenergized dreamer, 144-5
ingratitude, n240
Noteworthy acts: vi-ix
   conquers Morelos, 12-19
   defeats Narváez, 11-12
   modernizing projects xiv-xv
   formed character of his soldiers, 9-10
   orders punishment, 17
   kills first wife? 136, 169, n241
   usurps Mexican expedition, 169
   economic projects near Cuernavaca, 27, n140
   stipulations after death, 210-13
   develops water sources, 89
   peaceful alliances with Indians, 6-7; 61-2
   and concubines, 35-8, n50
   divides booty, 38-40
   tributes, 40, 54-5
   imposes taxes, 40-2
   removes enemies from central Mexico, 34, 42-3, 550
   distributes encomiendas, 49-57
   as New Spain's governor, 62-3
   protects Moctezuma's daughters, 73-5
   uses unpaid Indian labor, 98-200, n206
   helps select Belvís monks? 106-13
   welcomes monks, 122-3
   facilitates monks' travel, 131-2
   founds new cities, 142
   uses courts with encomiendas, 145
   prepares for friars, 146-7
   snubs king, 168
   and evangelization campaign, 176
   measures natives' public spaces, 180-3
   promotes Indians' rights, 185, 204
   doesn't pay laborers, 191-2, n252, n273
   important construction projects, 196-7
   introduces cattle, 199-200
   monopoly on cotton clothing, 200-1
   did not rob land, n119, n262
   explores Honduras, 42, 47, 133-35, n196, n243
   rebels against Spain?, n236
   discovery activities, 80-1 n244
   Writings: *Cartas* (or *Letters*), 111-2, 116, 121, 124, 259
   ordinances, 47
   "Carta reservada," 125, n184
   author of *Historia verdadera*?, 260-1
Court cases: treatment of Indians, 184
   porters, 189-90
   to regain encomiendas, 187-9
   regain sugar mill, 185-7
   Hernando's land, 188
   Indians file against Marquesado, 208-9
Relationships with: Adriano, 116-7
   Belvís monks, 116, 124, 128
   Carlos, 140-1, n246
   Cuernavaca chieftains, 20
   God, 140
   enemies, 29-30 37-8, 42, 133, 140
   Indians, 134, 185, 187-8, 191-2
   Indian laborers, 144, 199-200
   Las Casas, 232-4, 264
   Huejotzingo, 191-2
   Mendoza, n252
   Motolinía; Second Audiencia, 171-2
   soldiers, 9, n50
   Prescott praises, 204-5
   Zumárraga, 68, 169, 172

Cortés Monroe, Martín (father of Hernán), 116-8, n170
Coyoacán, city of, 11, 46
Cuauhtémoc, xiii, 29, 33-6
    Díaz's opinion, 35-6, 39-40
    execution, 133-4, n4
Cuernavaca chieftains, x, 16, 266
    See also Acamapitzin, San Martín Cortés, Yoatzín
    and Cortés, xii, 20-2, 25-7, 77ff, 83-5
    exemplary leadership, n43, 56-7, 160-2, 244
    conquer neighboring communities, 15-6
    nobles, 85ff
    change names with baptism, 92
    civility, 94-5
    practice slavery, 94
    govern for three centuries, 95-6
    measure public spaces, 180-1, 248, n264
    after Cortés's death, 211-8
    range of influence, n34
    homes, 83-4
    and construction of church, 99, 155-6
    evangelization campaign, xiv
    Indian events, 183-5
    file law suits against Cortés, n312
Cuernavaca, city of, xiv, 78ff, 81, n5, n35
Cuernavaca códices, 266
    See also Dubernard
Cueva, Melchor de la, 100, 156

D

Díaz del Castillo, Bernal, xi, 203-4
    and Pope Adriano, 117
    on peaceful conquest, 111
    and concubines, xiii

Historia verdadera, 30, 177, 259-60, 267
    authored by Cortés?, 260-1
    pride as conquistador, vii
    and Indians, 51, 63-4, 71-2
    and encomiendas, 54-5
    on Aztec cruelty, 61
    astounding memory, n28
    soldiers=hijos de algo, n71
Dominican Order, 130-2, n175
    against Indian baptisms, 92, 117
    and Cortés, 113-5
    in Morelos, 158, 176
    vs. Franciscans, 226
    and Las Casas, 234-5
disfavor with crown, 235
Dubernard Chauveau, Juan, xvi, 245ff, 266
    (See also *Códices*)
Duverger, Christian, 126, 260-1, 267, n7

E

Edad dorada.
    See Golden Age
Elliot, H. J., 175, n97
encomenderos
educate Indians, 148
    their decline, 216-9
Encomiendas, 33, 40-5, 49, 55, 217-9
    and Crown, 27, 51
    and Cortés, 54, 145
    monarchy against, 166
    growing abuses, 216-7
English colonies, n73
epidemics, xv, 213-5, n313, n314
Erasmus, Desiderio, n151
    influence in Spain, 104-6, n323
    and Belvís monks, 126-8
Evangelization campaign, ix, xiv, 102-131

INDEX

number of monks, 115
first steps, 129-30
noble Indian children assist, 162-3
Indian participation, 163-4
praise by Elliot, 175

F

Felipe II, king, xv
    and decline of Golden Age, 222-3, 266-7
feudalism, 30, 45, 58, 77, 85, 143, 176, 195
First Audencia
Franciscan friars.
    See Belvís Franciscan friars
Franciscan Order, n175
    respect for Cortés, n45
    and European humanism, 103-5
    early favor with crown, 119-21
    their Golden Age, 206-7
    their fall from favor, 219-21, 235
    internal divisions, 221, 225-6
    disputes with Dominicans, xvi, 235-7
Fuenleal.
    See Ramírez

G

Gante, Pedro de, ix, 262, n218
    and Colegio, 6-7, 150-1, n219
    1555 letter to king, 152-3, 192-3, 267
    and Erasmus, 106
    and Cortés, 153
    on pagan practices, 153-4
    attacks Las Casas, 224-6, 237
gardens, 18-9
Gibson, Charles, 264-5, 241-4, 266
    on Tlaxcala, 63-4
    on Aztecs, 244
    negative view of Cortés, 75, 244

Golden Age, vii, xv, 102, 265, 240, n191
Gómara. *See* López de Gómara
Guttenberg, Johannes, 103, 104
Guzmán, Nuño de. *See* Nuño
Grigorio, Don Antonio, 92
gun powder, 79-80

H

Haskett, Robert, 246, 265
Historia de Tlaxcala.
    See Muñoz
Historia verdadera.
    See Díaz del Castillo
Honduras (also Higueras), 41
    Cortés's expedition to, 81, 140
hospital, n268
Huejotzingo (Huitzozingo), city of
    letter to king, 57, 191-2, 266-7, n86, n285
Huizilac, town of, 250-1

I

Indians, 58-62
    favored Spanish, 58, 62-3
    Valladolid debates over, 59
    suffer in Cortés's absence, 133
    build churches, 149
    eager for baptism, 149, n213
    initiate court cases, 187
Indian community, 266
    See Huejotzingo
Inquisition in Mexico, 92
    under Cisneros, 115; in Spain 110
Isabela, Queen, 49, 103, 110
Isabela de Portugal (wife of King Carlos)
    promotes females, 131
    intervenes for Cortés, 190

J

Jesuits, 226
Jiménez de Cisneros, Cardinal.
    See Cisneros
Jojutla, village of, 91
Juitepec, village of, 81, 90

K

Kelly, John, 76

L

Las Casas, Bartolomé de, Dominican
    friar, 166, 228-34, 264, n323
    Brevísima historia, 235
    demoralizes Franciscans, 223-5
    early history, 228-30
    intellectual dishonesty, 233
Las islas. *See* Antillas
Lockhart, James, 266
López, shipbuilder, 11-12
López de Gómara, historiador, 13-4,
    21, 121, 134

M

Malinche (Indians called H.
    Cortés), 77
Mann, Charles C., 74
map, 76
Marina, Doña, 9, 25
Marqués del Valle. *See* Cortés, H.
Marquesa (wife of Cortés), 182-3, 266
    alone in Cuernavaca, 208-9
Marquesado, 26, 266; after Cortés's
    exit, 209-11
Martin, Cheryl English, 265, n119
Martínez, José Luis, 268
Medina, Alonso de, 131
Melgarejo, Fray, 14
Melgarejo, Dr. Bartolomé, 16, 212
Memoriales.
    See Motolinía

Mendieta, Fray Gerónimo de, ix, 45,
    68, 70-1, 262-3
    and Indians, 62-3
    and Colegio de Tlatelolco, 151-2
    and decline of Golden Age, 202-17
    and epidemics, 214-5
    on corrupt leadership, 215
Mendoza, Viceroy Antonio de, viii,
    n252
    and encomiendas, 57
    and Colegio de Tlatelolco, 152
metals, 80
Mexico's Independence, 263-4
Mexico, city of (also Tenochtitlán)
    rebuilding after Aztecs, 97-8, 142
    admirable construction, 206-7
Michoacán state of, 58
mining, 198
Mixtecs, 25
Moctezuma, 10, 25-6, 32, 73-5
    daughters, 73-6
    possessions in Cuernavaca, 87
monasteries, 76, 157
monks, 123
Montesinos, friar Antón, 114-5
More, Sir Thomas, 106
Morelos, state of, x, 1, 11-2, n7
    conquered, 12-19
    Indian towns, 22
    first churches, 147, 176-7, n210
Morley, Sylvanus G., 267
Motolinía, also Fray Toribio de
    Benavente, ix, 262
    1555 letter to king, 68-9, 237-8,
        267, n347
    writes about Indian labor, 99
    and Indian baptisms, 149
    activity in monasteries, 157-8
    letter to king praising Cortés,
        192-3
    attacks Las Casas, 224-5, 237
Muñoz Camargo, Diego, 128, 242-3

INDEX

N

náhuatl documents, xvi, xiii-xiv, xv, xvi, 249
Narváez, Pánfilo, 10-11, 170
New Laws of 1542, 219, n246
New Spain (Nueva España, Mexico), viii
 different Indian types, 21
 early leadership team, 174
 leadership attacked by Las Casas, 237-8
Nuño de Guzmán, 81-2, 171-3, 234

O

Oaxtepec, city of (also Huaxtepec), 13, 17, 18
 gardens, 12, 15-7
 hospital, n269
Olid, Cristóbal, 3, 24
Olmedo, Father Bartolomé (Merced Order), xii, 5, 7-10, 11, 15, 21, 92, 107, 111, 125, n159
Ovando, Licenciado Juan de, 161

P

Pacific Ocean, ports, 80, 97-9
 Cortés explores, 170
Peña, Francisco de la, 96
Phillip, king. *See* Felipe II
Pichardo, José Antonio, 247
Plagues. *See* epidemics
porters, 98, 189-90
Prescott, William H., 11, 204-5, 263
principales. See Cuernavaca chieftains

Q

Qujauhxomolco (today's San Buenaventura Coajomulco), 89
Qjuiñones, friar (Franciscan), 115
Quauhnahuac. See Cuernavaca
Quiroga, Vasco de, viii, 66, 261-2
 on Michoacán Indians, 60-6
 praises Franciscans, 154
 with Second Audiencia, 171-3
 acts in Michoacán, 173

R

Ramírez de Fuenleal, Sebastián, 171-3
Renaissance, 102-3, 118-9, 207
Ricard, Roberto, n93
Riley, G. Micheal, 247, 265, n117, n206
Rivera, Diego, n144
Ruiz Medrano, Ethelia, 234

S

Sahagún, Friar Bernardino de, ix, 18-9, 21, 26, 28-9, 262-3, n45, n330
 later spokesman for Franciscans, 225
 anthropologist, 154
 criticizes Franciscan baptisms, n330
saltpeter, 79, 198
San Martín Cortés, Toribio, 97, 100, 211, 247-8
 baptism, 122-3
 role in church, 164-5
 author of Códices de Cuernavaca, 247-8
San Martín, Gaspar de, 156
San Martín y Sandoval, Don Lucas, 85
Sandoval, Gonzalo de, 3, 13, 24
Serrano de Cardona, Antonio, 185-8
Second Audiencia (also Segunda), 171-4, 217, 234
Sepúlveda, Ginés de, 51
ship building, 197-8
silk production, 199-200
Sixteenth Century, xi
slavery in Mexico, 83, n199
soldiers, 1, 10, 45-9
 loyalty to Cortés, 2, 33-4, n54, n56

react to unjust rewards, 38-40
religiosity, 9
separation from Indians, 46
Cortés's faith in, 111
numbers, n30
bad examples, n51, n61
Spanish Crown, 110-11, 140
and Las Casas, 232-7
sugar, 88, 91, 198-200

T

Tapia, Andrés de, 3
Tascuco, city of, 13
Taxco, city of, 79, 87, 198
Tenochtitlán, city of.
See Mexico City
Teuantepeque, village of, 131
Texcoco, city of, 13, 18, 64
Tlaxcala. See Gibson
Tlaxcala, city of; people of, 6, 10, 16, 59, n317
Tlayacapan, city of, 6, 15-16, 58, 71, 175, 241-5
people of, 5, 8
chieftains betray, 175-8
government, 64-5
Tlalnepantla, village of, 13
Tlaltenango, village of, 89
Toluca, city of, 81
Tuchman, Barbara, xi, 103, 106
on Adriano, n171

U

Umbría, Gonzalo de, 81
Utopía. See More

V

Valencia, Fr. Martín de, ix, 104, 130, n168, n188
Valeriano, Baltasar, 164
Valladolid, city of, 59, 108

debates of 1550, 59
Vasco.
See Quiroga
Velasco, Viceroy Luis de, xii
Velázquez, Diego de, 2-3, 8, 169
Veracruz, city of, 2, 50

W

Warman, Marco, 265, n264
Womak, John Jr., n264

X

Xochimilco, city of, 11

Y

Yautepec, city of, 15-16, 81, 88, 90
Yecapixtla, city of, 14-16, 90, 15, 21, 88

Z

Zacatula, city of, 81
Zapata, Emiliano, 181
Zavala, Silvio, 264, 266
Tributos, 267-8, n199
Zumárraga, Juan de, viii, 262, n191
protector of Indians, 68, 137-8, 171-4
and Colegio de Tlatelolco, 151-2, 172
and Cortés, 68, 169, 172
1555 letter to king, 68, 192-3, 267-9
on Indians, 62-3, 71
pro education of females, 131
and Erasmus, 106, 172
against Augustinians, 159-60
heads inquisition, 172
executor of Cortés's estate, 172-3
criticizes Las Casas, 224-7, 237
Zúñiga, Doña Juana de (also La Marquesa, wife of Cortés).
See Cortés

www.ingramcontent.com/pod-product-compliance
Lightning Source LLC
LaVergne TN
LVHW091532070526
838199LV00001B/30